Taking Sides: Clashing Views on Social Issues, 19/e

Kurt Finsterbusch

http://create.mheducation.com

ISBN-10: 1259666409   ISBN-13: 9781259666407

Contents

Detailed Table of Contents

Unit: Culture and Values

Professor Gary Gutting, holder of the Notre Dame Endowed Chair in Philosophy, praises the modern economy for its amazing progress in production and consumer benefits but also recognizes its negative effects on our character and authentic well-being. It has led to economic insatiability and shrinking of the common good. Therefore, he favors less consumption. Michael Fisher, graduate student in American history at the University of Rochester, summarizes in this review article the thesis of James Livingston that the consumer culture is good, not bad. Though Fisher supports Livingston's thesis, he does not agree with Livingston's positive view of advertising. Nevertheless, he and Livingston favor more consumption.

Karen Hua, A staff writer for *Forbes*, concentrates on teens and finds them using social media to make friends and deepen friendships. She counters the viewpoint that social media provides superficial contacts by observing "that today's teenagers are forming deep, personal connections and relationships online." Stephen Marche, a journalist who is on the staff of The Atlantic, recognizes the amazing benefits of social media but reports on stories and studies which fined that Facebook and other social media can isolate us from people we know to people we meet online. Thus social media which are designed to increase our communication with our family and friends can actually make us lonelier.

Unit: Sex Roles, Gender, and the Family

Isabel V. Sawhill, a senior fellow in economic studies at the Brookings Institution, director of the Budgeting for National Priorities Project, and codirector of the Center on Children and Families, points out that marriages in college educated families are not declining but they are declining significantly for noncollege educated families, both white and black. W. Bradford Wilcox, associate professor of sociology and director of the National Marriage Project at the University of Virginia, describes the positive situation of families today. The majority of marriages are happy and are much more equal and fair than decades ago.

Gayle Tzemach Lemmon, best-selling author, journalist, and a Senior Fellow with the Council on Foreign Relations' Women and Foreign Policy program, discusses the issues in Sheryl Sandberg's famous book, *Lean In*. Sandberg's advice to career women is not to opt out but to lean in, that is, to firmly choose both career and parenting. Unfortunately men still run the country so the societal changes that could facilitate *Lean In* are missing. Full commitment to both career and family will not be easy. Anne-Marie Slaughter, the Bert G. Kerstetter '66 University Professor of Politics and International Affairs at Princeton University and formerly dean of Princeton's Woodrow Wilson School of Public and International Affairs, explains why Sandberg is wrong and women cannot successfully pursue career and family at the same time. They must decide which to do well and which to do adequately but not avidly.

Issue: Is Same-Sex Marriage Harmful to America?
Yes: Peter Sprigg, from "The Top Ten Harms of Same-Sex 'Marriage,'" *Family Research Council* (2013)
No: Jay Michaelson, from "Joe Biden Takes a Marriage Equality Victory Lap," *The Daily Beast* (2015)

Peter Sprigg, Senior Fellow for Policy Studies at the Family Research Council identifies 10 negative effects of same-sex marriages. Many of these worries concern how various institutions are likely to change as a result of same-sex marriages, and how authorities are likely to change their regulations and enforcement practices. Jay Michaelson supports Joe Biden, Vice President of the United States, who applauds the Supreme Court's decision to legalize same-sex marriage as a form of civil rights. Evan Wolfson, founder of Freedom to Marry organization, said that Biden deserves the most credit for the legalization of same-sex marriage.

Unit: Stratification and Inequality

Issue: Is Increasing Economic Inequality a Serious Problem?
Yes: Joseph E. Stiglitz, from "Slow Growth and Inequality Are Political Choices. We Can Choose Otherwise," *Washington Monthly* (2014)
No: Robert Rector and Rachel Sheffield, from "Understanding Poverty in the United States: Surprising Facts about America's Poor," *The Heritage Foundation* (2011)

Nobel laureate Joseph Stiglitz, professor of economics at Columbia University, demonstrates the vast inequality in America and argues that it results from exploitation and should be reduced. It has extensive negative impacts on many institutional areas such as health care. He suggests ways to fix these problems which the corporations will fight. Robert Rector is Senior Research Fellow in the Domestic Policy Studies Department, and Rachel Sheffield is a research assistant in the Richard and Helen DeVos Center for Religion and Civil Society at The Heritage Foundation. They argue that inequality is not so bad because the poor are rather well-off when we look at all the facts. The living conditions of the poor have improved for decades. Most of the poor have consumer items that were significant purchases for the middle class a few decades ago. They establish their thesis on countless facts such as "82 percent of poor adults reported never being hungry at any time in the prior year due to lack of money for food."

Issue: Has America Made Substantial Progress in the Rights of Blacks?
Yes: Noah C. Rothman, from "The 'Conversation about Race' That Isn't a Conversation: Twenty Years of Talk about Race Obscures This Country's Remarkable Progress," *Commentary* (2015)
No: Valerie Tarico, from "When Slavery Won't Die: The Oppressive Biblical Mentality America Can't Shake: An Interview with Black Theologian Kelly Brown Douglas on America's Greatest Sins," *AlterNet* (2015)

Noah C. Rothman, associate editor of HotAir.com, does not deny that strong racial prejudice still exists among whites, but he also shows many of the ways that behavior and institutions have become less discriminatory. Valerie Tarico is a psychologist and writer of two books and a number of articles. She begins with the painful story of Roof's shooting of nine people in a black church in Charleston because she wants to expose the racist thinking that is behind such acts. Her discussion with Kelly Brown Douglas also covers slavery and Trayvon Martin.

Issue: Has Gender Equality Come a Long Way?
Yes: Ronald Brownstein, from "Poll: American Men Embracing Gender Equality," *National Journal* (2015)
No: Leisa Peterson, from "Who Am I to Be Financially Feminist? (A Guide for Female Entrepreneurs)" *Huffington Post* (2015)

Ronald Brownstein, Atlantic Media's editorial director for strategic partnerships, reports on surprising findings of a recent poll that details major changes in gender attitudes of males and income, racial and ethnic groups. The survey suggests that men from all rungs on the economic and social ladder were open to the 'partnership of equals.' Leisa Peterson, money mindfulness expert and founder, TheWealthClinic, points out the many ways that she and other women today are discriminated against. She uses statistics and comparative studies to prove her thesis that women are worse off in several ways.

Unit: Political Economy and Institutions

Issue: Is Government Dominated by Big Business?
Yes: G. William Domhoff, from "Is the Corporate Elite Fractured, or Is There Continuing Corporate Dominance? Two Contrasting Views." *Class, Race and Corporate Power* (2015)
No: Mark S. Mizruchi, from "The Fracturing of the American Corporate Elite," Harvard University Press (2013)

Political sociologist G. William Domhoff presents two theories about who rules America. One is that the corporate elite are fractured and no longer stay united enough to rule America. The second is that the corporate elite are united enough to rule America. He argues for the second view. Mark S. Mizruchi, professor of sociology at Michigan University, argues the first view, that the corporate elite is fractured to the point that it does not rule America but uses its influence for the specific interests of individual corporations. This contributes to declining effectiveness of the American polity.

Jerry Z. Muller, professor of history at the Catholic University of America and author of *The Mind and the Market: Capitalism in Western Thought*, reports on how capitalism inevitably increases inequality because competition results in winners and losers. It is productive but it also increases commodification which erodes cultural values. It is a force for both good and bad. Chris Berg, a research fellow with the Institute of Public Affairs in Melbourne, Australia, and author of *In Defence of Freedom of Speech*, provides an enthusiastic defence of capitalism because it stimulates millions of innovations that improve millions of items that benefit us.

Chris Edwards, editor of Cato Institute's DownsizingGovernment.org, argues that the federal government runs badly. It is wasteful and inept. It does too much and does not have strong incentives for efficiency and effectiveness. Its problems include top down planning and bloated bureaucracy. Cut it back. Richard Eskrow, writer, a former Wall Street executive and a radio journalist, argues that the government must not be cut back because its services are badly needed. The anti-government side does want increases to the military budget, but the domestic side generates more jobs and growth.

Josh Sager, health policy intern at Community Catalyst, argues that most people on welfare want what all Americans want which is a job, the ability to provide for a family, and have pride in what they do. He denies the view of the right that they are lazy and enjoy being dependent and would get jobs when their welfare is taken away. Rather he advocates addressing the underlying causes of poverty. George F. Will, an American newspaper columnist with the *Washington Post* and political commentator with Fox News, points out the negative results of welfare. He blasts the American government for classifying large numbers of Americans as "needy." He gets his statistics from Nicholas Eberstadt, who documents the massive expansion of the welfare state and its erosion of recipients' character.

Ruth Conniff, editor and chief of *The Progressive*, criticizes No Child Left Behind for its excessive testing and teaching to the tests. She promotes a superior model of education which seeks to truly engage students and promote critical thinking. It gives teachers more control and thus treats them as professionals. This has worked in middle class schools and she advocates its use in poor areas. Russ Walsh, author, teacher, and coordinator of college reading at Rider University in Pennsylvania, reports on the book *Fear and Learning in America: Bad Data, Good Teachers, and the Attack on Public Education,* by John Kuhn. It blasts most school reform efforts as covers for corporate takeovers of the schools behind the rhetoric of reform.

Danny Crichton sees new technologies greatly increasing production and therefore consumption. Technologies will improve our lives. Digitally run robots are and will produce much faster than humans can and bring us into a wonderful world. Katherine Mangu-Ward sees technology as both good and bad. She is worried that the robots will take away many of our jobs and make most people unneeded in the labor force. What will happen? The results could pull our society apart.

Unit: Crime and Social Control

Issue: Are the Police in America to Be Condemned?

Yes: Nancy A. Heitzeg, from "'Broken Windows', Broken Lives and the Ruse of 'Public Order' Policing," *Truthout* (2015)

No: Nick Wing, from "If Most Police Officers Are 'Good Cops,' These Are Even Better," *Huffington Post* (2015)

Nancy A. Heitzeg, a professor of sociology and director of the critical studies of race/ethnicity program at St. Catherine University, presents and refutes the theory behind the "broken windows" approach to policing which is tough on crime and produces high imprisonment rates. She also presents several cases of police killing unarmed blacks and argues that the police need to be better controlled. Nick Wing, Senior Viral Editor at *The Huffington Post* emphasizes that most cops are good cops and act responsibly. He presents many reports by policemen and police chiefs which tell very positive stories about policemen to balance the very negative stories in the media.

Issue: Is American Justice Too Severe?

Yes: Eric Holder, from "Bold Steps to Reform and Strengthen American's Criminal Justice System," *Vital Speeches of the Day* (2013)

No: Zaid Jilani, from "Who Are the Biggest Killers in America? The Numbers Will Shock You," *AlterNet* (2015)

Eric Holder judges the current judicial system as broken and needing a major overhaul. The prison system needs to continue to punish and deter but also to rehabilitate. Their populations should be reduced which requires revised judicial laws and policies. "Too many Americans go to too many prisons for far too long, and for no truly good law enforcement reason." His reforms must also make communities safer. Zaid Jilani is an *AlterNet* staff writer who makes a good case that the really dangerous criminals are not the criminal poor but the rich and powerful. They make decisions that kill hundreds of thousands of people while murderers kill about 15,000 a year. For example, mal medical practice kills about 225,000 people a year. They also swindle, defraud, and cheat people out of $486 billion a year versus all property crimes mounting to $17.6 billion a year. These facts point out the real failure of the criminal justice system.

Issue: Is the United States in Significant Danger of Large-Scale Terrorist Attacks?

Yes: James R. Clapper, from "Statement for the Record: Worldwide Threat Assessment of the US Intelligence Community," Senate Intelligence Committee (2015)

No: Washington's Blog, from "There Are Far Fewer Terror Attacks Now Than in the 1970s," *Washington's Blog* (2015)

James R. Clapper, Director of national intelligence, gave this statement to Congress in 2015. It covers all types of terrorism from cyber terrorism to WMD and organized crime terrorism. Washington's Blog points out that terrorists' attacks have become practically non-existent since 2003 (shootings by psychos are not included in these statistics). Its point is that the threat of terrorism in the United States has been greatly exaggerated.

Unit: The Future: Population/Environment/Society

Issue: Does Immigration Benefit the Economy?

Yes: Robert Lynch and Patrick Oakford, from "The Economic Effects of Granting Legal Status and Citizenship to Undocumented Immigrants," Center for American Progress (2013)

No: Association for Mature American Citizens, from "How Much Does Illegal Immigration Cost You?" The Heritage Foundation (2015)

Robert Lynch, Everett E. Nuttle Professor and chair of the Department of Economics at Washington College, and Patrick Oakford, research assistant at the Center for American Progress, show that legal status and a road to citizenship for the unauthorized will bring about significant economic gains in terms of economic growth, earnings, tax revenues, and jobs and the sooner we provide legal status and citizenship, the greater the economic benefits will be for the nation. The main reason is that the immigrants will produce and earn significantly more than they cost and the results will ripple throughout the economy. The Association for Mature American Citizens argues that "Unlawful immigration and amnesty for current unlawful immigrants can pose large fiscal costs for U.S. taxpayers." The benefits would include Social Security, Medicare, welfare, education, police, and other services. Each such household would receive benefits that would exceed various payments to government of $14,387.

Preface

The English word *fanatic* is derived from the Latin *fanum*, meaning temple. It refers to the kind of madmen often seen in the precincts of temples in ancient times, the kind presumed to be possessed by deities or demons. The term first came into English usage during the seventeenth century, when it was used to describe religious zealots. Soon after, its meaning was broadened to include a political and social context. We have come to associate the term *fanatic* with a person who acts as if his or her views were inspired, a person utterly incapable of appreciating opposing points of view. The nineteenth-century English novelist George Eliot put it precisely: "I call a man fanatical when . . . he . . . becomes unjust and unsympathetic to men who are out of his own track." A fanatic may hear but is unable to listen. Confronted with those who disagree, a fanatic immediately vilifies opponents.

Most of us would avoid the company of fanatics, but who among us is not tempted to caricature opponents instead of listening to them? Who does not put certain topics off limits for discussion? Who does not grasp at euphemisms to avoid facing inconvenient facts? Who has not, in George Eliot's language, sometimes been "unjust and unsympathetic" to those on a different track? Who is not, at least in certain very sensitive areas, a *little* fanatical? The counterweight to fanaticism is open discussion. The difficult issues that trouble us as a society have at least two sides, and we lose as a society if we hear only one side. At the individual level, the answer to fanaticism is listening. And that is the underlying purpose of this book: to encourage its readers to listen to opposing points of view.

This book contains selections presented in a pro and con format. A variety of different controversial social issues are debated. The sociologists, political scientists, economists, and social critics whose views are debated here make their cases vigorously. In order to effectively read each selection, analyze the points raised, and debate the basic assumptions and values of each position, or, in other words, in order to think critically about what you are reading, you will first have to give each side a sympathetic hearing. John Stuart Mill, the nineteenth-century British philosopher, noted that the majority is not doing the minority a favor by listening to its views; it is doing *itself* a favor. By listening to contrasting points of view, we strengthen our own. In some cases, we change our viewpoints completely. But in most cases, we either incorporate some elements of the opposing

view—thus making our own richer—or else learn how to answer the objections to our viewpoints. Either way, we gain from the experience.

Organization of the book Each issue has an issue introduction, which sets the stage for the debate as it is argued in the YES and NO selections. Accompanying *Learning Outcomes* further help the reader to focus on just what he/she should "take away" from the issue debate. Each issue concludes with a section that explores the issue further and suggests questions which should help you to consider the issues from different angles. In reading the issue and forming your own opinions, you should not feel confined to adopt one or the other of the positions presented. There are positions in between the given views or totally outside them, and the suggestions for further reading that appear within the *Exploring the Issue* section at the end of each issue should help you find resources to continue your study of the subject. *Internet References* that are relevant to the issue are also included.

For more information on other McGraw-Hill Create™ titles and collections, visit http://create.mheducation.com.

Editor of This Volume

KURT FINSTERBUSCH is a professor of sociology at the University of Maryland at College Park. He received a BA in history from Princeton University in 1957, a BD from Grace Theological Seminary in 1960, and a PhD in sociology from Columbia University in 1969. He is the author of *Understanding Social Impacts* (Sage Publications, 1980), and he is the coauthor, with Annabelle Bender Motz, of *Social Research for Policy Decisions* (Wadsworth, 1980) and, with Jerald Hage, of *Organizational Change as a Development Strategy* (Lynne Rienner, 1987). He is the editor of *Annual Editions: Sociology* (McGraw-Hill/Contemporary Learning Series); *Annual Editions: Social Problems* (McGraw-Hill/Contemporary Learning Series); and *Sources: Notable Selections in Sociology*, 3rd ed. (McGraw-Hill/Dushkin, 1999).

Academic Advisory Board Members

Members of the Academic Advisory Board are instrumental in the final selection of articles for the Taking Sides series.

Their review of the articles for content, level, and appropriateness provides critical direction to the editor(s) and staff. We think that you will find their careful consideration reflected in this book.

Beth Macke
Kentucky Wesleyan College

Hua-Lun Huang
University of Louisiana

Marie Kathleen Daugherty
Donnelly College

Mary D. Young-Marcks
Southwest Michigan College

Rebecca Nees
Middle Georgia State College–Cochran

Rebecca Riehm
Jefferson Community College

Rosalind Kopfstein
Western Connecticut State University

Russ Ward
Maysville Community & Technical College

Introduction

Debating Social Issues

What Is Sociology?

"I have become a problem to myself," St. Augustine said. Put into a social and secular framework, St. Augustine's concern marks the starting point of sociology. We have become a problem to ourselves, and it is sociology that seeks to understand the problem and, perhaps, to find some solutions. The subject matter of sociology, then, is ourselves—people interacting with one another in groups and organizations.

Although the subject matter of sociology is very familiar, it is often useful to look at it in an unfamiliar light, one that involves a variety of theories and perceptual frameworks. In fact, to properly understand social phenomena, it *should* be looked at from several different points of view. In practice, however, this may lead to more friction than light, especially when each view proponent says, "I am right and you are wrong," rather than, "My view adds considerably to what your view has shown." Sociology, as a science of society, was developed in the nineteenth century. Auguste Comte (1798–1857), the French mathematician and philosopher who is considered to be the father of sociology, had a vision of a well-run society based on social science knowledge. Sociologists (Comte coined the term) would discover the laws of social life and then determine how society should be structured and run. Society would not become perfect, because some problems are intractable, but he believed that a society guided by scientists and other experts was the best possible society.

Unfortunately, Comte's vision was extremely naive. For most matters of state there is no one best way of structuring or doing things that sociologists can discover and recommend. Instead, sociologists debate more social issues than they resolve.

The purpose of sociology is to throw light on social issues and their relationship to the complex, confusing, and dynamic social world around us. It seeks to describe how society is organized and how individuals fit into it. But neither the organization of society nor the fit of individuals is perfect. Social disorganization is a fact of life—at least in modern, complex societies such as the one we live in. Here, perfect harmony continues to elude us, and "social problems" are endemic. The very institutions, laws, and policies that produce benefits also produce what sociologists call "unintended effects"—unintended and undesirable. The changes that please one sector of the society may displease another, or the changes that seem so indisputably healthy at first turn out to have a dark underside to them. The examples are endless. Modern urban life gives people privacy and freedom from snooping neighbors that the small town never afforded; yet that very privacy seems to breed an uneasy sense of anonymity and loneliness. Take another example: Hierarchy is necessary for organizations to function efficiently, but hierarchy leads to the creation of a ruling elite. Flatten out the hierarchy and you may achieve social equality—but at the price of confusion, incompetence, and low productivity.

This is not to say that all efforts to effect social change are ultimately futile and that the only sound view is the tragic one that concludes "nothing works." We can be realistic without falling into despair. In many respects, the human condition has improved over the centuries and has improved as a result of conscious social policies. But improvements are purchased at a price—not only a monetary price but one involving human discomfort and discontent. The job of policymakers is to balance the anticipated benefits against the probable costs. It can never hurt policymakers to know more about the society in which they work or the social issues they confront. That, broadly speaking, is the purpose of sociology. It is what this book is about. This volume examines issues that are central to the study of sociology.

Culture and Values

A common value system is the major mechanism for integrating a society, but modern societies contain so many different groups with differing ideas and values that integration must be built as much on tolerance of differences as on common values. Furthermore, technology and social conditions change, so values must adjust to new situations, often weakening old values. Some people (often called *conservatives*) will defend the old values. Others (often called *liberals*) will make concessions to allow for change. For example, the protection of human life is a sacred value to most people, but some would compromise that value when the life involved is a 90-year-old comatose man on life-support machines, who had signed a document indicating that he did not want to be kept alive under those conditions. The conservative would counter that once we make the value of human life relative, we become dangerously open to greater evils—that perhaps society will come to think it acceptable to terminate all sick, elderly people undergoing expensive treatments. This is only one example of how values are hotly debated today.

The first issue examines America's materialism and consumerism, which Gary Gutting asserts has negative impacts on our characters and the shrinking of the common good. Michael Fisher, presenting James Livingston's thesis on the benefits of high consumption, challenges the theory that austerity is character building. Rather, we should enjoy life to the fullest.

The next issue deals with social media and discusses its positive and negative effects. The list of effects is quite long, and opinions differ on how beneficial it is overall. A major use of social media is to connect with friends and family. This positive benefit is tempered somewhat by the fact that heavy social media use is associated with fewer face-to-face interactions with these very people. Social media is also very useful for many instrumental purposes, including getting information and conducting one's affairs. The debate, however, arises over the many negative aspects of the social media and how much they subtract from the positive benefits. There is a debate over how much social media hurts social relations relative to how much it helps social relationships. We obtain much information from social media, but we also obtain much misinformation from it. It leads to social connections but also to social isolation and depression and even personality disorders in some people (though not often). Further, the loss of privacy has badly hurt some people. It is very hard to pull all the effects of social media together and come up with a clear view of its overall impact on individuals and society.

Sex Roles, Gender, and the Family

An area that has experienced tremendous value change in the last several decades is sex roles and the family. Women in large numbers have rejected major aspects of their traditional gender roles and family roles while remaining strongly committed to much of the mother role and to many feminine characteristics. Men have changed much less, but their situation and attitudes have recently changed considerably.

The first issue examines the strength of the American family. Isabel Sawhill points out that the family is strong only among the college educated and very weak among the noncollege educated. Bradford Wilcox directly counters the troubled family thesis which he calls a myth. He shows that the majority of marriages are happy and accepted as fair.

The next issue discusses the current debate about whether women can strongly pursue (lean in) a career and have a rich family life at the same time. Anne-Marie Slaughter says that they cannot and Gayle Tzemach Lemmon says they can. She admits it will be hard but it is doable and promises great rewards.

The final issue examines the positive and negative effects of same-sex marriage. Peter S. Sprigg identifies 10 negative effects of same-sex marriage which would produce horrific results. Some of these negative effects are based on his assumptions about how various governments, agencies, and institutions would change as a result of same-sex marriages. Jay Michaelson supports Vice President Joe Biden in his celebration of the Supreme Court legalizing same-sex marriages by striking down laws against it. Biden strongly believes that gays deserve equal rights as much as straights.

Stratification and Inequality

The first issue centers around a sociological debate about whether or not increasing economic inequality is a serious problem. Joseph Stiglitz asserts that it is, while Robert Rector and Rachel Sheffield argue that the actual inequality is less than the perceived inequality. In fact the poor in America are rather well off when you look at what they have.

Today one of the most controversial issues regarding inequalities is the position of blacks in American society. Is the election of Barack Obama an indicator that America is now a post-racial society, meaning that blacks and whites are essentially on equal footing? In the next issue, Noah C. Rothman differentiates between the discussion of race which focuses on episodes that show the horrible racism that still operates in America and the solid gains of blacks in many areas that causes less of a stir. Valerie Tarico and her interviewee Kelly Brown Douglas disagree. They explore the underlining assumptions and beliefs that underlie some murderous events and discover the subconscious racism that explains the events.

The final issue deals with the gender inequality. One of the major forces slowing down the march toward gender equality is the continuing patriarchal thinking of men. Ronald Brownstein presents fascinating survey findings that show that men's opinions have shifted dramatically toward greater gender equality. Leisa Peterson argues from her personal story as well as sound data that women face considerable obstacles to their progress.

Political Economy and Institutions

Sociologists study not only the poor, the workers, and the victims of discrimination but also those at the top of society—those who occupy what the late sociologist C. Wright Mills used to call "the command posts." The question is whether the "pluralist" model or the "power elite" model is the one that best fits the facts in America. Does a single power elite rule the United States, or do many groups contend for power and influence so that the political process is accessible to all?

In the first issue, G. William Domhoff and Mark Mizruchi argue over the degree of unity and cooperation that the economic elite have. Both agree that the economic elite have a lot of power and dominate the political process but their power varies with the degree that they are united. Domhoff tries to show that they are very united and Mizruchi tries to show that they often are not united and sometimes do not lobby for their interests.

Another major political economy issue is whether capitalism has serious defects. In the next issue, Jerry Z. Muller explains how capitalism greatly increases inequality which creates political imbalances that undermine democracy. It also causes commodification and erodes moral and cultural values. David Berg strongly praises capitalism on how it stimulates innovation and risk taking which greatly advances societies.

The following issue addresses a major debate of the day: How big or small should the government be? Chris Edwards argues that the government is too big to work well. It has poor incentives and therefore is inefficient, inept, and wasteful. Cut it back and it will work better. Richardd Eskow argues the opposite policy. The government must not be cut back because its services are badly needed.

The United States is a capitalist welfare state, and the role of the state in welfare is examined in the next issue. The government provides welfare to people who cannot provide for their own needs in the labor market. This issue debates the wisdom of the Work Opportunity Reconciliation Act of 1996, which ended Aid to Families of Dependent Children (which was what most people equated with welfare). The debate is about the type of people who are on welfare. Josh Sager believes that the people on welfare want what most Americans want, which is a job, the ability to provide for a family, and have pride in what they do. He denies that they are lazy and prefer welfare to work. The real need is to address the underlying causes of poverty.

On the other hand, George Will sees welfare in very negative terms. With statistics he shows that the welfare system has expanded greatly and gives too much to many groups of people. Welfare erodes recipients' character.

Education is one of the biggest jobs of the government as well as the key to individual prosperity and the success of the economy. For decades the American system of education has been severely criticized. Such an important institution is destined to be closely scrutinized, and many reforms have been attempted over the years. The main policy trying to improve public schools in recent years has been the No Child Left Behind (NCLB), which is addressed by the next issue. On December 10, 2015 Congress passed the Every Student Succeeds Act which is an effort to improve the NCLB. It retains the program of testing Math and English and demanding improving scores especially for schools with low scores. It confers much more power to the states and local school districts for methods for implementing the tests and instituting sanctions. It tries to preserve the spirit of the NCLB but change its implementation. Ruth Conniff criticizes No Child Left Behind for its excessive testing and teaching to the tests. This approach emphasizes memorization but Conniff advocates truly engaging students and promoting critical thinking. Russ Walsh reports on the book, *Fear and Learning in America: Bad Data, Good Teachers, and the Attack on Public Education,* by John Kuhn. It blasts most school reform efforts as a smokescreen for corporate takeovers of the schools behind the rhetoric of reform. In effect he argues that we do not need "reform."

The next issue looks at the benefits and costs of new technologies that might change our lives. Will it be for better or worse? Danny Crichton sees technology in very positive terms while Katherine Mangu-Ward sees technology as both good and bad. Crichton sees new technologies greatly increasing production and therefore consumption. Technologies will improve our lives. Digitally run robots are and will produce much faster than humans can and bring us into a wonderful world. Mangu-Ward is worried that the robots will take away many of our jobs and make most people unneeded in the labor force. What will happen? The results could pull our society apart.

Crime and Social Control

Crime is interesting to sociologists because crimes are those activities that society makes illegal and will use force to stop. Sociologists ask why are some acts made illegal and others (even those that may be more harmful) not made illegal. Surveys indicate that concern about crime is extremely high in America. Is the fear of crime, however, rightly placed? Americans fear mainly street crime, but the review of research on the costs of crime by Jacek Czabanski shows that the complete cost of white-collar crime is much larger than the cost of street crime. His research shows that the full costs of crime are very high and constitute a significant portion of GDP. *The Economist* analyzes different statistics. It shows that crime has declined significantly throughout the developed world. These data justify major changes in the criminal justice system and how criminals should be treated.

Current events have forced America to look hard at the criminal justice system, which the next two issues do. The first asks the question about what to do about horrendous police behavior and the second asks what to do about the entire judicial system. First Nancy A. Heitzeg criticizes the current police of very extensive policing which has led to hassling people for minor crimes or just suspicions that ends in the suspect's death. Nick Wing argues that the public is overreacting to a few egregious police actions that have harmed suspects. Most cops are good cops and act responsibly. Let's not overreact. On the second question about the judicial system's defects Eric Holder judges the current judicial system as broken and needing a major overhaul. Punishments are too severe, prisons are too full, and the system is very racially biased. Zaid Jilani makes a good case that the major failure of the criminal justice system is its failure to prosecute the rich and powerful. They make decisions that kill hundreds of thousands of people a year and they swindle, defraud, and cheat people out of $486 billion a year and most of them get away free. This is our real justice problem.

The final issue deals with large-scale terrorist attacks which are perhaps the major problem in America today. The first article is the report by the director of national intelligence, which assesses the risks connected to all types of terrorism including from cyberterrorism to WMD and organized crime terrorism. The second article by Washington's Blog points out that terrorist attacks have become practically nonexistent since 2003, so the threat of terrorism in the United States has been greatly exaggerated.

The Future: Population/ Environment/Society

The first issue deals with population migration. Does the recent and current immigration into the United States benefit or harm our economy? Robert Lynch and Patrick Oakford show that immigrants help our economy when all costs and benefits are counted. The positive effect is greater if immigrants have a path to citizenship. The

Association for Mature American Citizens disagrees. It argues that "Unlawful immigration and amnesty for current unlawful immigrants can pose large fiscal costs for U.S. taxpayers." Their benefits would exceed their payments to government.

Many social commentators speculate on "the fate of the earth." The next issue on the state of the planet addresses this concern. Some environmentalists view the future in apocalyptic terms. They see the possibility that the human race could degrade the environment to the point that population growth and increasing economic production could overshoot the carrying capacity of the globe. The resulting collapse could lead to the extinction of much of the human race and the end of free societies. Other analysts believe that these fears are groundless. Daniel Immerwahr reviews the major environmental problems and argues that major cutbacks in resource use will be required to address them but perhaps the quality of our lives could improve at lower consumption levels. Ramez Naam discusses both great progress and problems of the past century but argues that ideas and innovations will solve most of the identified problems and bring great prosperity.

The final issue assesses the proper role of the United States in the world today. Should it be the world leader or share power? Salvatore Babones argues that America has been the hegemonic power since the collapse of the Soviet Union and is still the hegemonic power and should assert itself as such to keep the world from chaos and destruction. Will Ruger agrees that America stands alone in terms of power but advocates restraint in the use of that power. Our goals are better achieved when we share power.

The Social Construction of Reality

An important idea in sociology is that people construct social reality in the course of interaction by attaching social meanings to the reality they are experiencing and then responding to those meanings. Two people can walk down a city street and derive very different meanings from what they see around them. Both, for example, may see homeless people—but they may see them in different contexts. One fits them into a picture of once-vibrant cities dragged into decay and ruin because of permissive policies that have encouraged pathological types to harass citizens; the other observer fits them into a picture of an America that can no longer hide the wretchedness of its poor. Both feel that they are seeing something deplorable, but their views of what makes it deplorable are radically opposed. Their differing views of what they have seen will lead to very different prescriptions for what should be done about the problem.

The social construction of reality is an important idea for this book because each author is socially constructing reality and working hard to persuade you to see his or her point of view, that is, to see the definition of the situation and the set of meanings he or she has assigned to the situation. In doing this, each author presents a carefully selected set of facts, arguments, and values. The arguments contain assumptions or theories, some of which are spelled out and some of which are unspoken. The critical reader has to judge the evidence for the facts, the logic and soundness of the arguments, the importance of the values, and whether or not omitted facts, theories, and values invalidate the thesis. This book facilitates this critical thinking process by placing authors in opposition. This puts the reader in the position of critically evaluating two constructions of reality for each issue instead of one.

Conclusion

Writing in the 1950s, a period that was in some ways like our own, the sociologist C. Wright Mills said that Americans know a lot about their "troubles," but they cannot make the connections between seemingly personal concerns and the concerns of others in the world. If they could only learn to make those connections, they could turn their concerns into *issues*. An issue transcends the realm of the personal. According to Mills, "An issue is a public matter: some value cherished by publics is felt to be threatened. Often there is a debate about what the value really is and what it is that really threatens it." It is not primarily personal troubles but social issues that I have tried to present in this book. The variety of topics in it can be taken as an invitation to discover what Mills called "the sociological imagination." This imagination, said Mills, "is the capacity to shift from one perspective to another—from the political to the psychological; from examination of a single family to comparative assessment of the national budgets of the world. . . . It is the capacity to range from the most impersonal and remote transformations to the most intimate features of the human self—and to see the relations between the two." This book, with a range of issues well suited to the sociological imagination, is intended to enlarge that capacity.

Kurt Finsterbusch
University of Maryland, College Park

Unit 1

Culture and Values

*S*ociologists recognize that a fairly strong consensus on the basic values of a society contributes greatly to the smooth functioning of that society. The functioning of modern, complex urban societies, however, often depends on the tolerance of cultural differences and equal rights and protections for all cultural groups. In fact, such societies can be enriched by the contributions of different cultures. But at some point the cultural differences may result in a pulling apart that exceeds the pulling together.

Selected, Edited, and with Issue Framing Material by:
Kurt Finsterbusch, *University of Maryland, College Park*

ISSUE

Is It Necessary to Become Less Consumerist?

YES: Gary Gutting, from "Less, Please," *Commonweal* (2013)

NO: Michael Fisher, from "Review of James Livingston's *Against Thrift: Why Consumer Culture Is Good for the Economy, the Environment, and Your Soul*," Society for U.S. Intellectual History (2012)

Learning Outcomes

After reading this issue, you will be able to:

- Assess whether consumption is contributing significantly to environmental deterioration.
- Consider both the positive and negative effects of modern consumption on the consumers.
- Look at the different types of consumption and evaluate what type of needs it typically meets: whether basic needs like food, or functional needs like automobile transportation, or social needs like taking care of a family, or symbolic needs like goods and services which enhance one's status.
- Discern which consumption strengthens character and which consumption weakens character.
- Analyze when consumption has an addictive aspect to it.
- Explain the meaning of insatiable with respect to consumption.

ISSUE SUMMARY

YES: Professor Gary Gutting, holder of the Notre Dame Endowed Chair in Philosophy, praises the modern economy for its amazing progress in production and consumer benefits but also recognizes its negative effects on our character and authentic well-being. It has led to economic insatiability and shrinking of the common good. Therefore, he favors less consumption.

NO: Michael Fisher, graduate student in American history at the University of Rochester, summarizes in this review article the thesis of James Livingston that the consumer culture is good, not bad. Though Fisher supports Livingston's thesis, he does not agree with Livingston's positive view of advertising. Nevertheless, he and Livingston favor more consumption.

There are two major concerns about consumption in America today. First, does it currently having net negative effects on the environment? Second, does it, on net, have positive or negative impacts on our character and moral fiber? If it has significant negative impacts on the environment, then the next question is whether these negative impacts will overcome the regenerative powers of the environment and thus limit the quality of life of future generations. Abundant data show that humans have been overexploiting croplands for decades, leading to substantial worldwide soil loss and nutrient loss. Grasslands are overgrazed, forests are depleted, oceans are overfished, utilizable water is declining, and toxic pollution is increasing worldwide. Serious attention to these trends leads some analysts to give very pessimistic predictions for the future. For example, on October 29, 2013, I received an e-mail which reported on an article by Naomi Klein in *The Statesman* arguing that we must make radical changes to prevent climate change impacts from destroying the planet. Others recognize these adverse environmental trends, argue that they are less severe than the pessimists claim, and believe that new technologies will overcome these problems. The impact of consumption on our character is treated in this issue.

What are the effects of modern consumption patterns on consumers, culture, and society? In 1960 Vance Packard wrote *The Waste Makers,* which tried to document the transformation of the frugal society to the wasteful society. In the frugal society people bought only what they needed. To keep the economy booming, however, they had to buy more. According to Packer, "What was needed was strategies that would make Americans in large numbers into voracious, wasteful, compulsive consumers." The producers succeeded, the economy roared ahead, and people's desires became insatiable. Packer had chapters on hedonism, planned obsolescence, throwaway spirit, commercialization of American life, and vanishing resources. His greatest concern was on the transformation of people's values to an emphasis on "pleasure-mindedness, self indulgence, materialism" and the decline of self-denial. In the half century since Packard's shock at the changing culture around him, a fairly large literature on consumption has confirmed his observations and expanded his critique. It generally asserts that consumption affects people at deep psychological levels and has become an important basis for one's self-esteem and the esteem of others.

The consumption literature from Packard to today emphasizes numerous negative aspects of this cultural change. First, since 1957 average consumption per capita has tripled but happiness has slightly declined. Happiness does not seem to be related to income except at a very low consumption level where survival is at stake. Second, the desire for consumer goods and services has become insatiable. No matter how much one has it is never enough. We always want more or better things. We are never satisfied. Third, this literature argues that the endless work required for high consumption and the consumption experiences themselves squeeze out close relationships and time with loved ones which are major causes of happiness.

Gary Gutting draws upon a book by Robert and Edward Skidelsky called *How Much Is Enough?* to address these issues. The Skidelskys tie excessive consumption to capitalism, which is an excellent system for providing basic needs but ends up pushing excessive consumption. The result is tragic because people are transformed in negative ways in the process. "The Skidelskys argue that this destructive spiral is not inevitable" and suggest ways to better achieve the good life. The reading by Michael Fisher presenting the analysis of James Livingston advocates the opposite view. For them the good life is the result of the myriad of benefits that affluence (high production and consumption) provide. They take issue with the puritanical view that we must not focus on enjoying ourselves but limit and control ourselves. That may be appropriate for eras of scarcity of centuries ago but today we should enjoy the benefits of prosperity.

YES

Gary Gutting

Less, Please

Capitalism & the Good Life

Is capitalism an enemy of the good life? Marxists and other radicals think so. Toward the end of *How Much Is Enough?*, Robert and Edward Skidelsky (an economist father and his philosopher son) quote one such thinker:

> Working men have been surrendered, isolated and helpless, to the hard-heartedness of employers and the greed of unchecked competition . . . so that a small number of very rich men have been able to lay upon the teeming masses of the laboring poor a yoke little better than that of slavery.

Readers of *Commonweal* will be more likely than most to recognize the firebrand cited as Leo XIII in *Rerum novarum*.

The Skidelskys' own rhetoric is usually more restrained. The sober line of thought that underlies their engaging, informative, and stimulating book goes roughly as follows. Under capitalism, businesses sell us goods and service that are essential for living well, and most of us get the money to buy these things by working for businesses or, less often, profiting from investments in them. We need capitalism because no other economic system can produce sufficient goods to meet our essential material needs such as food, shelter, clothes, and medical care. But these goods are not enough. A good life mainly depends on intangibles such as love, friendship, beauty, and virtue—things capitalism cannot produce and money cannot buy. Given a sufficient minimum of material goods, the good life does not depend on the world of commerce.

Nonetheless, for most of us, work takes up the bulk of our time and energy, leaving comparatively little for living a good life. Some see their work itself as a pursuit of beauty, truth, or virtue. But most find what they do valuable primarily as a means of earning money to buy material necessities. And capitalist society itself insists that a good life requires much more than a minimum of material goods. A truly good life, it urges, requires fine food, a large and well-furnished home, stylish clothing, and a steady diet of diverting and enriching experiences derived from sports, culture, and travel—all of which are expensive.

We all agree that there's a limit beyond which more material goods would make little difference to the goodness of our lives. But almost all of us think we are considerably below that limit. In general, then, capitalism works against the good life from two directions. It requires us to engage in work that makes little contribution to our living well, beyond supplying our material necessities, and it urges us to believe, falsely, that a good life is mainly a matter of accumulating material possessions. The Skidelskys sum it up this way: "The irony is that . . . now that we have achieved abundance [in advanced capitalist countries], the habits bred into us by capitalism have left us incapable of enjoying it properly."

Their view of capitalism is critical rather than revolutionary. They decry its tendency to sacrifice the human good to the goods of the market, but think we can curb this tendency and harness capitalism's productive power for our pursuit of the good life. For them, the core problem with capitalism is "economic insatiability"—the intrinsic drive for increasing production (and therefore profits) without limit. The limitless demand for more can even lead, as we have recently seen, to economic catastrophe. More important, capitalism is morally deficient because its drivers are the vices of "greed and acquisitiveness," which pile up "goods" that take us away from the good life.

The insatiability of capitalism exploits the corresponding insatiability of individual desires. No matter how much I possess, I find myself desiring more than I have. As I become rich enough to satisfy all my old desires, I develop new ones. Moreover, beyond a certain level of wealth, I begin to desire the best of everything, where the "best" (rare wines, exclusive resorts, the paintings of Old Masters) are in such limited supply that hardly anyone can afford them. And in addition to our spontaneous individual desires, we develop other desires simply because there are things others have that we don't. Capitalism's endless need to sell more and more is met by our need to buy more and more.

The Skidelskys argue that this destructive spiral is not inevitable. It has arisen only because we have moved away from a properly human ideal of a good life. Their positive project draws on the traditions of premodern thought for a viable contemporary account of what makes for a good life. Their discussion, perceptive if schematic, produces a plausible list of seven "basic goods": health, security, respect, personal freedom (which they refer to, somewhat oddly, as "personality"), harmony with nature, friendship, and leisure (not idleness but freedom from wage-labor for work that is satisfying in itself). Their list has the distinct merit of allowing for the wide range of current disagreement on moral questions such as sexuality and personal rights. The authors also propose, with appropriate tentativeness, a variety of measures to curb capitalism's "insatiability." These include a basic wage (or personal endowment) for everyone, consumption taxes to curb excessive consumption, and severe restrictions on advertising.

This positive project has, of course, no point unless we accept the basic thesis that capitalism is a threat to a good life, and some of the Skidelskys' most crucial pages try to defuse two major objections to this claim. One objection comes from utilitarian thinkers, the other from liberal political theorists. I will assess the Skidelskys' position by reflecting on these two objections.

The first objection centers on a concept many readers will have found oddly absent from our discussion so far: happiness. Most modern people agree with utilitarian moral theorists that happiness is what everyone desires—and should desire—most. The Skidelskys would have no problem with this view if "happiness" were, like Aristotle's *eudaimonia*, merely a synonym for living a good life. But nowadays happiness is seen as a matter of subjective states of satisfaction, not objectively good achievements. The point of utilitarian morality is to maximize subjective satisfaction for everyone: "the greatest happiness for the greatest number." To do this, we need to find out what makes people happy and then supply them with whatever that is.

Economists and psychologists step forward for the first task, deploying "happiness surveys" to determine how various factors (health, wealth, sex, families, sports, reading, television, etc.) affect happiness. Once we know what we need to be happy, capitalist enterprises are ready to deliver the goods. To achieve their goal of maximizing profit, businesses must provide as many consumers as possible with as much satisfaction as they can. The capitalist is the merchant of happiness.

The Skidelskys are deeply skeptical of happiness science. They note that one of its most robust results is the "Easterlin paradox" (named for the economist Richard Easterlin, who formulated it in 1974). The paradox is that, in industrially advanced countries, major improvements in living standards have no long-term effect on happiness. This, the Skidelskys say, leads to a destructive dilemma. If the paradox is correct, then efforts to bring about improvements in living standards are futile. If it is not correct, then our best methods for discovering what makes people happy are inadequate. In either case, the utilitarian project of maximizing happiness is stymied.

This is an intriguing line of argument, but at best it undermines only the global project of producing happiness by altering the entire economic climate. It may still be possible to make numerous local improvements through actions focused on specific situations. In any case, the Skidelskys have a deeper critique of the happiness project: that the "supreme good" of humankind cannot be merely a succession of enjoyable psychological states. "We cannot think that all our suffering and labor has as its end something as trivial as a buzz or a tingle."

Although the Skidelskys don't mention him, Robert Nozick made the same point in *Anarchy, State, and Utopia* with his thought experiment of the Experience Machine. Suppose neuroscientists develop a machine that would allow you to have any subjective experiences you like—a great romantic love, writing a brilliant novel, saving your nation from destruction. You could even program an entire life filled with the most enjoyable experiences possible. But plugging into such a machine would not give you a good life, because you would never have actually done anything; you would have spent your days sitting in a laboratory enjoying a succession of feelings. The Skidelskys describe such illusory satisfactions as "the mirage of happiness." "If happiness is a mere private sensation, with no intrinsic connection to living well . . . why not admit up front that our concern is with the good life—and let happiness look after itself?"

Their critique, however, succeeds against only the naive claim that a good life consists merely of a succession of felicific fizzes. They agree that pleasurable feelings produced by objective achievements contribute to the good life, referring, for example, to the "glad apprehension . . . that my daughter has got into university, that my country has been liberated." But then why not admit that subjective pleasure in its own right is one of the essential components of a good life? Imagine the inverse of Nozick's Experience Machine: a device that does not interfere with my achieving great things in the real world but deactivates the pleasure centers of the brain so that I never enjoy anything I do. The result would be a far cry from anything we would regard as a good life. Nor is it enough to allow only the "glad apprehension" that something objectively good has occurred. Enjoying the taste of food helps make for a good life, even if I don't also feel satisfaction at having partaken of healthy nourishment.

The Skidelskys have at best shown that pleasurable feelings cannot be all there is to a good life, but pleasure may still have a major role; it may even deserve a place on their list of what makes for such a life. If this is so—and common sense along with most philosophy and psychology supports the idea—our account of the good life cannot discount the pleasures provided by the capitalist system of production.

But I presume the Skidelskys could accept these points as friendly amendments. There remains the second objection, which the Skidelskys themselves recognize as "the last, and deepest, objection to our project." This is the claim that their view rejects the fundamental insight of liberalism put forward by John Rawls, Amartya Sen, and Martha Nussbaum, among others. Here is the Skidelskys own deft statement of the objection:

> A liberal state . . . embodies no positive vision but only such principles as are necessary for people of different tastes and ideals to live together in harmony. To promote, as a matter of public policy, a positive idea of the good life is by definition illiberal, perhaps even totalitarian.

Their brief initial response to this objection is that it "rests on a thorough misconception of liberalism," which, throughout most of its history, has been "imbued with classical and Christian ideals of dignity, civility, and tolerance." They also cite, from the twentieth century, such "prototypical liberals as Keynes, Isaiah Berlin, and Lionel Trilling," who "took it for granted that upholding civilization was among the functions of the state." They note that Rawls in particular allows for a category of "primary goods," including "civic and political liberties, income and wealth, access to public office and 'the social bases of respect.'" These are necessary conditions for, as Rawls puts it, "forming a rational plan of life" and so must be desired by all rational agents, regardless of what basic goods they hope to achieve by carrying out their life plan. (Rawls presents his basic goods as resources everyone should have. Sen and Nussbaum maintain that beyond Rawls's resources, people also need the capabilities to make use of them.)

The Skidelskys rightly point out that contemporary liberals insist on primary goods rather than basic goods because they see autonomy—the right of people to choose their own conception of the good life—as an overarching value. Basic goods specify the content of a good life; the primary goods merely tell us what is needed to choose and work for any conception of a good life. The liberal emphasis on autonomy restricts government to promoting primary goods, while remaining neutral regarding basic goods and the various conceptions of the good life they specify.

The Skidelskys cite an example from Nussbaum that nicely focuses the difference between them. "A person who has opportunities for play," she says, "can always choose a workaholic life"—her point being that, as long as this choice is free and does not harm others, the state has no reason to oppose it. Such opposition would, in fact, be a paternalistic interference with personal autonomy. The Skidelskys disagree, arguing that "if the workaholic life is an impoverished one, as most people who have thought about the matter agree it is, then its adoption over finer lives, whether freely chosen or not, is surely something to worry us." As to the charge of paternalism, they point out that all Western nations have laws limiting the use of drugs, pornography, and alcohol, and use taxation as an incentive to promote or discourage behaviors such as home ownership and energy conservation.

This is not a convincing response. For one thing, the fact that we deplore a behavior is not a reason for violating autonomy to discourage it. For another, allowing a paternalistic approach to some evils is consistent with refusing to put the power of the state behind a comprehensive view of the human good. (Also, as the Skidelskys note, an entirely rigorous liberalism would discourage only behavior that it sees as dangerous to others.) In any case, the Skidelskys agree that, precisely because "the good life is by any reasonable definition an autonomous or self-determined one, there is only so much that the state, as a coercive body, can do to promote it."

For a deeper grasp of what's at stake in the liberal objection, we need to return to the Skidelskys' starting point: the relation of capitalism to the good life. As proponents of a free society, they agree that in the end individuals must make their own choices about how to pursue a good life. They are also unwilling to reject capitalism as the engine of our economic system. The capitalist system claims to be the servant of free choice, producing whatever consumers desire, to the extent that they desire it. But the claim is disingenuous. The goal of capitalist enterprises is to maximize profit, and they are willing—and often well equipped—to form consumer desires and public policy to achieve this goal. Advertising, public relations, and lobbying are their most effective weapons.

How can we maintain capitalism as our means of economic production and yet not allow it to determine our conception of the good life? The Skidelskys' approach derives from Keynes's 1930 essay "Economic Possibilities for Our Grandchildren," where he predicted that by 2030 the capitalist system would be able to meet all our material needs with the average employee working only about fifteen hours a week. This, he thought, would allow ample leisure time for people to pursue the good life. Keynes was right about the productive power of capitalism but wrong about the decrease in work hours, which have fallen only 20 percent since 1930. Why did Keynes go wrong about the balance of work and leisure? Because, the Skidelskys say, "a free-market economy both gives employers the power to dictate hours and terms of work and inflames our innate tendency to competitive, status-driven consumption."

In response, they propose their anti-insatiability conception of a good life and, as we have seen, suggest various legislative measures—primarily a guaranteed basic income that does not require employment (to make it easier for people to work less), as well as consumption taxes and strong restrictions on advertising (to reduce excessive consumption). But in a democracy such a legislative approach requires the support of most citizens, and that would be available only if the Skidelskys' goal were already achieved. The essential liberal objection to the Skidelskys is that their proposals are Utopian, given a population that overwhelmingly subscribes to the insatiability ethos of capitalism. The only people who would support their reforms are the small minority who have already renounced this ethos.

Let me suggest an alternative approach, one that is consistent with both the Skidelskys' appeal to traditional values and modern liberalism's emphasis on autonomy: a return to the weakened but still viable ideal of a liberal education.

We find enormous dissatisfaction with our educational system but there is still considerable respect for the idea that schooling should provide not so much vocational training as liberal learning. A liberal education forms citizens who have a broad understanding of the possibilities of human life as well as a critical ability to make informed choices among these possibilities. Such education will not necessarily inculcate the Skidelskys'—or any other—specific vision of the good life. But it will develop self-determining agents who can see through the blandishments of the market and insist that it provide what they have independently decided they need in order to lead a good life.

We cannot control the decisions of such agents, nor should we. They are free not only in the metaphysical sense of controlling their actions but also in the cultural sense of grasping, to some significant extent, the range of options available to them in their historical context. This latter freedom derives from access to our cultural history's enduring and ever-increasing legacy of literary, philosophical, political, religious, and scientific achievements. These achievements underlie the specific institutions and practices that define a person's world, but they also support radical critiques and alternatives to that world. Culture contains the seeds of revolution.

Here I am appealing to the same intellectual and moral heritage the Skidelskys draw on to formulate their conception of a good life. But they make the Utopian (ultimately Platonic) mistake of thinking that we can transform our world by legislating values from above. Rather, the transformation must come from below, forged by the very people it is meant to benefit. The liberal education I advocate is not that of old-world hereditary elites, bringing their inherited wisdom to the masses. It is inspired by the new-world ideal of an education equally open to everyone, limited only by one's ability and persistence. There is a risk that free citizens educated in this way will not arrive at the truth we have in mind. They may, free and informed, choose the material illusions of capitalism. But, in a democracy, an ideal of the good life has no force unless the people's will sustains it. Liberally educated consumers—and voters—are our only hope of subordinating capitalism to a humane vision of the good life.

GARY GUTTING holds the Notre Dame Endowed Chair in Philosophy and has authored seven books on philosophy.

Michael Fisher

 **NO**

Review of James Livingston's *Against Thrift: Why Consumer Culture Is Good for the Economy, the Environment, and Your Soul*

Goods Aplenty: *Against Thrift* and the Question, "What For?"

Following on the heels of his contentious rereading of late twentieth-century American thought and culture,[1] James Livingston has written a new book that promises to provoke much more than historiographic controversy. As the title suggests, *Against Thrift* is an ethical indictment and a political argument against the Protestant work ethic; yet it also prophesies a new moral order that might be just around the corner.

Livingston wants us to be happier, more carefree and better able to enjoy the pleasures of this life. In no uncertain terms, he thinks we ought to abandon the last vestiges of Puritanism that constrain our bodies and our minds in favor of a wholehearted embrace of spending—vigorous spending. Instead of saving and delaying gratification, he goads us: we should be focusing our scarce psychic and material resources on satisfying desire in the here and now. Why? Because the age-old assumption that work should come before play, that self-discipline and restraint are preferable to immediate gratification, is based on a series of false premises. So Livingston says and, for much of *Against Thrift,* he presumes to demonstrate. As he puts it in the introduction, "In this book, I make the case for consumer culture: why it's actually good for the economy, the environment, and our souls, among other things. In this sense, I'm trying to heal the split in our personalities by demonstrating that less work, less thrift, more leisure, and more spending are the cures for what ails us."[2]

What ails us in Livingston's view is partly economic and partly psychological (hence the supposed split in our personalities). But the twin ailments stem from a common cultural root. At least in theory, most Americans still buy the Puritan premise that disciplined frugality begets virtue whereas giving in to one's instincts begets vice. Because we remain beholden to the resulting economic mindset, which assumes that saving and investing in the future are the best ways to ensure long-term growth and security, we have trained ourselves psychologically to associate the deferral of emotional gratification—particularly the gratification that comes with buying consumer products—with goodness.

According to Livingston, this conventional wisdom informs everything from our personal morality to our response to the 2008 financial crisis; and the symmetry between the two examples is scarcely coincidental: "All adults—not just parents—have a powerful psychological urge to put their desires on hold, and that urge makes us receptive to the notion that we'd better be saving more and spending less, just like all the mainstream economists and reputable journalists keep telling us to. We know what will happen to our bank accounts, our waistlines, and our marriage vows if we stop listening to their insistent voice of reason."[3]

Against much popular (in fact Populist) opinion, Livingston argues quite convincingly that both the Great Depression and the Great Recession drew from this very thrift-centered mindset. We miss the connection, he says, only because we have yet to distance ourselves sufficiently from the late nineteenth century. Since the 1890s, when the original Populists almost succeeded in restructuring the existing relationship between labor and capital, American antimonopoly sentiment has gone hand in hand with the traditional argument against consumption; and the two have tended to reinforce each other. Particularly when the economy goes bust, as it did in 1929 and 2008, the majority of Americans blame corporate power and profligate consumers, and the underlying problem is said to be moral failings on the part of irresponsible individuals.

As Livingston documents throughout "Part One: Our Very Own Perestroika," this typical response—moral indignation against excessive spending, speculation, and greed—was especially widespread after the 2008 crisis. Yet it ignores several key pieces of historical evidence, most importantly the role of surplus capital, or what Livingston calls "redundant profits with no productive outlet, which eventually find their way into speculative markets that inflate bubbles." Here is his extended reading of both the Great Depression and the Great Recession:

> I explain both events as results of surplus capital generated by huge shifts in income shares away from labor, wages, and consumption, toward capital, profits, and corporate savings. And I draw the obvious conclusion from the historical comparison: if the New Deal succeeded by enfranchising working people and shifting income shares back toward wages and consumption—not by means of a 'financial fix'—then a massive redistribution of income away from capital, profits, and corporate savings is our best hope of addressing the causes of the recent crisis and laying the groundwork for balanced growth.[4]

In hardboiled form, this is Livingston's descriptive argument for why consumer culture is good for us, and it's difficult to refute. As Marx, Keynes, and even Milton Friedman all agree, he tells us, increasing aggregate consumption is the true handmaiden of long-term growth and security; it was what ended the Great Depression, and it is what will get us out of the current slump if we let it, that is if we give in to more of our desires and spend vigorously here and now. Our real obstacles are cultural and psychological, not economic, Livingston insists. But our atavistic resistance to instinctual gratification—in effect, our Puritan attraction to repression—runs deep. Without a total revaluation, or at least a major reshuffling, of values it's virtually immovable. Thankfully, Livingston is not one to shy away from ambitious intellectual tasks (his introduction is called "Waiting for Galileo"). In "Part Two: The Morality of Spending," he unveils his normative argument for consumer culture's goodness, this time with respect to our souls, and tries to re-designate consumption, instant gratification, and instinctual satisfaction as intrinsic moral goods.

As a self-described "radical empiricist,"[5] Livingston may object to this last claim. He doesn't believe in intrinsic moral goods the same way he doesn't believe in metaphysical ideals like Truth, Beauty, or Justice, he

might say. Yet by employing the word "Good" in his subtitle, he slyly evades the hard edge of his radical empiricism. He wants to enter into the debate over values, and in true Nietzschean form, his epistemological hang-ups about what actually constitutes "truth" take a backseat to the argument he wants to make convincing, indeed appetizing.

Whether his language is a subtle pragmatist's[6] trick or not, we ought to take Livingston at his word: he aims to convince us that spending is "moral," that consumer culture is "good," and that learning these lessons "might produce a new human nature that is more at ease in the world . . . a human being informed by a constant awareness of the needs of others, whether animal, vegetable, or mineral." To be fair, he frames this last bit provisionally; Livingston admits that "we just don't know what will happen when the renunciation of desire and the deferral of gratification and the delay of satisfaction are no longer necessary to organize society and build character."[7] But the reason he thinks this outcome is brightly possible is that he believes the liberation he prescribes is intrinsically good for us, not just pragmatically worthwhile. There is a difference, and Livingston's language makes his argument clear.

So how does his argument work? The first step involves what Livingston calls "the politics of more." Around the turn of the twentieth century, the Age of Scarcity passed into the Age of Abundance, and with this shift came a profound redefinition of American individualism. As Livingston describes it:

> Defenders of the old individualism, then and now, typically insisted that the site of self-discovery and self-determination—the address of autonomy—was work, where productive labor taught the moral lessons of punctuality, frugality, and honest effort, and meanwhile imposed external, objective, material limits on the imagination of the producer. Defenders of the new individualism moved this location, or rather scattered it, so that the site of self-discovery and self-determination could be leisure, the pleasurable scene of goods consumption, as well as work, the strenuous scene of goods production. Thus necessity and freedom, occupation and identity, even males and females, were now aligned at different angles.[8]

The Age of Abundance created the possibility for a new kind of self, a "social self" whose identity was primarily other-directed. For a social critic like Christopher Lasch, the erosion of traditional individual autonomy undermined psychic stability and led toward a culture of narcissism.[9]

Yet Livingston sees the transition in more sanguine terms. "The politics of 'more' defined autonomy . . . as a *collective* result of association with others—fellow workers, to be sure, but also people gathered with purposes or interests reaching beyond any workplace." Redefined as such, American individuals enjoyed new political opportunities as well as new aesthetic ones. But the basic change was psychological: "This new individual's identity was anything but private. It wasn't an enduring inner self you discovered by retreating from the outer world; it was instead a social construction, the result of interaction with others."[10]

In Livingston's account, the movement beyond scarcity—in America, the first stirrings of a mature surplus economy that advanced rapidly after 1900—etched the contours of the new moral horizon of consumer culture. In doing so, it also laid the seeds for two of the most important social movements of the twentieth century. Pointing to the Civil Rights Movement and the revolutions in Eastern Europe between 1968–1989, Livingston identifies a common pattern of resistance in which the (social) desire to take part in the joys of consumption "produced revolutionary *political* change." In both cases, he argues, African American music—what he calls "the black aesthetic"—was "the crucial medium in the redistribution of representational power accomplished by the movement." It gave African Americans and Eastern Europeans "the cultural credentials they needed to speak for the future, for the people, for the nation." And without the new technologies that allowed the black aesthetic to be mass distributed and mass consumed, neither movement could have succeeded. In short, Livingston thinks we owe both movements and their positive contributions to society to "the 'reification' or commodification of social life we (rightly) associate with consumer culture."[11] It goes without saying that this debt should make us more appreciative of the ways in which consumer culture is good for our souls.

Livingston is certainly right to point to the correlation between late twentieth-century social movements and expanding consumer consciousness. But he downplays the fact that Protestant Christianity was in many ways the deepest moral source of what came to pass in the American South between 1955–1963, and that Vaclav Havel had serious misgivings about the West's model of "consumer-led growth."[12] In Livingston's telling, it's as if the two movements arose from consumer longings alone, and *therefore* consumer culture stands acquitted of all the charges leveled against it. This curious logic points to a question Livingston never fully answers: independent of the ends to which people put them, is there a moral imperative embedded within consumer culture and the mass communication mediums that help diffuse it, or are these platforms morally neutral? Could they be used to produce any number of results, including the Civil Rights Movement? Or does some inherent moral property bend them toward manifesting greater respect for differences and deeper yearnings for democracy?

The question becomes especially pertinent when Livingston begins his defense of advertising, what he calls (again provisionally) "the thesaurus of our real feelings, the indispensable, vernacular language we use to plot our positions on the emotional atlas that is everyday life." By now it's clear what Livingston means by the eclipse of the former form of American individualism, and why he's glad about this as a radical empiricist. As he explains ever so delicately, there is not, and has never been, any "enduring, authentic, internal core of your self that you call your character." This is a myth we have inherited from history. In reality, "we all know that who we are depends, more or less, on what others make of us, how they see us, and that these others are mostly the absent causes we call strangers."[13] And we may as well embrace this. What David Riesman called the other-directed personality[14] is in fact the natural state of human existence, and this just happens to be good news for the advertising industry.

The reason Livingston calls advertising "the last utopian idiom of our time" is that he believes "it purveys a way of being in the world that is free of compulsion—free of necessary labor, the work you do because you have to—on the assumption that when at your leisure, you're free to choose an identity that might accord with the goods on offer." Yet what makes this way of being good for us? What about it furnishes the proper structure for our souls? Presumably Livingston's answer to these questions is: "like it or not, we create identities by means of commodities, buying and selling what we want to be." But isn't this a shallow vision of what human life can be? Not to mention what it ought to be? The freedom to buy, to satisfy desire by clicking an icon after seeing an ad on TV, sets a low bar for Utopia, much less for the attainment of what any of us might call the good life. Still, Livingston seems willing to compromise: "what advertising invokes is more of an idea than a place, more like a map or a video game than something you can experience in three dimensions. But for now, that's utopian enough."[15] At this point one wants to cry out, "no, it isn't." Why should we be willing to settle for so little so late?

If, as Livingston believes, we have reached a condition of post-scarcity, advertising brings us no closer to lasting salvation. The surface depth and masked anxieties of the lives it depicts in its many varieties conjures something closer to hell: coercive visions of the good life achieved through proximity to certain products; silent invitations to mimic the elegant gestures of a person who exists only in a photograph or a set of moving images; how do these social messages offer anything resembling liberation from "compulsion, necessity, fear?"[16]

Following Livingston's logic, we end up mired in a wasteland of goods aplenty. He defends other-direction as the necessary and binding condition of our lives, but the only compass he offers is an endless stream of barely distinguishable commodities, of consumer "goods." This leaves him heralding a wild west version of American individualism in which nothing exists outside the market of changing circumstance, where insatiable desire is our only guide. Fortunately, Livingston doesn't have to worry whether some permutations of social selfhood are bad for us because he doesn't believe in any fixed human nature. Instead he says "we might as well buckle up and prepare for takeoff," letting "change, flux, the dissolution of everything we take for granted" carry us forward. But toward what? Where does the unstated "premise of advertising: 'All that is solid melts into air'" ultimately lead?[17] After how many purchases do we ask the question, "what for?"

We get a hint in Livingston's coda, "Bataille Made Me Do It." After describing in great detail the lead-up to his "hamburger experiment," the change in his life that he says is "most relevant to the arguments of this book," the morality of spending finally reveals itself. It took a lot for Livingston to eat a hamburger again. As a dutiful husband and father, he denied himself the pleasure of animal flesh for years. But then things changed, and he decided it was time to loosen up and live a little. He scoured the best restaurant guides he could find, settling on a place called The Homestead "where the Kobe beef hamburger goes for twenty-one dollars as a lunch special and thirty-nine dollars on the dinner menu." Livingston and his girlfriend went for dinner. He ordered a martini straight up to dull the pre-gratification anxiety, but it didn't help. Nothing did. All he could do was face the moment when the burger came. And come it did:

It was delicious. Underdone, but delicious. All those fleeting bacon fumes from weekends past took up sudden residence in my mouth. But the meat was sliding around in there, as if the chef had somehow liquefied an honored part of a pampered, grass-fed cow. I was gargling beef. So I acceded to the unfreedom of my soul, took my girlfriend's advice, and sent the Kobe burger back

to the kitchen. On its return, it was much more solid and no less delicious. Even so, the junior partner in the table's choices [his girlfriend's burger] was clearly superior in every respect: the smaller, cheaper burger got the better of us. The sheer excess of the bigger, ridiculously expensive burger was worth the price, but just this once.[18]

The lesson from Livingston's hamburger experiment is abundantly clear. But one wonders if he registers it. Although it's delicious, his break from renunciation, from all the hidden vestiges of Puritan morality, culminates in a moment of bleak insecurity punctuated by a powerful compensatory desire for more sensory experience. As soon as he finishes, he's "already descending that slippery slope, thinking ahead to another, maybe better hamburger."[19]

If this is where consumer culture leads, we need a better set of goods than James Livingston can buy, much less sell. Perhaps it's time to redefine American individualism, again?

References

[1] James Livingston, *The World Turned Inside Out: American Thought and Culture at the End of the Twentieth Century* (Lanham, MD, 2009).
[2] James Livingston, *Against Thrift: Why Consumer Culture Is Good for the Economy, the Environment, and Your Soul* (New York, 2011), x.
[3] Ibid., xi.
[4] Ibid., 7.
[5] Ibid., xviii.
[6] Livingston's unique interpretation of pragmatism can be found in his earlier books *Pragmatism and the Political Economy of Cultural Revolution, 1850–1940* (Chapel Hill, NC, 1994) and *Pragmatism, Feminism, and Democracy: Rethinking the Politics of American History* (New York, 2001).
[7] Livingston, *Against Thrift*, xii.
[8] Ibid., 90.
[9] Christopher Lasch, *The Culture of Narcissism: American Life in an Age of Diminishing Expectations* (New York, 1979). For related accounts of the new psychology engendered by twentieth-century social and economic developments, see: David Riesman, *The Lonely Crowd: A Study of The Changing American Character* (New Haven, 1950); Philip Rieff, *Freud: The Mind of a Moralist* (New York, 1961) and *The Triumph of the Therapeutic: Uses of Faith After Freud* (Chicago, 1966); Richard Wightman Fox and T. Jackson Lears, Ed., *The Culture of Consumption: Critical Essays in American History 1880–1980* (New York, 1983);

Warren I. Susman, *Culture as History: The Transformation of American Society in the Twentieth Century* (New York, 1984); and Roland Marchand, *Advertising the American Dream: Making Way for Modernity 1920–1940* (Berkeley, 1985).

[10] Livingston, *Against Thrift*, 89.

[11] Ibid., 100, 104, 106. Surely Livingston would interpret Arab Spring along similar lines.

[12] Ibid., 114.

[13] Ibid., 115, 176, 177.

[14] In *The Lonely Crowd*.

[15] Livingston, *Against Thrift*, 116, 128.

[16] Ibid., 158.

[17] Ibid., 121.

[18] Ibid., 197, 207, 208.

[19] Ibid.

MICHAEL FISHER is a graduate student in American history at the University of Rochester who is working on his doctoral dissertation.

EXPLORING THE ISSUE

Is It Necessary to Become Less Consumerist?

Critical Thinking and Reflection

1. Evaluate your parents' consumption. Are most purchases sensible because they are very useful? Does the esteem of others influence much consumption?
2. Do you think that most people overconsume and on what items?
3. What are the activities that interfere with family closeness?
4. What consumption activities are you most critical of?
5. What is the overall impact your family has on the environment?
6. Why not enjoy life to the fullest? Is the United States too puritanical?

Is There Common Ground?

No one advocates poverty over affluence. Affluence has made so many good things available to billions of people including better health, longer life, adequate and beneficial food and water, access to education and information, ease of communicating with loved ones, awareness of many different peoples and cultures, and greater oversight of economic and political leaders. On the other side no one approves of overconsumption. Gutting more thoroughly explores the negative effects of over consumption on people while Fisher and Livingston do not accept the premise that high consumption erodes character. It only erodes a puritanical viewpoint which equates abundance with loss of self control.

This issue is a classic example of how a situation can have both positive and negative impacts. High production and consumption solves many problems of survival but can weaken the moral character of society. Capitalist economies must grow or fall into recession and even depression which greatly reduces the quality of life for millions. The common belief is that even when economic growth causes problems it is far better than no growth or decline.

Additional Resources

Benjamin R. Barber, *Consumed: How Markets Corrupt Children, Infantilize Adults, and Swallow Citizens Whole* (W. W. Norton, 2007)

Bill McKibben, "Reversal of Fortune," *Mother Jones* (March/April 2007)

Chris Hedges, "The Myth of Human Progress," *Truthdig* (January 20, 2013)

David Pearce Snyder, "A Rendezvous with Austerity: American Consumers Are About to Learn New Habits," *The Futurist* (July/August 2009)

Doug Brown, *Insatiable Is Not Sustainable* (Praeger, 2002)

Paul R. Ehrlich and Anne H. Ehrlich, Can a collapse of global civilization be avoided? Retrieved from rspb.royalsocietypublishing.org, accessed on August 7, 2013

Peter Dauvergne, "The Problem of Consumption," *Global Environmental Politics* (May 2010)

Ramez Naam, "How Innovation Could Save the Planet," *The Futurist* (March/April 2013)

Ronald Bailey, "How Free Markets and Human Ingenuity Can Save the Planet," a review of *The Infinite Resource: The Power of Ideas on a Finite Planet*, by Ramez Naam (April 12, 2013)

Worldwatch Institute, *2010 State of the World: Transforming Cultures from Consumerism to Sustainability* (W. W. Norton, 2010)

Internet References . . .

Sociosite

www.topsite.com/goto/sociosite.net

Sociology—Study Sociology Online

http://edu.learnsoc.org/

Sociology Web Resources

www.mhhe.com/socscience/sociology/resources/index.htm

Socioweb

www.topsite.com/goto/socioweb.com

Selected, Edited, and with Issue Framing Material by:
Kurt Finsterbusch, *University of Maryland, College Park*

ISSUE

Does Social Media Have Largely Positive Impacts on Its Users?

YES: Karen Hua, from "Where Millennials Make Friends and Mobilize for Change," *Forbes* (2015)

NO: Stephen Marche, from "Is Facebook Making Us Lonely?" *The Atlantic* (2012)

Learning Outcomes

After reading this issue, you will be able to:

- Understand how multifaceted the impacts of social media on people and on society are.
- Be aware of the great variety of opinions that leading experts on social media have about its consequences.
- Understand the primary ways that people use social media.
- Be able to discern how different groups of users differ and are similar in their use of social media.
- Explain how social media affects the development of various intellectual and social skills of its users.
- Speculate on how social media might affect society in the future.

ISSUE SUMMARY

YES: Karen Hua, a staff writer for *Forbes*, concentrates on teens and finds them using social media to make friends and deepen friendships. She counters the viewpoint that social media provides superficial contacts by observing "that today's teenagers are forming deep, personal connections and relationships online."

NO: Stephen Marche, a journalist who is on the staff of *The Atlantic*, recognizes the amazing benefits of social media but reports on stories and studies which fined that Facebook and other social media can isolate us from people we know to people we meet online. Thus social media which are designed to increase our communication with our family and friends can actually make us lonlier.

We will briefly provide a survey of many of the positive and negative results of social media. On the positive side is the abundant use of social media to communicate with family and friends and increase connections and strengthen relationships. It facilitates face-to-face interaction. It especially helps people who are socially isolated or shy to connect with people. It helps seniors to feel more connected to society. Social networking has also increased life satisfaction and reduced health problems. Social media has become a main source of information for many people and they can get information very fast. On average its use also improves school performance, though it can also be a distraction. It has been used by businesses to great effect and it can be argued that it has helped the economy with products, services, profits, and jobs. Even law enforcement has used it positively. It has played a major role in recent elections and has helped many groups organize and accomplish things. It has contributed to significant social changes and there are many stories about its help to charities and noble social actions. I add as an academic that social media is being used to disseminate a great deal of academic knowledge. Social media has also produced negative effects. It can negatively affect social relations. It causes people to spend less time in face-to-face interactions, especially in their homes (a small percentage of young people even respond to social media during sex). Social networking has been found to make some children more prone to depression and loneliness and can lead to stress. It correlates with personality disorders like ADHD, difficulty in face-to-face conversations, self-centered personalities, anxiety, and addictive behaviors. It encourages people to waste time. Heavy social media users have lower grades. It can cause many troubles for users including inadvertently engaging in criminal behavior including some cases of "sexting," assisting criminal actions against users (e.g., travel plans informing criminals when to rob their house), loss of privacy, being targeted by scam artists or other criminals, use of the Internet by potential employers or universities who find reasons not to hire potential employees or admit potential students, having revealing pictures and unattractive information widely distributed, facilitating cyberbullying, and reducing some workers' productivity. It often provides misinformation and questionable and even dangerous amateur advice. It can facilitate and spread hate groups and organized crime. It is impossible to weigh these and other negative effects of social media against the positive effects, but most people are avid users in spite of the risks, so consumers believe the net effects are clearly positive.

The pros and cons of social media is a vast topic with many angles and vast changes in the past few years. The rapid speed of change of these phenomena has limited the lessons from empirical research on its effects. As a result, poignant stories may have more prominence than thorough research and many of these on the focus on the impacts of social media on our relationships. Some of these are sad stories about withdrawal from close people to virtual friends. These are key to Stephen Marche's argument against social media. In contrast, Karen Hua is much more positive about the use of some social media. She finds that the majority use social media to increase social connections and facilitate their activities.

YES

Karen Hua

Where Millennials Make Friends and Mobilize for Change

Add "making friends" to the growing roster of reasons why teens can't seem to take their eyes off their screens. A new study, *Teens, Technology and Friendships,* . . . from Pew Research Center shows that 57% of teens (ages 13–17) have met at least one new friend online, with nearly 30% making five or more pals. Girls meet people primarily through social media, while boys tend to make acquaintances through gaming or eSports.

While the words "cyberbullying" and "online predator" are still chilling, this study reveals that today's teenagers are forming deep, personal connections and relationships online. "Adults in our society and parents have this idea that a lot of things teens are doing and video games are frivolous, a waste of time," says Amanda Lenhart, author of the study and associate director for research at Pew. "But these digital platforms are now incredibly important parts of how teens form meaningful relationships."

According to her findings, 72% of all teens spend time with friends on social media regularly. This behavior continues on college campuses across the country, and many online interactions have mobilized millennials into real-life communities. In fact, one in five teens have met an online friend in person; what would have been seen as a dangerous act years ago is now increasingly commonplace.

From Online to 'IRL'

The Harry Potter Alliance has done just that. What started as a collective, fervent passion for J.K. Rowling's franchise has transitioned from online to IRL (in real life)—inciting dozens of college chapters across the country. Founded by Andrew Slack in 2005, the non-profit company advocates for literacy and social awareness. Through the annual Accio Books campaign, chapters have donated almost 200,000 books to global disaster areas and local underprivileged communities. HPA's Odds in Our Favor campaign uses the popular Hunger Games franchise to promote economic inequality awareness.

Janae Phillips stepped up from her role as chapter organizer at the University of Arizona in 2014 to being the current national chapter director. She studied online communities as an ed-tech master's student.

Phillips describes HPA as a creative approach to activism, where members anywhere can reach out online for leadership advice and camaraderie, then mirror that back into their real life chapters. "The reason why we're able to develop (HPA's) community is because we have this shared interest and passion and fandom," she says. "It's a symbiotic relationship."

"It's unfortunate that the Internet has been around so long, yet is seen as so distinct," Phillips continues. "The online space to (millennials) is just part of their daily lives. The connections to real life are offline, too."

"The more prevalent something is online, the more prevalent it will be in real life," says Jessica Kotnour, a Kenyon College-bound student and HPA regional liaison. "We use Twitter to bring smaller causes to attention, and once you're aware of something online, you can make that change in real life." By using mainstream pop culture coupled with the megaphone of social media, the organization has a much wider reach to garner more support.

Melissa Anelli, HPA board president and co-owner of Mischief Management, an organization that bridges online fandom to real-life connections, emphasizes how her community sprouted from the liberal and activist morals of the Harry Potter books and other cult franchises. "The quality of a fandom with a shared interest goes back to the source material," she says. "The HPA is 'Dumbledore's Army' in the real world." Similarly, John and Hank Green's Nerdfighter community has spread from online fan groups (for John Green books and all things nerdy) to hundreds of global campuses that unite for community service.

At the University of Michigan, avid online fans [and] players of the League of Legends and Super Smash Bros. games have constructed real-life groups, as well. More than just a competitive team against other online players, Michigan's League of Legends club emphasizes community, says club president and rising computer science senior Patrick Huang. He defines his club simply as a way to meet people with a common interest in eSports—and the online component only strengthens their bond.

Huang met his first online friend at age 13, and after a series of video calls to verify authenticity and security, they've now met multiple times and are still friends to this day. He also met his current college roommate as an online gaming competitor, too, until they met and clicked in person at school. "People nowadays spend a lot of time on Netflix," Huang explains as an example. "But playing (video) games with friends is given a negative connotation, when it's actually even more social."

KAREN HUA is a staff writer for *Forbes* and a college student at the University of Michigan

Stephen Marche  **NO**

Is Facebook Making Us Lonely?

Social media—from Facebook to Twitter—have made us more densely networked than ever. Yet for all this connectivity, new research suggests that we have never been lonelier (or more narcissistic)—and that this loneliness is making us mentally and physically ill. A report on what the epidemic of loneliness is doing to our souls and our society.

Yvette Vickers, a former *Playboy* playmate and B-movie star, best known for her role in *Attack of the 50 Foot Woman*, would have been 83 last August, but nobody knows exactly how old she was when she died. According to the Los Angeles coroner's report, she lay dead for the better part of a year before a neighbor and fellow actress, a woman named Susan Savage, noticed cobwebs and yellowing letters in her mailbox, reached through a broken window to unlock the door, and pushed her way through the piles of junk mail and mounds of clothing that barricaded the house. Upstairs, she found Vickers's body, mummified, near a heater that was still running. Her computer was on too, its glow permeating the empty space.

The *Los Angeles Times* posted a story headlined "Mummified Body of Former Playboy Playmate Yvette Vickers Found in Her Benedict Canyon Home," which quickly went viral. Within two weeks, by Technorati's count, Vickers's lonesome death was already the subject of 16,057 Facebook posts and 881 tweets. She had long been a horror-movie icon, a symbol of Hollywood's capacity to exploit our most basic fears in the silliest ways; now she was an icon of a new and different kind of horror: our growing fear of loneliness. Certainly she received much more attention in death than she did in the final years of her life. With no children, no religious group, and no immediate social circle of any kind, she had begun, as an elderly woman, to look elsewhere for companionship. Savage later told *Los Angeles* magazine that she had searched Vickers's phone bills for clues about the life that led to such an end. In the months before her grotesque death, Vickers had made calls not to friends or family but to distant fans who had found her through fan conventions and Internet sites.

Vickers's web of connections had grown broader but shallower, as has happened for many of us. We are living in an isolation that would have been unimaginable to our ancestors, and yet we have never been more accessible. Over the past three decades, technology has delivered to us a world in which we need not be out of contact for a fraction of a moment. In 2010, at a cost of $300 million, 800 miles of fiber-optic cable was laid between the Chicago Mercantile Exchange and the New York Stock Exchange to shave three milliseconds off trading times. Yet within this world of instant and absolute communication, unbounded by limits of time or space, we suffer from unprecedented alienation. We have never been more detached from one another, or lonelier. In a world consumed by ever more novel modes of socializing, we have less and less actual society. We live in an accelerating contradiction: the more connected we become, the lonelier we are. We were promised a global village; instead we inhabit the drab cul-de-sacs and endless freeways of a vast suburb of information.

At the forefront of all this unexpectedly lonely interactivity is Facebook, with 845 million users and $3.7 billion in revenue last year. The company hopes to raise $5 billion in an initial public offering later this spring, which will make it by far the largest Internet IPO in history. Some recent estimates put the company's potential value at $100 billion, which would make it larger than the global coffee industry—one addiction preparing to surpass the other. Facebook's scale and reach are hard to comprehend: last summer, Facebook became, by some counts, the first Web site to receive 1 trillion page views in a month. In the last three months of 2011, users generated an average of 2.7 billion "likes" and comments every day. On whatever scale you care to judge Facebook—as a company, as a culture, as a country—it is vast beyond imagination.

Despite its immense popularity, or more likely because of it, Facebook has, from the beginning, been under something of a cloud of suspicion. The depiction of

Mark Zuckerberg, in *The Social Network,* as a bastard with symptoms of Asperger's syndrome, was nonsense. But it felt true. It felt true to Facebook, if not to Zuckerberg. The film's most indelible scene, the one that may well have earned it an Oscar, was the final, silent shot of an anomic Zuckerberg sending out a friend request to his ex-girlfriend, then waiting and clicking and waiting and clicking—a moment of superconnected loneliness preserved in amber. We have all been in that scene: transfixed by the glare of a screen, hungering for response.

When you sign up for Google+ and set up your Friends circle, the program specifies that you should include only "your real friends, the ones you feel comfortable sharing private details with." That one little phrase, *Your real friends*—so quaint, so charmingly mothering—perfectly encapsulates the anxieties that social media have produced: the fears that Facebook is interfering with our real friendships, distancing us from each other, making us lonelier; and that social networking might be spreading the very isolation it seemed designed to conquer.

FACEBOOK ARRIVED IN THE MIDDLE of a dramatic increase in the quantity and intensity of human loneliness, a rise that initially made the site's promise of greater connection seem deeply attractive. Americans are more solitary than ever before. In 1950, less than 10 percent of American households contained only one person. By 2010, nearly 27 percent of households had just one person. Solitary living does not guarantee a life of unhappiness, of course. In his recent book about the trend toward living alone, Eric Klinenberg, a sociologist at NYU, writes: "Reams of published research show that it's the quality, not the quantity of social interaction, that best predicts loneliness." True. But before we begin the fantasies of happily eccentric singledom, of divorcées dropping by their knitting circles after work for glasses of Drew Barrymore pinot grigio, or recent college graduates with perfectly articulated, Steampunk-themed, 300-square-foot apartments organizing croquet matches with their book clubs, we should recognize that it is not just isolation that is rising sharply. It's loneliness, too. And loneliness makes us miserable.

We know intuitively that loneliness and being alone are not the same thing. Solitude can be lovely. Crowded parties can be agony. We also know, thanks to a growing body of research on the topic, that loneliness is not a matter of external conditions; it is a psychological state. A 2005 analysis of data from a longitudinal study of Dutch twins showed that the tendency toward loneliness has roughly the same genetic component as other psychological problems such as neuroticism or anxiety.

Still, loneliness is slippery, a difficult state to define or diagnose. The best tool yet developed for measuring the condition is the UCLA Loneliness Scale, a series of 20 questions that all begin with this formulation: "How often do you feel . . . ?" As in: "How often do you feel that you are 'in tune' with the people around you?" And: "How often do you feel that you lack companionship?" Measuring the condition in these terms, various studies have shown loneliness rising drastically over a very short period of recent history. A 2010 AARP survey found that 35 percent of adults older than 45 were chronically lonely, as opposed to 20 percent of a similar group only a decade earlier. According to a major study by a leading scholar of the subject, roughly 20 percent of Americans—about 60 million people—are unhappy with their lives because of loneliness. Across the Western world, physicians and nurses have begun to speak openly of an epidemic of loneliness.

The new studies on loneliness are beginning to yield some surprising preliminary findings about its mechanisms. Almost every factor that one might assume affects loneliness does so only some of the time, and only under certain circumstances. People who are married are less lonely than single people, one journal article suggests, but only if their spouses are confidants. If one's spouse is not a confidant, marriage may not decrease loneliness. A belief in God might help, or it might not, as a 1990 German study comparing levels of religious feeling and levels of loneliness discovered. Active believers who saw God as abstract and helpful rather than as a wrathful, immediate presence were less lonely. "The mere belief in God," the researchers concluded, "was relatively independent of loneliness."

But it is clear that social interaction matters. Loneliness and being alone are not the same thing, but both are on the rise. We meet fewer people. We gather less. And when we gather, our bonds are less meaningful and less easy. The decrease in confidants—that is, in quality social connections—has been dramatic over the past 25 years. In one survey, the mean size of networks of personal confidants decreased from 2.94 people in 1985 to 2.08 in 2004. Similarly, in 1985, only 10 percent of Americans said they had no one with whom to discuss important matters, and 15 percent said they had only one such good friend. By 2004, 25 percent had nobody to talk to, and 20 percent had only one confidant.

In the face of this social disintegration, we have essentially hired an army of replacement confidants, an entire class of professional carers. As Ronald Dworkin pointed out in a 2010 paper for the Hoover Institution, in the late '40s, the United States was home to 2,500 clinical psychologists, 30,000 social workers, and fewer than 500 marriage and family therapists. As of 2010, the country had 77,000 clinical psychologists, 192,000 clinical social workers, 400,000 nonclinical social workers, 50,000 marriage and family therapists, 105,000 mental-health counselors, 220,000 substance-abuse counselors, 17,000 nurse psychotherapists, and 30,000 life coaches. The majority of patients in therapy do not warrant a psychiatric diagnosis. This raft of psychic servants is helping us through what used to be called regular problems. We have outsourced the work of everyday caring.

We need professional carers more and more, because the threat of societal breakdown, once principally a matter of nostalgic lament, has morphed into an issue of public health. Being lonely is extremely bad for your health. If you're lonely, you're more likely to be put in a geriatric home at an earlier age than a similar person who isn't lonely. You're less likely to exercise. You're more likely to be obese. You're less likely to survive a serious operation and more likely to have hormonal imbalances. You are at greater risk of inflammation. Your memory may be worse. You are more likely to be depressed, to sleep badly, and to suffer dementia and general cognitive decline. Loneliness may not have killed Yvette Vickers, but it has been linked to a greater probability of having the kind of heart condition that did kill her.

And yet, despite its deleterious effect on health, loneliness is one of the first things ordinary Americans spend their money achieving. With money, you flee the cramped city to a house in the suburbs or, if you can afford it, a McMansion in the exurbs, inevitably spending more time in your car. Loneliness is at the American core, a by-product of a long-standing national appetite for independence: The Pilgrims who left Europe willingly abandoned the bonds and strictures of a society that could not accept their right to be different. They did not seek out loneliness, but they accepted it as the price of their autonomy. The cowboys who set off to explore a seemingly endless frontier likewise traded away personal ties in favor of pride and self-respect. The ultimate American icon is the astronaut: Who is more heroic, or more alone? The price of self-determination and self-reliance has often been loneliness. But Americans have always been willing to pay that price.

Today, the one common feature in American secular culture is its celebration of the self that breaks away from the constrictions of the family and the state, and, in its greatest expressions, from all limits entirely. The great American poem is Whitman's "Song of Myself." The great American essay is Emerson's "Self-Reliance." The great American novel is Melville's *Moby-Dick*, the tale of a man on a quest so lonely that it is incomprehensible to those around him. American culture, high and low, is about self-expression and personal authenticity. Franklin Delano Roosevelt called individualism "the great watchword of American life."

Self-invention is only half of the American story, however. The drive for isolation has always been in tension with the impulse to cluster in communities that cling and suffocate. The Pilgrims, while fomenting spiritual rebellion, also enforced ferocious cohesion. The Salem witch trials, in hindsight, read like attempts to impose solidarity—as do the McCarthy hearings. The history of the United States is like the famous parable of the porcupines in the cold, from Schopenhauer's *Studies in Pessimism*—the ones who huddle together for warmth and shuffle away in pain, always separating and congregating.

We are now in the middle of a long period of shuffling away. In his 2000 book *Bowling Alone,* Robert D. Putnam attributed the dramatic post-war decline of social capital—the strength and value of interpersonal networks—to numerous interconnected trends in American life: suburban sprawl, television's dominance over culture, the self-absorption of the Baby Boomers, the disintegration of the traditional family. The trends he observed continued through the prosperity of the aughts, and have only become more pronounced with time: the rate of union membership declined in 2011, again; screen time rose; the Masons and the Elks continued their slide into irrelevance. We are lonely because we want to be lonely. We have made ourselves lonely.

The question of the future is this: Is Facebook part of the separating or part of the congregating; is it a huddling-together for warmth or a shuffling-away in pain?

WELL BEFORE FACEBOOK, digital technology was enabling our tendency for isolation, to an unprecedented degree. Back in the 1990s, scholars started calling the contradiction between an increased opportunity to connect and a lack of human contact the "Internet paradox." A prominent 1998 article on the phenomenon by a team of researchers at Carnegie Mellon showed that increased Internet usage was already coinciding with increased loneliness. Critics of the study pointed out that the two groups that participated in the study—high-school journalism students who were heading to university and socially active members of community-development boards—were statistically likely to become lonelier over time. Which brings us to a more fundamental question: Does the Internet make people lonely, or are lonely people more attracted to the Internet?

The question has intensified in the Facebook era. A recent study out of Australia (where close to half the population is active on Facebook), titled "Who Uses Facebook?," found a complex and sometimes confounding relationship between loneliness and social networking. Facebook users had slightly lower levels of "social loneliness"—the sense of not feeling bonded with friends—but "significantly higher levels of family loneliness"—the sense of not feeling bonded with family. It may be that Facebook encourages more contact with people outside of our household, at the expense of our family relationships—or it may be that people who have unhappy family relationships in the first place seek companionship through other means, including Facebook. The researchers also found that lonely people are inclined to spend more time on Facebook: "One of the most noteworthy findings," they wrote, "was the tendency for neurotic and lonely individuals to spend greater amounts of time on Facebook per day than non-lonely individuals." And they found that neurotics are more likely to prefer to use the wall, while extroverts tend to use chat features in addition to the wall.

Moira Burke, until recently a graduate student at the Human-Computer Institute at Carnegie Mellon, used to run a longitudinal study of 1,200 Facebook users. That study, which is ongoing, is one of the first to step outside the realm of self-selected college students and examine the effects of Facebook on a broader population, over time. She concludes that the effect of Facebook depends on what you bring to it. Just as your mother said: you get out only what you put in. If you use Facebook to communicate directly with other individuals—by using the "like" button, commenting on friends' posts, and so on—it can increase your social capital. Personalized messages, or what Burke calls "composed communication," are more satisfying than "one-click communication"—the lazy click of a like. "People who received composed communication became less lonely, while people who received one-click communication experienced no change in loneliness," Burke tells me. So, you should inform your friend in writing how charming her son looks with Harry Potter cake smeared all over his face, and how interesting her sepia-toned photograph of that tree-framed bit of skyline is, and how cool it is that she's at whatever concert she happens to be at. That's what we all want to hear. Even better than sending a private Facebook message is the semi-public conversation, the kind of back-and-forth in which you half ignore the other people who may be listening in. "People whose friends write to them semi-publicly on Facebook experience decreases in loneliness," Burke says.

On the other hand, non-personalized use of Facebook—scanning your friends' status updates and updating the world on your own activities via your wall, or what Burke calls "passive consumption" and "broadcasting"—correlates to feelings of disconnectedness. It's a lonely business, wandering the labyrinths of our friends' and pseudo-friends' projected identities, trying to figure out what part of ourselves we ought to project, who will listen,

and what they will hear. According to Burke, passive consumption of Facebook also correlates to a marginal increase in depression. "If two women each talk to their friends the same amount of time, but one of them spends more time reading about friends on Facebook as well, the one reading tends to grow slightly more depressed," Burke says. Her conclusion suggests that my sometimes unhappy reactions to Facebook may be more universal than I had realized. When I scroll through page after page of my friends' descriptions of how accidentally eloquent their kids are, and how their husbands are endearingly bumbling, and how they're all about to eat a home-cooked meal prepared with fresh local organic produce bought at the farmers' market and then go for a jog and maybe check in at the office because they're so busy getting ready to hop on a plane for a week of luxury dogsledding in Lapland, I do grow slightly more miserable. A lot of other people doing the same thing feel a little bit worse, too.

Still, Burke's research does not support the assertion that Facebook creates loneliness. The people who experience loneliness on Facebook are lonely away from Facebook, too, she points out; on Facebook, as everywhere else, correlation is not causation. The popular kids are popular, and the lonely skulkers skulk alone. Perhaps it says something about me that I think Facebook is primarily a platform for lonely skulking. I mention to Burke the widely reported study, conducted by a Stanford graduate student, that showed how believing that others have strong social networks can lead to feelings of depression. What does Facebook communicate, if not the impression of social bounty? Everybody else looks so happy on Facebook, with so many friends, that our own social networks feel emptier than ever in comparison. Doesn't that *make* people feel lonely? "If people are reading about lives that are much better than theirs, two things can happen," Burke tells me. "They can feel worse about themselves, or they can feel motivated."

Burke will start working at Facebook as a data scientist this year.

JOHN CACIOPPO, THE director of the Center for Cognitive and Social Neuroscience at the University of Chicago, is the world's leading expert on loneliness. In his landmark book, *Loneliness*, released in 2008, he revealed just how profoundly the epidemic of loneliness is affecting the basic functions of human physiology. He found higher levels of epinephrine, the stress hormone, in the morning urine of lonely people. Loneliness burrows deep: "When we drew blood from our older adults and analyzed their white cells," he writes, "we found that loneliness somehow penetrated the deepest recesses of the cell to alter the way genes were being expressed." Loneliness affects not only the brain, then, but the basic process of DNA transcription. When you are lonely, your whole body is lonely.

To Cacioppo, Internet communication allows only ersatz intimacy. "Forming connections with pets or online friends or even God is a noble attempt by an obligatorily gregarious creature to satisfy a compelling need," he writes. "But surrogates can never make up completely for the absence of the real thing." The "real thing" being actual people, in the flesh. When I speak to Cacioppo, he is refreshingly clear on what he sees as Facebook's effect on society. Yes, he allows, some research has suggested that the greater the number of Facebook friends a person has, the less lonely she is. But he argues that the impression this creates can be misleading. "For the most part," he says, "people are bringing their old friends, and feelings of loneliness or connectedness, to Facebook." The idea that a Web site could deliver a more friendly, interconnected world is bogus. The depth of one's social network outside Facebook is what determines the depth of one's social network within Facebook, not the other way around. Using social media doesn't create new social networks; it just transfers established networks from one platform to another. For the most part, Facebook doesn't destroy friendships—but it doesn't create them, either.

In one experiment, Cacioppo looked for a connection between the loneliness of subjects and the relative frequency of their interactions via Facebook, chat rooms, online games, dating sites, and face-to-face contact. The results were unequivocal. "The greater the proportion of face-to-face interactions, the less lonely you are," he says. "The greater the proportion of online interactions, the lonelier you are." Surely, I suggest to Cacioppo, this means that Facebook and the like inevitably make people lonelier. He disagrees. Facebook is merely a tool, he says, and like any tool, its effectiveness will depend on its user. "If you use Facebook to increase face-to-face contact," he says, "it increases social capital." So if social media let you organize a game of football among your friends, that's healthy. If you turn to social media instead of playing football, however, that's unhealthy.

"Facebook can be terrific, if we use it properly," Cacioppo continues. "It's like a car. You can drive it to pick up your friends. Or you can drive alone." But hasn't the car increased loneliness? If cars created the suburbs, surely they also created isolation. "That's because of how we use cars," Cacioppo replies. "How we use these technologies can lead to more integration, rather than more isolation."

The problem, then, is that we invite loneliness, even though it makes us miserable. The history of our use of technology is a history of isolation desired and achieved.

When the Great Atlantic and Pacific Tea Company opened its A&P stores, giving Americans self-service access to groceries, customers stopped having relationships with their grocers. When the telephone arrived, people stopped knocking on their neighbors' doors. Social media bring this process to a much wider set of relationships. Researchers at the HP Social Computing Lab who studied the nature of people's connections on Twitter came to a depressing, if not surprising, conclusion: "Most of the links declared within Twitter were meaningless from an interaction point of view." I have to wonder: What other point of view is meaningful?

LONELINESS IS CERTAINLY not something that Facebook or Twitter or any of the lesser forms of social media is doing to us. We are doing it to ourselves. Casting technology as some vague, impersonal spirit of history forcing our actions is a weak excuse. We make decisions about how we use our machines, not the other way around. Every time I shop at my local grocery store, I am faced with a choice. I can buy my groceries from a human being or from a machine. I always, without exception, choose the machine. It's faster and more efficient, I tell myself, but the truth is that I prefer not having to wait with the other customers who are lined up alongside the conveyor belt: the hipster mom who disapproves of my high-carbon-footprint pineapple; the lady who tenses to the point of tears while she waits to see if the gods of the credit-card machine will accept or decline; the old man whose clumsy feebleness requires a patience that I don't possess. Much better to bypass the whole circus and just ring up the groceries myself.

Our omnipresent new technologies lure us toward increasingly superficial connections at exactly the same moment that they make avoiding the mess of human interaction easy. The beauty of Facebook, the source of its power, is that it enables us to be social while sparing us the embarrassing reality of society—the accidental revelations we make at parties, the awkward pauses, the farting and the spilled drinks and the general gaucherie of face-to-face contact. Instead, we have the lovely smoothness of a seemingly social machine. Everything's so simple: status updates, pictures, your wall.

But the price of this smooth sociability is a constant compulsion to assert one's own happiness, one's own fulfillment. Not only must we contend with the social bounty of others; we must foster the appearance of our own social bounty. Being happy all the time, pretending to be happy, actually attempting to be happy—it's exhausting. Last year a team of researchers led by Iris Mauss at the University of Denver published a study looking into "the paradoxical effects of valuing happiness." Most goals in life show a direct correlation between valuation and achievement. Studies have found, for example, that students who value good grades tend to have higher grades than those who don't value them. Happiness is an exception. The study came to a disturbing conclusion:

> Valuing happiness is not necessarily linked to greater happiness. In fact, under certain conditions, the opposite is true. Under conditions of low (but not high) life stress, the more people valued happiness, the lower were their hedonic balance, psychological well-being, and life satisfaction, and the higher their depression symptoms.

The more you try to be happy, the less happy you are. Sophocles made roughly the same point.

Facebook, of course, puts the pursuit of happiness front and center in our digital life. Its capacity to redefine our very concepts of identity and personal fulfillment is much more worrisome than the data-mining and privacy practices that have aroused anxieties about the company. Two of the most compelling critics of Facebook—neither of them a Luddite—concentrate on exactly this point. Jaron Lanier, the author of *You Are Not a Gadget*, was one of the inventors of virtual-reality technology. His view of where social media are taking us reads like dystopian science fiction: "I fear that we are beginning to design ourselves to suit digital models of us, and I worry about a leaching of empathy and humanity in that process." Lanier argues that Facebook imprisons us in the business of self-presenting, and this, to his mind, is the site's crucial and fatally unacceptable downside.

Sherry Turkle, a professor of computer culture at MIT who in 1995 published the digital-positive analysis *Life on the Screen*, is much more skeptical about the effects of online society in her 2011 book, *Alone Together:* "These days, insecure in our relationships and anxious about intimacy, we look to technology for ways to be in relationships and protect ourselves from them at the same time." The problem with digital intimacy is that it is ultimately incomplete: "The ties we form through the Internet are not, in the end, the ties that bind. But they are the ties that preoccupy," she writes. "We don't want to intrude on each other, so instead we constantly intrude on each other, but not in 'real time.'"

Lanier and Turkle are right, at least in their diagnoses. Self-presentation on Facebook is continuous, intensely mediated, and possessed of a phony nonchalance that eliminates even the potential for spontaneity. ("Look how casually I threw up these three photos from the party at which I took 300 photos!") Curating the exhibition of the self has become a 24/7 occupation. Perhaps not

surprisingly, then, the Australian study "Who Uses Facebook?" found a significant correlation between Facebook use and narcissism: "Facebook users have higher levels of total narcissism, exhibitionism, and leadership than Facebook nonusers," the study's authors wrote. "In fact, it could be argued that Facebook specifically gratifies the narcissistic individual's need to engage in self-promoting and superficial behavior."

Rising narcissism isn't so much a trend as the trend behind all other trends. In preparation for the 2013 edition of its diagnostic manual, the psychiatric profession is currently struggling to update its definition of narcissistic personality disorder. Still, generally speaking, practitioners agree that narcissism manifests in patterns of fantastic grandiosity, craving for attention, and lack of empathy. In a 2008 survey, 35,000 American respondents were asked if they had ever had certain symptoms of narcissistic personality disorder. Among people older than 65, 3 percent reported symptoms. Among people in their 20s, the proportion was nearly 10 percent. Across all age groups, one in 16 Americans has experienced some symptoms of NPD. And loneliness and narcissism are intimately connected: a longitudinal study of Swedish women demonstrated a strong link between levels of narcissism in youth and levels of loneliness in old age. The connection is fundamental. Narcissism is the flip side of loneliness, and either condition is a fighting retreat from the messy reality of other people.

A considerable part of Facebook's appeal stems from its miraculous fusion of distance with intimacy, or the illusion of distance with the illusion of intimacy. Our online communities become engines of self-image, and self-image becomes the engine of community. The real danger with Facebook is not that it allows us to isolate ourselves, but that by mixing our appetite for isolation with our vanity, it threatens to alter the very nature of solitude. The new isolation is not of the kind that Americans once idealized, the lonesomeness of the proudly nonconformist, independent-minded, solitary stoic, or that of the astronaut who blasts into new worlds. Facebook's isolation is a grind. What's truly staggering about Facebook usage is not its volume—750 million photographs uploaded over a single weekend—but the constancy of the performance it demands. More than half its users—and one of every 13 people on Earth is a Facebook user—log on every day. Among 18-to-34-year-olds, nearly half check Facebook minutes after waking up, and 28 percent do so before getting out of bed. The relentlessness is what is so new, so potentially transformative. Facebook never takes a break. We never take a break. Human beings have always created elaborate acts of self-presentation. But not all the time, not every morning, before we even pour a cup of coffee. Yvette Vickers's computer was on when she died.

Nostalgia for the good old days of disconnection would not just be pointless, it would be hypocritical and ungrateful. But the very magic of the new machines, the efficiency and elegance with which they serve us, obscures what isn't being served: everything that matters. What Facebook has revealed about human nature—and this is not a minor revelation—is that a connection is not the same thing as a bond, and that instant and total connection is no salvation, no ticket to a happier, better world or a more liberated version of humanity. Solitude used to be good for self-reflection and self-reinvention. But now we are left thinking about who we are all the time, without ever really thinking about who we are. Facebook denies us a pleasure whose profundity we had underestimated: the chance to forget about ourselves for a while, the chance to disconnect.

STEPHEN MARCHE journalist who is on the staff of *The Atlantic*, writes a monthly column for *Esquire*, and a weekly column for the *National Post*. He has written three books including *The Hunger of the Wolf* (2015)

EXPLORING THE ISSUE

Does Social Media Have Largely Positive Impacts on Its Users?

Critical Thinking and Reflection

1. Should social media be considered simply a tool that users can use for either good or evil?
2. How can the negative consequences of social media be reduced?
3. What role can education play in reducing the negative aspects of social media and increasing its positive aspects?
4. What have been the positive and negative results of your own use of social media?
5. What activities have been reduced by the time spent on social media?
6. How has social media impacted your community? Your nation?
7. Have you or your friends been embarrassed or harmed through your use of social media?

Is There Common Ground?

Both YES and NO selections recognize many of the benefits of social media.

Marche also emphasize the many negative impacts of social media and Hua does not. Hua would not deny that social media does have negative impacts but treats them as less important than the positive impacts. Both selections consider the impacts on social connectedness as the key issue to examine, especially on family and close friends. Both agree that it is also useful for news, information, and helping conduct personal business. It also stimulates the economy and facilitates business, governments, and civil sector activities. For example, I conveniently paid property taxes online.

Additional Resources

Pew Internet (pewinternet.org), a project of the Pew Research Center, produces many articles a year on this topic. Another major resource is socialnetworking.procon.org. It is the most informative website on the pros and cons of social media with 173 footnotes, but it does not provide useful links. Its useful references include LexisNexis Risk Solutions, "Role of Social Media in Law Enforcement Significant and Growing," www.lexisnexis.com, July 18, 2012; Shelley Galasso Bonanno, *Social Media's Impact on Relationships* (PsychCentral, 2015); Mary Wilks, "Online Social Networking's Effect on Adolescent Social Development," www.eckerd.edu (accessed December 5, 2012); Levi R. Baker and Debra L. Oswald, "Shyness and Online Social Networking Services," *Journal of Social and Personal Relationships* (November 2010); "The Impact of Social Media on Relationships," Newsletter of Relationship Rules, December 25, 2014; "Economist Debates: Social Networking," *The Economist*, www.economist.com, February 13, 2012; Tony Dokoupil, "Is the Onslaught Making Us Crazy?" *Newsweek*, July 16, 2012; Kerric Harvey, ed., *Encyclopaedia of Social Media and Politics*, (Sage, 2014).

Other useful references are José van Dijck, *The Culture of Connectivity: A Critical History of Social Media* (Oxford University Press, 2013); Tim Jordan, *Internet, Society and Culture* [electronic resource]: *Communicative Practices Before and After the Internet* (Bloomsbury Publishing, 2013); Francis L. F. Lee, ed., *Frontiers in New Media Research* (Routledge, 2013); Allison Cerra, *Identity Shift: Where Identity Meets Technology in the Networked-Community Age* (John Wiley & Sons, 2012); Andrew Keen, *Digital Vertigo: How Today's Online Social Revolution Is Dividing, Diminishing, and Disorienting Us* (Constable, 2012); Pamela Lund, *Massively Networked: How the Convergence of Social Media and Technology Is Changing Your Life*, 2nd ed. (PLI Media, 2012); Hana S. Noor Al-Deen, and John Allen Hendricks, eds., *Social Media: Usage and Impact* (Lexington Books, 2012); Nora Young, *The Virtual Self: How Our Digital Lives Are Altering the World Around Us* (McClelland & Stewart, 2012).

Internet References . . .

Sociology—Study Sociology Online

http://edu.learnsoc.org/

Sociology Web Resources

www.mhhe.com/socscience/sociology/resources
/index.htm

Sociosite

www.topsite.com/goto/sociosite.net

Socioweb

www.topsite.com/goto/socioweb.com

Unit 2

UNIT

Sex Roles, Gender, and the Family

*T*he modern feminist movement has advanced the causes of women to the point where there are now more women in the workforce in the United States than ever before. Professions and trades that were traditionally regarded as the provinces of men have opened up to women, and women now have easier access to the education and training necessary to excel in these new areas. But what is happening to sex roles, and what are the effects of changing sex roles? How have men and women been affected by the stress caused by current sex roles, the demand for the right to same-sex marriages, and the deterioration of the traditional family structure? The issues in this unit address these sorts of questions.

Selected, Edited, and with Issue Framing Material by:
Kurt Finsterbusch, *University of Maryland, College Park*

ISSUE

Is the American Family in Trouble?

YES: Isabel V. Sawhill, from "The New White Negro: What It Means That Family Breakdown Is Now Biracial," *Washington Monthly* (2013)

NO: W. Bradford Wilcox, from "Unequal, Unfair, and Unhappy: The 3 Biggest Myths about Marriage Today," *The Atlantic* (2013)

Learning Outcomes

After reading this issue, you will be able to:

- Estimate the general quality of marriages in America.
- Discern which groups have the least successful marriages generally.
- Know the major reasons due to which marriages fail.
- Be able to counter the myth that most marriages are bad.

ISSUE SUMMARY

YES: Isabel V. Sawhill, a senior fellow in economic studies at the Brookings Institution, director of the Budgeting for National Priorities Project, and codirector of the Center on Children and Families, points out that marriages in college educated families are not declining but they are declining significantly for noncollege educated families, both white and black.

NO: W. Bradford Wilcox, associate professor of sociology and director of the National Marriage Project at the University of Virginia, describes the positive situation of families today. The majority of marriages are happy and are much more equal and fair than decades ago.

The state of the American family deeply concerns many Americans. About 40 percent of marriages end in divorce, and only 27 percent of children born in 1990 are expected to be living with both parents by the time they reach age 17. Most Americans, therefore, are affected personally or are close to people who are affected by structural changes in the family. Few people can avoid being exposed to the issue: violence in the family and celebrity divorces are standard fare for news programs, and magazine articles decrying the breakdown of the family appear frequently. Politicians today try to address the problems of the family. Academics have affirmed that the family crisis has numerous significant negative effects on children, spouses, and the rest of society.

But is the situation as bad as portrayed? Divorces are much easier to get than in the 1950s, and therefore, increased until the nineties. But is it not better to have a choice to stay or leave than to have no choice and be trapped in a bad marriage? Many of you reading this come from divorced homes and can evaluate how much you and your family suffered and whether you have been scarred for life. All of you can look around you and judge for yourselves how your acquaintances have been affected by divorce or other family issues.

One reason family strength is a very important issue is the important role that the family plays in the functioning of society. For a society to survive, its population must reproduce (or take in many immigrants), and its young must be trained to perform adult roles and to have the values and attitudes that will motivate them to contribute to society. Procreation and socialization are two vital roles that families traditionally have performed. In addition, the family provides economic and emotional support for its members, which is vital to their effective functioning in society. Stable, well-functioning families best perform these roles and divorce and family conflict jeopardize them.

Although most experts agree that the American family is in crisis, there is little agreement about what, if anything, should be done about it. After all, most of these problems result from the choices that people make to try to increase their well-being. People end unhappy marriages. When they do, most parents also carefully consider the best interests of their children. These considerations obviously prevent or delay many divorces and probably should prevent many more. Obviously, however,

many situations are improved by divorce, especially if the divorce and aftermath arrangements are conducted in a compassionate manner. So which way is best is a judgment call, both by the potentially divorcing parents and by the academics who study the issue.

In the selections that follow, Isabel V. Sawhill shows that modern marriages have problems as divorce rates demonstrate. Her main point, however, is that marriage problems are much more prevalent in the lower class than in the middle or upper classes for both whites and blacks. In sum, Sawhill reports that marriage is in trouble but mainly in the lower class. W. Bradford Wilcox paints a brighter picture. He shows that "Most husbands and wives make about equal total contributions to the paid and unpaid work needed to sustain a family. Most judge their marriages to be fair and are happily married."

YES

Isabel V. Sawhill

The New White Negro: What It Means That Family Breakdown Is Now Biracial

In 1965, Daniel Patrick Moynihan released a controversial report written for his then boss, President Lyndon Johnson. Entitled "The Negro Family: The Case for National Action," it described the condition of lower-income African American families and catalyzed a highly acrimonious, decades-long debate about black culture and family values in America.

The report cited a series of staggering statistics showing high rates of divorce, unwed childbearing, and single motherhood among black families. "The white family has achieved a high degree of stability and is maintaining that stability," the report said. "By contrast, the family structure of lower class Negroes is highly unstable, and in many urban centers is approaching complete breakdown."

Nearly fifty years later, the picture is even more grim and the statistics can no longer be organized neatly by race. In fact, Moynihan's bracing profile of the collapsing black family in the 1960s looks remarkably similar to a profile of the average white family today. White households have similar—or worse—statistics of divorce, unwed childbearing, and single motherhood as the black households cited by Moynihan in his report. In 2000, the percentage of white children living with a single parent was identical to the percentage of black children living with a single parent in 1960: 22 percent.

What was happening to black families in the '60s can be reinterpreted today not as an indictment of the black family but as a harbinger of a larger collapse of traditional living arrangements—of what demographer Samuel Preston, in words that Moynihan later repeated, called "the earthquake that shuddered through the American family."

That earthquake has not affected all American families the same way. While the Moynihan report focused on disparities between white and black, increasingly it is class, and not just race, that matters for family structure. Although blacks as a group are still less likely to marry than whites, gaps in family formation patterns by class have increased for both races, with the sharpest declines in

marriage rates occurring among the least educated of both races. For example, in 1960, 76 percent of adults with a college degree were married, compared to 72 percent of those with a high school diploma—a gap of only 4 percentage points. By 2008, not only was marriage less likely, but that gap had quadrupled, to 16 percentage points, with 64 percent of adults with college degrees getting married compared to only 48 percent of adults with a high school diploma. A report from the National Marriage Project at the University of Virginia summed up the data well: "Marriage is an emerging dividing line between America's moderately educated middle and those with college degrees." The group for whom marriage has largely disappeared now includes not just unskilled blacks but unskilled whites as well. Indeed, for younger women without a college degree, unwed childbearing is the new normal.

These differences in family formation are a problem not only for those concerned with "family values" per se, but also for those concerned with upward mobility in a society that values equal opportunity for its children. Because the breakdown of the traditional family is overwhelmingly occurring among working-class Americans of all races, these trends threaten to make the U.S. a much more class-based society over time. The well-educated and upper-middle-class parents who are still forming two-parent families are able to invest time and resources in their children—time and resources that lower- and working-class single mothers, however impressive their efforts to be both good parents and good breadwinners, simply do not have.

The striking similarities between what happened to black Americans at an earlier stage in our history and what is happening now to white working-class Americans may shed new light on old debates about cultural versus structural explanations of poverty. What's clear is that economic opportunity, while not the only factor affecting marriage, clearly matters.

The journalist Hanna Rosin describes the connection between declining economic opportunities for men and declining rates of marriage in her book *The End of Men*. Like Moynihan, she points to the importance of job opportunities for men in maintaining marriage as an institution. The disappearance of well-paying factory jobs has, in her view, led to the near collapse of marriage in towns where less educated men used to be able to support a family and a middle-class lifestyle, earning $70,000 or more in a single year. As these jobs have been outsourced or up-skilled, such men either are earning less or are jobless altogether, making them less desirable marriage partners. Other researchers, including Kathryn Edin at Harvard, Andrew Cherlin at Johns Hopkins, and Charles Murray of the American Enterprise Institute, drawing on close observations of other working-class communities, have made similar arguments.

Family life, to some extent, adapts to the necessities thrown up by the evolution of the economy. Just as joblessness among young black men contributed to the breakdown of the black family that Moynihan observed in the '60s, more recent changes in technology and global competition have hollowed out the job market for less educated whites. Unskilled white men have even less attachment to the labor force today than unskilled black men did fifty years ago, leading to a decline in their marriage rates in a similar way.

In 1960, the employment rate of prime-age (twenty-five to fifty-five) black men with less than a high school education was 80 percent. Fast-forward to 2000, and the employment rate of white men with less than a high school education was much lower, at 65 percent—and even for white high school graduates it was only 84 percent. Without an education in today's economy, being white is no guarantee of being able to find a job.

That's not to say that race isn't an issue. It's clear that black men have been much harder hit by the disappearance of jobs for the less skilled than white men. Black employment rates for those with less than a college education have sunk to near-catastrophic levels. In 2000, only 63 percent of black men with only a high school diploma (compared with 84 percent of white male graduates) were employed. Since the recession, those numbers have fallen even farther. And even black college graduates are not doing quite as well as their white counterparts. Based on these and other data, I believe it would be a mistake to conclude that race is unimportant; blacks continue to face unique disadvantages because of the color of their skin. It ought to be possible to say that class is becoming more important, but that race still matters a lot.

Most obviously, the black experience has been shaped by the impact of slavery and its ongoing aftermath. Even after emancipation and the civil rights revolution in the 1960s, African Americans faced exceptional challenges like segregated and inferior schools and discrimination in the labor market. It would take at least a generation for employers to begin to change their hiring practices and for educational disparities to diminish; even today these remain significant barriers. A recent audit study found that white applicants for low-wage jobs were twice as likely to be called in for interviews as equally qualified black applicants.

Black jobless rates not only exceed those of whites; in addition, a single-minded focus on declining job prospects for men and its consequences for family life ignores a number of other factors that have led to the decline of marriage. Male employment prospects can lead to more marriages, but scholars such as Harvard's David Ellwood and Christopher Jencks have argued that economic factors alone cannot explain the wholesale changes in the frequency of single parenting, unwed births, divorce, and marriage, especially among the least educated, that are leading to growing gaps between social classes. So what else explains the decline of marriage?

First, and critically important in my view, is the changing role of women. In my first book, *Time of Transition: The Growth of Families Headed by Women*, published in 1975, my coauthor and I argued that it was not just male earnings that mattered, but what men could earn relative to women. When women don't gain much, if anything, from getting married, they often choose to raise children on their own. Fifty years ago, women were far more economically dependent on marriage than they are now. Today, women are not just working more, they are better suited by education and tradition to work in such rapidly growing sectors of the economy as health care, education, administrative jobs, and services. While some observers may see women taking these jobs as a matter of necessity—and that's surely a factor—we shouldn't forget the revolution in women's roles that has made it possible for them to support a family on their own.

In a fascinating piece of academic research published in the *Journal of Human Resources* in 2011, Scott Hankins and Mark Hoekstra discovered that single women who won between $25,000 and $50,000 in the Florida lottery were 41 percent to 48 percent less likely to marry over the following three years than women who won less than $1,000. We economists call this a "natural experiment," because it shows the strong influence of women's ability to support themselves without marriage—uncontaminated by differences in personal attributes that may also affect one's ability or willingness to marry. My own earlier research also suggested that the relative incomes of wives and husbands predicted who would divorce and who would not.

Women's growing economic independence has interacted with stubborn attitudes about changing gender roles. When husbands fail to adjust to women's new breadwinning responsibilities (who cooks dinner or stays home with a sick child when both parents work?) the couple is more likely to divorce. It may be that well-educated younger men and women continue to marry not only because they can afford to but because many of the men in these families have adopted more egalitarian attitudes. While a working-class male might find such attitudes threatening to his manliness, an upper-middle-class man often does not, given his other sources of status. But when women find themselves having to do it all—that is, earn money in the workplace and shoulder the majority of child care and other domestic responsibilities—they raise the bar on whom they're willing to marry or stay married to.

These gender-related issues may play an even greater role for black women, since while white men hold slightly more high school diplomas and baccalaureate degrees than white women, black women are much better educated than black men. That means it's more difficult for well-educated black women to find black partners with comparable earning ability and social status. In 2010, black women made 87 percent of what black men did, whereas white women made only 70 percent of what white men earned. For less educated black women, there is, in addition, a shortage of black men because of high rates of incarceration. One estimate puts the proportion of black men who will spend some time in prison at almost one third.

In a forthcoming book, *Doing the Best I Can: Fatherhood in the Inner City*, Timothy Nelson and Edin, the Harvard sociologist, describe in great detail the kind of role reversal that has occurred among low-income families, both black and white. What they saw were mothers who were financially responsible for children, and fathers who were trying to maintain ties to their children in other ways, limited by the fact that these fathers have very little money, are often involved in drugs, crime, or other relationships, and rarely live with the mother and child.

In other words, low-income fathers are not only withdrawing from the traditional breadwinner role, they're staging a wholesale retreat—even as they make attempts to remain involved in their children's lives.

Normative changes figure as well. As the retreat from marriage has become more common, it's also become more acceptable. That acceptance came earlier among blacks than among whites because of their own distinct experiences. Now that unwed childbearing is becoming the norm among the white working class as well, there is no longer much of a stigma associated with single parenting, and there is a greater willingness on the part of the broader community to accept the legitimacy of single-parent households.

Despite this change in norms, however, most Americans, whatever their race or social class, still aspire to marriage. It's just that their aspirations are typically unrealistically high and their ability to achieve that ideal is out of step with their opportunities and lifestyle. As scholars such as Cherlin and Edin have emphasized, marriage is no longer a precursor to adult success. Instead, when it still takes place, marriage is more a badge of success already achieved. In particular, large numbers of young adults are having unplanned pregnancies long before they can cope with the responsibilities of parenthood. Paradoxically, although they view marriage as something they cannot afford, they rarely worry about the cost of raising a child.

Along with many others, I remain concerned about the effects on society of this wholesale retreat from stable two-parent families. The consequences for children, especially, are not good. Their educational achievements, and later chances of becoming involved in crime or a teen pregnancy are, on average, all adversely affected by growing up in a single-parent family. But I am also struck by the lessons that emerge from looking at how trends in family formation have differed by class as well as by race. If we were once two countries, one black and one white, we are now increasingly becoming two countries, one advantaged and one disadvantaged. Race still affects an individual's chances in life, but class is growing in importance. This argument was the theme of William Julius Wilson's 1980 book, *The Declining Significance of Race*. More recent evidence suggests that, despite all the controversy his book engendered, he was right.

To say that class is becoming more important than race isn't to dismiss race as a very important factor. Blacks have faced, and will continue to face, unique challenges. But when we look for the reasons why less skilled blacks are failing to marry and join the middle class, it is largely for the same reasons that marriage and a middle-class lifestyle is eluding a growing number of whites as well. The jobs that unskilled men once did are gone, women are increasingly financially independent, and a broad cultural shift across America has created a new normal.

ISABEL V. SAWHILL is a senior fellow in economic studies at the Brookings Institution and director of the Budgeting for National Priorities Project. She also codirects the Center on Children and Families and has authored several important books and many reports and articles.

W. Bradford Wilcox

 **NO**

Unequal, Unfair, and Unhappy: The 3 Biggest Myths about Marriage Today

Most married couples with children are satisfied with their relationships.

Of course, it's true that some marriages are unequal and unfair, leaving a minority of wives (and husbands) unhappy. And most husbands and wives experience moments or even periods of frustration with their work-family arrangements. Nevertheless, the big picture for marriage in America—for those Americans fortunate enough to have tied the knot—is markedly more rosy than Mundy's portrait would suggest. Most husbands and wives make about equal total contributions to the paid and unpaid work needed to sustain a family, judge their marriages to be fair, and are happily married.

Take family work. When you combine paid work, housework, and childcare, today's married parents both put in about 55 hours, according to a recent report from the Pew Research Center. It's true that married mothers do more of the housework and childcare, but in most households this doesn't amount to an onerous burden for them. That's because most married mothers do *not* work full-time (43 percent work full-time) and do *not* wish to work full-time (just 23 percent wish to work full-time, a fact rarely mentioned in media accounts of work and family life).

The rough parity in total family work hours enjoyed by most couples, combined with the fact that most married mothers don't wish to work full-time, may explain why most husbands and wives judge their marriages to be fair. In fact, 73 percent of married fathers and 68 percent of married mothers reported that their marriage was fair, according to the 2010–2011 Survey of Marital Generosity.

Perhaps in part because husbands' and wives' perceptions of equity are important predictors of contemporary marital happiness, most married parents report that they are satisfied with their marriages. Specifically, 80 percent of today's married fathers and 77 percent of today's married mothers say they are satisfied or very satisfied with their marriage.

Thus, in average families across the nation, married men *and* married women work roughly the same total hours for their families, judge their marriages to be fair, and enjoy happy marriages.

So, why was Mundy so off the mark in her depiction of contemporary marriage? The most notable exception to the positive marriage portrait I have painted here can be found among married couples with children where both spouses work full-time—the one group that featured prominently in the statistics cited by Mundy. In these marriages, there really is a "second shift" for many married mothers; wives in these marriages do about five hours more of total work per week and enjoy six hours less free time per week than their husbands, according to research by sociologist Suzanne Bianchi. Such marriages may indeed be more vulnerable to the kinds of tensions and unhappiness Mundy dwelled upon.

But for most married men and women today, marriage looks pretty good. It may not be a "24/7 Sleepover Party," but it is basically equal, fair, and happy. And that's the real and often unreported good news about marriage in America today.

W. Bradford Wilcox, associate professor of sociology and director of the National Marriage Project at the University of Virginia, has authored two books and many articles.

EXPLORING THE ISSUE

Is the American Family in Trouble?

Critical Thinking and Reflection

1. Which is more hurtful for children, having their parents divorcing or having their parents frequently fighting and angry at each other? How does your judgment change if spouse abuse is part of the picture? How does your judgment change if child abuse is part of the picture?
2. Do you favor or oppose laws that make divorce easier and why?
3. What factors contribute to the current relatively high divorce rates? How can these factors be changed to reduce divorce rates?
4. What are the impacts of divorces on society?
5. Do you think that marriage is in trouble?
6. How are changing values and culture patterns affecting marriages?
7. How is the economy affecting marriages?

Is There Common Ground?

Because about 45 percent of first marriages and about 60 percent of second marriages end in divorce, it is a major problem for the individuals involved and, potentially, for the society as a whole. Everyone agrees that happy marriages are far better than divorces. Everyone also agrees that the welfare of the children is critical to our judgments on the issues of family functioning and divorce. The debate, therefore, is over which of two bad situations (divorce or bad marriages) is the least bad. This is a difficult issue to clearly judge. Crucial to the answer is how bad is the marriage before the divorce and how bad are the arrangements after the divorce? Furthermore, many of the consequences of divorce are difficult to measure accurately.

Additional Resources

There was a deluge of books on families, divorce, and children in the 1990s and many fewer in the 2000s. Many of the earlier works are still very relevant. Most writings emphasize the negative effects of divorce, especially for children. These include: Maggie Gallagher, *The Abolition of Marriage: How We Destroy Lasting Love* (Regnery, 1996); Barbara Dafoe Whitehead, *The Divorce Culture: How Divorce Became an Entitlement and How It Is Blighting the Lives of Our Children* (Alfred A. Knopf, 1997); Richard T. Gill, *Posterity Lost: Progress, Ideology, and the Decline of the American Family* (Rowman & Littlefield, 1997); James Q. Wilson, *The Marriage Problem: How Our Culture Has Weakened Families* (HarperCollins, 2002); Judith Wallerstein, *The Unexpected*

Legacy of Divorce (Hyperion, 2000); Elizabeth Marquardt, *Between Two Worlds: The Inner Lives of Children of Divorce* (Crown, 2006); and Linda Waite and Maggie Gallagher, *The Case for Staying Married* (Oxford University Press, 2005).

The writings that minimize the harmful effects of divorce include: John H. Harvey, *Children of Divorce: Stories of Loss and Growth* (Routledge, 2010); Constance Ahrons, *We're Still Family: What Grown Children Have to Say About Their Parents' Divorce* (HarperCollins, 2004); E. L. Kain, *The Myth of Family Decline* (D. C. Heath, 1990); and Mavis Hetherington and John Kelly, *For Better or for Worse: Divorce Reconsidered* (W. W. Norton, 2002).

David Popenoe and Jean Bethke Elshtain's book *Promises to Keep: Decline and Renewal of Marriage in America* (Rowman & Littlefield, 1996) discusses the negative impacts of divorce but also discusses signs of the renewal of marriage.

For a thorough treatment of divorce and its consequences, see: Alison Clark-Stewart, *Divorce: Causes and Consequences* (Yale University Press, 2006).

The legal aspects of divorce are covered by: Joanna L. Grossman in *Inside the Castle: Law and the Family in 20th Century America* (Princeton University Press, 2011).

Works that analyze changes in marriage and the family along with divorce include: Rebecca L. Davis, *More Perfect Unions: The American Search for Marital Bliss* (Harvard University Press, 2011); Tamara Metz, *Untying the Knot: Marriage, the State and the Case for Their Divorce* (Princeton University Press, 2010); Kristin Celello, *Making Marriage Work: A History of Marriage and Divorce in the Twentieth-Century United States* (University of North Carolina

Press, 2009); Andrew J. Cherlin, *The Marriage-Go-Round: The State of Marriage and the Family in America Today* (Alfred A. Knopf, 2009); Betty Farrell's *Family: The Making of an Idea, an Institution, and a Controversy in American Culture* (Westview Press, 1999); Karla B. Hackstaff's *Marriage in a Culture of Divorce* (Temple University Press, 1999); Jessica Weiss's *To Have and to Hold: Marriage, the Baby Boom, and Social Change* (University of Chicago Press, 2000); Barbara J. Risman's *Gender Vertigo: American Families in Transition* (Yale University Press, 1998); Ronald D. Taylor and Margaret C. Wang, eds., *Resilience Across Contexts: Family, Work, Culture, and Community* (Lawrence Erlbaum, 2000); Linda J. Waite and Maggie Gallagher, *The Case for Marriage: Why Married People Are Happier, Healthier, and Better Off Financially* (Doubleday, 2000); Daniel P. Moynihan et al., eds.,

Future of the Family (Russell Sage Foundation, 2004); and Lynne M. Casper and Suzanne M. Bianchi, *Continuity and Change in the American Family* (Sage, 2002).

For counsel on how to strengthen marriages, see: David P. Gushee, *Getting Marriage Right: Realistic Counsel for Saving and Strengthening Relationships* (Baker Books, 2004).

For information on divorce among seniors, see: Deirdre Bair, *Calling It Quits: Late-Life Divorce and Starting Over*, 1st ed. (Random House, 2007).

For advice on handling divorce issues, see: Mark A. Fine and John H. Harvey, eds., *Handbook of Divorce and Relationship Dissolution* (Lawrence Erlbaum, 2006).

Finally, for information on the adjustment of children, see: Robert E. Emery, *Marriage, Divorce, and Children's Adjustment*, 2nd ed. (Sage, 1999).

Internet References . . .

National Council on Family Research

www.ncfr.com

Sociology—Study Sociology Online

http://edu.learnsoc.org/

Sociology Web Resources

www.mhhe.com/socscience/sociology/resources
/index.htm

Sociosite

www.topsite.com/goto/sociosite.net

Socioweb

www.topsite.com/goto/socioweb.com

Selected, Edited, and with Issue Framing Material by:
Kurt Finsterbusch, *University of Maryland, College Park*

ISSUE

Can Women Have It All?

YES: Gayle Tzemach Lemmon, from "Sheryl Sandberg's Radically Realistic 'And' Solution for Working Mothers," *The Atlantic* (2013)

NO: Anne-Marie Slaughter, from "Why Women Still Can't Have It All," *The Atlantic* (2012)

Learning Outcomes
After reading this issue, you will be able to:
• Understand how people (in this case women) deal with the stress of situations involving the conflict between two very important values. Women have to make life-changing decisions regarding the balance of work and family responsibilities.
• Understand how the conditions affecting these choices have changed over time.
• Explore how the workplaces and family units are changing to accommodate women's needs in this set of conflicting demands.
• Explain, if possible, why these institutions are not more accommodating.
• Form an opinion about whether this issue is largely an individual problem or largely an institutional problem or is both.
• Evaluate what the role of husbands is in this situation.
• Discuss how men tend to handle the stress between work and family.

ISSUE SUMMARY

YES: Gayle Tzemach Lemmon, best-selling author, journalist, and a Senior Fellow with the Council on Foreign Relations' Women and Foreign Policy program, discusses the issues in Sheryl Sandberg's famous book, *Lean In*. Sandberg's advice to career women is not to opt out but to lean in, that is, to firmly choose both career and parenting. Unfortunately men still run the country so the societal changes that could facilitate *Lean In* are missing. Full commitment to both career and family will not be easy.

NO: Anne-Marie Slaughter, the Bert G. Kerstetter '66 University Professor of Politics and International Affairs at Princeton University and formerly dean of Princeton's Woodrow Wilson School of Public and International Affairs, explains why Sandberg is wrong and women cannot successfully pursue career and family at the same time. They must decide which to do well and which to do adequately but not avidly.

The fascinating aspect of social life is how many different trends and changes significantly affect how we live and the choices we make. For example, consider married women and their work–family choices. Ever since the 1950s, married women have increasingly participated in the labor force. Why? The reasons are numerous. Women want the money for themselves. Women need the money for the family. Women want the challenge of a career. Women want the social life that work provides. Women want independence. The list of reasons goes on and on. These reasons change, however, as the context changes.

For example, since 1965 the median price of the one-family home compared to the average income of private nonagricultural workers had doubled in real terms before the housing market crashed. Thus, the single earner family is having much more difficulty buying a house. This trend helps explain why married women increasingly enter or stay in the labor force. Attitudes have also changed. In 1968, a large survey asked young people what they expected to be doing at age 35. About 30 percent of the 20- to 21-year-olds said that they would be working. Seven years later, 65 percent of 20- to 21-year-olds said they would be working. That is an astounding change. The statistical result is that in 1900, women 16 and over constituted 18 percent of the labor force; in 1950, women constituted 30 percent; and since 1995, women have constituted 45–47 percent of the labor force.

Educational changes in the past half century have also been dramatic. Females have overtaken males in most aspects of education. Women are now outnumbering men in college and currently earn 58 percent of all bachelor's degrees, 60 percent of all master's degrees, and 52 percent of PhDs. Women are also more focused on professional degrees while in college as demonstrated by their selection of majors. In 1966, 40 percent of college women graduates majored in education and 17 percent majored in English/literature, but only 2 percent majored in business. Women have stopped shying away from the business world. The percentage of female BA business degrees went from 9 percent in 1971 to 49 percent in 1997, while it went from 4 percent to 39 percent for MA business degrees and from 5 percent to 70 percent for law degrees. Another trend affecting choices and behaviors is the increasing scarcity of time. The percentage of males working more than 50 hours a week increased from 21.0 to 26.5 and for females from 5.2 to 11.3 during 1970–2000.

Two issues that have received major media attention explore the circumstances of the work–family choice. First, in the 1990s, employers talked about a mommy track for women employees who would be allowed an easier workload that would reduce the conflict between work and family but would slow down their advancement and hold down their income. Second, in the past decade investigators noticed that capable women with prosperous husbands "opted out" of the work world and stayed home with the kids. They had the circumstances that allowed them to make this choice. Could it be that if all women had such circumstances then the majority of them would make the same choice? This is the issue which is debated in the following selections. Gayle Tzemach Lemmon strongly supports Sheryl Sandberg's message in her famous book, *Lean In*, which advises career women not to opt out but to lean in, i.e., to firmly choose both career and parenting. It will not be easy but it is much better than the opt out alternative. Anne-Marie Slaughter attacks Sandberg's thesis. She tries to show that women cannot successfully pursue both career and family at the same time. They will fail at one or both objectives. They must decide which to do well and which to do adequately but not avidly.

YES

Gayle Tzemach Lemmon

Sheryl Sandberg's Radically Realistic "And" Solution for Working Mothers

At a wedding this summer, while I was eight months pregnant with twins, an older gentleman sitting next to me asked me whether I still worked in finance.

No, I told him, at the moment I was focused on my next book project, think-tank work, and several magazine pieces.

"Well," he said with a gentle, nearly sympathetic, smile, "in any case, soon you will be pushing three babies in a stroller, right? Won't leave time for much else."

Annoyance swelled up into my already enormous stomach. When our table rose to watch the bride cut the cake I scurried two seats over to my husband and fumed. "I was so irritated I couldn't even come up with a clever answer, other than to say that the kids have a father, too," I said. "No one would *ever* say something like that to you."

My husband laughed and told me not to pay any attention. "It's just because people think that women can only be one thing."

And therein lies the rub.

Somehow, today—even while women learn and earn in greater numbers than ever before—the idea that women live in an "either/or" world stubbornly hangs on. A woman can either be a mother or a professional. Career-driven or family-oriented. A great wife or a great worker. Not both. In other words, the choices are Donna Reed and Murphy Brown (pre-baby). Precious few Clair Huxtables out there.

That is the challenge Sheryl Sandberg's book sets out to tackle. In a women-in-the-workplace discussion consisting mostly of "either/ors," her argument in the upcoming book *Lean In* injects the word "and" into the conversation in a way that urges women to bring their "whole selves" to work. Choice is good, *and* so is aspiration. Ambition is great, and so is telling your boss that you want to have children. Working hard at your job is important, and so is finding a way to leave the office early enough to be home for dinner with your kids.

Already, weeks before the book's publication, criticism is within easy earshot. A 20-something friend told me that several women she respected greatly argued that Sandberg is hardly representative of others and that her advice is impractical for the non-wealthy. But it seems to me that this criticism misses the point. What Sandberg offers is a view that shows 20-somethings like my friend that choices and trade-offs surely exist, but that the "old normal" of blunting ambition so that you can fit in one category or another does not have to be the way it is. And that each of us has a say in what comes next. And that includes men.

We live in an era of immense change when it comes to what women do, how they do it, and with whom. 2011 marked the first year in which more women than men had advanced degrees. Between 1970 and 2009 the number of jobs held by women leapt from 37 percent to close to 48 percent. The boost in productivity resulting from women's increased labor participation accounts for 25 percent of U.S. GDP. Women own nearly 8 million businesses, enterprises that provide more than 20 million jobs. And as researcher Liza Mundy noted in her recent book, nearly 40 percent of wives in the U.S. now earn more than their husbands; Mundy predicts in a generation breadwinning wives will be the majority. Yet no real evolution in our expectations for women's lives and women's ambitions has accompanied these numbers, as Anne-Marie Slaughter's zeitgeist-channeling 2012 *Atlantic* story "Why Women Still Can't Have It All" points out.

Sandberg's proposition, though, looks a lot more like most women's lives than the "either/or" model into which women's lives get shoved. Many women navigate the "ands" every day, juggling a work life and a family life whose demands have meshed into one another in our constantly connected, 24/7-everything world. They don't have the luxury of choosing one or the other because they are too busy doing both. And as I have argued here at *The Atlantic*, all of these are undoubtedly high-class conversations the women I grew up with never had the chance to have.

Still, it is relevant to all women that, as Sandberg notes, "the blunt truth is that men still run the world." Women are fewer than 5 percent of all Fortune 500 CEOs and hold less than 20 percent of all executive board seats. Half the population accounts for barely 10 percent of all heads of state. And it was enormous progress for women to reach the 20-percent mark in the U.S. Senate last year. These dismal numbers and the lack of power they indicate are why it matters that the land of "and" is not only where women live now, but where they should want to stay and prosper. When 50 percent of the country has a kiddie seat at the head table, making room for others gets a whole lot harder. (Sandberg argues that women should, quite literally, sit "at the table" of power in which decisions get made.) Creating a world in which the next generation of talent gets to exercise its potential instead of bumping its head against career-stifling stereotypes or soul-crushing ceilings is in everyone's interest—and the American economy's.

Still, though, even when you succeed in winning fame and fortune in the world of "and", sometimes others make it "either/or" for you.

In a recent *Rolling Stone* piece on the end of the long-running television program *30 Rock*, show creator Tina Fey said the show had run its course, and dropping ratings meant no more. She wanted to do some movies and develop a multi-camera TV show while staying close to home and her two small children.

Her fellow *30 Rock* actor Alec Baldwin had a different and somewhat more detailed explanation.

Baldwin, the magazine wrote, is "convinced that having a second child, in 2011, may have been the breaking point for Fey. 'I saw a real difference in her,' says Baldwin. 'Tina always had her antenna up, but this year was the first time where she came in and laid down on the couch on set, and you could tell, she's a mom. She's fucking wiped out.'"

GAYLE TZEMACH LEMMON is a best-selling author, journalist, and a Senior Fellow with the Council on Foreign Relations' Women and Foreign Policy Program.

Anne-Marie Slaughter

 **NO**

Why Women Still Can't Have It All

It's time to stop fooling ourselves, says a woman who left a position of power: the women who have managed to be both mothers and top professionals are superhuman, rich, or self-employed. If we truly believe in equal opportunity for all women, here's what has to change.

Eighteen months into my job as the first woman director of policy planning at the State Department, a foreign-policy dream job that traces its origins back to George Kennan, I found myself in New York, at the United Nations' annual assemblage of every foreign minister and head of state in the world. On a Wednesday evening, President and Mrs. Obama hosted a glamorous reception at the American Museum of Natural History. I sipped champagne, greeted foreign dignitaries, and mingled. But I could not stop thinking about my 14-year-old son, who had started eighth grade three weeks earlier and was already resuming what had become his pattern of skipping homework, disrupting classes, failing math, and tuning out any adult who tried to reach him. Over the summer, we had barely spoken to each other—or, more accurately, he had barely spoken to me. And the previous spring I had received several urgent phone calls—invariably on the day of an important meeting—that required me to take the first train from Washington, D.C., where I worked, back to Princeton, New Jersey, where he lived. My husband, who has always done everything possible to support my career, took care of him and his 12-year-old brother during the week; outside of those midweek emergencies, I came home only on weekends.

As the evening wore on, I ran into a colleague who held a senior position in the White House. She has two sons exactly my sons' ages, but she had chosen to move them from California to D.C. when she got her job, which meant her husband commuted back to California regularly. I told her how difficult I was finding it to be away from my son when he clearly needed me. Then I said, "When this is over, I'm going to write an op-ed titled 'Women Can't Have It All.'"

She was horrified. "You *can't* write that," she said. "You, of all people." What she meant was that such a statement, coming from a high-profile career woman—a role model—would be a terrible signal to younger generations of women. By the end of the evening, she had talked me out of it, but for the remainder of my stint in Washington, I was increasingly aware that the feminist beliefs on which I had built my entire career were shifting under my feet. I had always assumed that if I could get a foreign-policy job in the State Department or the White House while my party was in power, I would stay the course as long as I had the opportunity to do work I loved. But in January 2011, when my two-year public-service leave from Princeton University was up, I hurried home as fast as I could.

A rude epiphany hit me soon after I got there. When people asked why I had left government, I explained that I'd come home not only because of Princeton's rules (after two years of leave, you lose your tenure), but also because of my desire to be with my family and my conclusion that juggling high level government work with the needs of two teenage boys was not possible. I have not exactly left the ranks of full-time career women: I teach a full course load; write regular print and online columns on foreign policy; give 40 to 50 speeches a year; appear regularly on TV and radio; and am working on a new academic book. But I routinely got reactions from other women my age or older that ranged from disappointed ("It's such a pity that you had to leave Washington") to condescending ("I wouldn't generalize from your experience. *I've* never had to compromise, and *my* kids turned out great").

The first set of reactions, with the underlying assumption that my choice was somehow sad or unfortunate, was irksome enough. But it was the second set of reactions—those implying that my parenting and/ or my commitment to my profession were somehow substandard—that triggered a blind fury. Suddenly, finally, the penny dropped. All my life, I'd been on the other side of this exchange. I'd been the woman smiling the faintly superior smile while another woman told me she had decided to take some time out or pursue a less competitive career track so that she could spend more time with her family. I'd been the woman congratulating herself on her unswerving commitment to the feminist cause, chatting smugly with her dwindling number of college or law-school friends who had reached and maintained their place on the highest rungs of their profession. I'd been the one telling young women at my lectures that you *can* have it all and do it all, regardless of what field you are in. Which means I'd been part, albeit unwittingly, of making millions of women feel that *they* are to blame if they cannot manage to rise up the ladder as fast as men and also have a family and an active home life (and be thin and beautiful to boot).

Last spring, I flew to Oxford to give a public lecture. At the request of a young Rhodes Scholar I know, I'd agreed to talk to the Rhodes community about "work-family balance." I ended up speaking to a group of about 40 men and women in their mid-20s. What poured out of me was a set of very frank reflections on how unexpectedly hard it was to do the kind of job I wanted to do as a high government official and be the kind of parent I wanted to be, at a demanding time for my children (even though my husband, an academic, was willing to take on the lion's share of parenting for the two years I was in Washington). I concluded by saying that my time in office had convinced me that further government service would be very unlikely while my sons were still at home. The audience was rapt, and asked many thoughtful questions. One of the first was from a young woman who began by thanking me for "not giving just one more fatuous 'You can have it all' talk." Just about all of the women in that room planned to combine careers and family in some way. But almost all assumed and accepted that they would have to make compromises that the men in their lives were far less likely to have to make.

The striking gap between the responses I heard from those young women (and others like them) and the responses I heard from my peers and associates prompted me to write this article. Women of my generation have clung to the feminist credo we were raised with, even as our ranks have been steadily thinned by unresolvable tensions between family and career, because we are determined not to drop the flag for the next generation. But when many members of the younger generation have

stopped listening, on the grounds that glibly repeating "you can have it all" is simply airbrushing reality, it is time to talk.

I still strongly believe that women can "have it all" (and that men can too). I believe that we can "have it all at the same time." But not today, not with the way America's economy and society are currently structured. My experiences over the past three years have forced me to confront a number of uncomfortable facts that need to be widely acknowledged—and quickly changed.

Before my service in government, I'd spent my career in academia: as a law professor and then as the dean of Princeton's Woodrow Wilson School of Public and International Affairs. Both were demanding jobs, but I had the ability to set my own schedule most of the time. I could be with my kids when I needed to be, and still get the work done. I had to travel frequently, but I found I could make up for that with an extended period at home or a family vacation.

I knew that I was lucky in my career choice, but I had no idea how lucky until I spent two years in Washington within a rigid bureaucracy, even with bosses as understanding as Hillary Clinton and her chief of staff, Cheryl Mills. My workweek started at 4:20 on Monday morning, when I got up to get the 5:30 train from Trenton to Washington. It ended late on Friday, with the train home. In between, the days were crammed with meetings, and when the meetings stopped, the writing work began—a never-ending stream of memos, reports, and comments on other people's drafts. For two years, I never left the office early enough to go to any stores other than those open 24 hours, which meant that everything from dry cleaning to hair appointments to Christmas shopping had to be done on weekends, amid children's sporting events, music lessons, family meals, and conference calls. I was entitled to four hours of vacation per pay period, which came to one day of vacation a month. And I had it better than many of my peers in D.C.; Secretary Clinton deliberately came in around 8 a.m. and left around 7 p.m., to allow her close staff to have morning and evening time with their families (although of course she worked earlier and later, from home).

In short, the minute I found myself in a job that is typical for the vast majority of working women (and men), working long hours on someone else's schedule, I could no longer be both the parent and the professional I wanted to be—at least not with a child experiencing a rocky adolescence. I realized what should have perhaps been obvious: having it all, at least for me, depended almost entirely on what type of job I had. The flip side is the harder truth: having it all was not possible in many types of jobs, including high government office—at least not for very long.

I am hardly alone in this realization. Michèle Flournoy stepped down after three years as undersecretary of defense for policy, the third-highest job in the department, to spend more time at home with her three children, two of whom are teenagers. Karen Hughes left her position as the counselor to President George W. Bush after a year and a half in Washington to go home to Texas for the sake of her family. Mary Matalin, who spent two years as an assistant to Bush and the counselor to Vice President Dick Cheney before stepping down to spend more time with her daughters, wrote: "Having control over your schedule is the only way that women who want to have a career and a family can make it work."

Yet the decision to step down from a position of power—to value family over professional advancement, even for a time—is directly at odds with the prevailing social pressures on career professionals in the United States. One phrase says it all about current attitudes toward work and family, particularly among elites. In Washington, "leaving to spend time with your family" is a euphemism for being fired. This understanding is so ingrained that when Flournoy announced her resignation last December, *The New York Times* covered her decision as follows:

> Ms. Flournoy's announcement surprised friends and a number of Pentagon officials, but all said they took her reason for resignation at face value and not as a standard Washington excuse for an official who has in reality been forced out. "I can absolutely and unequivocally state that her decision to step down has nothing to do with anything other than her commitment to her family," said Doug Wilson, a top Pentagon spokesman. "She has loved this job and people here love her."

Think about what this "standard Washington excuse" implies: it is so unthinkable that an official would *actually* step down to spend time with his or her family that this must be a cover for something else. How could anyone voluntarily leave the circles of power for the responsibilities of parenthood? Depending on one's vantage point, it is either ironic or maddening that this view abides in the nation's capital, despite the ritual commitments to "family values" that are part of every political campaign. Regardless, this sentiment makes true work-life balance exceptionally difficult. But it cannot change unless top women speak out.

Only recently have I begun to appreciate the extent to which many young professional women feel under assault by women my age and older. After I gave a recent speech in New York, several women in their late 60s or early 70s came up to tell me how glad and proud they were to see me speaking as a foreign-policy expert. A couple of them went on, however, to contrast my career with the path being traveled by "younger women today." One expressed dismay that many younger women "are just not willing to get out there and do it." Said another, unaware of the circumstances of my recent job change: "They think they have to choose between having a career and having a family."

A similar assumption underlies Facebook Chief Operating Officer Sheryl Sandberg's widely publicized 2011 commencement speech at Barnard, and her earlier TED talk, in which she lamented the dismally small number of women at the top and advised young women not to "leave before you leave." When a woman starts thinking about having children, Sandberg said, "she doesn't raise her hand anymore . . . She starts leaning back." Although couched in terms of encouragement, Sandberg's exhortation contains more than a note of reproach. We who have made it to the top, or are striving to get there, are essentially saying to the women in the generation behind us: "What's the matter with you?"

They have an answer that we don't want to hear. After the speech I gave in New York, I went to dinner with a group of 30-somethings. I sat across from two vibrant women, one of whom worked at the UN and the other at a big New York law firm. As nearly always happens in these situations, they soon began asking me about work-life balance. When I told them I was writing this article, the lawyer said, "I look for role models and can't find any." She said the women in her firm who had become partners and taken on management positions had made tremendous sacrifices, "many of which they don't even seem to realize . . . They take two years off when their kids are young but then work like crazy to get back on track professionally, which means that they see their kids when they are toddlers but not teenagers, or really barely at all." Her friend nodded, mentioning the top professional women she knew, all of whom essentially relied on round-the-clock nannies. Both were very clear that they did not want that life, but could not figure out how to combine professional success and satisfaction with a real commitment to family.

I realize that I am blessed to have been born in the late 1950s instead of the early 1930s, as my mother was, or the beginning of the 20th century, as my grandmothers were. My mother built a successful and rewarding career as a professional artist largely in the years after my brothers and I left home—and after being told in her 20s that she could not go to medical school, as her father had done and her brother would go on to do, because, of course, she was going to get married. I owe my own freedoms and opportunities to the pioneering generation of women ahead of me—the women now in their 60s, 70s, and 80s who faced overt sexism of a kind I see only when watching *Mad Men*, and who knew that the only way to make it as a woman was to act exactly like a man. To admit to, much less act on, maternal longings would have been fatal to their careers.

But precisely thanks to their progress, a different kind of conversation is now possible. It is time for women in leadership positions to recognize that although we are still blazing trails and breaking ceilings, many of us are also reinforcing a falsehood: that "having it all" is, more than anything, a function of personal determination. As Kerry Rubin and Lia Macko, the authors of *Midlife Crisis at 30,* their cri de coeur for Gen-X and Gen-Y women, put it:

> What we discovered in our research is that while the empowerment part of the equation has been loudly celebrated, there has been very little honest discussion among women of our age about the real barriers and flaws that still exist in the system despite the opportunities we inherited.

I am well aware that the majority of American women face problems far greater than any discussed in this article. I am writing for my demographic—highly educated, well-off women who are privileged enough to have choices in the first place. We may not have choices about whether to do paid work, as dual incomes have become indispensable. But we have choices about the type and tempo of the work we do. We are the women who could be leading, and who should be equally represented in the leadership ranks.

Millions of other working women face much more difficult life circumstances. Some are single mothers; many struggle to find any job; others support husbands who cannot find jobs. Many cope with a work life in which good day care is either unavailable or very expensive; school schedules do not match work schedules; and schools themselves are failing to educate their children. Many of these women are worrying not about having it all, but rather about holding on to what they do have. And although women as a group have made substantial gains in wages, educational attainment, and prestige over the past three decades, the economists Justin Wolfers and Betsey Stevenson have shown that women are less happy today than their predecessors were in 1972, both in absolute terms and relative to men.

The best hope for improving the lot of all women, and for closing what Wolfers and Stevenson call a "new gender gap"—measured by well-being rather than wages—is to close the leadership gap: to elect a woman president and 50 women senators; to ensure that women are equally represented in the ranks of corporate executives and judicial leaders. Only when women wield power in sufficient numbers will we create a society that genuinely works for all women. That will be a society that works for everyone.

The Half-Truths We Hold Dear

Let's briefly examine the stories we tell ourselves, the clichés that I and many other women typically fall back on when younger women ask us how we have managed to "have it all." They are not necessarily lies, but at best partial truths. We must clear them out of the way to make room for a more honest and productive discussion about real solutions to the problems faced by professional women.

It's Possible If You Are Just Committed Enough

Our usual starting point, whether we say it explicitly or not, is that having it all depends primarily on the depth and intensity of a woman's commitment to her career. That is precisely the sentiment behind the dismay so many older career women feel about the younger generation. *They are not committed enough,* we say, to make the trade-offs and sacrifices that the women ahead of them made.

Yet instead of chiding, perhaps we should face some basic facts. Very few women reach leadership positions. The pool of female candidates for any top job is small, and will only grow smaller if the women who come after us decide to take time out, or drop out of professional competition altogether, to raise children. That is exactly what has Sheryl Sandberg so upset, and rightly so. In her words, "Women are not making it to the top. A hundred and ninety heads of state; nine are women. Of all the people in parliament in the world, 13 percent are women. In the corporate sector, [the share of] women at the top—C-level jobs, board seats—tops out at 15, 16 percent."

Can "insufficient commitment" even plausibly explain these numbers? To be sure, the women who do make it to the top are highly committed to their profession. On closer examination, however, it turns out that most of them have something else in common: they are genuine superwomen. Consider the number of women recently in the top ranks in Washington—Susan Rice, Elizabeth Sherwood-Randall, Michelle Gavin, Nancy-Ann Min DeParle—who are Rhodes Scholars. Samantha Power, another senior White House official, won a Pulitzer Prize at age 32. Or consider Sandberg herself, who graduated with the prize given to Harvard's top student of economics. These women cannot possibly be the standard against which even very talented professional women should measure themselves. Such a standard sets up most women for a sense of failure.

What's more, among those who have made it to the top, a balanced life still is more elusive for women than it is for men. A simple measure is how many women in top positions have children compared with their male colleagues. Every male Supreme Court justice has a family. Two of the three female justices are single with no children. And the third, Ruth Bader Ginsburg, began her career as a judge only when her younger child was almost grown. The pattern is the same at the National Security Council: Condoleezza Rice, the first and only woman national-security adviser, is also the only national-security adviser since the 1950s not to have a family.

The line of high-level women appointees in the Obama administration is one woman deep. Virtually all of us who have stepped down have been succeeded by men; searches for women to succeed men in similar positions come up empty. Just about every woman who could plausibly be tapped is already in government. The rest of the foreign-policy world is not much better; Micah Zenko, a fellow at the Council on Foreign Relations, recently surveyed the best data he could find across the government, the military, the academy, and think tanks, and found that women hold fewer than 30 percent of the senior foreign-policy positions in each of these institutions.

These numbers are all the more striking when we look back to the 1980s, when women now in their late 40s and 50s were coming out of graduate school, and remember that our classes were nearly 50–50 men and women. We were sure then that by now, we would be living in a 50–50 world. Something derailed that dream.

Sandberg thinks that "something" is an "ambition gap"—that women do not dream big enough. I am all for encouraging young women to reach for the stars. But I fear that the obstacles that keep women from reaching the top are rather more prosaic than the scope of their ambition. My longtime and invaluable assistant, who has a doctorate and juggles many balls as the mother of teenage twins, e-mailed me while I was working on this article: "You know what would help the vast majority of women with work/family balance? MAKE SCHOOL SCHEDULES MATCH WORK SCHEDULES." The present system, she noted, is based on a society that no longer exists—one in which farming was a major occupation and stay-at-home moms were the norm. Yet the system hasn't changed.

Consider some of the responses of women interviewed by Zenko about why "women are significantly underrepresented in foreign policy and national security positions in government, academia, and think tanks."

Juliette Kayyem, who served as an assistant secretary in the Department of Homeland Security from 2009 to 2011 and now writes a foreign-policy and national-security column for *The Boston Globe,* told Zenko that among other reasons,

> the basic truth is also this: the travel sucks. As my youngest of three children is now 6, I can look back at the years when they were all young and realize just how disruptive all the travel was. There were also trips I couldn't take because I was pregnant or on leave, the conferences I couldn't attend because (note to conference organizers: weekends are a bad choice) kids would be home from school, and the various excursions that were offered but just couldn't be managed.

Jolynn Shoemaker, the director of Women in International Security, agreed: "Inflexible schedules, unrelenting travel, and constant pressure to be in the office are common features of these jobs."

These "mundane" issues—the need to travel constantly to succeed, the conflicts between school schedules and work schedules, the insistence that work be done in the office—cannot be solved by exhortations to close the ambition gap. I would hope to see commencement speeches that finger America's social and business policies, rather than women's level of ambition, in explaining the dearth of women at the top. But changing these policies requires much more than speeches. It means fighting the mundane battles—every day, every year—in individual workplaces, in legislatures, and in the media.

It's Possible If You Marry the Right Person

Sandberg's second message in her Barnard commencement address was: "The most important career decision you're going to make is whether or not you have a life partner and who that partner is." Lisa Jackson, the administrator of the Environmental Protection Agency, recently drove that message home to an audience of Princeton students and alumni gathered to hear her acceptance speech for the James Madison Medal. During the Q&A session, an audience member asked her how she managed her career and her family. She laughed and pointed to her husband in the front row, saying: "There's my work-life balance." I could never have had the career I have had without my husband, Andrew Moravcsik, who is a tenured professor of politics and international affairs at Princeton. Andy has spent more time with our sons than I have, not only on homework, but also on baseball, music lessons, photography, card games, and more. When each of them had to bring in a foreign dish for his fourth-grade class dinner, Andy made his grandmother's Hungarian *palacsinta;* when our older son needed to memorize his lines for a lead role in a school play, he turned to Andy for help.

Still, the proposition that women can have high-powered careers as long as their husbands or partners are willing to share the parenting load equally (or disproportionately) assumes that most women will *feel* as comfortable as men do about being away from their children, as long as their partner is home with them. In my experience, that is simply not the case.

Here I step onto treacherous ground, mined with stereotypes. From years of conversations and observations, however, I've come to believe that men and women respond quite differently when problems at home force them to recognize that their absence is hurting a child, or at least that their presence would likely help. I do not believe fathers love their children any less than mothers do, but men do seem more likely to choose their job at a cost to their family, while women seem more likely to choose their family at a cost to their job.

Many factors determine this choice, of course. Men are still socialized to believe that their primary family obligation is to be the breadwinner; women, to believe that their primary family obligation is to be the caregiver. But it may be more than that. When I described the choice between my children and my job to Senator Jeanne Shaheen, she said exactly what I felt: "There's really no choice." She wasn't referring to social expectations, but to a maternal imperative felt so deeply that the "choice" is reflexive.

Men and women also seem to frame the choice differently. In *Midlife Crisis at 30*, Mary Matalin recalls her days working as President Bush's assistant and Vice President Cheney's counselor:

> Even when the stress was overwhelming—those days when I'd cry in the car on the way to work, asking myself "Why am I doing this?"—I always knew the answer to that question: I believe in this president.

But Matalin goes on to describe her choice to leave in words that are again uncannily similar to the explanation I have given so many people since leaving the State Department:

> I finally asked myself, "Who needs me more?" And that's when I realized, it's somebody else's turn to do this job. I'm indispensable to my kids, but I'm not close to indispensable to the White House.

To many men, however, the choice to spend more time with their children, instead of working long hours on issues that affect many lives, seems selfish. Male leaders are routinely praised for having sacrificed their personal life on the altar of public or corporate service. That sacrifice, of course, typically involves their family. Yet their children, too, are trained to value public service over private responsibility. At the diplomat Richard Holbrooke's memorial service, one of his sons told the audience that when he was a child, his father was often gone, not around to teach him to throw a ball or to watch his games. But as he grew older, he said, he realized that Holbrooke's absence was the price of saving people around the world—a price worth paying.

It is not clear to me that this ethical framework makes sense for society. Why should we want leaders who fall short on personal responsibilities? Perhaps leaders who invested time in their own families would be more keenly aware of the toll their public choices—on issues from war to welfare—take on private lives. (Kati Marton, Holbrooke's widow and a noted author, says that although Holbrooke adored his children, he came to appreciate the full importance of family only in his 50s, at which point he became a very present parent and grandparent, while continuing to pursue an extraordinary public career.) Regardless, it is clear which set of choices society values more today. Workers who put their careers first are typically rewarded; workers who choose their families are overlooked, disbelieved, or accused of unprofessionalism.

In sum, having a supportive mate may well be a necessary condition if women are to have it all, but it is not sufficient. If women feel deeply that turning down a promotion that would involve more travel, for instance, is the right thing to do, then they will continue to do that. Ultimately, it is society that must change, coming to value choices to put family ahead of work just as much as those to put work ahead of family. If we really valued those choices, we would value the people who make them; if we valued the people who make them, we would do everything possible to hire and retain them; if we did everything possible to allow them to combine work and family equally over time, then the choices would get a lot easier.

It's Possible If You Sequence It Right

Young women should be wary of the assertion "You can have it all; you just can't have it all at once." This 21st-century addendum to the original line is now proffered by many senior women to their younger mentees. To the extent that it means, in the words of one working mother, "I'm going to do my best and I'm going to keep the long term in mind and know that it's not always going to be this hard to balance," it is sound advice. But to the extent that it means that women can have it all if they just find the right sequence of career and family, it's cheerfully wrong. ·

The most important sequencing issue is when to have children. Many of the top women leaders of the generation just ahead of me—Madeleine Albright, Hillary Clinton, Ruth Bader Ginsburg, Sandra Day O'Connor, Patricia Wald, Nannerl Keohane—had their children in their 20s and early 30s, as was the norm in the 1950s through the 1970s. A child born when his mother is 25 will finish high school when his mother is 43, an age at which, with full-time immersion in a career, she still has plenty of time and energy for advancement.

Yet this sequence has fallen out of favor with many high-potential women, and understandably so. People tend to marry later now, and anyway, if you have children earlier, you may have difficulty getting a graduate degree, a good first job, and opportunities for advancement in the crucial early years of your career. Making matters worse, you will also have less income while raising your children, and hence less ability to hire the help that can be indispensable to your juggling act.

When I was the dean, the Woodrow Wilson School created a program called Pathways to Public Service, aimed at advising women whose children were almost grown about how to go into public service, and many women still ask me about the best "on-ramps" to careers in their mid-40s. Honestly, I'm not sure what to tell most of them. Unlike the pioneering women who entered the workforce after having children in the 1970s, these women are competing with their younger selves. Government and NGO jobs are an option, but many careers are effectively closed off. Personally, I have never seen a woman in her 40s enter the academic market successfully, or enter a law firm as a junior associate, Alicia Florrick of *The Good Wife* notwithstanding.

These considerations are why so many career women of my generation chose to establish themselves in their careers first and have children in their mid-to-late 30s. But that raises the possibility of spending long, stressful years and a small fortune trying to have a baby. I lived that nightmare: for three years, beginning at age 35, I did everything possible to conceive and was frantic at the thought that I had simply left having a biological child until it was too late.

And when everything does work out? I had my first child at 38 (and counted myself blessed) and my second at 40. That means I will be 58 when both of my children are out of the house. What's more, it means that many peak career opportunities are coinciding precisely with their teenage years, when, experienced parents advise, being available as a parent is just as important as in the first years of a child's life.

Many women of my generation have found themselves, in the prime of their careers, saying no to opportunities they once would have jumped at and hoping those chances come around again later. Many others who have decided to step back for a while, taking on consultant positions or part-time work that lets them spend more time with their children (or aging parents), are worrying about how long they can "stay out" before they lose the competitive edge they worked so hard to acquire.

Given the way our work culture is oriented today, I recommend establishing yourself in your career first but still trying to have kids before you are 35—or else freeze your eggs, whether you are married or not. You may well be a more mature and less frustrated parent in your 30s or 40s; you are also more likely to have found a lasting life partner. But the truth is, neither sequence is optimal, and both involve trade-offs that men do not have to make.

You should be able to have a family if you want one—however and whenever your life circumstances allow—and still have the career you desire. If more women could strike this balance, more women would reach leadership positions. And if more women were in leadership positions, they could make it easier for more women to stay in the workforce. The rest of this essay details how.

Changing the Culture of Face Time

Back in the Reagan administration, a *New York Times* story about the ferociously competitive budget director Dick Darman reported, "Mr. Darman sometimes managed to convey the impression that he was the last one working in the Reagan White House by leaving his suit coat on his chair and his office light burning after he left for home." (Darman claimed that it was just easier to leave his suit jacket in the office so he could put it on again in the morning, but his record of psychological manipulation suggests otherwise.)

The culture of "time macho"—a relentless competition to work harder, stay later, pull more all-nighters, travel around the world and bill the extra hours that the international date line affords you—remains astonishingly prevalent among professionals today. Nothing captures the belief that more time equals more value better than the cult of billable hours afflicting large law firms across the country and providing exactly the wrong incentives for employees who hope to integrate work and family. Yet even in industries that don't explicitly reward sheer quantity of hours spent on the job, the pressure to arrive early, stay late, and be available, always, for in-person meetings at 11 a.m. on Saturdays can be intense. Indeed, by some measures, the problem has gotten worse over time: a study by the Center for American Progress reports that nationwide, the share of all professionals—women and men—working more than 50 hours a week has increased since the late 1970s.

But more time in the office does not always mean more "value added"—and it does not always add up to a more successful organization. In 2009, Sandra Pocharski, a senior female partner at Monitor Group and the head of the firm's Leadership and Organization practice, commissioned a Harvard Business School professor to assess the factors that helped or hindered women's effectiveness and advancement at Monitor. The study found that the company's culture was characterized by an "always on" mode of working, often without due regard to the impact on employees. Pocharski observed:

> Clients come first, always, and sometimes burning the midnight oil really does make the difference between success and failure. But sometimes we were just defaulting to behavior that overloaded our people without improving results much, if at all. We decided we needed managers to get better at distinguishing between these categories, and to recognize the hidden costs of assuming that "time is cheap." When that time doesn't add a lot of value and comes at a high cost to talented employees, who will leave when the personal cost becomes unsustainable—well, that is clearly a bad outcome for everyone.

I have worked very long hours and pulled plenty of all-nighters myself over the course of my career, including a few nights on my office couch during my two years in D.C. Being willing to put the time in when the job simply has to get done is rightfully a hallmark of a successful professional. But looking back, I have to admit that my assumption that I would stay late made me much less efficient over the course of the day than I might have been, and certainly less so than some of my colleagues, who managed to get the same amount of work done and go home at a decent hour. If Dick Darman had a boss who clearly valued prioritization and time management, he might have found reason to turn out the lights and take his jacket home.

Long hours are one thing, and realistically, they are often unavoidable. But do they really need to be spent at the office? To be sure, being in the office *some* of the time is beneficial. In-person meetings can be far more efficient than phone or e-mail tag; trust and collegiality are much more easily built up around the same physical table; and spontaneous conversations often generate good ideas and lasting relationships. Still, armed with e-mail, instant messaging, phones, and videoconferencing technology, we should be able to move to a culture where the office is a base of operations more than the required locus of work.

Being able to work from home—in the evening after children are put to bed, or during their sick days or snow days, and at least some of the time on weekends—can be the key, for mothers, to carrying your full load versus letting a team down at crucial moments. State-of-the-art videoconferencing facilities can dramatically reduce the need for long business trips. These technologies are making inroads, and allowing easier integration of work and family life. According to the Women's Business Center, 61 percent of women business owners use technology to "integrate the responsibilities of work and home"; 44 percent use technology to allow employees "to work off-site or to have flexible work schedules." Yet our work culture still remains more office-centered than it needs to be, especially in light of technological advances.

One way to change that is by changing the "default rules" that govern office work—the baseline expectations about when, where, and how work will be done. As behavioral economists well know, these baselines can make an enormous difference in the way people act. It is one thing, for instance, for an organization to allow phone-ins to a meeting on an ad hoc basis, when parenting and work schedules collide—a system that's better than nothing, but likely to engender guilt among those calling in, and possibly resentment among those in the room. It is quite another for that organization to declare that its policy will be to schedule in-person meetings, whenever possible, during the hours of the school day—a system that might normalize call-ins for those (rarer) meetings still held in the late afternoon.

One real-world example comes from the British Foreign and Commonwealth Office, a place most people are more likely to associate with distinguished gentlemen in pinstripes than with progressive thinking about work-family balance. Like so many other places, however, the FCO worries about losing talented members of two-career couples around the world, particularly women. So it recently changed its basic policy from a default rule that jobs have to be done on-site to one that assumes that some jobs might be done remotely, and invites workers to make the case for remote work. Kara Owen, a career foreign-service officer who was the FCO's diversity director and will soon become the British deputy ambassador to France, writes that she has now done two remote jobs. Before her current maternity leave, she was working a London job from Dublin to be with her partner, using teleconferencing technology and timing her trips to London to coincide "with key meetings where I needed to be in the room (or chatting at the pre-meeting coffee) to have an impact, or to do intensive 'network maintenance.'" In fact, she writes, "I have found the distance and quiet to be a real advantage in a strategic role, providing I have put in the investment up front to develop very strong personal relationships with the game changers." Owen recognizes that not every job can be done this way. But she says that for her part, she has been able to combine family requirements with her career.

Changes in default office rules should not advantage parents over other workers; indeed, done right, they can improve relations among co-workers by raising their awareness of each other's circumstances and instilling a sense of fairness. Two years ago, the ACLU Foundation of Massachusetts decided to replace its "parental leave" policy with a "family leave" policy that provides for as much as 12 weeks of leave not only for new parents, but also for employees who need to care for a spouse, child, or parent with a serious health condition. According to Director Carol Rose, "We wanted a policy that took into account the fact that even employees who do not have children have family obligations." The policy was shaped by the belief that giving women "special treatment" can "backfire if the broader norms shaping the behavior of all employees do not change." When I was the dean of the Wilson School, I managed with the mantra "Family comes first"—any family—and found that my employees were both productive and intensely loyal.

None of these changes will happen by themselves, and reasons to avoid them will seldom be hard to find. But obstacles and inertia are usually surmountable if leaders are open to changing their assumptions about the workplace. The use of technology in many high-level government jobs, for instance, is complicated by the need to have access to classified information. But in 2009, Deputy Secretary of State James Steinberg, who shares the parenting of his two young daughters equally with his wife, made getting such access at home an immediate priority so that he could leave the office at a reasonable hour and participate in important meetings via videoconferencing if necessary. I wonder how many women in similar positions would be afraid to ask, lest they be seen as insufficiently committed to their jobs.

Revaluing Family Values

While employers shouldn't privilege parents over other workers, too often they end up doing the opposite, usually subtly, and usually in ways that make it harder for a primary caregiver to get ahead. Many people in positions of power seem to place a low value on child care in comparison with other outside activities. Consider the following proposition: An employer has two equally talented and productive employees. One trains for and runs marathons when he is not working. The other takes care of two children. What assumptions is the employer likely to make about the marathon runner? That he gets up in the dark every day and logs an hour or two running before even coming into the office, or drives himself to get out there even after a long day. That he is ferociously disciplined and willing to push himself through distraction, exhaustion, and days when nothing seems to go right in the service of a goal far in the distance. That he must manage his time exceptionally well to squeeze all of that in.

Be honest: Do you think the employer makes those same assumptions about the parent? Even though she likely rises in the dark hours before she needs to be at work, organizes her children's day, makes breakfast, packs lunch, gets them off to school, figures out shopping and other errands even if she is lucky enough to have a housekeeper—and does much the same work at the end of the day. Cheryl Mills, Hillary Clinton's indefatigable chief of staff, has twins in elementary school; even with a fully engaged husband, she famously gets up at four every morning to check and send e-mails before her kids wake up. Louise Richardson, now the vice chancellor of the University of St. Andrews, in Scotland, combined an assistant professorship in government at Harvard with mothering three young children. She organized her time so ruthlessly that she always keyed in 1:11 or 2:22 or 3:33 on the microwave rather than 1:00, 2:00, or 3:00, because hitting the same number three times took less time.

Elizabeth Warren, who is now running for the U.S. Senate in Massachusetts, has a similar story. When she had two young children and a part-time law practice, she struggled to find enough time to write the papers and articles that would help get her an academic position. In her words:

> I needed a plan. I figured out that writing time was when Alex was asleep. So the minute I put him down for a nap or he fell asleep in the baby swing, I went to my desk and started working on something—footnotes, reading, outlining, writing . . . I learned to do everything else with a baby on my hip.

The discipline, organization, and sheer endurance it takes to succeed at top levels with young children at home is easily comparable to running 20 to 40 miles a week. But that's rarely how employers see things, not only when making allowances, but when making promotions. Perhaps because people *choose* to have children? People also choose to run marathons.

One final example: I have worked with many Orthodox Jewish men who observed the Sabbath from sundown on Friday until sundown on Saturday. Jack Lew, the two-time director of the Office of Management and Budget, former deputy secretary of state for management and resources, and now White House chief of staff, is a case in point. Jack's wife lived in New York when he worked in the State Department, so he would leave the office early enough on Friday afternoon to take the shuttle to New York and a taxi to his apartment before sundown. He would not work on Friday after sundown or all day Saturday. Everyone who knew him, including me, admired his commitment to his faith and his ability to carve out the time for it, even with an enormously demanding job.

It is hard to imagine, however, that we would have the same response if a mother told us she was blocking out mid-Friday afternoon through the end of the day on Saturday, every week, to spend time with her children. I suspect this would be seen as unprofessional, an imposition of unnecessary costs on co-workers. In fact, of course, one of the great values of the Sabbath—whether Jewish or Christian—is precisely that it carves out a family oasis, with rituals and a mandatory setting-aside of work.

Our assumptions are just that: things we believe that are not necessarily so. Yet what we assume has an enormous impact on our perceptions and responses. Fortunately, changing our assumptions is up to us.

Redefining the Arc of a Successful Career

The American definition of a successful professional is someone who can climb the ladder the furthest in the shortest time, generally peaking between ages 45 and 55. It is a definition well suited to the mid-20th century, an era when people had kids in their 20s, stayed in one job, retired at 67, and were dead, on average, by age 71.

It makes far less sense today. Average life expectancy for people in their 20s has increased to 80; men and women in good health can easily work until they are 75. They can expect to have multiple jobs and even multiple careers throughout their working life. Couples marry later, have kids later, and can expect to live on two incomes. They may well retire *earlier*—the average retirement age has gone down from 67 to 63—but that is commonly "retirement" only in the sense of collecting retirement benefits. Many people go on to "encore" careers.

Assuming the priceless gifts of good health and good fortune, a professional woman can thus expect her working life to stretch some 50 years, from her early or mid-20s to her mid-70s. It is reasonable to assume that she will build her credentials and establish herself, at least in her first career, between 22 and 35; she will have children, if she wants them, sometime between 25 and 45; she'll want maximum flexibility and control over her time in the 10 years that her children are 8 to 18; and she should plan to take positions of maximum authority and demands on her time after her children are out of the house. Women who have children in their late 20s can expect to immerse themselves completely in their careers in their late 40s, with plenty of time still to rise to the top in their late 50s and early 60s. Women who make partner, managing director, or senior vice president; get tenure; or establish a medical practice before having children in their late 30s should be coming back on line for the most demanding jobs at almost exactly the same age.

Along the way, women should think about the climb to leadership not in terms of a straight upward slope, but as irregular stair steps, with periodic plateaus (and even dips) when they turn down promotions to remain in a job that works for their family situation; when they leave high-powered jobs and spend a year or two at home on a reduced schedule; or when they step off a conventional professional track to take a consulting position or project-based work for a number of years. I think of these plateaus as "investment intervals." My husband and I took a sabbatical in Shanghai, from August 2007 to May 2008, right in the thick of an election year when many of my friends were advising various candidates on foreign-policy issues. We thought of the move in part as "putting money in the family bank," taking advantage of the opportunity to spend a close year together in a foreign culture. But we were also investing in our children's ability to learn Mandarin and in our own knowledge of Asia.

Peaking in your late 50s and early 60s rather than your late 40s and early 50s makes particular sense for women, who live longer than men. And many of the stereotypes about older workers simply do not hold. A 2006 survey of human-resources professionals shows that only 23 percent think older workers are less flexible than younger workers; only 11 percent think older workers require more training than younger workers; and only 7 percent think older workers have less drive than younger workers.

Whether women will really have the confidence to stair-step their careers, however, will again depend in part on perceptions. Slowing down the rate of promotions, taking time out periodically, pursuing an alternative path during crucial parenting or parent-care years—all have to become more visible and more noticeably accepted as a pause rather than an opt-out. (In an encouraging sign, *Mass Career Customization*, a 2007 book by Cathleen Benko and

Anne Weisberg arguing that "today's career is no longer a straight climb up the corporate ladder, but rather a combination of climbs, lateral moves, and planned descents," was a *Wall Street Journal* best seller.)

Institutions can also take concrete steps to promote this acceptance. For instance, in 1970, Princeton established a tenure-extension policy that allowed female assistant professors expecting a child to request a one-year extension on their tenure clocks. This policy was later extended to men, and broadened to include adoptions. In the early 2000s, two reports on the status of female faculty discovered that only about 3 percent of assistant professors requested tenure extensions in a given year. And in response to a survey question, women were much more likely than men to think that a tenure extension would be detrimental to an assistant professor's career.

So in 2005, under President Shirley Tilghman, Princeton changed the default rule. The administration announced that all assistant professors, female and male, who had a new child would *automatically* receive a one-year extension on the tenure clock, with no opt-outs allowed. Instead, assistant professors could request early consideration for tenure if they wished. The number of assistant professors who receive a tenure extension has tripled since the change.

One of the best ways to move social norms in this direction is to choose and celebrate different role models. New Jersey Governor Chris Christie and I are poles apart politically, but he went way up in my estimation when he announced that one reason he decided against running for president in 2012 was the impact his campaign would have had on his children. He reportedly made clear at a fund-raiser in Louisiana that he didn't want to be away from his children for long periods of time; according to a Republican official at the event, he said that "his son [missed] him after being gone for the three days on the road, and that he needed to get back." He may not get my vote if and when he does run for president, but he definitely gets my admiration (providing he doesn't turn around and join the GOP ticket this fall).

If we are looking for high-profile female role models, we might begin with Michelle Obama. She started out with the same résumé as her husband, but has repeatedly made career decisions designed to let her do work she cared about and also be the kind of parent she wanted to be. She moved from a high-powered law firm first to Chicago city government and then to the University of Chicago shortly before her daughters were born, a move that let her work only 10 minutes away from home. She has spoken publicly and often about her initial concerns that her husband's entry into politics would be bad for their family life, and

about her determination to limit her participation in the presidential election campaign to have more time at home. Even as first lady, she has been adamant that she be able to balance her official duties with family time. We should see her as a full-time career woman, but one who is taking a very visible investment interval. We should celebrate her not only as a wife, mother, and champion of healthy eating, but also as a woman who has had the courage and judgment to invest in her daughters when they need her most. And we should expect a glittering career from her after she leaves the White House and her daughters leave for college.

Rediscovering the Pursuit of Happiness

One of the most complicated and surprising parts of my journey out of Washington was coming to grips with what I really wanted. I had opportunities to stay on, and I could have tried to work out an arrangement allowing me to spend more time at home. I might have been able to get my family to join me in Washington for a year; I might have been able to get classified technology installed at my house the way Jim Steinberg did; I might have been able to commute only four days a week instead of five. (While this last change would have still left me very little time at home, given the intensity of my job, it might have made the job doable for another year or two.) But I realized that I didn't just *need* to go home. Deep down, I *wanted* to go home. I wanted to be able to spend time with my children in the last few years that they are likely to live at home, crucial years for their development into responsible, productive, happy, and caring adults. But also irreplaceable years for me to enjoy the simple pleasures of parenting—baseball games, piano recitals, waffle breakfasts, family trips, and goofy rituals. My older son is doing very well these days, but even when he gives us a hard time, as all teenagers do, being home to shape his choices and help him make good decisions is deeply satisfying.

The flip side of my realization is captured in Macko and Rubin's ruminations on the importance of bringing the different parts of their lives together as 30-year-old women:

> If we didn't start to learn how to integrate our personal, social, and professional lives, we were about five years away from morphing into the angry woman on the other side of a mahogany desk who questions her staff's work ethic after standard 12-hour workdays, before heading home to eat moo shoo pork in her lonely apartment.

Women have contributed to the fetish of the one-dimensional life, albeit by necessity. The pioneer generation of feminists walled off their personal lives from their professional personas to ensure that they could never be discriminated against for a lack of commitment to their work. When I was a law student in the 1980s, many women who were then climbing the legal hierarchy in New York firms told me that they never admitted to taking time out for a child's doctor appointment or school performance, but instead invented a much more neutral excuse.

Today, however, women in power can and should change that environment, although change is not easy. When I became dean of the Woodrow Wilson School, in 2002, I decided that one of the advantages of being a woman in power was that I could help change the norms by deliberately talking about my children and my desire to have a balanced life. Thus, I would end faculty meetings at 6 p.m. by saying that I had to go home for dinner; I would also make clear to all student organizations that I would not come to dinner with them, because I needed to be home from six to eight, but that I would often be willing to come back after eight for a meeting. I also once told the Dean's Advisory Committee that the associate dean would chair the next session so I could go to a parent-teacher conference.

After a few months of this, several female assistant professors showed up in my office quite agitated. "You *have* to stop talking about your kids," one said. "You are not showing the gravitas that people expect from a dean, which is particularly damaging precisely because you are the first woman dean of the school." I told them that I was doing it deliberately and continued my practice, but it is interesting that gravitas and parenthood don't seem to go together.

Ten years later, whenever I am introduced at a lecture or other speaking engagement, I insist that the person introducing me mention that I have two sons. It seems odd to me to list degrees, awards, positions, and interests and *not* include the dimension of my life that is most important to me—and takes an enormous amount of my time. As Secretary Clinton once said in a television interview in Beijing when the interviewer asked her about Chelsea's upcoming wedding: "That's my real life." But I notice that my male introducers are typically uncomfortable when I make the request. They frequently say things like "And she particularly wanted me to mention that she has two sons"—thereby drawing attention to the unusual nature of my request, when my entire purpose is to make family references routine and normal in professional life.

This does not mean that you should insist that your colleagues spend time cooing over pictures of your baby or listening to the prodigious accomplishments of your kindergartner. It does mean that if you are late coming in one week, because it is your turn to drive the kids to school, that you be honest about what you are doing. Indeed, Sheryl Sandberg recently acknowledged not only that she leaves work at 5:30 to have dinner with her family, but also that for many years she did not dare make this admission, even though she would of course make up the work time later in the evening. Her willingness to speak out now is a strong step in the right direction.

Seeking out a more balanced life is not a women's issue; balance would be better for us all. Bronnie Ware, an Australian blogger who worked for years in palliative care and is the author of the 2011 book *The Top Five Regrets of the Dying*, writes that the regret she heard most often was "I wish I'd had the courage to live a life true to myself, not the life others expected of me." The second-most-common regret was "I wish I didn't work so hard." She writes: "This came from every male patient that I nursed. They missed their children's youth and their partner's companionship."

Juliette Kayyem, who several years ago left the Department of Homeland Security soon after her husband, David Barron, left a high position in the Justice Department, says their joint decision to leave Washington and return to Boston sprang from their desire to work on the *"happiness project,"* meaning quality time with their three children. (She borrowed the term from her friend Gretchen Rubin, who wrote a best-selling book and now runs a blog with that name.)

It's time to embrace a national happiness project. As a daughter of Charlottesville, Virginia, the home of Thomas Jefferson and the university he founded, I grew up with the Declaration of Independence in my blood. Last I checked, he did not declare American independence in the name of life, liberty, and professional success. Let us rediscover the pursuit of happiness, and let us start at home.

Innovation Nation

As I write this, I can hear the reaction of some readers to many of the proposals in this essay: It's all fine and well for a tenured professor to write about flexible working hours, investment intervals, and family-comes-first management. But what about the real world? Most American women cannot demand these things, particularly in a bad economy, and their employers have little incentive to grant them voluntarily. Indeed, the most frequent reaction I get in putting forth these ideas is that when the choice is whether to hire a man who will work whenever and wherever needed, or a woman who needs more flexibility, choosing the man will add more value to the company.

In fact, while many of these issues are hard to quantify and measure precisely, the statistics seem to tell a different story. A seminal study of 527 U.S. companies, published in the *Academy of Management Journal* in 2000, suggests that "organizations with more extensive work-family policies have higher perceived firm-level performance" among their industry peers. These findings accorded with a 2003 study conducted by Michelle Arthur at the University of New Mexico. Examining 130 announcements of family-friendly policies in *The Wall Street Journal,* Arthur found that the announcements alone significantly improved share prices. In 2011, a study on flexibility in the workplace by Ellen Galinsky, Kelly Sakai, and Tyler Wigton of the Families and Work Institute showed that increased flexibility correlates positively with job engagement, job satisfaction, employee retention, and employee health.

This is only a small sampling from a large and growing literature trying to pin down the relationship between family-friendly policies and economic performance. Other scholars have concluded that good family policies attract better talent, which in turn raises productivity, but that the policies themselves have no impact on productivity. Still others argue that results attributed to these policies are actually a function of good management overall. What is evident, however, is that many firms that recruit and train well-educated professional women are aware that when a woman leaves because of bad work-family balance, they are losing the money and time they invested in her.

Even the legal industry, built around the billable hour, is taking notice. Deborah Epstein Henry, a former big-firm litigator, is now the president of Flex-Time Lawyers, a national consulting firm focused partly on strategies for the retention of female attorneys. In her book *Law and Reorder,* published by the American Bar Association in 2010, she describes a legal profession "where the billable hour no longer works"; where attorneys, judges, recruiters, and academics all agree that this system of compensation has perverted the industry, leading to brutal work hours, massive inefficiency, and highly inflated costs. The answer—already being deployed in different corners of the industry—is a combination of alternative fee structures, virtual firms, women-owned firms, and the outsourcing of discrete legal jobs to other jurisdictions. Women, and Generation X and Y lawyers more generally, are pushing for these changes on the supply side; clients determined to reduce legal fees and increase flexible service are pulling on the demand side. Slowly, change is happening.

At the core of all this is self-interest. Losing smart and motivated women not only diminishes a company's talent pool; it also reduces the return on its investment in training and mentoring. In trying to address these issues, some firms are finding out that women's ways of working may just be better ways of working, for employees and clients alike.

Experts on creativity and innovation emphasize the value of encouraging nonlinear thinking and cultivating randomness by taking long walks or looking at your environment from unusual angles. In their new book, *A New Culture of Learning: Cultivating the Imagination for a World of Constant Change,* the innovation gurus John Seely Brown and Douglas Thomas write, "We believe that connecting play and imagination may be the single most important step in unleashing the new culture of learning."

Space for play and imagination is exactly what emerges when rigid work schedules and hierarchies loosen up. Skeptics should consider the "California effect." California is the cradle of American innovation—in technology, entertainment, sports, food, and lifestyles. It is also a place where people take leisure as seriously as they take work; where companies like Google deliberately encourage play, with Ping-Pong tables, light sabers, and policies that require employees to spend one day a week working on whatever they wish. Charles Baudelaire wrote: "Genius is nothing more nor less than childhood recovered at will." Google apparently has taken note.

No parent would mistake child care for childhood. Still, seeing the world anew through a child's eyes can be a powerful source of stimulation. When the Nobel laureate Thomas Schelling wrote *The Strategy of Conflict,* a classic text applying game theory to conflicts among nations, he frequently drew on child-rearing for examples of when deterrence might succeed or fail. "It may be easier to articulate the peculiar difficulty of constraining [a ruler] by the use of threats," he wrote, "when one is fresh from a vain attempt at using threats to keep a small child from hurting a dog or a small dog from hurting a child."

The books I've read with my children, the silly movies I've watched, the games I've played, questions I've answered, and people I've met while parenting have broadened my world. Another axiom of the literature on innovation is that the more often people with different perspectives come together, the more likely creative ideas are to emerge. Giving workers the ability to integrate their non-work lives with their work—whether they spend that time mothering or marathoning—will open the door to a much wider range of influences and ideas.

Enlisting Men

Perhaps the most encouraging news of all for achieving the sorts of changes that I have proposed is that men are joining the cause. In commenting on a draft of this article, Martha Minow, the dean of the Harvard Law School, wrote me that one change she has observed during 30 years of teaching law at Harvard is that today many young men are asking questions about how they can manage a work-life balance. And more systematic research on Generation Y confirms that many more men than in the past are asking questions about how they are going to integrate active parenthood with their professional lives.

Abstract aspirations are easier than concrete trade-offs, of course. These young men have not yet faced the question of whether they are prepared to give up that more prestigious clerkship or fellowship, decline a promotion, or delay their professional goals to spend more time with their children and to support their partner's career.

Yet once work practices and work culture begin to evolve, those changes are likely to carry their own momentum. Kara Owen, the British foreign-service officer who worked a London job from Dublin, wrote me in an e-mail:

> I think the culture on flexible working started to change the minute the Board of Management (who were all men at the time) started to work flexibly—quite a few of them started working one day a week from home.

Men have, of course, become much more involved parents over the past couple of decades, and that, too, suggests broad support for big changes in the way we balance work and family. It is noteworthy that both James Steinberg, deputy secretary of state, and William Lynn, deputy secretary of defense, stepped down two years into the Obama administration so that they could spend more time with their children (for real).

Going forward, women would do well to frame work-family balance in terms of the broader social and economic issues that affect both women and men. After all, we have a new generation of young men who have been raised by full-time working mothers. Let us presume, as I do with my sons, that they will understand "supporting their families" to mean more than earning money.

I HAVE BEEN BLESSED to work with and be mentored by some extraordinary women. Watching Hillary Clinton in action makes me incredibly proud—of her intelligence, expertise, professionalism, charisma, and command of any audience. I get a similar rush when I see a frontpage picture of Christine Lagarde, the managing director of the International Monetary Fund, and Angela Merkel, the chancellor of Germany, deep in conversation about some of the most important issues on the world stage; or of Susan Rice, the U.S. ambassador to the United Nations, standing up forcefully for the Syrian people in the Security Council.

These women are extraordinary role models. If I had a daughter, I would encourage her to look to them, and I want a world in which they are extraordinary but not unusual. Yet I also want a world in which, in Lisa Jackson's words, "to be a strong woman, you don't have to give up on the things that define you as a woman." That means respecting, enabling, and indeed celebrating the full range of women's choices. "Empowering yourself," Jackson said in her speech at Princeton, "doesn't have to mean rejecting motherhood, or eliminating the nurturing or feminine aspects of who you are."

I gave a speech at Vassar last November and arrived in time to wander the campus on a lovely fall afternoon. It is a place infused with a spirit of community and generosity, filled with benches, walkways, public art, and quiet places donated by alumnae seeking to encourage contemplation and connection. Turning the pages of the alumni magazine (Vassar is now coed), I was struck by the entries of older alumnae, who greeted their classmates with *Salve* (Latin for "hello") and wrote witty remembrances sprinkled with literary allusions. Theirs was a world in which women wore their learning lightly; their news is mostly of their children's accomplishments. Many of us look back on that earlier era as a time when it was fine to joke that women went to college to get an "M.R.S." And many women of my generation abandoned the Seven Sisters as soon as the formerly all-male Ivy League universities became coed. I would never return to the world of segregated sexes and rampant discrimination. But now is the time to revisit the assumption that women must rush to adapt to the "man's world" that our mothers and mentors warned us about.

I continually push the young women in my classes to speak more. They must gain the confidence to value their own insights and questions, and to present them readily. My husband agrees, but he actually tries to get the young men in his classes to act more like the women—to speak less and listen more. If women are ever to achieve real equality as leaders, then we have to stop accepting male behavior and male choices as the default and the ideal. We must insist on changing social policies and bending career tracks to accommodate *our* choices, too. We have the power to do it if we decide to, and we have many men standing beside us.

We'll create a better society in the process, for *all* women. We may need to put a woman in the White House before we are able to change the conditions of the women working at Walmart. But when we do, we will stop talking about whether women can have it all. We will properly focus on how we can help all Americans have healthy, happy, productive lives, valuing the people they love as much as the success they seek.

Anne-Marie Slaughter is the Bert G. Kerstetter '66 University Professor of Politics and International Affairs at Princeton University and formerly dean of Princeton's Woodrow Wilson School of Public and International Affairs. She is currently the president and CEO of the New America Foundation, a public policy institute and idea incubator based in Washington and New York.

EXPLORING THE ISSUE

Can Women Have It All?

Critical Thinking and Reflection

1. The debate about leaning in is largely limited to professional women because that is the group that can afford to choose to lean in or opt out. What hypotheses would you make about the desires of nonprofessional women based on the behavior of professional women?
2. Note two facts. First, the percentage of mothers with at-home children that were working in the labor force increased until the 1990s and then leveled off. Second, a noticeable number of professional women who could afford to were opting out. Linda Hirshman concludes from these facts that "the belief that women are responsible for childrearing and homemaking was largely untouched by decades of workplace feminism." Do a critique of this conclusion.
3. How does the fact that many mothers return to the labor force when their children are of school age and more return when their children leave home impact your view of this debate?
4. What public policies would improve the lives of women with work/family tensions?
5. What is your judgment about the companies that have a "mommy track" policy?

Is There Common Ground?

Both authors want what is best for women and are upset about the situation that they analyze. Both would like societal arrangements to reduce the conflict between work and family. Both want women to be able to have it all. Their debate is over how possible it is to have it all. Gayle Tzemach Lemmon thinks they can have it all but it will not be easy. They will have to "lean in," which involves strength and determination. Anne-Marie Slaughter argues that the cost is generally too high. Women should put family first and career second. They can still have careers but must pursue them in ways that do not sacrifice too much for the family. I know that I would feel very deprived if I had to quit my professor's job to raise children even though children are a great joy. But I do not have to make this choice. This is what is obviously unfair about this issue. It is mostly a female problem. Men are not expected to quit their jobs and stay home and raise their children. Some, in fact, are doing just this since their wives are making far more money than they can, but this is rare. Society and religious groups generally preach that the wife should put family before work, so the stress is generally on women.

Additional Resources

Women who quit careers to go home to raise a family are said to "opt out." For analyses of the opt out phenomenon look at: Pamela Stone, *Opting Out?: Why Women Really*

Quit Careers and Head Home (University of California Press, 2007); Lisa A. Mainiero and Sherry E. Sullivan, *The Opt-Out Revolt* (Davies-Black, 2006); Phyllis Moen, *The Career Mystique* (Rowan & Littlefield, 2005); Ann Crittenden, *The Price of Motherhood* (Metropolitan Books, 2001); and Susan Chira, *A Mother's Place: Choosing Work and Family Without Guilt or Shame* (Perennial, 1999).

Some who advocate for "leaning in" and against opting out are: Leslie Bennetts, who strongly advises women not to give up their careers in *The Feminine Mistake* (Voice/Hyperion, 2007), and Sylvia Ann Hewlett does the same in *Off-Ramps and On-Ramps: Keeping Talented Women on the Road to Success* (Harvard Business School Press, 2007).

For discussions of the demands of work and family on women, see: Suzanne M. Bianchi, John P. Robinson, and Melissa Milkie, *Changing Rhythms of Family Life* (American Sociological Association, 2006); Susan Thistle, *From Marriage to the Market* (University of California Press, 2006); Arlie Russell Hochschild, *The Second Shift* (Penguin Books, 2003); and Anna Fels, *Necessary Dreams: Ambition in Women's Changing Lives* (Pantheon Book, 2004). Mary Eberstadt is the major critic of the working mothers who leave much of the childrearing to others. See her *Home-Alone America: The Hidden Toll of Daycare, Behavioral Drugs, and Other Parent Substitutes* (Penguin, 2004).

On the issue of time scarcity and time use, which factors into the debate on the tension between work and family, see: *Fighting for Time: Shifting Boundaries of Work and Social Life,* edited by Cynthia Fuchs-Epstein and Arne L. Kalleberg (Russell Sage Foundation, 2004); Phyllis Moen, *It's About Time: Couples and Careers* (Cornell University Press, 2003); Harriet B. Presser, *Working in a 24/7 Economy: Challenges for American Families* (Russell Sage Foundation, 2003); John Robinson and Geoffrey Godbey, *Time for* *Life: The Surprising Ways Americans Use Their Time,* 2nd ed. (State University Press, 1999); Juliet Schor, *The Overworked American: The Unexpected Decline of Leisure* (Basic Books, 1991); and Jerry A. Jacobs and Kathleen Gerson, *The Time Divide: Work, Family, and Gender Inequality* (Harvard University Press, 2004).

Internet References . . .

National Council on Family Research

www.ncfr.com

Sociology—Study Sociology Online

http://edu.learnsoc.org/

Sociology Web Resources

www.mhhe.com/socscience/sociology/resources/index.htm

Sociosite

www.topsite.com/goto/sociosite.net

Socioweb

www.topsite.com/goto/socioweb.com

Selected, Edited, and with Issue Framing Material by:
Kurt Finsterbusch, *University of Maryland, College Park*

ISSUE

Is Same-Sex Marriage Harmful to America?

YES: Peter Sprigg, from "The Top Ten Harms of Same-Sex 'Marriage,'" Family Research Council (2013)

NO: Jay Michaelson, from "Joe Biden Takes a Marriage Equality Victory Lap," *The Daily Beast* (2015)

Learning Outcomes

After reading this issue, you will be able to:

- Understand the potential force of traditions in delegitimizing proposed changes that counter them.
- Understand the importance of other traditions and strongly held values in supporting changes that seem to oppose accepted traditions.
- Observe how the way the issue is defined affects the success or failure of the change efforts.
- Analyze how the political system and its laws can be ahead of the public on changing institutions or can lag behind the public.
- Understand the arguments and the values that underpin the support for and the opposition against same-sex marriage.

ISSUE SUMMARY

YES: Peter Sprigg, Senior Fellow for Policy Studies at the Family Research Council, identifies 10 negative effects of same-sex marriages. Many of these worries concern how various institutions are likely to change as a result of same-sex marriages, and how authorities are likely to change their regulations and enforcement practices.

NO: Jay Michaelson supports Joe Biden, Vice President of the United States, who applauds the Supreme Court's decision to legalize same-sex marriage as a form of civil rights. Evan Wolfson, founder of Freedom to Marry organization, said that Biden deserves the most credit for the legalization of same-sex marriage.

In 1979, in Sioux Falls, South Dakota, Randy Rohl and Grady Quinn became the first acknowledged homosexual couple in America to receive permission from their high school principal to attend the senior prom together. The National Gay Task Force hailed the event as a milestone in the progress of human rights. It is unclear what the voters of Sioux Falls thought about it, because it was not put up to a vote. However, if their views were similar to those of voters in Dade County, Florida; Houston, Texas; Wichita, Kansas; and various localities in the state of Oregon, they probably were not pleased. In referenda held in these and other areas, voters have reversed decisions by legislators

and local boards that banned discrimination by sexual preference.

Yet the attitude of Americans toward the rights of homosexuals is not easy to pin down. Voters have also defeated resolutions such as the one in California in 1978 that would have banned the hiring of homosexual schoolteachers, or the one on the Oregon ballot in 1992 identifying homosexuality as abnormal, wrong, unnatural, and perverse. In some states, notably Colorado, voters have approved initiatives widely perceived as antihomosexual. But, almost invariably, these resolutions have been carefully worded so as to appear to oppose special rights for homosexuals. In general, polls show that a large majority of Americans believe that homosexuals should have equal rights with heterosexuals with regard to job opportunities. On the other hand, many view homosexuality as morally wrong. These developments prompted President Bush to propose a constitutional amendment limiting marriage to the union of a man and a woman, but this law did not pass Congress.

The rights of gays have been rapidly changing in the past 15 years, culminating in the legalization of same-sex marriage by the Supreme Court in September 2015. In 2001 the "Don't Ask, Don't Tell" policy was rescinded, which allowed gays and lesbians to be in the military. Same-sex sexual activity was made legal by the Supreme Court in 2003. The federal hate-crime law has included sexual orientation and gender identity cases since 2009. Same-sex marriage has been legally recognized by the federal government since 2013. The rights of gays have also advanced throughout the world but not everywhere. In 66 countries homosexual acts are legal but in 12 countries these acts can be punished by death. In 100 countries homosexual acts are legal but other restrictions may apply. In 21 countries same-sex marriage is allowed.

Along with these legal changes surveys show massive changes in public attitudes. Pew Research shows that in 2001, 57 percent of Americans opposed same-sex marriage and only 35 percent supported it. In 2015, however, 55 percent supported same-sex marriage and only 39 percent opposed it. This is a massive change in 14 years. The change occurs in all groups but it is strongly reflected in generational changes. Of the generation born in 1981 or later 70 percent supported same-sex marriage, 59 percent of the 1965–80 generation supported it, 45 percent of the 1946–64 generation supported it, and 39 percent of the 1925–45 generation supported it. All these groups increased their support by 10 percent or more from 2001 to 2015. There are wide differences between religious groups but all religious groups have increased their support. Least supportive are the white evangelicals, whose support went from 13 to 24 percent while the unaffiliated went from 61 to 82 percent. Differences are notable between the political parties: Democrats: 66 percent supported, Independents: 62 percent, Republicans: 31 percent.

The issue of same-sex marriage fascinates sociologists because it represents a basic change in a major social institution and is being played out on several fields: legal, cultural/moral, and behavioral. The legal debate has been decided by the Supreme Court; the cultural/moral debate is open to all of us; and the behavioral debate will be conducted by the activists on both sides. In the readings that follow, Peter Sprigg argues that marriage must remain heterosexual while Jay Michaelson supports Vice President Joe Biden, who celebrates the legalization of same-sex marriage.

YES

Peter Sprigg

The Top Ten Harms of Same-Sex "Marriage"

Some advocates of same-sex "marriage" scoff at the idea that it could harm anyone. Here are ten ways in which society could be harmed by legalizing same-sex "marriage." Most of these effects would become evident only in the long run, but several would occur immediately.

Immediate Effects

Taxpayers, Consumers, and Businesses Would Be Forced to Subsidize Homosexual Relationships

One of the key arguments often heard in support of homosexual civil "marriage" revolves around all the government "benefits" that homosexuals claim they are denied. Many of these "benefits" involve one thing—taxpayer money that homosexuals are eager to get their hands on. For example, one of the goals of homosexual activists is to take part in the biggest government entitlement program of all—Social Security. Homosexuals want their partners to be eligible for Social Security survivors benefits when one partner dies.

The fact that Social Security survivors benefits were intended to help stay-at-home mothers who did not have retirement benefits from a former employer has not kept homosexuals from demanding the benefit.[1] Homosexual activists are also demanding that children raised by a homosexual couple be eligible for benefits when one of the partners dies—even if the deceased partner was not the child's biological or adoptive parent. . . .

Imagine, though, what the impact on employee benefit programs would be if homosexual "marriage" is legalized nationwide. Right now, marriage still provides a clear, bright line, both legally and socially, to distinguish those who receive dependent benefits and those who don't. But if homosexual couples are granted the full legal status of civil "marriage," then employers who do not want to grant benefits to homosexual partners—whether out of principle, or simply because of a prudent economic judgment—would undoubtedly be coerced by court orders to do so.

Schools Would Teach That Homosexual Relationships Are Identical to Heterosexual Ones

The advocates of same-sex "marriage" argue that it will have little impact on anyone other than the couples who "marry." However, even the brief experience in Massachusetts, where same-sex "marriage" was imposed by the state's Supreme Judicial Court and began on May 17, 2004, has demonstrated that the impact of such a social revolution will extend much further—including into the public schools. In September 2004, National Public Radio reported, "Already, some gay and lesbian advocates are working on a new gay-friendly curriculum for kindergarten and up." They also featured an interview with Deb Allen, a lesbian who teaches eighth-grade sex education in Brookline, Mass. Allen now feels "emboldened" in teaching a "gay-friendly" curriculum, declaring, "If somebody wants to challenge me, I'll say, 'Give me a break. It's legal now.'" Her lessons include descriptions of homosexual sex given "thoroughly and explicitly with a chart." Allen reports she will ask her students, "Can a woman and a woman have vaginal intercourse, and they will all say no. And I'll say, 'Hold it. Of course, they can. They can use a sex toy. They could use'—and we talk—and we discuss that. So the answer there is yes."[2]. . .

Freedom of Conscience and Religious Liberty Would Be Threatened

Another important and immediate result of same-sex "marriage" would be serious damage to religious liberty. . . .

Some of these threats to religious liberty can arise from "nondiscrimination" laws based on sexual orientation, even without same-sex "marriage." But when homosexual "marriage" becomes legal, then laws which once applied to homosexuals only as individuals then apply to homosexual couples as well. So, for example, when Catholic Charities in Boston insisted that they would stay true to principle and refuse to place children for adoption with same-sex couples, they were told by the state that they could no longer do adoptions at all.[3]

In other cases, a variety of benefits or opportunities that the state makes available to religious nonprofits could be withheld based on the organization's refusal to treat same-sex couples and "marriages" the same as opposite-sex marriages. Organizations might be denied government grants or aid otherwise available to faith-based groups; they might be denied access to public facilities for events; and they might even have their tax-exempt status removed.[4] That is what happened to the Ocean Grove Camp Meeting Association in New Jersey when they refused to rent facilities for a lesbian "civil union" ceremony.[5] . . .

Religious liberty is one of the deepest American values. We must not sacrifice it on the altar of political correctness that homosexual "marriage" would create.

Long-Term Effects

Fewer People Would Marry

Even where legal recognition and marital rights and benefits are available to same-sex couples (whether through same-sex civil "marriages," "civil unions," or "domestic partnerships"), *relatively few same-sex couples even bother to seek such recognition or claim such benefits.*

The most simple way to document this is by comparing the number of same-sex couples who have sought such legal recognition in a given state[6] with the number of "same-sex unmarried-partner households" in the most recent U.S. Census.[7]

When a relatively small percentage of same-sex couples—even among those already living together as partners—even bother to seek legal recognition of their relationships, while an overwhelming majority of heterosexual couples who live together are legally married, it suggests that homosexuals are far more likely than heterosexuals to *reject the institution of marriage* or its legal equivalent. . . .

These figures show that a large percentage, and possibly even an outright majority, of homosexuals—even those already living with a partner—neither need nor desire to participate in the institution of marriage. Legalizing same-sex "marriage" would be very effective in sending a message of endorsement of homosexual behavior. But the indifference of most homosexuals to "marriage" would send a message to society that marriage does not matter—that it is no longer the normative setting for sexual relations and child-rearing, but is instead nothing more than one relationship option among many, made available as a government entitlement program to those who seek taxpayer-funded benefits.

Couples who could marry, but choose instead to cohabit without the benefit of marriage, harm the institution of marriage by setting an example for other couples, making non-marital cohabitation seem more acceptable as well. If same-sex "marriage" were legalized, the evidence suggests that the percentage of homosexual couples who would choose cohabitation over "marriage" would be much larger than the current percentage of heterosexual couples who choose cohabitation over marriage. It is likely that the poor example set by homosexual couples would, over time, lead to lower marriage rates among heterosexuals as well.[8]

Fewer People Would Remain Monogamous and Sexually Faithful

One value that remains remarkably strong, even among people who have multiple sexual partners before marriage, is the belief that marriage itself is a sexually exclusive relationship. Among married heterosexuals, having sexual relations with anyone other than one's spouse is still considered a grave breach of trust and a violation of the marriage covenant by the vast majority of people.

Yet the same cannot be said of homosexuals—particularly of homosexual men. Numerous studies of homosexual relationships, including "partnered" relationships, covering a span of decades, have shown that sex with multiple partners is tolerated and often expected, even when one has a "long-term" partner. Perhaps the most startling of these studies was published in the journal *AIDS*. In the context of studying HIV risk behavior among young homosexual men in the Netherlands (coincidentally, the first country in the world to legalize homosexual civil "marriage"), the researchers found that homosexual men who were *in partnered relationships* had an *average* of eight sexual partners *per year* outside of the primary relationship.[9] (It must be conceded that having such a partnership did have some "taming" effect upon such men—those without a "permanent" partner had an average of 22 sexual partners per year.) This is an astonishing contrast to the typical behavior of married heterosexuals, among whom 75% of the men and 85% of the women report *never* having had extra-marital sex even once during the entire duration of their marriage.[10] . . .

Fewer People Would Remain Married for a Lifetime

Lawrence Kurdek, a homosexual psychologist from Ohio's Wright State University,[11] who has done extensive research on the nature of homosexual relationships, has correctly stated, "Perhaps the most important 'bottom-line' question about gay and lesbian couples is whether their relationships last."[12] After extensive research, he determined that "it is safe to conclude that gay and lesbian couples dissolve their relationships more frequently than heterosexual couples, especially heterosexual couples with children."[13]

Once again, abundant research has borne out this point. Older studies came to similar conclusions. In one study of 156 male couples, for instance, only seven had been together for longer than five years (and none of those seven had remained sexually faithful to each other).[14] . . .

How would this affect heterosexual couples? If the unstable nature of homosexual partnerships becomes part of the ideal of marriage that is being held up to society, it will inevitably affect the future behavior of everyone in society—heterosexuals included. Therefore, we can predict the following:

If homosexual "marriage" is legalized, the percentage of homosexual couples that remain together for a lifetime will always be lower than the percentage of heterosexual couples that do so; but the percentage of heterosexual couples demonstrating lifelong commitment will also decline, to the harm of society as a whole.

Fewer Children Would Be Raised by a Married Mother and Father

The greatest tragedy resulting from the legalization of homosexual "marriage" would not be its effect on adults, but its effect on children. For the first time in history, society would be placing its highest stamp of official government approval on the *deliberate* creation of *permanently* motherless or fatherless households for children.

There simply cannot be any serious debate, based on the mass of scholarly literature available to us, about the ideal family form for children. It consists of a mother and father who are committed to one another in marriage. Children raised by their married mother and father experience lower rates of many social pathologies, including:

- premarital childbearing;[15]
- illicit drug use;[16]
- arrest;[17]
- health, emotional, or behavioral problems;[18]
- poverty;[19]
- or school failure or expulsion.[20]

These benefits are then passed on to future generations as well, because children raised by their married mother and father are themselves less likely to cohabit or to divorce as adults.[21]

In a perfect world, every child would have that kind of household provided by his or her own loving and capable biological parents (and every husband and wife who wanted children would be able to conceive them together). Of course, we do not live in a perfect world. . . .

As scholar Stanley Kurtz says,

If, as in Norway, gay "marriage" were imposed here by a socially liberal cultural elite, it would likely speed us on the way toward the classic Nordic pattern of less frequent marriage, more frequent out-of-wedlock birth, and skyrocketing family dissolution. In the American context, this would be a disaster.[22]

More Children Would Grow Up Fatherless

This harm is closely related to the previous one, but worth noting separately. As more children grow up without a married mother and father, they will be deprived of the tangible and intangible benefits and security that come from that family structure. However, most of those who live with only one biological parent will live with their mothers. In the general population, 79% of single-parent households are headed by the mother, compared to only 10% which are headed by the father.[23] Among homosexual couples, as identified in the 2000 census, 34% of lesbian couples have children living at home, while only 22% of male couples were raising children.[24] The encouragement of homosexual relationships that is intrinsic in the legalization of same-sex "marriage" would thus result in an increase in the number of children who suffer a specific set of negative consequences that are clearly associated with fatherlessness.

Homosexual activists say that having both a mother and a father simply does not matter—it is having two loving parents that counts. But social science research simply does not support this claim. Dr. Kyle Pruett of Yale Medical School, for example, has demonstrated in his book *Fatherneed* that fathers contribute to parenting in ways that mothers do not. Pruett declares, "From deep within their biological and psychological being, children need to connect to fathers . . . to live life whole."[25]

Children—both sons and daughters—suffer without a father in their lives. The body of evidence supporting this conclusion is both large and growing.[26] For example, research has shown that "youth incarceration risks in a national male cohort were elevated for adolescents in father-absent households," even after controlling for other factors.[27] Among daughters, "father absence was strongly associated with elevated risk for early sexual activity and adolescent pregnancy."[28] Author David Blankenhorn puts these risks more succinctly: "One primary result of growing fatherlessness is more boys with guns. Another is more girls with babies."[29] Even researchers who are supportive of homosexual parenting have had to admit that "children raised in fatherless families from infancy," while closer to their mothers, "perceived themselves to be less cognitively and physically competent than their peers from father-present families."[30]

Some lesbian couples are deliberately *creating* new children in order to raise them fatherless from birth. It is quite striking to read, for example, the model "Donor Agreement" for sperm donors offered on the Human Rights Campaign website, and to see the lengths to which they will go to legally insure that the actual biological father plays no role in the life of a lesbian mother's child.[31] Yet a recent study of children conceived through sperm donation found, "Donor offspring are significantly more likely than those raised by their biological parents to struggle with serious, negative outcomes such as delinquency, substance abuse, and depression, even when controlling for socioeconomic and other factors."[32] Remarkably, 38% of donor offspring born to lesbian couples in the study agreed that "it is wrong deliberately to conceive a fatherless child."[33]

Birth Rates Would Fall

One of the most fundamental tasks of any society is to reproduce itself. That is why virtually every human society up until the present day has given a privileged social status to male-female sexual relationships—the only type capable of resulting in natural procreation. This privileged social status is what we call "marriage."

Extending the benefits and status of "marriage" to couples who are intrinsically incapable of natural procreation (i.e., two men or two women) would dramatically change the social meaning of the institution. It would become impossible to argue that "marriage" is about encouraging the formation of life-long, potentially procreative (i.e., opposite-sex) relationships. The likely long-term result would be that fewer such relationships would be formed, fewer such couples would choose to procreate, and fewer babies would be born.

There is already evidence of at least a *correlation* between low birth rates and the legalization of same-sex

"marriage." At this writing, five U.S. states grant marriage licenses to same-sex couples. As of 2007, the last year for which complete data are available, four of those five states ranked within the bottom eight out of all fifty states in both birth rate (measured in relation to the total population) and fertility rate (measured in relation to the population of women of childbearing age).[34] . . .

The contribution of same-sex "marriage" to declining birth rates would clearly lead to significant harm for society.

Demands for Legalization of Polygamy Would Grow

If the natural sexual complementarity of male and female and the theoretical procreative capacity of an opposite-sex union are to be discarded as principles central to the definition of marriage, then what is left? According to the arguments of the homosexual "marriage" advocates, only love and companionship are truly necessary elements of marriage.

But if that is the case, then why should *other* relationships that provide love, companionship, and a lifelong commitment not *also* be recognized as "marriages"—including relationships between adults and children, or between blood relatives, or between three or more adults? And if it violates the equal protection of the laws to deny homosexuals their first choice of marital partner, why would it not do the same to deny pedophiles, polygamists, or the incestuous the right to marry the person (or persons) of their choice?

Of these, the road to polygamy seems the best-paved—and it is the most difficult for homosexual "marriage" advocates to deny. If, as they claim, it is arbitrary and unjust to limit the *gender* of one's marital partner, it is hard to explain why it would not be equally arbitrary and unjust to limit the *number* of marital partners.

There are also two other reasons why same-sex "marriage" advocates have trouble refuting warnings of a slippery slope toward polygamy. The first is that there is far more precedent cross-culturally for polygamy as an accepted marital structure than there is for homosexual "marriage." The second is that there is a genuine movement for polygamy or "polyamory" in some circles. . . .

The "gay" oriented newspaper the *Washington Blade* has also featured this topic in a full-page article under the headline "Polygamy advocates buoyed by gay court wins." It quotes Art Spitzer of the American Civil Liberties Union acknowledging, "Yes, I think [the Supreme Court decision in *Lawrence v. Texas*] would give a lawyer a foothold to argue such a case. The general framework of that case, that states can't make it a crime to engage in private consensual intimate relationships, is a strong argument."[35]

This argument is already being pressed in the courts. Two convicted bigamists in Utah, Tom Green and Rodney Holm, have appealed to have their convictions overturned—citing the Supreme Court's decision in the *Lawrence* case as precedent.[36] And another attorney has filed suit challenging the refusal of the Salt Lake County clerk to grant a marriage license for G. Lee Cook to take a second wife.[37]

Make no mistake about it—if same-sex "marriage" is not stopped now, we will have the exact same debate about "plural" marriages only one generation from now.

References

1. One of the architects of Social Security, Abraham Epstein, said, "[T]he American standard assumes a normal family of man, wife, and two or three children, with the father fully able to provide for them out of his own income." Abraham Epstein, *Insecurity: A Challenge to America* (New York: Harrison Smith and Robert Haas, 1933), 101–102; cited in Allan Carlson, *The "American Way": Family and Community in the Shaping of the American Identity* (Wilmington, DE: ISI Books, 2003), 69. See generally Carlson's entire chapter on "'Sanctifying the Traditional Family': The New Deal and National Solidarity," 55–77.
2. "Debate in Massachusetts over how to address the issue of discussing gay relationships and sex in public school classrooms," *All Things Considered*, National Public Radio, September 13, 2004.
3. Maggie Gallagher, "Banned in Boston: The coming conflict between same-sex marriage and religious liberty," *The Weekly Standard* Vol. 11, Issue 33, May 15, 2006; online at: http://weeklystandard.com/Content/Public/Articles/000/000/012/191kgwgh.asp
4. Roger Severino, "Or for Poorer? How Same-Sex Marriage Threatens Religious Liberty," *Harvard Journal of Law and Public Policy* 30, Issue 3 (Summer 2007), 939–82.
5. Jill P. Capuzzo, "Group Loses Tax Break Over Gay Union Issue," *The New York Times*, September 18, 2007, p. B2. Online at: http://www.nytimes.com/2007/09/18/nyregion/18grove.html?_r=1&scp=1&sq=Ocean%20Grove%20Camp%20Meeting%20&%20civil%20union&st=cse
6. This is a matter of public record, although some states do not track same-sex "marriages" separately from opposite-sex ones.
7. The 2000 Census was the first in which cohabiting individuals (both opposite-sex and same-sex) were given the option of declaring themselves to be "partners." Since people who are merely roommates or housemates can still identify themselves as such, the presumption is that the term "partners" will only be used by those in a sexual relationship. See Tavia

Simmons and Martin O'Connell, "Married-Couple and Unmarried Partner Households: 2000," *Census 2000 Special Reports* CENSR-5 (Washington, DC: U.S. Census Bureau). Online at: http://www.census.gov/prod/2003pubs/censr_5.pdf
8. For example, in the Netherlands, the percentage of heterosexual couples rejecting marriage jumped by more than a third, from 13% to 18%, between 1995 and 2004—during the very time period when same-sex "marriage" was legalized. "Types of households in the Netherlands 1995–2004," op. cit.
9. Maria Xiridou, et al., "The Contribution of Steady and Casual Partnerships to the Incidence of HIV Infection among Homosexual Men in Amsterdam," *AIDS* 17 (2003): 1031.
10. E. O. Laumann et al., *The Social Organization of Sexuality: Sexual Practices in the United States* (Chicago: University of Chicago Press, 1994): 216.
11. Peter Freiberg, "Couples study shows strengths," *The Washington Blade*, March 16, 2001.
12. Lawrence Kurdek, "What Do We Know about Gay and Lesbian Couples?" *Current Directions in Psychological Science* 14 (2005): 252.
13. Lawrence Kurdek, "Are Gay and Lesbian Cohabiting Couples *Really* Different from Heterosexual Married Couples?" *Journal of Marriage and Family* 66 (November 2004): 896.
14. David P. McWhirter and Andrew M. Mattison, *The Male Couple: How Relationships Develop* (Englewood Cliffs: Prentice-Hall, 1984): 252, 253.
15. Kristin A. Moore, "Nonmarital School-Age Motherhood: Family, Individual, and School Characteristics," *Journal of Adolescent Research* 13, October 1998: 433–457.
16. John P. Hoffman and Robert A. Johnson, "A National Portrait of Family Structure and Adolescent Drug Use," *Journal of Marriage and the Family* 60, August 1998: 633–645.
17. Chris Coughlin and Samuel Vucinich, "Family Experience in Preadolescence and the Development of Male Delinquency," *Journal of Marriage and the Family* 58, May 1996: 491–501.
18. Debra L. Blackwell, "Family structure and children's health in the United States: Findings from the National Health Interview Survey, 2001–2007," *Vital and Health Statistics*, Series 10, No. 246 (Hyattsville, MD: National Center for Health Statistics, December 2010). Online at: http://www.cdc.gov/nchs/data/series/sr_10/sr10_246.pdf
19. Federal Interagency Forum on Child and Family Statistics, *America's Children: Key Indicators of Well-Being 2001*, Washington, D.C., p. 14.
20. Deborah A. Dawson, "Family Structure and Children's Health and Well-Being: Data from the 1988 National Health Interview Survey on Child Health," *Journal of Marriage and the Family* 53, August 1991: 573–584.

21. Paul R. Amato and Alan Booth, *A Generation at Risk: Growing Up in an Era of Family Upheaval,* Cambridge, Massachusetts: Harvard University Press, 1997, pp. 111–115.

22. Stanley Kurtz, "The End of Marriage in Scandinavia: The 'conservative case' for same-sex marriage collapses," *The Weekly Standard* 9, No. 20 (February 2, 2004): 26–33.

23. Rose M. Kreider, "Living Arrangements of Children: 2004," *Current Population Reports* P70–114 (Washington, DC: U.S. Census Bureau), February 2008, Figure 1, p. 5.

24. Simmons and O'Connell, op. cit., Table 4, p. 9.

25. Kyle D. Pruett, *Fatherneed: Why Father Care Is as Essential as Mother Care for Your Child* (New York: The Free Press, 2000), p. 16.

26. A good recent summary is Paul C. Vitz, *The Importance of Fathers: Evidence and Theory from Social Science* (Arlington, VA: Institute for the Psychological Sciences, June 2010); online at: http://www.profam.org/docs/thc.vitz.1006.htm

27. Cynthia C. Harper and Sara S. McLanahan, "Father Absence and Youth Incarceration," *Journal of Research on Adolescence* 14(3), 2004, p. 388.

28. Bruce J. Ellis, John E. Bates, Kenneth A. Dodge, David M. Fergusson, L. John Horwood, Gregory S. Pettit, Lianne Woodward, "Does Father Absence Place Daughters at Special Risk for Early Sexual Activity and Teenage Pregnancy?" *Child Development* Vol. 74, Issue 3, May 2003; abstract online at: http://onlinelibrary.wiley.com/doi/10.1111/1467-8624.00569/abstract

29. David Blankenhorn, *Fatherless America: Confronting Our Most Urgent Social Problem* (New York: BasicBooks, 1995), p. 45.

30. Susan Golombok, Fiona Tasker, Clare Murray, "Children Raised in Fatherless Families from Infancy: Family Relationships and the Socioemotional Development of Children of Lesbian and Single Heterosexual Mothers," *Journal of Child Psychologyc and Psychiatry* Vol. 38, Issue 7 (October 1997); abstract online at: http://onlinelibrary.wiley.com/doi/10.1111/j.1469-7610.1997.tb01596.x/abstract

31. Human Rights Campaign, *Donor Agreement*; online at: http://www.hrc.org/Template.cfm?Section=Search_the_Law_Database&Template=/ContentManagement/ContentDisplay.cfm&ContentID=18669

32. Elizabeth Marquardt, Norval D. Glenn, and Karen Clark, *My Daddy's Name Is Donor: A New Study of Young Adults Conceived Through Sperm Donation* (New York: Institute for American Values, 2010) p. 9.

33. Ibid., Table 2, p. 110.

34. Joyce A. Martin, Brady E. Hamilton, Paul D. Sutton, Stephanie J. Ventura, T. J. Mathews, Sharon Kirmeyer, and Michelle J. K. Osterman, U.S. Department of Health and Human Services, Centers for Disease Control and Prevention, National Center for Health Statistics, National Vital Statistics System, "Births: Final Data for 2007," *National Vital Statistics Reports* Vol. 58, No. 24, August, 2010, Table 11. Rankings calculated by the author.

35. Joe Crea, "Polygamy advocates buoyed by gay court wins: Some see sodomy, marriage opinions as helping their cause," *Washington Blade* (December 26, 2003): 14.

36. Both appeals failed—but legalization of same-sex "marriage" would create a stronger argument than the one based on *Lawrence v. Texas*, which was not related to marriage. See: Warren Richey, "Supreme Court declines polygamy case: The husband of three wives claimed the court's landmark ruling on gays applies to polygamists," *The Christian Science Monitor,* February 27, 2007; online at: http://www.csmonitor.com/2007/0227/p25s01-usju.html; and Brooke Adams, "Polygamist Green wants 'a private, quiet life' after Tuesday parole," *Salt Lake Tribune,* August 6, 2007. Online. Nexis

37. Alexandria Sage, "Attorney challenges Utah ban on polygamy, cites Texas sodomy case," *Associated Press* (January 12, 2004).

PETER SPRIGG serves as vice president for policy at the Family Research Council and oversees FRC research, publications, and policy formulation. He is also the author of the book *Outrage: How Gay Activists and Liberal Judges Are Trashing Democracy to Redefine Marriage* (Regnery, 2004) and the coeditor of the book *Getting It Straight: What the Research Shows About Homosexuality*.

Jay Michaelson

Joe Biden Takes a Marriage Equality Victory Lap

On Thursday in Manhattan, the vice president looked back at the long battle—and what's next. But what really made this win inevitable was when love became the essence of marriage.

In a way, Jane Austen won the right to same-sex marriage.

Not Austen specifically, of course—though Mr. Darcy has been the object of much gay and straight adoration—but the centuries-long movement of which she is a part: the humanistic, romantic idea that love should conquer law.

Such was my impression at Thursday night's marriage equality victory lap at the swanky Cipriani New York, put on by the advocacy organization Freedom to Marry and its founder/guru, Evan Wolfson. He's the man who, more than any other individual, including Jane Austen, deserves the most credit for winning national marriage equality.

As Vice President Joe Biden, Wolfson, and others recognized, there were many, many factors that caused marriage equality to become the law of the land on June 26, 2015. But as Biden said, in a way, at the core of the movement has been a very straightforward proposition. Recalling a time when he and his father saw two men kissing, Biden said Thursday: "I looked at my Dad, and he said, 'they love each other—it's simple.'"

Of course, as Biden quickly added, the long march to marriage equality hasn't been that simple. Dozens of lawsuits have been filed, millions of philanthropic dollars spent, and a myriad of cultural moments marked, from *La Cage Aux Folles* to Ellen DeGeneres. "This is the civil rights issue of our generation," Biden told the cheering crowd. "And what you have accomplished didn't just take moral courage. It took physical courage."

That, too, is true. Recall ACT-UP activists demanding that an uncharacteristically speechless Ronald Reagan utter the word "AIDS." (It took him until September 1985, at which point 12,000 people had died.) Remember also the original transgender rioters at Stonewall and the first gay rights protest in front of the White House, in 1957, when 10 people risked their livelihoods to demand legal equality.

But what won the day, in the end, was neither constitutional legal theory nor radical societal change. It was clear at Cipriani that what won the day was—trigger alert, cynics—love.

Consider this version of the story. The arguments against same-sex marriage are many, but the majority of them insist it isn't really marriage at all but something lesser. This isn't love, it's lust, like bestiality or incest. ("Man on dog," in Rick Santorum's epitaph-worthy phrase.) Homosexuals were said to be perverts, psychological deviants, or sex fiends.

Only, gradually, it became clear that they aren't—at least, not in significantly greater number than heterosexuals.

In fact, as people got to know gays and lesbians, either personally or through the media, it turned out that most, though not all, were actually a little dull. They wanted love, equal rights, basic dignity. They wanted to live and let live.

(This outraged the non-dull gays, the radicals who wanted a movement of sexual liberation, but they turned out to be in the minority.)

Eventually, the arguments against gay marriage started to seem either mean, or abstract, or both. Sure, the Bible seems to say bad things about lascivious homosexual behavior, but that's not what Aunt Nancy and Aunt Lisa have, right?

And no one really took those abstractions about "gender complementarity" and procreation too seriously. They seemed like rationales for prejudice. How can you compare some philosophical argument with Jim Oberge fell, flying his dying partner out of state so they could get married, only to have the marriage ignored by his home state of Ohio? Or with Edie Windsor?

Which is where Jane Austen comes in. If love really does conquer all—even if, in Austen, Shakespeare, and others, the lovers pay a serious price—then surely it conquers some abstract bloviating about the Bible. (Of course, it also didn't help that so many anti-gay pastors and politicians turned out to be closeted gays and so many priests turned out to be child molesters.)

And if marriage, again following Austen, is primarily about love, then how can it be denied to two consenting adults who are obviously, manifestly, in love?

I was personally involved in the marriage struggle—as a full-time activist, but playing a very bit part—from around 2008 to 2013. And I heard this firsthand from religious people, time and time again: "I used to believe it was wrong, but then my [daughter][friend][uncle] came out, and I had to think again."

I came to see victory as inexorable because there really was a truth of the matter, and it really was on our side. Our opponents were lying about our lives. If we just told the truth, we wouldn't win over everyone, but we'd win over enough.

Easy to say in 2015. But in 1983, when Evan Wolfson wrote his quixotic law review article arguing for a constitutional right to same-sex marriage, everyone thought he was crazy. As late as the 1990s, I myself thought marriage was the wrong battle to fight—too contentious, too soaked in the language of religion.

We were all wrong, and Wolfson was right.

Really, it was a two-pronged battle. The first prong was the set of cultural changes I've talked about already. The second was, indeed, a matter of law, and canny political strategy. Wolfson went state by state, winning some battles in the courts and a few in the legislature. He focused exclusively on marriage, building coalitions with willing conservatives—alienating many progressives in the process—and putting aside differences on other issues. He convinced several large LGBT organizations, each with their own interests, to coordinate their efforts.

And he made crucial legal arguments.

On Thursday in Biden's remarks, which seemed to be largely off the cuff, he pointed out that in the 1987 confirmation hearings of Robert Bork, he and the would-be Supreme Court justice had a passionate disagreement about the nature of constitutional rights. Bork, an originalist like Antonin Scalia, said the only rights guaranteed by the Constitution are those written in the Constitution. (Scalia said the same thing in his *Obergefell* dissent.)

Biden disagreed. Citing Wolfson's law review article, he said human rights are given by God and that the Constitution merely guarantees that they cannot be taken

away. Exactly what those rights are—what "equal protection of the laws" means, for example—is subject to the evolution of moral and legal reasoning. Not judicial fiat, as the *Obergefell* dissenters charged, but argumentation, reason, and reflection on the ambit of human rights.

For decades after the Fourteenth Amendment was passed, Jim Crow laws oppressed those the amendment was specifically designed to protect. Were those laws really constitutional, simply because they weren't enumerated in the text of the Constitution or were present when it passed? Surely not. Surely, even if "equal protection" and "due process" meant one thing in 1868, they encompassed these later developments, as well.

Well, Biden won the battle, and Bork lost. And as the vice president pointed out, the man Reagan nominated in his place was Anthony Kennedy, the deciding vote in *Obergefell* and the author of all four major Supreme Court opinions on LGBT equality.

A cynic would say Biden just took even more credit for marriage equality—on top of the credit he already gets (and deserves) for beating his boss to the punch and saying in May 2012 that he believed that all couples, gay or straight, should be able to legally marry.

But Biden also noted that legal philosophy was never the driving force in the struggle. "The country has always been ahead of the court," he said. And he generously shared credit with the ballroom full of activists, donors, and ordinary citizens, many of whom had been fighting this battle for 30 years, well before it seemed inevitable to Johnny-Come-Latelys like me.

Biden insisted on looking forward to the next battle: anti-discrimination protection. "There are 32 states where you can get married in the morning and get fired in the afternoon," he said. "We most expose the darkness to justice."

At the same time, the reception was a kind of victory lap—combined with a retirement party for Freedom to Marry, which is admirably closing its doors, having accomplished its mission. The sponsor-provided vodka flowed freely, and Carly Rae Jepsen entertained the crowd.

I'm a pretty cynical guy, but I was honored to be among them.

JAY MICHAELSON is a writer and LGBT activist who writes on spirituality, Judaism, sexuality, and law. Michaelson is legal affairs and religion columnist at The Daily Beast and a contributing editor to The Forward, newspaper.

JOE BIDEN is the Vice President of the United States. He was elected to the U. S. Senate from Delaware in 1972.

EXPLORING THE ISSUE

Is Same-Sex Marriage Harmful to America?

Critical Thinking and Reflection

1. What is your theory about homosexuality? Do you think it is a choice or is there a biological basis for it? Can homosexuals be reprogrammed to be heterosexuals? (The research is not decisive on this point. No gene for homosexuality has been discovered yet, but people do vary considerably in their levels of various hormones.)
2. Does your theory influence your opinion on the debate issue?
3. Can the civil rights of homosexuals on the issue of unions be protected in any other way than by same-sex marriages?
4. No proposed law would require religious leaders to marry same-sex couples. Do you think this largely nullifies the religious objection to same-sex marriage?
5. Evaluate the argument that homosexual marriage is a threat to heterosexual marriage. Has it had negative effects on heterosexual marriages so far as you can tell?

Is There Common Ground?

The issue of the rights of homosexuals creates a social dilemma. Most people would agree that all members of society should have equal rights. However, the majority may disapprove of the lifestyles of a minority group and pass laws against some of their behaviors. The question is, when do these laws violate civil rights? Are laws against same-sex marriage such a violation? The courts are the key to this debate.

Another common set of values is the right to life, liberty, and the pursuit of happiness. Life is not threatened in this issue but liberty and happiness are. Thus, the liberty and happiness of homosexuals should be promoted unless that would harm heterosexuals. We must ask, therefore, who is hurt by same-sex marriages? Are heterosexuals being hurt? As far as I know, I have not been hurt as a heterosexual. I know some people who are upset by same-sex marriage laws, but I know more who are upset by the lack of such laws. Do these feelings have any standing in the moral argument?

Additional Resources

There is a considerable literature on homosexuality and the social and legal status of homosexuals, so we will mainly cite works since 2012: Debra A. Miller, ed.,

Gay Marriage, (Greenhaven Press, 2012); Emily R. Gill, *An Argument for Same-Sex Marriage* (Georgetown University Press, 2012); Katrina Kimport, *Queering Marriage* (Rutgers University Press, 2014); Mary Bernstein and Verta Taylor, eds., *The Marrying Kind? Debating Same-Sex Marriage Within the Lesbian and Gay Movement* (University of Minnesota Press, 2013); Leigh Moscowitz, *The Battle over Marriage: Gay Rights Activism Through the Media* (Rowman & Littlefield, 2013); Jason Pierceson, *Same-Sex Marriage in the United States: The Road to the Supreme Court* (Rowman & Littlefield, 2013); Pamela J. Lannutti, *Experiencing Same-Sex Marriage: Individuals, Couples and Social Networks* (Peter Lang, 2014); and Brian Heaphy, Carol Smart, and Anna Einarsdottir, *Same-Sex Marriages: New Generations, New Relationships* (Palgrave Macmillan, 2013). A good history of the issue is Leila J. Rupp and Susan K. Freeman, eds., *Understanding and Teaching U.S. Lesbian, Gay, Bisexual, Transgender History* (University of Wisconsin Press, 2014).

Most works are pro gay rights. For opposition to same-sex marriage, see Jaye Cee Whitehead, *The Nuptial Deal: Same-Sex Marriage and Neo-Liberal Governance* (University of Chicago Press, 2012).

Internet References . . .

Sociology—Study Sociology Online

> http://edu.learnsoc.org/

Sociology Web Resource

> www.mhhe.com/socscience/sociology
> /resources/index.htm

Sociosite

> www.topsite.com/goto/sociosite.net

Socioweb

> www.topsite.com/goto/socioweb.com

Unit 3

UNIT

Stratification and Inequality

*W*hy is there so much poverty in a society as rich as ours? Why has there been such a noticeable increase in inequality over the past quarter century? Although the ideal of equal opportunity for all is strong in the United States, many charge that the American political and economic systems are unfair. Does extensive poverty demonstrate that policymakers have failed to live up to U.S. egalitarian principles? Are American institutions deeply flawed in that they provide fabulous opportunities for the educated and rich and meager opportunities for the uneducated and poor? Is the American stratification system at fault or are the poor themselves at fault? And what about the racial gap? The civil rights movement and the Civil Rights Act have made America more fair than it was, so why does a sizable racial gap remain? Various affirmative action programs have been implemented to remedy unequal opportunities, but some argue that this is discrimination in reverse. In fact, California passed a referendum banning affirmative action. Where should America go from here? Social scientists debate questions such as these in this unit.

Selected, Edited, and with Issue Framing Material by:
Kurt Finsterbusch, *University of Maryland, College Park*

ISSUE

Is Increasing Economic Inequality a Serious Problem?

YES: Joseph E. Stiglitz, from "Slow Growth and Inequality Are Political Choices. We Can Choose Otherwise," *Washington Monthly* (2014)

NO: Robert Rector and Rachel Sheffield, from "Understanding Poverty in the United States: Surprising Facts About America's Poor," The Heritage Foundation (2011)

Learning Outcomes

After reading this issue, you will be able to:

- Know the basic facts about the level of income inequality in America and how it compares with the degree of income inequality in other developed countries.
- Explain the high levels of inequality in America and predict whether those same forces will increase inequality in the future.
- Identify what commentators claim are the benefits of income inequality and what are the adverse effects.
- Present the pros and cons of the trickle-down theory.
- Understand what policies, institutions, or technologies can increase or decrease income inequality in America.
- Critique the thesis that the poor are to be blamed for their poverty.

ISSUE SUMMARY

YES: Nobel laureate Joseph Stiglitz, professor of economics at Columbia University, demonstrates the vast inequality in America and argues that it results from exploitation and should be reduced. It has extensive negative impacts on many institutional areas such as health care. He suggests ways to fix these problems which the corporations will fight.

NO: Robert Rector is Senior Research Fellow in the Domestic Policy Studies Department, and Rachel Sheffield is a research assistant in the Richard and Helen DeVos Center for Religion and Civil Society at the Heritage Foundation. They argue that inequality is not so bad because the poor are rather well-off when we look at all the facts. The living conditions of the poor have improved for decades. Most of the poor have consumer items that were significant purchases for the middle class a few decades ago. They establish their thesis on countless facts such as "82 percent of poor adults reported never being hungry at any time in the prior year due to lack of money for food."

The cover of the January 29, 1996, issue of *Time* magazine bears a picture of 1996 Republican presidential candidate Steve Forbes and large letters reading: "DOES A FLAT

TAX MAKE SENSE?" During his campaign, Forbes expressed his willingness to spend $25 million of his own wealth in pursuit of the presidency, with the major focus of his presidential campaign being a flat tax that would reduce taxes substantially for the rich. It seems reasonable to say that if the rich pay less in taxes, others would have to pay more. Is it acceptable for the tax burden to be shifted away from the rich in America? Forbes believed that the flat tax would benefit the poor as well as the rich. He theorized that the economy would surge ahead because investors would shift their money from relatively nonproductive, but tax-exempt, investments to productive investments. Although Forbes has disappeared from the political scene, his basic argument still thrives today. It is an example of the trickle-down theory, which states that helping the rich stimulates the economy, which in turn helps the poor. In fact, the trickle-down theory is the major rationalization for the view that great economic inequality benefits all of society.

Inequality is not a simple subject. For example, America is commonly viewed as having more social equality than do the more hierarchical societies of Europe and Japan, but America has more income inequality than almost all other industrial societies. This apparent contradiction becomes understandable when one recognizes that American equality is not in income, but in the opportunity to obtain higher incomes. The issue of economic inequality is further complicated by other categories of equality/inequality, which include political power, social status, and legal rights.

Americans believe that everyone should have an equal opportunity to compete for jobs and rewards. This belief is backed up by free public school education, which provides poor children with a ladder to success, and by laws that forbid discrimination. Americans, however, do not agree on many specific issues regarding opportunities or rights. For example, should society compensate for handicaps such as disadvantaged family backgrounds or the legacy of past discrimination? This issue has divided the country. Americans do not agree on programs such as income-based scholarships, quotas, affirmative action, or the Head Start compensatory education program for poor preschoolers.

America's commitment to political equality is strong in principle, although less strong in practice. Everyone over 18 years old gets one vote, and all votes are counted equally. However, the political system tilts in the direction of special interest groups; those who do not belong to such groups are seldom heard. Furthermore, as in the case of Forbes, money plays an increasingly important role in political campaigns.

The final dimension of equality/inequality is status. Inequality of status involves differences in prestige, and it cannot be eliminated by legislation. Ideally, the people who contribute the most to society are the most highly esteemed. To what extent does this principle hold true in the United States?

The Declaration of Independence proclaims that "all men are created equal," and the Founding Fathers who wrote the Declaration of Independence went on to base the laws of the land on the principle of equality. The equality they were referring to was equality of opportunity and legal and political rights for white, property-owning males. In the two centuries following the signing of the Declaration, nonwhites and women struggled for and won considerable equality of opportunity and rights. Meanwhile, income gaps in the United States have been widening.

In the readings that follow the fact of inequality is hotly debated. Joseph Stiglitz presents data showing the vast inequality in America and then argues that it is hurting America. It has negatively affected many institutions and life chances and must be reduced. Robert Rector and Rachel Sheffield, on the other hand, argue that American inequality may look bad but the reality is better than it looks. In fact, the poor are richer that we think. Most of them have most of the items that a middle-class person would have had several decades ago.

YES ⬅

Joseph E. Stiglitz

Slow Growth and Inequality Are Political Choices. We Can Choose Otherwise

A rich country with millions of poor people. A country that prides itself on being the land of opportunity, but in which a child's prospects are more dependent on the income and education of his or her parents than in other advanced countries. A country that believes in fair play, but in which the richest often pay a smaller percentage of their income in taxes than those less well off. A country in which children every day pledge allegiance to the flag, asserting that there is "justice for all," but in which, increasingly, there is only justice for those who can afford it. These are the contradictions that the United States is gradually and painfully struggling to come to terms with as it begins to comprehend the enormity of the inequalities that mark its society—inequities that are greater than in any other advanced country.

Those who strive not to think about this issue suggest that this is just about the "politics of envy." Those who discuss the issue are accused of fomenting class warfare. But as we have come to grasp the causes and consequences of these inequities we have come to understand that this is not about envy. The extreme to which inequality has grown in the United States and the manner in which these inequities arise undermine our economy. Too much of the wealth at the top of the ladder arises from exploitation—whether from the exercise of monopoly power, from taking advantage of deficiencies in corporate governance laws to divert large amounts of corporate revenues to pay CEOs' outsized bonuses unrelated to true performance, or from a financial sector devoted to market manipulation, predatory and discriminatory lending, and abusive credit card practices. Too much of the poverty at the bottom of the income spectrum is due to economic discrimination and the failure to provide adequate education and health care to the nearly one out of five children growing up poor.

The growing debate about inequality in America today is, above all, about the nature of our society, our vision of who we are, and others' vision of us. We used to think of ourselves as a middle-class society, where each generation was better off than the last. At the foundation of our democracy was the middle class—the modern-day version of the small, property-owning American farmer whom Thomas Jefferson saw as the backbone of the country. It was understood that the best way to grow was to build out from the middle—rather than trickle down from the top. This commonsense perspective has been verified by studies at the International Monetary Fund, which demonstrate that countries with greater equality perform better—higher growth, more stability. It was one of the main messages of my book *The Price of Inequality*. Because of our tolerance for inequality, even the quintessential American Dream has been shown to be a myth: America is less of a land of opportunity than even most countries of "old Europe."

The articles in this special edition of the *Washington Monthly* describe the way that America's inequality plays out at each stage of one's life, with several articles focusing in particular on education. We now know that there are huge disparities even as children enter kindergarten. These grow larger over time, as the children of the rich, living in rich enclaves, get a better education than the one received by those attending schools in poorer areas. Economic segregation has become the order of the day, so much so that even those well-off and well-intentioned selective colleges that instituted programs of economic affirmative action—explicitly trying to increase the fraction of their student body from lower socioeconomic groups—have struggled to do so. The children of the poor can afford neither the advanced degrees that are increasingly required for employment nor the unpaid internships that provide the alternative route to "good" jobs.

Similar stories could be told about each of the dimensions of America's outsized inequality. Take health care. America is unique among the advanced countries in not recognizing access to health care as a basic human right. And that means if you are a poor American, your prospects of getting adequate, let alone good, medical care are worse than in other advanced countries. Even after passage of the Affordable Care Act (ACA), almost two dozen states have rejected expanding vitally needed Medicaid, and more than forty million Americans still lacked health insurance at the beginning of 2014. The dismal statistics concerning America's health care system are well known: while we spend more—far more—on health care (both per capita and as a percentage of gross domestic product) than other countries, health outcomes are worse. In Australia, for instance, spending on health care per capita is just over two-thirds that in the United States, yet health outcomes are better—including a life expectancy that is a remarkable three years longer.

Two of the reasons for our dismal health statistics are related to inequalities at the top and the bottom of our society—monopoly profits reaped by drug companies, medical device makers, health insurers, and highly concentrated provider networks drive prices, and inequality, up while the lack of access to timely care for the poor, including preventive medicine, makes the population sicker and more costly to treat. The ACA is helping on both accounts. The health insurance exchanges are designed to promote competition. And the whole act is designed to increase access. The numbers suggest it's working. As for costs, the widespread predictions that Obamacare would cause massive health care inflation have proven false, as the rate of increase in health care prices has remained comparatively moderate over the last several years, showing once again that there is no necessary trade-off between fairness and efficiency. The first year of the ACA showed significant increases in coverage—far more significant in those states that implemented the Medicaid expansion than in those that refused to do so. But the ACA was a compromise, leaving out dental and long-term extended care insurance.

Inequities in health care, then, are still with us, beginning even before birth. The poor are more likely to be exposed to environmental hazards, and mothers have less access to good prenatal care. The result is infant mortality rates that are comparable to some developing countries alongside a higher incidence of low birth weight (systemically correlated with poor lifetime prospects) than in other advanced countries. Lack of access to comprehensive health care for the 20 percent of American children growing up in poverty, combined with lack of access to adequate nutrition, makes success in school even less likely. With the cheapest form of food often being unhealthy carbohydrates, the poor are more likely to face problems of childhood diabetes and obesity. The inequities continue throughout life—culminating in dramatically different statistics on life expectancy.

All well and good, you might say: it would be nice if we could give free health care to all, free college education to all, but these are dreams that have to be tamed by the harsh realities of what we can afford. Already the country has a large deficit. Proposals to create a more equal society would make the large deficit even larger—so the argument goes. America is especially constrained because it has assumed the costly mission of ensuring peace and security for the world.

This is nonsense, on several counts.

The real strength of the United States is derived from its "soft power," not its military power. But growing inequality is sapping our standing in the world from within. Can an economic system that provides so little opportunity—where real median household income (half above, half below, after adjusting for inflation) is lower today than it was a quarter century ago—provide a role model that others seek to emulate, even if a few at the very top have done very well?

Moreover, what we can afford is as much a matter of priorities as anything else. Other countries, such as the nations of Scandinavia, have, for instance, managed to provide good health care to all, virtually free college education for all, and good public transportation, *and* have done just as well, or even better, on standard metrics of economic performance: incomes per head and growth are at least comparable. Even some countries that are far poorer than the United States (such as Mauritius, off the east cost of Africa) have managed to provide free college education and better access to health care. A nation must make choices, and these countries have made different ones: they may spend less on their military, they may spend less on prisons, they may tax more.

Besides, many of the distributional issues are related not to how much we spend but who we spend it on. If we include within our expenditures the "tax expenditures" buried in our tax system, we effectively spend a lot more on the housing of the rich than is generally recognized. Interest deductability on a mega-mansion could easily be worth $25,000 a year. And alone among advanced economies, the United States tends to invest more in schools with richer student bodies than in those with mostly poor students—an effect of U.S. school districts' dependence on local tax bases for funding. Interestingly, according to some calculations, the entire deficit can be attributed to our inefficient and inequitable health care system: if we had a better health care system—of the kind that provided more equality at lower cost, such as those in so many European countries—we arguably wouldn't even have a federal budget deficit today.

Or consider this: if we provided more opportunity to the poor, including better education and an economic system that ensured access to jobs with decent pay, then perhaps we would not spend so much on prisons—in some states spending on prisons has at times exceeded that on universities. The poor instead would be better able to seize new employment opportunities, in turn making our economy more productive. And if we had better public transportation systems that made it easier and more affordable for working-class people to commute to where jobs are available, then a higher percentage of our population would be working and paying taxes. If, like the Scandinavian countries, we provided better child care and had more active labor market policies that assisted workers in moving from one job to another, we would have a higher labor force participation rate—and the enhanced growth would yield more tax revenues. It pays to invest in people.

This brings me to the final point: we could impose a fair tax system, raising more revenue, improving equity, and boosting economic growth while reducing distortions in our economy and our society. (That was the central finding of my 2014 Roosevelt Institute white paper, "Reforming Taxation to Promote Growth and Equity.") For instance, if we just imposed the same taxes on the returns to capital that we impose on those who work for a living, we could raise some $2 trillion over ten years. "Loopholes" does not adequately describe the flaws in our tax system; "gaps" might be better. Closing them might end the specter of the very rich almost proudly disclosing that they pay a tax rate on their disclosed income at half the rate of those with less income, and that they keep their money in tax havens like the Cayman Islands. No one can claim that the inhabitants of these small islands know how to manage money better than the wizards of Wall Street; but it seems as though that money grows better in the sunshine of these beach resorts!

One of the few advantages of there being so much money at the top of the income ladder, with close to a quarter of all income going to the top 1 percent, is that slight increases in taxes at the top can now raise large amounts of money. And because so much of the money at the top comes from exploitation (or as economists prefer to call it, "rent seeking"—that is, seizing a larger share of the national pie rather than increasing its size), higher taxes at the top do not seem to have much of an adverse effect on economic performance.

Then there's our corporate tax rate. If we actually made corporations pay what they are supposed to pay and eliminated loopholes we would raise hundreds of billions of dollars. With the right redesign, we could even get more employment and investment in the United States. True, U.S. corporations face one of the higher *official* corporate tax rates among the advanced countries; but the reality is otherwise—as a share of corporate income actually paid, our federal corporate taxes are just 13 percent of reported worldwide income. By most accounts, the amount of taxes actually paid (as a percentage of profits) is no higher than the average of other advanced countries. Apple Inc., Google Inc., and General Electric Co. have become the poster children of American ingenuity—making products that are the envy of the rest of the world. But they are using too much of that ingenuity to figure out how to avoid paying their fair share of taxes. Yet they and other U.S. corporations make full use of ideas and innovations produced with the support of the U.S. government, starting with the Internet itself. At the same time they rely on the talent produced by the country's first-rate universities, all of which receive extensive support from the federal government. They even turn to the U.S. government to demand better treatment from our trading partners.

Corporations argue that they would not engage in so much despicable tax avoidance if tax rates were lower. But there is a far better solution, and one that the individual U.S. states have discovered: have corporations pay taxes based on the economic activity they conduct in the United States, on the basis of a simple formula reflecting their sales, their production, and their research activities here, and tax corporations that invest in the United States at lower rates than those that don't. In this way we could increase investment and employment here at home—a far cry from the current system, in which we in effect encourage even U.S. corporations to produce elsewhere. (Even if U.S. taxes are no higher than the average, there are some tax havens—like Ireland—that are engaged in a race to the bottom, trying to recruit companies to make their country their tax home.) Such a reform would end the corporate stampede toward "inversions," changing a corporation's tax home to avoid taxes. Where they claim their home office is would make little difference; only where they actually do business would.

Other sources of revenue would benefit our economy and our society. Two basic principles of taxation are that it is better to tax bad things than good; and it is better to tax factors in what economists call "inelastic supply"—meaning that the amounts produced and sold won't change when taxes are imposed on them. Thus, if we taxed pollution in all of its forms—including carbon emissions—we could raise hundreds of billions of dollars every year, and have a better environment. Similarly, appropriately designed taxes on the financial sector would not only raise considerable amounts of money but also discourage banks from imposing costs on others—as when they polluted the global economy with toxic mortgages.

The $700 billion bank bailout pales in comparison to what the bankers' fecklessness has cost our economy and our society—trillions of dollars in lost GDP, millions of Americans thrown out of their homes and jobs. Yet few in the financial world have been held accountable.

If we required the banks to pay but a fraction of the costs they have imposed on others, we would then have further funds to undo some of the damage that they caused by their discriminatory and predatory lending practices, which moved money from the bottom of the economic pyramid to the top. And by imposing even slight taxes on Wall Street's speculative activities via a financial transactions tax, we would raise much-needed revenue, decrease speculation (thus increasing economic stability), and encourage more productive use of our scarce resources, including the most valuable one: talented young Americans.

Similarly, by taxing land, oil, and minerals more—and forcing those who extract resources from public land to pay the full values of these resources, which rightly belong to *all* the people, we could then spend those proceeds for public investments—for instance, in education, technology, and infrastructure—without resulting in less land, less oil, fewer minerals. (Even if they are taxed more, these resources won't go on strike; they won't leave the country!) The result: increased long-term investments in our economy would pay substantial future dividends in higher economic productivity and growth—and if the money was spent right, we could have more shared prosperity.

The question is not whether we can afford to do more about our inequality; it is whether we can afford *not* to do more. The debate in America is not about eliminating inequality. It is simply about moderating it and restoring the American Dream.

JOSEPH E. STIGLITZ, a Nobel laureate in economics, is University Professor at Columbia University. His most recent book, co-authored with Bruce Greenwald, is *Creating a Learning Society: A New Approach to Growth, Development, and Social Progress.*

Robert Rector and Rachel Sheffield  **NO**

Understanding Poverty in the United States: Surprising Facts About America's Poor

Today, the Census Bureau released its annual poverty report, which declared that 46.2 million (roughly one in seven) Americans were poor in 2010. The numbers were up sharply from the previous year's total of 43.6 million. Although the current recession has increased the numbers of the poor, high levels of poverty predate the recession. In most years for the past two decades, the Census Bureau has declared that at least 35 million Americans lived in poverty.

Yet what do these numbers actually mean? What does it mean to be poor in America? For most Americans, the word "poverty" suggests near destitution: an inability to provide nutritious food, clothing, or reasonable shelter for one's family. For example, the Poverty Pulse poll by the Catholic Campaign for Human Development in 2005 asked the general public: "How would you describe being poor in the U.S.?" The overwhelming majority of responses focused on homelessness, hunger or not being able to eat properly, and not being able to meet basic needs. Yet if poverty means lacking nutritious food, adequate warm housing, and clothing, relatively few of the 46 million people identified by the Census Bureau as being "in poverty" could be characterized as poor.

The Census Bureau's poverty report is widely publicized by the press. Regrettably, the report provides only a bare count of the number of Americans defined as poor by the government. It provides no data on or description of their actual living conditions. However, several other federal surveys provide detailed information on the living conditions of the poor. These surveys provide a very different sense of American poverty. They reveal that the actual standard of living of America's poor—in terms of amenities in the home, housing, food consumption, and nutrition—is far higher than expected.

These surveys show that most people whom the government defines as "in poverty" are not actually poor in any ordinary sense of the term. While material hardship does exist in the United States, it is restricted in scope and severity. Regrettably, the mainstream press rarely reports on these detailed surveys of living conditions.

TALKING POINTS

- The typical poor American lives in an air-conditioned house or apartment that is in good repair and has cable TV, a car, multiple color TVs, a DVD player, a VCR, and many other appliances. Half of the poor have computers, and one-third have wide-screen plasma TVs.
- Some 96 percent of poor parents report their chilldren were never hungry at any time in the prior year.
- A poor child is more likely to have cable TV, a computer, a wide-screen plasma TV, an Xbox, or a TiVo in the home than to be hungry.
- Poor Americans have more living space in their homes than the average non-poor Swede, Frenchman, or German.
- Sound anti-poverty policy must be based on accurate information and address the causes of poverty, not merely the symptoms. Exaggerating the extent and severity of hardships will not benefit society, the taxpayers, or the poor.

Amenities in Poor Households

Chart 1 shows ownership of property and consumer durables among poor households based on data from the 2009 American Housing Survey, which was conducted by the U.S. Department of Housing and Urban Development and the Census Bureau, and the 2009 Residential Energy Consumption Survey, which was conducted by the U.S. Department of Energy. These surveys show that:

- 80 percent of poor households have air conditioning. By contrast, in 1970, only 36 percent of the U.S. population enjoyed air conditioning.

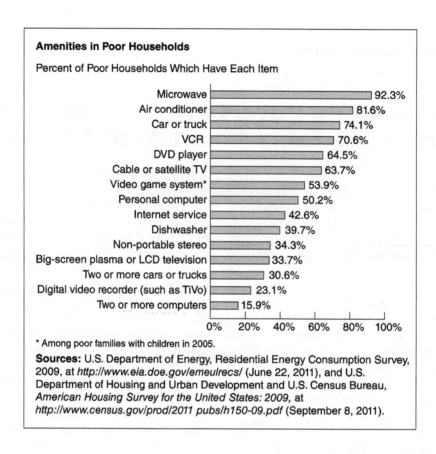

Amenities in Poor Households

Percent of Poor Households Which Have Each Item

Item	Percent
Microwave	92.3%
Air conditioner	81.6%
Car or truck	74.1%
VCR	70.6%
DVD player	64.5%
Cable or satellite TV	63.7%
Video game system*	53.9%
Personal computer	50.2%
Internet service	42.6%
Dishwasher	39.7%
Non-portable stereo	34.3%
Big-screen plasma or LCD television	33.7%
Two or more cars or trucks	30.6%
Digital video recorder (such as TiVo)	23.1%
Two or more computers	15.9%

0%   20%   40%   60%   80%   100%

* Among poor families with children in 2005.

Sources: U.S. Department of Energy, *Residential Energy Consumption Survey, 2009,* at *http://www.eia.doe.gov/emeulrecs/* (June 22, 2011), and U.S. Department of Housing and Urban Development and U.S. Census Bureau, *American Housing Survey for the United States: 2009,* at *http://www.census.gov/prod/2011 pubs/h150-09.pdf* (September 8, 2011).

- 92 percent of poor households have a microwave.
- Nearly three-fourths have a car or truck, and 31 percent have two or more cars or trucks.
- Nearly two-thirds have cable or satellite TV.
- Two-thirds have at least one DVD player, and 70 percent have a VCR.
- Half have a personal computer, and one in seven have two or more computers.
- More than half of poor families with children have a video game system, such as an Xbox or PlayStation.
- 43 percent have Internet service.
- 40 percent have an automatic dishwasher.
- One-third have a wide-screen plasma or LCD TV.
- Around one-fourth have a digital video recorder, such as a TiVo.
- More than half have a cell phone.

Of course, nearly all poor households have commonplace amenities such as color TVs, telephones, and kitchens equipped with an oven, stove, and refrigerator.

In 2005, more than half of poor households had at least five of the following 10 conveniences: a computer, cable or satellite TV, air conditioning, Internet service, a large-screen TV, non-portable stereo, computer printer, separate freezer or second refrigerator, microwave, and at least one color TV. One-fourth of the poor had seven or more of these 10 items in their homes. . . .

Steady Improvement in Living Conditions

Are the numbers in Chart 1 a fluke? Have they been inflated by working-class families with lots of conveniences in the home who have lost jobs in the recession and temporarily joined the ranks of the poor? No. The data indicate that the broad array of modern conveniences in the homes of the poor is the result of decades of steady progress in the living standards of the poor. Year by year, the poor tend to be better off. Consumer items that were luxuries or significant purchases for the middle class a few decades ago have become commonplace in poor households.

In part, this is caused by a normal downward trend in prices after a new product is introduced. Initially, new products tend to be expensive and therefore available only to the affluent. Over time, prices fall sharply, and the product saturates the entire population including poor households. As a rule of thumb, poor households tend to obtain modern conveniences about a dozen years after the middle class. Today, most poor families have conveniences that were major purchases or unaffordable to the middle class not too long ago.

Liberals use the declining relative prices of many amenities to argue that it is no big deal that poor households have air conditioning, computers, and cable TV. They contend that even though most poor families have houses full of modern conveniences, the average poor family still suffers from serious deprivation in basic needs, such as food, nutrition, and housing. While such an outcome is theoretically possible, this paper demonstrates that this is not the case. In fact, the overwhelming majority of poor households have an adequate and reasonably steady supply of food, are not hungry, and are well housed.

Poverty and Malnutrition

Malnutrition (also called undernutrition) is a condition of reduced health due to a chronic shortage of calories and nutriments. There is little or no evidence of poverty-induced malnutrition in the United States. It is often believed that a lack of financial resources forces poor people to eat low-quality diets that are deficient in nutriments and high in fat, but survey data show that nutriment density (amount of vitamins, minerals, and protein per kilocalorie of food) does not vary by income class. Nor do the poor consume higher-fat diets than do members of the middle class. The percentage of persons with high fat intake (as a share of total calories) is virtually the same for low-income and upper-middle-income persons. However, overconsumption of calories is a major problem among the poor, as it is in the general U.S. population.

Examination of the average nutriment consumption of Americans reveals that age and gender play a far greater role than income class in determining nutritional intake. For example, the nutriment intakes of adult women in the upper middle class (incomes above 350 percent of the poverty level—roughly $76,000 for a family of four in today's dollars) more closely resemble the intakes of poor women than those of upper-middle-class men, children, or teens. The average nutriment consumption of upper-middle-income preschoolers is virtually identical with that of poor preschoolers, but not with the consumption of adults or older children in the upper middle class.

This same pattern holds for adult males, teens, and most other age and gender groups. In general, children

who are 0–11 years old have the highest average level of nutriment intakes relative to the recommended daily allowance (RDA), followed by adult and teen males. Adult and teen females have the lowest level of intakes. This pattern holds for all income classes.

Nutrition and Poor Children

Government surveys provide little evidence of widespread undernutrition among poor children. In fact, they show that the average nutriment consumption among the poor closely resembles consumption among the upper middle class. Children in families with incomes below the poverty level actually consume more meat than do children in upper-middle-class families. . . .

Poverty and Consistency of Food Supply

Most poor Americans are not undernourished, but experience an abundance of food over time rather than chronic shortfalls of food. However, even though the poor generally have an ample food supply, some do suffer from temporary food shortages. For example, even if a poor household has an adequate or good overall food supply when measured over a moderate period, it still might need to cut back meals or go without if food stamps run out at the end of the month. This problem of temporary food shortages leads some advocates to claim that there is widespread "hunger" in the United States.

The current deep recession and prolonged high levels of unemployment have made it much more difficult for families to have a steady supply of food. Many families have been forced to eat less expensive food than they are accustomed to eating. Nonetheless, USDA survey data show that most households, poor or non-poor, do not suffer even temporarily from food shortages. During the recession in 2009, 95 percent of all U.S. households report that they had "enough food to eat," although not always the kinds of food that they would have preferred. Some 3.9 percent of all households report they "sometimes" did not have enough food to eat, while 1 percent said they "often" did not have enough food.

Among the poor, the figures are slightly lower: 83.4 percent of poor households asserted that they always had "enough food to eat," although a full 38 percent of these did not always have the foods they would have preferred. Some 13 percent of poor households stated that they "sometimes" did not have enough food, and 3.7 percent said that they "often" did not have enough food. The bottom line is that, although a significant portion of poor households do report temporary food shortages, five out of six poor households stated that they had enough food to eat even in the middle of a recession.

Poverty and Temporary Food Shortages

The USDA also measures temporary food shortages within households, a condition it calls "very low food security." According to the USDA, in households with very low food security, the "eating patterns of one or more household members were disrupted and their food intake reduced, at least some time during the year, because they couldn't afford enough food."

At times, these households worried that food would run out, ate unbalanced meals, and relied on cheaper foods. In addition, adults usually cut back on the size of their meals or skipped meals to save money. In a majority of these households, adults reported feeling hungry at times but not eating due to a lack of food. In the overwhelming majority of households with very low food security, adults ate less while shielding children from reductions in food intake.

Very low food security is almost always an intermittent and episodic problem for families rather than a chronic condition. The average family with very low food security experienced disrupted food intakes in seven months of the year, for one to seven days per month. . . .

In 2009, the USDA also asked parents living in poverty the following question about their children: "In the last 12 months, were the children ever hungry but you just couldn't afford more food?" Some 96 percent of poor parents responded that their children had never been hungry during the previous year due to a lack of food resources. Only 4 percent of poor parents responded that their children had been hungry at some point in the year.

Poverty and Homelessness

The mainstream press and activist groups frequently conflate poverty with homelessness. News stories about poverty often feature homeless families living "on the street." This depiction is seriously misleading because only a small portion of persons "living in poverty" will become homeless over the course of a year. The overwhelming majority of the poor reside throughout the year in non-crowded housing that is in good repair.

The *2009 Annual Homeless Assessment Report to Congress* published by the U.S. Department of Housing and Urban Development (HUD) states that on a given night in 2009, some 643,000 persons in the U.S. were

homeless (without permanent domicile). This means that at any given time, one out of 470 persons in the general population or one out of 70 persons with incomes below the poverty level was homeless.

Moreover, two-thirds of the 643,000 homeless persons were residing in emergency shelters or transitional housing. Only 240,000 were without shelter; these "unsheltered" individuals were "on the street," meaning that they were living in cars, abandoned buildings, alleyways, parks, or similar places. At any point in 2009, roughly one person out of 1,250 in the general population or one out of 180 poor persons was homeless in the literal sense of being on the street and without shelter.

Homelessness is usually a transitional condition. Individuals typically lose housing, reside in an emergency shelter for a few weeks or months, and then reenter permanent housing. The transitional nature of homelessness means that many more people become temporarily homeless over the course of a year than are homeless at any single point in time. Thus, HUD reports that 1.56 million persons resided in an emergency shelter or transitional housing at least one night during 2009. The year-round total of individuals who ever stayed in a shelter or transitional housing was nearly four times larger than the 403,000 who resided in such facilities on an average night.

Based on the year-round data on shelter use, roughly one person in 195 in the general population resided in an emergency shelter or transitional housing for at least one night during a full 12-month period. Roughly one in 25 poor persons (4 percent of all poor persons) resided in an emergency shelter or transitional housing for at least one night during the full year.

Although news stories often suggest that poverty and homelessness are similar, this is inaccurate. In reality, the gap between the living conditions of a homeless person and the typical poor household are proportionately as great as the gap between the poor household and a middle-class family in the suburbs.

Housing Conditions and Poverty

When the mainstream media do not portray the poor as homeless, they will often present them as living in dismal conditions such as an overcrowded, dilapidated trailer. Again, government survey data provide a very different picture. Most poor Americans live in conventional houses or apartments that are in good repair. 49.5 percent of poor households live in single-family homes, either unattached single dwellings or attached units such as townhouses.

Another 41 percent live in apartments, and 9.5 percent live in mobile homes.

Poverty and Crowding

Both the overall U.S. population and the poor in America live in very spacious housing. 71 percent of all U.S. households have two or more rooms per tenant. Among the poor, this figure is 65 percent.

Crowding is quite rare. Only 2.2 percent of all households and 6.2 percent of poor households are crowded with less than one room per person. By contrast, social reformer Jacob Riis, writing on tenement living conditions around 1890 in New York City, described crowded families living with four or five persons per room and some 20 square feet of living space per person. . . .

Conclusion

The living conditions of the poor as defined by the government bear little resemblance to notions of "poverty" promoted by politicians and political activists. If poverty is defined as lacking adequate nutritious food for one's family, a reasonably warm and dry apartment, or a car to go to work when one is needed, then the United States has relatively few poor persons. Real material hardship does occur, but it is limited in scope and severity.

In 2005, the typical poor household as defined by the government had a car and air conditioning. For entertainment, the household had two color TVs, cable or satellite TV, a DVD player, and a VCR. If children—especially boys—were in the home, the family had a game system, such as an Xbox or PlayStation. In the kitchen, the household had a refrigerator, an oven and stove, and a microwave. Other household conveniences included a clothes washer, clothes dryer, ceiling fans, a cordless phone, and a coffee maker.

The home of the typical poor family was not overcrowded and was in good repair. The family was able to obtain medical care when needed. By its own report, the family was not hungry and had sufficient funds during the previous year to meet all essential needs.

Poor families certainly struggle to make ends meet, but in most cases, they are struggling to pay for air conditioning and the cable TV bill as well as to put food on the table. While poor households certainly are not sitting in the lap of luxury, their actual living standards are far different from the images of dire deprivation promoted by activists and the mainstream media.

However, the average poor family does not represent every poor family. There is a range of living conditions within the poverty population. Although most poor families are well housed, a small minority are homeless. Although most poor families are well fed and have a fairly stable food supply, a sizeable minority experiences temporary shortages in food supply at various times during the year.

Nonetheless, the living standards of most poor households are far different from what the public imagines and differ greatly from the images of dramatic hardship conveyed by advocacy groups and the mainstream media. Why, then, does the Census Bureau routinely report that over 35 million Americans live in poverty? Its annual poverty report is inaccurate and misleading in part because nearly all of the welfare state is excluded from its poverty calculations. The Census Bureau identifies a family as "poor" if its income falls below specific thresholds; however, in counting a family's income, the Census Bureau omits nearly all welfare benefits. In 2010, government spent $871 billion on means-tested welfare programs that provided cash, food, housing, medical care, and social services to poor and low-income Americans. Virtually none of this assistance is counted as income for purposes of the Census Bureau's estimations of poverty or inequality.

In 2010, government means-tested assistance averaged nearly $9,000 for each poor and low-income American. Many "poor" families have higher than expected living standards in part because they receive considerable government aid that is "off the books" for purposes of counting poverty. Do the higher living standards of the poor mean that the welfare state has been successful?

The answer is: yes and no. Not even the government can spend $9,000 per person without having a significant effect on living conditions. But the original goal of the War on Poverty was not to prop up living standards artificially through an ever-expanding welfare state. President Lyndon Johnson intended for the War on Poverty to make Americans self-sufficient and prosperous through their own abilities, not through increased reliance on government aid. Ironically, Johnson actually planned to reduce, not increase, welfare dependence. His declared goal for the War on Poverty was "making taxpayers out of taxeaters."

Since the beginning of the War on Poverty, the U.S. has spent over $17 trillion on anti-poverty programs. In terms of its original goal of making poor Americans self-sufficient and prosperous through their own abilities, the War on Poverty has been a colossal failure. In many low-income communities, the work ethic has eroded and marriage has collapsed. As result, lower-income groups are less capable of self-sufficient prosperity today than they were when the War on Poverty began.

Congress should reorient the massive welfare state to promote self-sufficient prosperity rather than expanded dependence. As the recession ends, able-bodied recipients should be required to work or prepare for work as a condition of receiving aid. Even more important, the welfare system needs to abandon its 50-year-old tradition of ignoring, dismissing, and penalizing marriage. It should embark on a new course to strengthen and rebuild marriage in low-income communities.

ROBERT RECTOR is Senior Research Fellow in the Domestic Policy Studies Department in the Richard and Helen DeVos Center for Religion and Civil Society at the Heritage Foundation and has been a leading authority on poverty, welfare programs, and immigration in America for three decades.

RACHEL SHEFFIELD is a research assistant in the Richard and Helen DeVos Center for Religion and Civil Society at the Heritage Foundation.

EXPLORING THE ISSUE

Is Increasing Economic
Inequality a Serious Problem?

Critical Thinking and Reflection

1. How did a country with such a strong commitment to equality come to have such a high level of inequality?
2. What are the arguments for the trickle-down theory and what are the arguments against it?
3. How does the growing inequality in America affect the functioning of our major institutions and areas of life?
4. How can the adverse effects of inequality be mitigated by policies or regulations?
5. Currently many activists are claiming that the 1 percent is screwing the 99 percent. What evidence supports this claim and what evidence contradicts it?
6. What should be done about the growing inequality, or should nothing be done?

Is There Common Ground?

There is not much common ground between the two selections. Stiglitz says the inequality is very bad and its consequences are very bad. Rector and Sheffield say that the inequality is not so bad and its consequences are not so bad. Both sides want America to be prosperous, and that includes a prosperous lower class. Stiglitz says that most Americans are worse off than a decade ago and especially the lower class. Rector and Sheffield say that the poor are far better off than most people realize because they actually own many things that were hard for the middle class to own decades ago. They back this point up with generous statistics. Most of the poor have cable, a car, DVD player, video player, personal computer, air conditioner, and a microwave. Their homes are filled with abundant possessions. In fact, they say that "for decades, the living conditions of the poor have steadily improved." They are also relatively well-off in the basics. "Most of the poor do not experience hunger or food shortages . . . 96 percent of poor parents stated that their children were never hungry at any time during the year because they could not afford food." They are well-off even in their housing. "The average poor American has more living space than the typical non-poor person in Sweden, France, or the United Kingdom." These and other statistics do not erase the vast inequality in incomes in America but they make a good case for seeing the inequality as not so bad.

Stiglitz has income inequality statistics on his side showing its negative effects on living conditions. Thus,

inequality must be reduced and he prescribes the ways to do that.

So the two sides have very different views of America today and would probably disagree on what to do about commonly recognized problems. Both want a strong and prosperous America and a well-off lower class but differ on what are the best ways to achieve it. All agree that they should get educational assistance. Do free public schools accomplish that? Some European countries make education free through college. Should America do the same? Are food stamps, free school lunches, Head Start, and welfare for the needy enough at their current levels to enable poor young people to climb the ladder of success? Everyone recognizes that there is a danger that help can create dependency, so how much is enough and not too much?

Additional Resources

Inequality, stratification, and social mobility are central concerns of sociology, and they are addressed by a large body of literature. Important discussions of income inequality include Rebecca M. Blank, *Changing Inequality* (University of California Press, 2011); Nathan J. Kelly, *The Politics of Income Inequality in the United States* (Cambridge University Press, 2009); Congressional Budget Office, "The Distribution of Household Income and Federal Taxes 2011," November 2014; John Cassidy, "American Inequality in Six Charts," *The New Yorker* (November 18, 2013); Luxembourg Income Study Center, "Income Inequality in the U.S. in Cross-National Perspective," April

2015; Thomas Piketty, *Capital in the Twenty-First Century* (Belknap Press 2014); David M. Kotz, *The Rise and Fall of Neoliberal Capitalism* (Harvard University Press, 2015); and Emmanuel Saez, *Striking It Richer: The Evolution of Top Incomes in the United States* (University of California at Berkeley, 2013).

Internet References . . .

Sociology—Study Sociology Online

http://edu.learnsoc.org/

Sociology Web Resources

www.mhhe.com/socscience/sociology/resources/index.htm

Sociosite

www.topsite.com/goto/sociosite.net

Socioweb

www.topsite.com/goto/socioweb.com

Selected, Edited, and with Issue Framing Material by:
Kurt Finsterbusch, *University of Maryland, College Park*

ISSUE

Has America Made Substantial Progress in the Rights of Blacks?

YES: Noah C. Rothman, from "The 'Conversation about Race' That Isn't a Conversation: Twenty Years of Talk about Race Obscures This Country's Remarkable Progress," *Commentary* (2015)

NO: Valerie Tarico, from "When Slavery Won't Die: The Oppressive Biblical Mentality America Can't Shake: An Interview with Black Theologian Kelly Brown Douglas on America's Greatest Sins," AlterNet (2015)

Learning Outcomes

After reading this issue, you will be able to:

- Apprehend the changes in the civil rights of blacks in America in the past half century.
- Evaluate the discrimination, biases, prejudices, stereotypes, and values that still hold blacks back.
- Know basic facts about current racial inequalities and a sense of the extent of change since the 1950s.
- Understand how change is resisted.
- Understand how public figures affect children's perceptions and thereby their lives.
- Discern what can be accomplished by new policies and what cannot be accomplished by them.
- Understand indirect victimization and judge its importance in current racial inequality.

ISSUE SUMMARY

YES: Noah C. Rothman, associate editor of HotAir.com, does not deny that strong racial prejudice still exists among whites, but he also shows many of the ways that behavior and institutions have become less discriminatory.

NO: Valerie Tarico is a psychologist and writer of two books and a number of articles. She begins with the painful story of Dylann Roof's shooting of nine people in a black church in Charleston because she wants to expose the racist thinking that is behind such acts. Her discussion with Kelly Brown Douglas also covers slavery and Trayvon Martin.

This debate analyzes interracial (and interethnic) relations, but our focus will be on black–white relations. Our starting point is the question, "What does the election of Barack Obama indicate about race relations in America today?" A black was elected to the highest position in America. This was impossible to imagine 50 years ago. Clearly America has changed. There were important precursors to the Obama presidency such as very popular Oprah Winfrey and many other popular black entertainers. Blacks have also become prominent political leaders such as Colin Powell, Condoleezza Rice, and Ben Carson. The public image of blacks has greatly improved. *The Cosby Show* had something to do with this. As a viewer I identified with Dr. Huxtable and his family as well as many other black actors and actresses in movies and TV shows over the years. The images that young people see are quite different from what I saw when I was growing up. The first movie that I saw about interracial marriage was *Guess Who's Coming to Dinner* with Spencer Tracy, Katherine Hepburn, and Sidney Poitier. It came out in 1967, and was a bombshell at the time—very tense. Many people could not handle it.

Today the situation is totally different. Interracial and interethnic marriages are more common and thus more normal, and this reflects changes in interracial attitudes and laws. Interracial marriages were illegal in many states until the Supreme Court declared these laws unconstitutional in 1967. Change in interracial marriages has been slow, however, since only 2.9 percent of the population were interracial in 2010. On the other hand, 5.6 percent of the population under age 18 are interracial. According to the 2010 census, 8.5 percent of married black men and 3.9 percent of married black women had a white spouse. According to the 2008 Pew Research Center Report based on the Census Bureau's 2008 American Community Survey:

> Among all newlyweds in 2008, 9% of whites, 16% of blacks, 26% of Hispanics and 31% of Asians married someone whose race or ethnicity was different from their own. . . . Among all newlyweds in 2008, intermarried pairings were primarily White-Hispanic (41%) as compared to White-Asian (15%), White-Black (11%), and Other Combinations (33%). . . . Rates of intermarriages among newlyweds in the U.S. more than doubled between 1980 (6.7%) and 2008 (14.6%). . . . Most Americans say they approve of racial or ethnic intermarriage—not just in the abstract, but in their own families. More than six-in-ten say

it would be fine with them if a family member told them they were going to marry someone from any of three major race/ethnic groups other than their own. More than a third of adults (35%) say they have a family member who is married to someone of a different race. Blacks say this at higher rates than do whites; younger adults at higher rates than older adults; and Westerners at higher rates than people living in other regions of the country.

These statistics demonstrate that considerable change has occurred, and also show that there is room for a great deal more change. The United States is moving toward a post-racial society, but it is debatable whether it is moving enough to get there this century.

Noah C. Rothman discusses race relations in the United States at two levels. The more open and superficial level includes the many dramatic newsworthy episodes that impact our consciences and that provoke the media coverage of race. At that level race relations are at a low point. Rothman, however, emphasizes the deeper level, which receives little attention, and he shows that race relations at that level have improved considerably over the past two decades. Valerie Tarico, on the other hand, immerses herself in the tragedies and delves into the psychologies and cultural values which explain these violent actions. This is an issue that it is hard to be calm about.

YES ↵   Noah C. Rothman

The "Conversation about Race" That Isn't a Conversation: Twenty Years of Talk about Race Obscures This Country's Remarkable Progress

Two thousand fourteen was an explosive and regrettable year for the politics of race in America. The fatal police shooting of black Missouri teenager Michael Brown on August 9 sparked ongoing riots in his hometown of Ferguson and beyond. After grand juries decided not to indict police officers for either the fatal shooting of Brown or the death of the 43-year-old New Yorker Eric Garner during an arrest, the country was hit with a wave of protest the likes of which we have not seen since the 1992 Los Angeles riots and whose geographic breadth was altogether new—from the blocking of bridges and highways in Los Angeles and New York City to "die-ins" in Seattle. But if the scope of turmoil was novel, the reaction from pundits, politicians, and academics was all too familiar. They called once again for a "national conversation" on race.

The *New York Times* columnist Nicholas Kristof penned a five-part epic—from August to November—on how "whites don't get it." To rectify this problem, he called for "a new commission [that] could jumpstart an overdue national conversation." Peniel Joseph, of Tufts University, called the violence in Ferguson a "teachable political moment" that should give rise to the creation of a "National Dialogue on Race Day" on American college campuses. "The ultimate goal is to create a sustained conversation that will carry policy implications on a range of issues locally and nationally," he wrote for TheRoot.com. Finally, the president of the United States weighed in. "What we need is a sustained conversation," Barack Obama urged in December, "to move forward in a constructive fashion."

As the history of these proposed "conversations" shows, those seeking an honest give-and-take on national race relations would do well to look to other venues. For two decades, our tortured and contrived "conversations"

have misled rather than enlightened. While there have been some well-intentioned advocates of having a "national conversation," most of those who propose such an undertaking are not looking for candor or reconciliation. Rather, the prominent instigators of the national conversation are using it as a means of furthering a vision of United States as a hopelessly racist society. Meanwhile, those who resist the outcome these instigators desire are then charged with ignorance or cowardice or banished from the discussion altogether.

Appeals for these supposedly cathartic and therapeutic discourses date back to the final decade of the past century. Before 1994, the *New York Times* had never printed the now-ubiquitous phrase "national conversation on race." We can place this phrase's origin in remarks delivered two years earlier by the New Jersey Democrat Bill Bradley, who stood in the well of the Senate after the acquittal of four Los Angeles cops in the beating of Rodney King and demanded that the country have a frank discussion about its racial divisions. "If we as a nation continue to ignore the racial reality of our times, tip-toe around it, demagogue it, or flee from it, we're going to pay an enormous price," Bradley asserted in a speech that was as highly praised as it was devoid of substance.

The next year, newly elected president Bill Clinton appointed University of Pennsylvania law professor Lani Guinier to serve as assistant attorney general for civil rights. The revelation that she had become an advocate for proportional representation in Congress to thwart the "tyranny of the majority" made her confirmation impossible, and Clinton pulled her nomination. Thereafter, Guinier devoted her career to calling for a "national conversation" on race. In short order, Clinton began to appropriate Guinier's language and actually crafted a national policy around her proposals. In 1997, Clinton called for a yearlong conversation on race. He appointed the distinguished black historian John Hope Franklin to lead it.*

Franklin's national conversation proved to be an ideologically tendentious effort—and it would remain the standard model going forward. He refused to allow opponents of affirmative action to participate, famously declaring that they would have "nothing to contribute" to a 1997 forum on racial diversity. He accused minorities of betrayal if they criticized racial quotas: "Some blacks have a price," Franklin claimed. "It's just tragic when anyone sells themselves out." An editorial in the *Arkansas Democrat-Gazette*, Clinton's hometown paper, pronounced Franklin "rancorous, intolerant, accusatory, insulting, and divisive."

While Franklin took the discussion through ugly terrain, others were veering toward the ludicrous. This, too, has been a fixture of the national conversation. First Lady Hillary Clinton injected herself into the deliberation when she insisted that her rejected overtures of friendship toward a *white* sports teammate in college actually lent her genuine credibility to speak on the issue.

When President Clinton tried to right this listing ship, he succeeded only by dealing a death blow to his initiative. At a town-hall meeting in Akron in the final weeks of 1997, Clinton was confronted by Abigail Thernstrom and Ward Connerly, both prominent critics of affirmative action. Clinton came back at them aggressively. "Do you favor the United States Army abolishing the affirmative-action program that produced Colin Powell?" he asked. "Yes, or no?" Thernstrom triumphed with her reply: "I do not think that it is racial preferences that made Colin Powell. The overwhelming majority of Americans want American citizens to be treated as individuals."

Proponents of the national conversation didn't want debate; they wanted a confession. And so they judged Clinton, and the country, as failures on this first official outing. "President Clinton's lofty goal of a national conversation on race is failing to have any substantive effect because most Americans are unprepared to think about their own personal prejudices," wrote Maurice Berger, author of *White Lies: Race and the Myths of Whiteness*, in the *Los Angeles Times*. Further repudiation came from Clinton's closest associate: In January 2000, Vice President Al Gore told the *Atlanta Journal-Constitution* that Clinton's attempt to spur a dialogue on race was "a good beginning" before pledging to continue the effort in "not exactly in the same form."

The "conversation" ebbed after the 2000 campaign and disappeared almost entirely after the September 11 attacks. National discussion centered instead on terrorism and war in the Muslim world. During this period, however, racial divisions grew more extreme on the nation's intellectually sequestered college campuses.

President George W. Bush's reelection in 2004 offered him an opportunity to open his own national debate on ethnic tensions. He told the press he intended to invest his freshly acquired political capital in addressing the disparity of outcomes among different races in the public-education system. But exogenous events preempted the dialogue Bush had hoped to initiate.

In 2005 came Hurricane Katrina. A stream of images showing black Louisianans displaced and desperate in the wake of nature's wrath set the country on edge. "Much as pictures of horses and German shepherds turned on protesters shamed the nation into confronting racial prejudice in the 1960s, the image of impoverished hurricane victims waiting in vain for government help is forcing a national conversation on race and urban poverty," read a statement released by the Congressional Black Caucus.

Few prominent political and cultural figures acknowledged the hyperbole in this and other similar assertions. Fewer still reflected on the fact that New Orleans's black mayor, Ray Nagin, was responsible— along with the state's governor, Kathleen Blanco—for the local government's inaction. Instead, Hurricane Katrina was used to highlight the ongoing plight of blacks in a bigoted United States. "I was taken aback when reporters and others watching this tragedy were saying: 'This is not America,'" said California Representative Barbara Lee. "I thought, 'Wait a minute. This is the America I know. This is the America that each and every member of the Congressional Black Caucus knows all too well.'"

In response, Bush nodded in the direction of the "national conversation" once again. "This poverty has roots in generations of segregation and discrimination that closed many doors of opportunity," he told attendees of the 2005 National Prayer Breakfast. "As we clear away the debris of a hurricane, let us also clear away the legacy of inequality." But coming from a controversial Republican president who had essentially been blamed for an act of God, the exhortation found no purchase among liberals and leftists. Their understanding of the national conversation didn't include the president who had been condemned for looking down at the hurricane from a helicopter. During a live telethon for Katrina victims, the rapper Kanye West went off script, looked dead at the camera, and simply offered, "George Bush doesn't care about black people." West's statement more or less summed up the tenor of the national conversation on race during Bush's second term.

Many in the chattering classes greeted Barack Obama's candidacy warmly, partly *because* it would spark the anticipated conversation on race. Undoubtedly, the idealists among them hoped a leader had emerged who would remake the nation along post-racial lines. "I think a lot of Americans are uncomfortable having an authentic conversation about race and would like to 'move on' without necessarily facing the complex mix of unexpressed emotions and viewpoints inherent in the legacy of racism," the civil-rights advocate J.G. Boccella asserted in a February 2008 column for the *Pittsburgh Post-Gazette*. "Maybe, instead of an Obama presidency being a chance to skip over the tricky parts and stop talking about race, it could be an opportunity to take the conversation to the next level."

Those further to the left hoped for a direct confrontation with America's racist nature. The opaque Obama didn't offer much reason to suspect he would move in one direction or another, but the discovery of controversial remarks from his long-time pastor Jeremiah Wright pointed to anything but a move toward a post-racial America. "God damn America, as long as she tries to act like she is God, and she is supreme," said Wright. "The United States government has failed the vast majority of her citizens of African descent." The Obama campaign was thrust into a crisis.

In March 2008, Obama responded with a lengthy televised speech. Over the course of 37 minutes, he became an even-handed, one-man embodiment of the national conversation on race. He decried the casual racial stereotyping in which the members of his white grandmother's generation engaged. But he also called Wright's comments offensive. Obama discussed the expectations placed on him, noting that he's been criticized as both "too black" and "not black enough." Though he denounced the "original sin of slavery," the future president granted that there was hope for the nation yet.

Whatever the speech's substantive merits, it was a political masterstroke and pulled Obama out of the perilous spiral into which Wright's words had pulled him. "Brilliant," the *Philadelphia Inquirer* exclaimed. Obama's "frankness" on race could only be likened to that of Presidents Johnson and Lincoln, the *New York Times* averred. The speech also opened the window to restart the national conversation in the country at large. The national conversation on race is renewed, declared the *Baltimore Sun's* Fraser Smith. Obama had delivered unto the nation a "long-awaited invitation to begin an honest, calm national dialogue about race," the *Chicago Tribune* affirmed.

But, as before, "honest, calm national dialogue about race" is not what the conversation's prominent endorsers sought. It wasn't long before familiar patterns reemerged,

and the conversation began to disappoint its champions. "We need more than another conversation; we need a 'teach-in,'" Robin D.G. Kelley asserted in *U.S. News and World Report*. "We have seen a distinct difference in commentary on Rev. Wright from people who have spent time in black churches and those who have not," said PBS host Gwen Ifill.

Many liberal pundits continued to be anything but calm even as they praised that quality in Obama. Obama's backers accused his critics of latent racial antipathy. "Obama has been running as a post-racial candidate from the start," said presidential historian Douglas Brinkley. "But the fact of the matter is that some voters—we can't know yet how many—will not get past his race. And I very much believe that the McCain–Palin ticket is tapping into that." The *Times*, too, warned its readers that the "extent of the racial divide" would become clear only on Election Day when returns quantified residual racism in the United States. One senses in these comments a vague and shameful hope that a persistent and insoluble racism does permeate America.

Indeed, once the United States had elected its first black president, some worried that the country would take this (rightly, in fact) as evidence of tremendous national progress on race and therefore dismiss the need for having the "national conversation." They were surely delighted to discover in the early months of the Obama presidency that a new ceaseless dialogue on race in America had only just begun. "In things racial, we have always been, and continue to be, in too many ways, essentially a nation of cowards," said Attorney General Eric Holder, prodding open the discussion. When Harvard professor Henry Louis Gates was detained for attempting to break into his own house in 2009, Obama rushed to insert himself into the fracas. In a prime-time news conference, he insisted that the white police officer had "acted stupidly" in suspecting the black academic of wrongdoing.

But as is their wont, the conversationists expressed dissatisfaction once again. As Democratic fortunes waned in the summer of 2010, Obama and the nation he led were deemed failures on race. "Expecting an American conversation on race in this country is like expecting financial advice from someone who prefers to not check his or her bank balance," wrote the *Atlantic's* Ta-Nehisi Coates. "This is a country too ignorant of itself to grapple with race in any serious way." (Coates would go on to write a lengthy essay in favor of reparations for black Americans, making clear his idea of where a "serious" national conversation should lead.)

The shooting death of black Florida teen Trayvon Martin (by a Hispanic man) in February 2012 opened the national conversation yet again. But this time, those who issued their appeals hoped that the president who had let them down would take a back seat. "There needs to be a national conversation on race, but the president isn't necessarily the one who has to lead it," said Wisconsin Representative Gwen Moore. With characteristic crassness, New York Representative Charlie Rangel agreed that Obama's involvement would not be constructive. "That's like a man about to be lynched wants to give a talk about civil rights," he said. Barack Obama had been dismissed for failing to advance the discussion of race in America.

By the time Obama's supporters embarked on the task of securing his reelection, the national conversation on race had plainly become divorced from objective reality. With a black president having served a full term, agitators didn't have much to work with on the surface, and so they had to dig. On the left, divining racism out of "code words" became a pseudo-intellectual sport. During an MSNBC panel discussion on the undue influence of exurban America on the political process, Michael Eric Dyson, of Georgetown University, teased out the supposedly racist language often used to discuss cities. "Who lives in urban America?" he asked pointedly. "This is 'welfare queen'-lite. You don't even have to say it. All you have to say is 'urban.'" While covering the 2012 Republican National Convention, MSNBC host Chris Matthews noted, "They keep saying 'Chicago,' by the way, have you noticed?" *Game Change* author John Heilemann added further clarification: "There's a lot of black people in Chicago"

Confounding the expectations of prejudice-mongers once again, Obama was reelected president of the United States. But having a twice-elected black president did little to quell the push for a national conversation on race. The continued fascination with racial offense would be stoked in part by random news events and sensationalized oddball cases. The NFL's Washington Redskins faced a new round of outrage over their name; television chef Paula Deen came under fire for having used racial epithets in conversation years earlier; and Los Angeles Clippers owner Donald Sterling came in for broad public ridicule when a female companion released secretly audiotaped segments of his bizarre and offensive racial rants. All of this served to keep the "national conversation" going at what, in retrospect, looks like a low boil.

IN 2014, the months-long public scolding of the police for their role in the deaths of Brown and Garner culminated in a sermon from New York City Mayor Bill de Blasio. Owing to "centuries of racism," the mayor said, he had had to teach his biracial son to fear the police force that de Blasio himself led. This was one more heaping brace of kindling added to a growing fire. While protesters called

for the retributive murder of police, someone took up the charge. When officers Wenjian Liu and Rafael Ramos were assassinated while sitting in their cruiser in Brooklyn, many drew a line from de Blasio's official characterization of the police to the two victims.

For the national conversation's skeptics, this horrific attack—one inspired, if not wholly motivated by, a popular culture infatuated with blaming law enforcement—proved decisive. The obsession with finding America guilty of broad and institutional racism was a dishonest and dangerous pursuit that had finally claimed lives. "It is impossible to overstate how inflammatory and ignorant de Blasio's statements are," wrote the Manhattan Institute's Heather Mac Donald in the *New York Daily News*. Days earlier she had compellingly observed in that there is "no institution in New York more dedicated to the proposition that black lives matter than the NYPD."

But for the national conversation's advocates, the shootings were an unwelcome obstacle to their self-reinforcing, decades-old lecture on race relations. "Conservatives are seizing on NYPD murders to silence any discussion about race in America," declared Think Progress's Igor Volsky hours after the shootings. Fearing that the targeted murder of police in New York might "derail" anti-police demonstrations, CBS News pondered whether "any gains made in the protest movement would be lost." Speaking to a Boston-area NPR affiliate, the city's ministerial leaders said they hoped the murders would not "derail a long overdue conversation around race." All this before the officers' bodies were buried.

Such blind insistence on a national conversation on race is not only distasteful; it has served to obscure the remarkable progress that has been made in America. While unacceptable racial inequalities persist, outcomes for African Americans have improved over the decades. By 2005, the income and wage gaps between blacks and whites had shrunk to their lowest points in American history. Progress toward parity was only arrested by the onset of the recession in 2007. The 2010 census revealed that African Americans, while less likely to receive a college degree than other demographics, are now more likely than any other demographic to have received some college education.

On the eve of the racially charged 2012 election cycle, 50 percent of Americans told Gallup pollsters that race relations had "greatly improved," while another 39 percent said that racial comity had improved "somewhat." In that same year, 76 percent said "new civil rights laws" were no longer necessary. Only 21 percent disagreed, down dramatically from the 38 percent who supported new civil rights laws as recently as 1993. In 2011, the majority of Americans believed that racial tensions between blacks and whites would "eventually [be] worked out." These and other signs of progress are somehow not considered germane to those chasing the ever-elusive national conversation.

The latest racial firestorms are largely based on either arguable assertions or outright fabrications. The claim that Michael Brown had his hands up in a display of submission when he was shot is a demonstrable myth. Though both were unarmed, Brown and Eric Garner were also both resisting arrest when they were killed. Neither officer was indicted despite significant black represent-ation on both grand juries. And those who claim that Garner died as a result of an officer's application of a prohibited choke hold must contend with the fact that the 350-pound, hyper-tense asthmatic who died in the ambulance of a heart attack is as likely to have succumbed to extreme stress and physical exertion brought about by his ordeal.

But when the "conversation" veers into areas of disagreement or conflict, its advocates always declare it a failure. Nuanced discussion of the Brown or Garner cases is not permitted. As we have seen in Missouri and New York, this is a great hindrance to calm and under-standing. The national conversation on race is, at best, disingenuous pageantry. At its worst, however, it throws up an ugly obstacle in America's ongoing march toward freedom and justice for all its citizens.

Note:

* When it was said that Clinton was flirting with issuing a formal apology for American slavery, paleoconservatives such as Patrick Buchanan offered distasteful criticisms of the president for undervaluing the European effort to spread Western civilization to Africa. This argument helped isolate Buchanan on the right and push him out of the party's mainstream, which was a clarifying moment for American conservatism.

NOAH C. ROTHMAN is the associate editor of HotAir.com and a political commentator.

Valerie Tarico

When Slavery Won't Die: The Oppressive Biblical Mentality America Can't Shake: An Interview with Black Theologian Kelly Brown Douglas on America's Greatest Sins

"*You rape our women and you're taking over our country. And you have to go.*" So said white supremacist Dylann Roof to black members of Emanuel AME Church in Charleston as he systematically executed nine, leaving one woman and a five-year-old child to bear witness to the slaughter.

The horror of the mass murder defies rational analysis. And yet, if we have any hope of a better future, we must analyze it—not just the circumstances or persons or events that led to this particular slaughter on this particular day, but the root attitudes and assumptions—the ancient strands of brutality and inequality that are woven into the fabric of our society.

In her article, "The Lethal Gentleman: The 'Benevolent Sexism' Behind Dylann Roof's Racism," sociologist Lisa Wade outlines how racism and sexism intersect in Roof's comments. The phrase "benevolent sexism" sounds jarring, but it is the term social scientists use when people attribute "positive traits to women that, nonetheless, justify their subordination to men:" *Women are beautiful and fragile; women are good with children; women are emotionally weak; God made woman as the perfect 'helpmeet' for man.* Roof's implication that white women need protecting from rape falls into this category.

One striking aspect of sexism and racism in Roof's statement is the sense of ownership it conveys: "Our women" in "our country" need to be protected from black men who either don't know their place or won't stay in it. White men can and should kill black men because they are having sex in our home territory with women who belong to us. We own America and we own the women who live here, and black men don't because if all was right in the world we would own them too.

The idea that women and minorities (along with children and members of other species) at some level *belong* to men of the dominant tribe can be traced all the way back to the culture and laws of the Iron Age and the concept of chattel. The term *chattel* is related to the term *cattle*, and human chattel, like cows, exist to serve their owners and must stay where they belong. In this view, dominant men have a right or even responsibility to enforce social hierarchy. If women or slaves or children or ethnic and religious minorities or livestock step out of line, they must be punished to keep society in its proper order.

I have written in the past about how Iron Age chattel culture underlies Religious Right priorities that might otherwise seem at odds: Why do the same people who oppose abortion also oppose protections and rights for children once they are born? What do opposition to marriage equality and opposition to contraception have in common? Why is the line between marriage and slavery so blurry in the Bible? How was American slavery influenced by the Iron Age worldview? Why does biblical literalism so often incline people to embrace sexual and racial inequality?

From within Christianity, Episcopal theologian and author Kelly Brown Douglas has written extensively about some of these same questions, with a particular focus on sexuality and the Black body. After the Trayvon Martin killing, she channeled her grief into a book, *Stand Your Ground: Black Bodies and the Justice of God.* In the interview that follows, Brown Douglas talks about the ancient concept of chattel, how it leads to the assumption that black bodies are "guilty, hypersexual, and dangerous," and how it underlies the slaughter, from Florida to New York to Charleston, that has left America reeling.

Tarico: You are the mother of a black son, so the horrendous epidemic of shootings we all have witnessed in recent years strikes very close to your heart.

Brown Douglas: I just couldn't shake the Trayvon Martin killing. At the time my son was 21 and I knew—as a 6' tall young man with locks that people would perceive him as a threat. My husband and I have tried to help our son understand how others perceive him as a black male. As his mother, I find myself continually reminding him that, while I will defend him to his death I don't want to defend him in his death. I have said, *If you are ever stopped by the police, even if they tell you to get on your knees, do it. A moment of humiliation could save your life.* When he's out there's not a moment that I don't fear for him, not because of anything he would do—he is a very responsible person—but because of how people might perceive him. So I am passionate about what is going on now, what is going on with our children. Somehow we have to change this world to make it safe for our children.

Tarico: In *Stand Your Ground,* you explore cultural values and beliefs that contribute to America's plague of racial violence including the sense of exceptionalism and manifest destiny—the idea that Anglo-Saxon European culture is fundamentally good, a light unto the world, something to be exported. When any of us has that kind of self-perception, it's hard to see ourselves as the bad guy, hard to see when we're doing harm.

Brown Douglas: To stop the harm, one of the first things that we have to understand is the complexity of violence. We have to understand that this Anglo-Saxon exceptionalism is inherently violent because it is unjust particularly as it suggests that certain people deserve the benefits of being treated with decency and dignity while others do not. Systems of injustice—racism, sexism, heterosexism—the ways that these systems manifest themselves systemically and structurally is violent. Anything that does harm to another is violent.

We seldom name the violence that is imbedded in the structures and systems of our society. We don't ask, where is the violence behind the violence? Yes, there are too many guns, and we should change that. But I'm speaking about the violence of injustice. Inasmuch as we don't begin to dismantle unjust discriminatory systems then we will consistently have violent eruptions that people respond to with more violence. Systemic and structural violence perpetuates a cycle of violence on all levels of society.

Tarico: Our handed-down cultural and religious traditions contain the concept of chattel, the idea that some people (and other species) exist for the benefit of others. Slavery is an extreme example of this. But even beyond overt slavery, you and I both write about how the residual of this concept continues to ripple down in our society.

Brown Douglas: When we talk about American slavery we have to talk about chattel slavery. Chattel doesn't mean simply that one person serves another, it means that one belongs to another. Black people were property. They were never meant to own their own labor or their own bodies. While I truly appreciate the way that female and black bodies intersect, the black body *came to this country as property.* When we talk about chattel in U.S. history, the only people who were considered nonhuman were those of African descent.

Tarico: Yes! Mercifully, by the time this country was founded, outright ownership of women was no longer the overt norm. In the Old Testament, women were literally governed by property law rather than personhood rights. A man, a father, essentially sold his daughter to another man to be a wife or slave. She was a valuable reproductive technology that produced economically valuable offspring that also belonged to the patriarch, who could beat or sell them or send them into war or even sacrifice them.

The notion of women as fully autonomous persons rather than property has taken centuries to emerge. During the American colonial era, single women could own real estate and other assets, but thanks to a legal concept called coverture, married women couldn't. "All men are created equal" really meant *men,* well, men who were white. A woman couldn't get a credit card on her own in the U.S. until 1974! When I was young, a woman couldn't obtain birth control without her husband's permission because her reproductive capacity belonged to him. Women in the South, including black women, have been of the last to get rights to control their own property and bodies. But that is a long way from literally being bought and sold in chains, as in the slave trade!

So this idea of people owning people is changing. But, damn, the process is slow. From your point of view, where do you see the residual of chattel culture in America today?

Brown Douglas: What we see is that some people have certain privileges because of who they are while other people are penalized because of who they are. Clearly the white male heterosexual body is the most privileged body and in as much as you lose one of those attributes you lose certain privileges. In your person you have less freedom, less right to the wages of freedom in your body. That is what we are struggling through in this country.

Tarico: The rape culture that we are struggling with on college campuses is rooted in the idea that men are entitled to women's bodies. Economic exploitation is rooted in the idea that might makes right, that powerful people have a right to exploit and consume the time, energy, productive capacity and reproductive capacity of the less powerful. The same could be said about environmental exploitation, that those who are most powerful have the right to exploit, consume, and take what they can; that other beings and their desires are secondary, if they matter at all.

As a theologian, you say that one way chattel culture gets justified is via "natural law" theology. What is that?

Brown Douglas: Natural law theology is a way of sanctifying this hierarchy of exploitation. It suggests that this wasn't just a human creation, but divine law. This was the way God designed things to be. For example, the whole idea was that God created black people as slaves not as full human beings. Slavery was legitimated specifically through Christianity.

Tarico: What are some echoes of natural law theology in the way that conservatives think today? How does it get translated into the modern language of the Religious Right?

Brown Douglas: We know that the discourse around women has been that God created women to serve men and to reproduce. Women have had to fight that battle for years, and continue to fight the battle that they were indeed not created to be subservient to men or to be reproductive machines. That is about natural law. The other way you see it is that marriage is supposed to be between a man and a woman—that's God's law according to various religious communities. Those are ways that we see "natural law" functioning in our culture today.

In racial relations, if one scanned some of the white supremacy rhetoric you see that too. Historically it is part of the rhetoric of the Klan. Today most people don't argue that in polite conversation, but we see it all the time when we place this religious canopy over discrimination. We sanctify discriminatory patterns. *If God wanted men and women to be equal, God would have created women to be different—not to be the bearers of children.* Or, *God created Adam and Eve not Adam and Steve.* Those are remnants of natural law. It functions in those places where people attempt to elevate social constructs and human laws so that they seem as if they are divine laws.

Tarico: I write mostly about women—about reproductive freedom and empowerment, and in our fight to create a new norm of chosen childbearing, this notion of women as chattel is hugely problematic. Specific verses from the Bible get cited to justify the GOP's assault on women. "Women will be saved through childbearing," for example. In the sphere of racial relations and justice, this notion of human chattel also gets tied in with sexuality—how black sexuality is seen, why blacks are seen as dangerous.

Brown Douglas: One thing that you'll notice is that marginalized oppressed people often are sexualized by the dominant narrative. You see that with LGBT people—the rhetoric is that they are indiscriminately promiscuous—as

with black people and women. A couple of traditional cultural narratives come together here. In the conservative religious mindset, the only good sex is procreative sex. If you suggest that people are engaging in sexual activity for non-procreative reasons that's sinful and lustful—that's the Apostle Paul.

On top of that is this oppression narrative in which identity and sexuality get bound together. The late French philosopher Michel Foucault asked, Why is it that sexuality has become so significant in Western society that it becomes the source not just of reproduction but of truth? Why has it become the way the way people think of themselves and others? Foucalt suggests that it is because sexuality is where the body and identity come together. If you can control the sexuality of a group of people, then you can control that Women are said to be driven by their passions and women's sexuality has to be controlled, and is only acceptable if it's procreative, which means men are controlling it. Sexualizing black people allowed black women to be used as breeders. It became a rationale for a black man to be lynched—because he was preying on white women. This is one way we have an overlap in how all women and black men are perceived as well as other marginalized groups. I wrote a book, *Sexuality and the Black Church*, in which I discuss this in more depth.

Tarico: How does this all play into a presumption of guilt? At the opening to your chapter on the black body, you echo L. Z. Granderson's question, *Why are black murder victims put on trial?* Why *are* black murder victims put on trial?

Brown Douglas: Black people don't have the presumption of innocence. The concept of black people as chattel, that black people are not meant to occupy a free space and are dangerous when doing so, has been transformed into a notion of black people as criminal. If a black person has been accused of something then people assume that he or she is probably guilty, and our media representations of black people continue to reinforce this in the collective unconscious. There have been various studies which reveal that people have visceral automatic reactions to black bodies in which they see them as threatening. In one study police officers who were shown pictures of white and black men with and without guns were more likely to perceive that a black male had a gun even when he didn't and to miss a gun in the hands of a white male even when he had one. The stereotypes of the criminal black male and the angry black woman lead to the presumption of guilt.

Tarico: I write largely for an audience of non-theists and people who describe themselves as former Christians. Many of them look at the black community's response to an incident like the mass murder in Charleston and say, *I don't get it. How can so many Black people be Christian when Christianity has been such a tool of racial oppression against blacks? How can oppressed racial minorities embrace a sacred text that talks about chosen people and privileged blood lines?* What do you say to that?

Brown Douglas: That is the very question that compelled another book of mine called, *What's Faith Got to Do with It?* In the Black Christian tradition, the first time that black people encountered God was not through their slaveholders. They knew God in freedom, as they encountered God through their African traditional religions. As black Christianity emerged during slavery, it emerged from an entirely different place than white Christianity. Black people understood that they were meant to be free, so God stood for freedom. Throughout history you see a black critique of White Christianity. The sum of the critique is this: If Christianity is used to oppress another that's not Christianity. What I ask is, How can one embrace a culture of oppression and claim to be Christian?

Tarico: What do you say to your own son about all of this?

Brown Douglas: I always told my son every morning as he was growing up, *There is no one greater than you but God and you are sacred.* I've always tried to teach him that he is not greater than anyone, that we are equal. God created us all, and the very breath we breathe comes from God—that is what makes us all sacred. Even when someone treats you as less than human, you must still affirm their humanity. I am working overtime these last two years to help him understand that, yes, this nation is racist and people do racist things but not all people are like that. And so, I try to teach him to respect people as he would respect himself, to affirm his humanity and to finds ways to affirm that of others. Most of all, I try to teach him not to get trapped in the cycle of hate because in the end, hate is self-destructive.

VALERIE TARICO is a psychologist and writer in Seattle, Washington, founder of Wisdom Commons, and writer of two books and a number of articles.

EXPLORING THE ISSUE

Has America Made Substantial Progress in the Rights of Blacks?

Critical Thinking and Reflection

1. What criteria should a scholar use to judge a social movement's success?
2. What are the advantages and disadvantages of movement leaders setting movement goals higher than it is possible to achieve?
3. Can civil rights equity be legislated? Can integration be legislated? If integration can be legislated in the economy, can it also be legislated in the churches?
4. Does complete integration require that intermarriages become as common as intramarriages?
5. Are black self-images on a par with white self-images? If not, why?
6. Consider the power of symbols in national life.
7. The election of Obama had the potential to unite our country racially and ethnically. Why are we more divided than ever?

Is There Common Ground?

Both authors agree that much progress has been made in the civil rights of blacks. The main difference in their opinions regards how far this country has come and how far it has yet to go. America is somewhere between Jim Crow and post-racialism. According to Rothman, America is closer to King's mountaintop than Jim Crow. It comes down to what you emphasize: half empty or half full. I went to Princeton University in 1953 and there was only one black in my class. In fact the first African American undergraduate to enter Princeton during peacetime arrived only 6 years earlier. According to an article in the *Princeton Alumni Weekly* in 2010, "The percentage of minority students—defined by Princeton University as Asian-Americans, African-Americans, Hispanics, Native Americans, and those who self-identify as multiracial—make up 37 percent of students in the Class of 2013. Asian-American students are the largest ethnic minority in the freshman class (17.7 percent), followed by African-Americans (7.3 percent), Hispanics (6.8 percent), and Native Americans (0.5 percent). In recent years the University has allowed students to identify themselves as multiracial, and more than 5 percent of freshmen do so." Check the history of your college or employer and you will see a dramatic story. The story of your neighborhood will probably also involve racial changes but in several different directions. The story of your church or other religious body will probably show the least change, and that is a story in itself. From what has happened around you, how much do you think America has moved toward a post-racial society?

Additional Resources

The following books bitterly proclaim that the treatment of blacks is definitely unfair: Ellen Berrey, *The Enigma of Diversity: The Language of Race and the Limits of Racial Justice* (The University of Chicago Press, 2015); Eduardo Bonilla-Silva, *Racism Without Racists: Color-Blind Racism and the Persistence of Racial Inequality in America,* 4th ed. (Rowman & Littlefield, 2014); John D. Foster, *White Race Discourse: Preserving Racial Privilege in a Post-Racial Society* (Lexington Books, 2013); Daria Roithmayr, *Reproducing Racism: How Everyday Choices Lock in White Advantage* (New York University Press, 2014); Gregory S. Parks and Matthew W. Hughey, eds., *12 Angry Men: True Stories of Being a Black Man in America Today* (New Press, 2010); Michael C. Dawson, *Not in Our Lifetimes: The Future of Black Politics* (University of Chicago Press, 2011); Joe R. Feagan, *Racist America: Roots, Current Realities, and Future Reparations* (Routledge, 2010); and Roy H. Kaplan, *The Myth of Post-Racial America: Searching for Equality in the Age of Materialism* (Rowman & Littlefield Education, 2011).

The historical perspective is presented in Greta De Jong, *Invisible Enemy: The African American Freedom Struggle After 1965* (Wiley-Blackwell, 2010); and Cynthia Griggs Fleming, *Yes We Did?: From King's Dream to Obama's Promise* (University of Kentucky Press, 2009). *The Obamas and a (Post) Racial America?* edited by Gregory S. Parks and

Matthew W. Highey (Oxford University Press, 2011) focuses on the role of the Obamas in altering racial relations.

This debate connects strongly with black politics, which is the focus of several books including Desmond S. King, *Still a House Divided: Race and Politics in Obama's America* (Princeton University Press, 2011); Theodore James Davis, *Black Politics Today: The Era of Socioeconomic Transition* (Routledge, 2012); and the broader issue of racism is analyzed in George Lipsitz, *How Racism Takes Place* (Temple University Press, 2011) and Roy L. Brooks, *Racial Justice in the Age of Obama* (Princeton University Press, 2009).

Internet References . . .

Sociology—Study Sociology Online

http://edu.learnsoc.org/

Sociology Web Resources

www.mhhe.com/socscience/sociology
/resources/index.htm

Sociosite

www.topsite.com/goto/sociosite.net

Socioweb

www.topsite.com/goto/socioweb.com

Selected, Edited, and with Issue Framing Material by:
Kurt Finsterbusch, *University of Maryland, College Park*

ISSUE

Has Gender Equality Come a Long Way?

YES: Ronald Brownstein, from "Poll: American Men Embracing Gender Equality," *National Journal* (2015)

NO: Leisa Peterson, from "Who Am I to Be Financially Feminist? (A Guide for Female Entrepreneurs)," *Huffington Post* (2015)

Learning Outcomes

After reading this issue, you will be able to:

- Discuss the changes in men's attitudes toward partnership marriages.
- Identify several widespread attitudes that still disadvantage women.
- Explain why women earn less money than men, or at least know the main theories that explain these differences.
- Understand the various possible meanings of "equal pay" and understand the difficulties of legislating equal pay for comparable work.
- Debate the pros and cons of women's work/family choices.
- Understand the motives that underlie women's work/family choices.

ISSUE SUMMARY

YES: Ronald Brownstein, Atlantic Media's editorial director for strategic partnerships, reports on surprising findings of a recent poll that details major changes in gender attitudes of males and income, racial, and ethnic groups. "The survey suggests that men from all rungs on the economic and social ladder were open to the 'partnership of equals.'"

NO: Leisa Peterson, money mindfulness expert and founder, WealthClinic, points out the many ways that she and other women today are discriminated against. She uses statistics and comparative studies to prove her thesis that women are worse off in several ways.

Gender equality is a complex issue with many aspects. Here we first focus on wage inequality. According to the 2012 *Statistical Abstract,* the median income of full-time women workers was 71.8 percent of median income of full-time men workers. This is a troubling fact that needs to be explained. It calls into question the success of the feminist movement. It calls into question the effectiveness of the antidiscrimination laws and their enforcement. It may not be the result of discrimination but may indicate that women are choosing to limit their participation in the labor force to less demanding and less stressful jobs. It may be driven by the same forces that lead to the "opting out"

phenomena. Another possibility is that the discrimination against women that still exists makes women want to reduce their participation in the labor force.

Most commentators approach this issue in agreement on several basic issues. First, discrimination is wrong. Equal pay for equal work has been a feminist demand from the beginning and very few of either gender would argue against this principle today. Second, both work and family are important to most adults. Third, most married persons experience tension between work and family. Fourth, the "traditional" family value system resulted in less tension between work and family than today's value system. Traditionally, the husband was the provider and the wife was the homemaker. Today, both tend to be providers and active parents. In spite of these agreements, commentators today provide very different judgments about the gender wage gap and other gender inequality issues. The argument starts with the meaning of equal work. Feminists argue that it should include equal pay for comparable work, but many object to this standard. Many argue that the market should determine what different occupations should be paid. The Equal Pay Act states, "Employers may not pay unequal wages to men and women who perform jobs that require substantially equal skill, effort, and responsibility, and that are performed under similar working conditions within the same establishment." It therefore proposes the comparable work rule. It also states, "Pay differentials are permitted when they are based on seniority, merit, quantity or quality of production, or a factor other than sex." This provision provides the grounds for more definitional debates. Another issue is how willing should the employer be to facilitate various special considerations that wives might need to accommodate her family role such as a greater use of sick days or unavailability for out-of-town travel? So what is fair? This is a matter of values, not science.

The following articles address the attitudes of men and women toward the changing reality around gender issues. Brownstein uses a survey to show that a surprising number of white, black, and Latino men have positive views of greater gender equality at and in the office. Peterson uses statistics, personal experience, and comparative studies to show many attitudes and behaviors remain very prejudiced against women.

YES ↵

Ronald Brownstein

Poll: American Men Embracing Gender Equality

The gender revolution has met the demographic revolution.

A new survey of men's attitudes toward women, family, and relations between the sexes has found much more similarity than difference among the perspectives of whites, African-Americans, Hispanics, and other minorities.

That convergence suggests that changes in family and gender dynamics are permeating minority and working-class communities that many researchers have long assumed held more culturally traditional or conservative views about the role of women.

The poll, conducted by the Democratic polling firm Hart Research Associates for The Shriver Report, founded by Maria Shriver, explored men's attitudes about an unusually wide range of issues related to gender roles in society. In the survey, the samples of African-American and Hispanic men were too small to allow for statistically valid results for each of those groups individually. But The Shriver Report provided Next America with combined results among minorities that did provide a statistically valid sample to compare with whites; it also provided statistically valid results among whites with and without four-year college degrees.

Many key questions in the survey underscored how much all of those groups have converged around a new consensus on gender relations. That agreement offered a stark contrast to the routine chasms in attitudes between whites and minorities, and often between college and noncollege whites, on many political questions. "In every community, women have gone out and are working and very often they are making more than their husbands or their partners," Shriver said in an interview. "I think people assume that Latinos and African Americans are more culturally conservative on certain issues. But I think the 21st-century man, as we are calling him, is very different from five, six, nine years ago [in all racial communities]."

Put another way, the survey suggests that men from all rungs on the economic and social ladder were open to the "partnership of equals" that is often assumed to thrive most in white-collar and upper middle-class families where both spouses earn substantial incomes.

One survey question, for instance, asked men to rate how comfortable they would be in a series of potential life experiences. Responding to those questions, 85 percent of white men and 82 percent of minority men said they would be comfortable with a wife or partner who worked outside the home; 74 percent of white men and 71 percent of minority men said they would be comfortable having a woman as a boss; and 77 percent of white men and 75 percent of minority men said they would be comfortable with a partner or spouse who earned more than they did.

About an equal, though substantially smaller, share of white (at 46 percent) and nonwhite men (at 40 percent) also said they were comfortable with the prospect of "being a stay at home dad and not working outside of the home to focus on raising a child." Similarly small percentages of white (38 percent) and minority men (37 percent) agreed that they feel "uncomfortable around homosexual men."

Although the samples were too small for detailed analysis, the results showed very small differences between African Americans and Hispanics on all of those questions (except that Hispanics were less likely than African Americans or whites to say they were uncomfortable around gay men). The variation on these questions was also modest among whites with and without a four-year college degree (though noncollege white men were notably less comfortable about the prospect of working for a woman).

The poll also found more agreement than disagreement across racial lines on the qualities men said they wanted in a wife or partner. Asked to identify the top two or three qualities they would want in a partner, similar shares of white and minority men picked "intelligent" (75 percent white, 64 percent minority); "sweet" (32 vs. 37); "nurturing" (28 vs. 24); "principled"

(26 vs. 27); and "homemaker" (14 vs. 14). Wider differences emerged in some other areas. Whites were more likely to emphasize "attractive" (49 percent vs. 35 percent among minorities), while minority men were more likely to stress "strong" (36 minority vs. 24 white) and "independent" (40 minority vs. 31 white). Black and Hispanic men differed little on these issues, too, though the former put more emphasis on "strong" and the latter more on "sweet."

White and minority men also mostly converged in the qualities they said they would prize in a daughter—though in each case, those qualities diverged in revealing ways from their priorities in a spouse or partner. In thinking about a daughter, both white and minority men put top priority on intelligence (78 percent among whites, 87 percent among nonwhites), independence (66 white, 65 minority), and strength (47 white, 49 minority). White men put greater emphasis on "principled" (40 percent vs. 24 percent for minorities), while minorities put relatively more stress on "sweet" (26 percent for minorities vs. 16 percent for whites).

Jeff Horwitt, who directed the survey for Hart Research Associates, noted that both white and minority men mostly prized qualities in a daughter that correlate with success in the workplace. "Reading the survey as a whole," Horwitt wrote last week in *The Wall Street Journal*, "the qualities that men want most in a daughter—intelligent, independent, strong, and principled—are the qualities that help women thrive in the workplace." In the interview, Shriver summed up the contrast in attitudes more archly: "Men are saying they don't want their daughters to be beholden to a guy like them."

White and minority men mostly agreed as well on a question that asked them to define "what . . . it means to be a strong man in today's world." About one-fifth of both groups picked providing financially for their families or "having the confidence to be free to follow your own path." Another one-in-nine whites and about one-in-six minorities selected "having the emotional strength to deal with stressful situations." The largest group among both whites (at 49 percent) and nonwhites (at 39 percent) said the most important way to demonstrate strength today was "having a strong personal character and sense of integrity." College and noncollege white men again differed relatively, except that the former placed greater emphasis on personal character. Hispanics tilted relatively more toward emotional strength while African Americans put greater stress on character.

Two summary questions in the survey also produced mostly convergence across racial lines. Asked about the difficulty of being a man today compared to "your father's generation," the two groups almost completely agreed on whether it was harder (45 percent among both whites and minorities), easier (19 whites and 22 nonwhites), or about the same (36 whites vs. 33 nonwhite).

Likewise, whites and minorities varied only modestly when the poll asked men whether it was "more important to you as a man" to "provide" for one's family and spouse or partner, or to "be present" for them. Each group divided about in half: 47 percent of whites and 45 percent of nonwhites said it was more important to provide, while 53 percent of the former and 55 percent of the latter said it was more important to "be present."

African Americans tilted more toward providing, while Hispanics edged more toward "being present"; noncollege whites were also much more likely than their college-educated counterparts to stress providing. For both African Americans and noncollege whites, the relative emphasis on providing may reflect the difficulty each group has faced doing so in the modern economy.

Still, the overall picture in all racial communities was that men are mostly accepting, if sometimes confused, about women's growing financial independence and prominence in the workplace and are seeking ways to engage with their partners and families as something other than just emotionally distant economic providers. "The men know that women have changed the dynamic in the home and in the workplace," Shriver said. "They are struggling to figure out what it means for them overall . . . , [but] men have caught up with the change much more than they are given credit for."

The survey polled 818 adult men from April 10 through 13; it was conducted online, which most analysts do not consider as accurate as polls conducted through landline and cell phones. But in their release, the sponsors argue that "a self-administered online survey is particularly useful to explore potentially controversial and sensitive topics such as attitudes about gender and sex."

RONALD BROWNSTEIN, Atlantic media's editorial director for strategic partnerships and is in charge of long-term editorial strategy. He also writes for the *National Journal*, *Quartz*, and *The Atlantic*.

Leisa Peterson  **NO**

Who Am I to Be Financially Feminist? (A Guide for Female Entrepreneurs)

Feminists are given a bad rap. When I was growing up, women who wanted to excel in the workforce were demonized as anti-family, bra burning egoists. Women have made many inroads since then but even so, women who seek equal rights are still degraded as "feminazis" by others and even disparaged by our misguided selves (you've seen the "I am not a feminist" movement?).

Sadly, feminism exists for a reason. Gender inequality is one of the most persistent human rights violations of our time, and in the U.S. it isn't getting any better. In fact, it's getting worse. According to a recent report released by the World Economic Forum, the U.S. ranks 17th among 22 industrialized nations in labor force participation for women. This is in stark comparison to our nation's number six rank in the 1990s.

The $.77 a white female earns in comparison to every $1.00 a white male earns equates to a lifetime loss in gross income of about $1.2 million for a college graduate and $2 million for a professional school graduate. And it is even worse for black and Latina women.

But I'm not a sociologist. I'm a wealth coach. So why do I care about the current state of the feminist movement?

Here's why: Because how women are perceived in the workplace has a direct correlation with how equally we're compensated—even when we run our own businesses.

That's right. Even when we seek to escape the old boys club and strike out on our own, women still often make less than our male counterparts.

I worked in the corporate world—in a male-dominated field—for 23 years. I know from first-hand experience that it can feel like women have to be more manly to gain success. That's why, with hopes of being rewarded for their skills, so many promising female corporate employees end up trying to be someone they're not. Instead, what often happens is women end up dealing with the double standards that exist for behaviors, unfair judgments, and ruthless competition from colleagues of both genders.

According to a 2012 *Harvard Business Review* survey of 7,280 leaders, even though women were often rated as being better overall leaders than their male counterparts, many women in leadership positions don't feel their appointments are safe. There is constant pressure to perform mistake-free and, because many feel their positions are vulnerable, women tend to take feedback to heart.

When women opt out of their corporate environments, those feelings don't get left behind with the no-longer-needed hanging file folders. Instead, they get packed in to who they are, and they carry them, even when setting out on a new entrepreneurial venture.

Some of the most prevalent concerns my female clients come to me with stem from what I see as a chronic problem: We don't feel our own value and so we come to doubt our self worth.

To get grounded and begin to recover from these limiting beliefs, I ask my female entrepreneurial clients to engage in a powerful mini meditation. You, too, can do it, right from wherever you are. First, close your eyes for a moment and then take in a nice, deep breath. Plant your feet firmly on the ground and then take one more really deep breath to release any tension you are holding on to. Then, ask yourself how many times you have asked yourself the following questions:

- Who am I to question things that have been done the same way forever?
- Who am I to double, triple, or quadruple my fees?
- Who am I to run a successful company that grosses multiple millions of dollars?
- Who am I to follow my passion and make money doing it?

What else have you said to yourself? Fill in your own blank—Who am I to. . . . And add that in to the meditation.

Begin to notice the limiting beliefs that hold you back. Then, consider what might happen if you shifted your thoughts to empowering beliefs that focus on the importance and value you bring to the world.

I've done this work myself and the end result is powerfully transformative.

From completing this work, clients I've coached have:

- Noticed new life possibilities
- Been heard more by others
- Seen ideas gain traction and take off
- Gained confidence in the contributions they offer to clients and the world
- Learned to value the services they provide and set higher client rates

This work doesn't just help us in our professional lives. When we start to show up in a bigger way, we can help our families and communities in bigger ways. We can provide greater financial support by paying our kids' tuition, for example, or by writing large checks to further causes we care about.

For today's financial feminists, it's time to shift away from a mindset limited by who we are not—and instead move toward a self-image that's shaped by who we really are.

LEISA PETERSON is a Money Mindfulness Expert and Founder of the WealthClinic. Previously she had many years as an executive and financial manager.

EXPLORING THE ISSUE

Has Gender Equality Come a Long Way?

Critical Thinking and Reflection

1. How can any inequality be justified? Does the gender wage gap fit under one of these justifications of inequality?
2. Why are current values about gender roles better than traditional values which were more patriarchal?
3. Are values entirely relative or are there logical standards that can justify some values and actions and condemn other values and actions? God can make some values absolute but can secular reasoning also make some values superior to others?
4. What obligations do women have? What obligations do men have? Why do women have more obligations to childrearing and housework than men? Do men have more obligations to work outside the home than women, and if so, why?
5. What work/family arrangements best serve the general good (good of society)?

Is There Common Ground?

Equality is a commonly held value in America. Very few would argue against different groups getting equal treatment including equal pay for equal work. That agreement breaks down when the equality formula is equal pay for comparable work. Many think that "comparable" is used politically and often is unfair. There is also general agreement that disadvantaged people should be given some assistance such as Head Start to make their competition with advantaged people more fair. There is vehement disagreement, however, over how much assistance is fair. Some complain that current policies are reverse discrimination. Another issue is what is fair in the gender relations in the home. Here traditional values make the man the head of the home, but these values are receding. Now each married couple must work out their own arrangement. There usually is conflict in this process, but the degree of agreement is increasing.

Another area of agreement in America is that women are on a par with men as having moral value. In some societies, women are the property of their husband or father and have very few rights. Here they have rights and supposedly equal value. Nevertheless, in the 1950s, they did not have equal rights in the workplace and few paid attention. As women went to college in large numbers and young people spoke out against the war, traditions, authorities, and injustices in the 1960s, a new women's movement developed that changed the political

landscape. Equal treatment in the workplace became a hot issue with no strong moral arguments against it. The progress of women has been impressive except for the "glass ceiling" that limited women's promotions at the highest levels. Now this is part of the present debate about the justice or injustice of the gender wage gap. A similar situation is occurring on the home front.

Additional Resources

Gender discrimination has been greatly reduced in the last several decades, but it still remains. Several works that research this problem include Cecilia L. Ridgeway, *Framed by Gender: How Gender Inequality Persists in the Modern World* (Oxford University Press, 2011); Robert L. Kaufman, *Race, Gender, and the Labor Market: Inequalities at Work* (Lynne Rienner Publishers, 2010); Sarah Jane, "White Men Are Not in Decline," *The Atlantic*, December 20, 2012; Lis W. Wiehl, *The 51% Minority: How Women Still Are Not Equal and What You Can Do About It* (Ballantine Books, 2007); Deborah L. Rhode, *What Women Want: An Agenda for the Women's Movement* (Oxford University Press, 2014); Philip Cohen, "America Is Still a Patriarchy," *The Atlantic*, November 19, 2012; Christina Hoff Sommers, "The Boys at the Back," *New York Times*, February 2, 2013; John Spritzler, "A Misunderstanding About "Patriarchy;" www.NewDemocracyWorld, May 27, 2013; Ariel Smilowitz, "For U.S. Women, Inequality Takes Many Forms," *Huffington Post*, April 14, 2015.

Internet References . . .

Sociology: Sociology—Study Sociology Online

http://edu.learnsoc.org/

Sociology Web Resources

www.mhhe.com/socscience/sociology/resources/index.htm

Sociosite

www.topsite.com/goto/sociosite.net

Socioweb

www.topsite.com/goto/socioweb.com

Unit 4

UNIT

Political Economy and Institutions

*W*hat is the proper role of government in the economy? Some believe that the government must correct for the many failures of the market, while others think that the government usually complicates the workings of the free market and reduces its effectiveness.

Selected, Edited, and with Issue Framing Material by:
Kurt Finsterbusch, *University of Maryland, College Park*

ISSUE

Is Government Dominated by Big Business?

YES: G. William Domhoff, from "Is the Corporate Elite Fractured, or Is There Continuing Corporate Dominance? Two Contrasting Views." *Class, Race and Corporate Power* (2015)

NO: Mark S. Mizruchi, from "The Fracturing of the American Corporate Elite," Harvard University Press (2013)

Learning Outcomes

After reading this issue, you will be able to:

- Know which groups have been identified as the ones with the greatest influence over the U.S. government and the main evidence supporting the thesis of their inordinate influence.
- Understand the tactics that are used to influence government policies and the administration of these policies.
- Understand the concept of negative power and use it to explain how minority groups can stop policies that are perceived as likely to adversely affect them.
- Identify the limits to the power of big corporations in influencing government policies.
- Analyze the recent bank bailout and its aftermath on the one hand and the stimulus package to generate jobs on the other. Comment on the rebound of the stock market (although still fragile) and the continued high unemployment.
- Analyze the consequences of the current structure of power in America.

ISSUE SUMMARY

YES: Political sociologist G. William Domhoff presents two theories about who rules America. One is that the corporate elite is fractured and no longer stays united enough to rule America. The second is that the corporate elite is united enough to rule America. He argues for the second view.

NO: Mark S. Mizruchi, professor of sociology at Michigan University, argues the first view, that the corporate elite is fractured to the point that it does not rule America but uses its influence for the specific interests of individual corporations. This contributes to declining effectiveness of the American polity.

Since the framing of the U.S. Constitution in 1787, there have been periodic charges that America is unduly influenced by wealthy financial interests. Richard Henry Lee, a signer of the Declaration of Independence, spoke for many Anti-Federalists (those who opposed ratification of the Constitution) when he warned that the proposed charter shifted power away from the people and into the hands of the "aristocrats" and "moneyites."

Before the Civil War, Jacksonian Democrats denounced the eastern merchants and bankers who, they charged, were usurping the power of the people. After the Civil War, a number of radical parties and movements revived this theme of antielitism. The ferment—which was brought about by the rise of industrial monopolies, government corruption, and economic hardship for western farmers—culminated in the founding of the People's Party at the beginning of the 1890s. The Populists, as they were more commonly called, wanted economic and political reforms aimed at transferring power away from the rich and back to "the plain people."

By the early 1900s, the People's Party had disintegrated, but many writers and activists have continued to echo the Populists' central thesis: that the U.S. democratic political system is in fact dominated by business elites. Yet the thesis has not gone unchallenged. During the 1950s and the early 1960s, many social scientists subscribed to the pluralist view of America.

Pluralists argue that because there are many influential elites in America, each group is limited to some extent by the others. There are some groups, like the business elites, that are more powerful than their opponents, but even the more powerful groups are denied their objectives at times. Labor groups are often opposed to business groups; conservative interests challenge liberal interests, and vice versa; and organized civil libertarians sometimes fight with groups that seek government-imposed bans on pornography or groups that demand tougher criminal laws. No single group, the pluralists argue, can dominate the political system.

Pluralists readily acknowledge that American government is not democratic in the full sense of the word; it is not driven by the majority. But neither, they insist, is it run by a conspiratorial "power elite." In the pluralist view, the closest description of the American form of government would be neither majority rule nor minority rule but minorities rule. (Note that in this context, "minorities" does not necessarily refer to race or ethnicity but to any organized group of people with something in common—including race, religion, or economic interests—not constituting a majority of the population.) Each organized minority enjoys some degree of power in the making of public policy. In extreme cases, when a minority feels threatened, its power may take a negative form: the power to derail policy. When the majority—or, more accurately, a coalition of other minorities—attempts to pass a measure that threatens the vital interests of an organized minority, that group may use its power to obstruct their efforts. (Often cited in this connection is the use of the Senate filibuster, which is the practice of using tactics during the legislative process that cause extreme delays or prevent action, thus enabling a group to "talk to death" a bill that threatens its vital interests.) But in the pluralist view, negative power is not the only driving force: When minorities work together and reach consensus on certain issues, they can institute new laws and policy initiatives that enjoy broad public support. Pluralism, although capable of producing temporary gridlock, ultimately leads to compromise, consensus, and moderation.

Critics of pluralism argue that pluralism is an idealized depiction of a political system that is in the grip of powerful elite groups. Critics fault pluralist theory for failing to recognize the extent to which big business dominates the policy-making process. In the selections that follow, G. William Domhoff supports the power elite view, acknowledges some effects of fracturing, but argues that the power elite is united enough to rule. Mark S. Mizruchi, in opposition, argues that the power elite did rule around 1980 but their fracturing since then has greatly lessened their control.

YES

G. William Domhoff

Is the Corporate Elite Fractured, or Is There Continuing Corporate Dominance? Two Contrasting Views

Introduction

This article compares two recent analyses of continuity and change in the American power structure since 1900, with a focus on the postwar decades and the years between 1990 and 2010. The first analysis defines the "corporate elite" as a subset of top executives and directors in the Fortune 1000, which was unified, moderate, and pragmatic in the postwar era. It further claims that the corporate elite has been fracturing and fragmenting in recent decades due to its decisive triumphs in the 1970s and 1980s, which made cohesion less necessary. Although corporations remain the most powerful organizations in the United States, their leaders are too divided and concerned with their own companies to contribute to the common good, as they once did. The loss of a united and moderate corporate elite is a "significant source of the current crisis in American democracy and a major cause of the predicament in which the twenty-first century United States finds itself."

The alternative view, called corporate-dominance theory in some books and in this article, claims that the United States continues to be dominated by the owners and top-level executives in corporations, banks, agri-businesses, and commercial real estate.[1] "Domination" is defined as "the institutionalized outcome of great distributive power," which is in turn defined as the ability "to establish the organizations, rules, and customs through which everyday life is conducted." Methodologically, great distributive power is understood as an underlying "trait" or "property" of a collectivity called the "corporate community," which includes all the financial companies and other corporations that are linked by common ownership or interlocking directorates. Research is carried out by means of a series of if-then statements using as many independent power indicators as possible. These power indicators include various benefit distributions (e.g., the wealth and income distributions), overrepresentation in

government positions, and success in specific policy and legislative arguments.

In this theory, corporate domination is maintained through a leadership group called "the power elite," defined as those people who serve as directors or trustees in profit and nonprofit institutions controlled by the corporate community. This control is exercised through stock ownership, financial support, involvement on the board of directors, or some combination of these factors. The power elite has moderately conservative and ultra-conservative policy leanings within it, as indexed by the policy preferences expressed by specific organizations; however, some large corporations have directorships in both moderate and ultraconservative policy-discussion organizations. This view was developed on the basis of the systematic reading of business magazines by C. Wright Mills, not on the basis of claims about corporate liberals by one subset of 1960s historians.

According to the fractured-elite analysis, three factors contributed to the corporate elite's cohesion and moderation in the post–World War II era that stretched from the mid-1940s to the mid-1970s, at which point the corporate elite made a more conservative turn: (1) an activist federal government that was able to regulate the economy to maintain high levels of employment and an adequate safety net; (2) the challenges from a strong union movement, which was able to negotiate a capital-labor accord that led to higher wages, greater social benefits, and increasing income equality; and (3) a handful of large commercial banks, whose boards of directors were able to create cohesion among various types of corporations because of their network centrality, depth of information, and wider business outlook.

On the other hand, the corporate-dominance view argues that common interests, common opponents (not just unions), social interactions in exclusive settings, and meetings within policy-discussion groups lead to both social and policy cohesion, with social cohesion contributing to the ability to create policy cohesion. Further, there never was a capital-labor accord because corporations never stopped trying to eliminate unions, and the federal government was constrained on all but a few pieces of employment and social-benefits legislation in the postwar era by the corporate community in general. This corporate constraint was exercised in good part through its electoral support for, and close ties to, the conservative coalition in Congress, which consisted of a majority of Southern Democrats and a majority of Republicans voting against a majority of non-Southern Democrats from the late 1930s to the mid-1990s.

In addition, corporate-dominance theory claims that a corporate-supported policyplanning network formulated and lobbied for the many pro-corporate government policies that were implemented between 1910 and 2010, not the boards of directors of banks. According to this perspective, the power elite is at least as unified and powerful since 1980 as in the past, as indexed by the decline in union density, the increasing concentration of the income distribution, and most important of all in terms of this article, their ability to achieve their policy goals—eliminate the remaining union presence, extend international trade and continue the movement of production to low-wage countries when useful, reduce their personal income taxes and corporate taxes, and limit government programs for retirees and low-income workers.

The fractured-elite perspective is presented in a recent book, one that provides far more than a theoretical analysis. It is a call to the corporate elite by its author, sociologist Mark Mizruchi, "to save the world as we know it," which is claimed to be necessary because there is not enough time remaining to create a strong social movement to force the corporate elite to make the needed changes. The first page of the Preface praises the corporate elite for its earlier "moderate and pragmatic approach that helped the society to prosper, both economically and politically," but criticizes it for an "abdication of responsibility" since the 1980s. It chastises the corporate leaders for allowing themselves to be "bullied and cowed" by right-wing extremists, and for being "ineffectual" and self-interested. It claims that the corporate elite is "leading us toward the fate of the earlier Roman, Dutch, and Habsburg Spanish Empires" by "starving the treasury and accumulating vast resources for itself." Mizruchi's book concludes with the admonition that "It is long past time for its members to exercise some enlightened self-interest in the present."

On the other hand, there are few or no criticisms of corporate leaders in the books that present the corporate-dominance perspective. Instead, these books are concerned with understanding the nature and operation of power within the overall social structure, not only with the impact of the power elite on American society. To the degree that there are criticisms in the work that presents the corporate-dominance perspective, they are usually if not always based on analytical comparisons of corporate-dominance theory with alternative theories of power.

The analysis in this article follows the outline in the book on the fractured-elite perspective. It begins with a discussion of the rise of corporate moderates between 1900 and the end of World War II because the fractured-elite theory's misunderstandings of this time period lead it to an inadequate characterization of the postwar era. It then shows where and how the fractured-elite account goes wrong in its analysis of the three main topics it addresses for the postwar era: the role of the federal government, the impact of organized labor, and the policy influence of the members of the boards of commercial banks. It then presents evidence that the policy-planning network, which consists of nonprofit foundations, think tanks, and policy-discussion groups, and is financed and directed by corporate leaders, has a more important role in generating policy cohesion around common interests than do banks and their boards of directors. Finally, it examines several key policy issues that arose between 1990 and 2010 to demonstrate that the corporate elite continues to have a collective impact and is not fractured. . . .

The Corporate Moderates and the Postwar Economy

The fractured-elite perspective stresses that the corporate moderates accepted the idea that there had to be more government involvement in the economy than ultraconservatives believed was necessary, including an expansion of Social Security and the use of deficit spending. However, it does not discuss the crucial differences between the way in which the corporate moderates and the liberal-labor alliance wanted to manage the economy, thereby overlooking the class conflict that played out within government on key economic issues. The corporate moderates were for very specific kinds of government involvement, and they largely succeeded in having their way. This point is best demonstrated by the way in which the corporate moderates disagreed with both the ultraconservatives and the liberal-labor alliance on fiscal and monetary policy. In other words, there were acceptable and unacceptable versions of Keynesianism as far as the corporate moderates were concerned. It is on this point that CED policy statements and archival files provide a very good window into the mindset of the corporate moderates as to what they thought was at stake.

Although CED trustees had crafted their own version of Keynesianism by 1943–1944, their views are best articulated in two policy statements that were published after the war ended. The first of the two, *Taxes and the Budget: A Program for Prosperity in a Free Economy* created a halfway position between the ultraconservatives, who wanted balanced budgets, and the liberal and left Keynesians, who wanted to manage future economic downturns through tax cuts for low- and middle-income workers, increases in government spending, and the provision of government jobs. In addition, the liberal Keynesians wanted to head off periods of demand-pull inflation by raising taxes on the well-to-do and cutting government expenditures, which would decrease buying power and at the same time perhaps provide enough of a government surplus to pay down the federal debt. CED trustees opposed all of these liberal-labor policy preferences without at the same time embracing economic orthodoxy about balancing the budget each year.

The CED trustees believed that the ultraconservatives' economic plans would slow the economy, and thereby risk falling profits, depression, and renewed social disruption. However, they did not adopt the liberals' approach because of its emphasis on manipulating the tax rate and using increases and decreases in government spending to heat up or cool down the economy. They feared that repeated economic forecasts of inadequate demand by liberal experts might lead to policies that would increase government expenditures year after year. In the interest of limiting such expenditures as much as possible, the CED suggested its own formula for a "stabilizing budget policy," which called for setting tax rates at a level that would balance the budget over a period of several years while providing for a high level of employment. This new method of balancing the budget over time supposedly would be accomplished by allowing tax receipts to be lower in times of economic recession, thereby leading to automatic deficit spending by the federal government. This is often the form of deficit spending that the fractured-elite account is in effect alluding to when it discusses support for social spending by corporate moderates. Such temporary deficit spending, including higher outlays for unemployment benefits, would then presumably lead to higher tax collections once the economy recovered, thereby making it possible to decrease government debt and to eliminate excess purchasing power.

A year later CED provided a 75-page synthesis of its full program in *Monetary and Fiscal Policy for Greater Economic Stability*. The report rejected the need for annual balanced budgets while at the time criticizing the efforts at demand management by the liberal and left Keynesians. It instead placed strong emphasis on the use of monetary policy to stimulate the economy when necessary, or to reduce demand if inflation increased. The CED policy statement claimed that the Federal Reserve Board and its Open Market Committee could move more quickly than Congress, and that monetary policy has a more immediate impact. Historical studies show that this rationale was adopted by every administration from Eisenhower through Carter, and that the post-1948 Truman Administration was influenced by it as well, perhaps in part because several CED trustees served as directors of regional Fed banks and a CED trustee was appointed to chair the Fed in early 1948.

In principle, the mix of fiscal and monetary policies advocated by the CED did not necessitate any expansion of the traditional functions of government, as CED trustees clearly understood at the time. Moreover, the emphasis on monetary policy meant that the Fed could induce recessions by raising interest rates, which in effect made unemployment for workers, not higher taxes for the corporate owners and executives, the accepted way in which inflation would be controlled. Put another way, even though the corporate moderates were willing to resort to their version of fiscal policy in some circumstances, there was a general corporate preference for monetary policy over fiscal policy 20–25 years before the crisis of the late 1960s and early 1970s unfolded.

Why did Corporate Moderates Abandon Commercial Keynesianism?

According to the fractured-elite perspective, Keynesianism continued to be favored by corporate moderates until at least 1971, but around that time it supposedly began to fail as theory and practice. Corporate-dominance theory argues that both of these assertions are false. The most powerful corporate moderates, the chief executives of large industrial corporations, rapidly abandoned Keynesianism for an emphasis on high interest rates and balanced budgets in the late 1960s and early 1970s, but Keynesian economists, including a prominent CED advisor, had a solid analysis of what happened to the economy in the 1970s. The fractured-elite version begins with the key issue, the demand-pull inflation that began in 1966 due to increased spending for the Vietnam War (but not the War on Poverty, as the fractured-elite analysis claims) and the tightening of labor markets. But it does not mention that President Johnson was hesitant to call for the wage-price controls that were used to control inflation in World War II and the Korean War, and that the conservative coalition stalled on the tax hikes finally called for by President Johnson and many corporate moderates in 1967 in order to cool off demand-pull inflation in commercial-Keynesian fashion.

The inevitable increase in inflation (from 1.0 percent in January 1965, to 4.7 percent in December 1968) had worldwide consequences because it also caused inflation for the country's trading partners. At the same time, the federal government was demanding that they hold on to the dollars they were earning through exports to the United States, which were increasing as a result of the continuing lowering of tariffs negotiated by corporate moderates in the aftermath of their all-out efforts to pass the Trade Expansion Act of 1962. The flood of "Eurodollars" fed into the Eurodollar market that the London financial district and the Bank of England had slowly constructed in the late 1950s and early 1960s to boost the profits of British banks by circumventing the Bretton Woods agreements and any attempts at controlling American banks by the American government. Ironically, the British banks made a considerable portion of their rising profits after 1968 by lending Eurodollars to American banks, which dampened the intended effects of high interest rates on inflation in the United States. In June 1969, six months after Nixon took office, the bankers in charge of his Treasury Department concluded that the administration should deal with a burgeoning balance-of-payments problem by honoring the government's agreement to exchange dollars for gold as long as it could for geopolitical reasons, but should close the gold window immediately and without negotiations when it became necessary to do so for domestic economic reasons.

The Nixon Administration first tackled inflation with an approach long recommend by advocates of commercial Keynesianism, higher interest rates and budget balancing, but inflation rose from 4.4 percent in January 1969, to 6.2 percent one year later, and was only back to 4.4 percent in July 1971. During the same 31-month period, unemployment grew from 3.4 percent to 6.0 percent. To deal with these problems, and help ensure his reelection, Nixon instituted a temporary wage-price freeze and called for a tax cut in August 1971. He also announced that the United States would no longer exchange American gold for American dollars held by other nations, which left the country's shocked allies with no positive alternatives to capitulating to this exercise of American power by putting the value of their currencies at the mercy of market forces. Together, these new policies were meant to give corporations and the Nixon Administration more flexibility in dealing with inflation and unions at home while improving the competitiveness of American corporations abroad, and they succeeded. Inflation dipped as low as 2.7 percent 11 months after Nixon announced the new policies and stood at a tolerable 3.4 percent when he was reelected. The sequence of events outlined in this and the previous paragraph, which was triggered by attempting to fight an imperial war without inflation controls, deserves far more weight than the fractured-elite account gives it in evaluating the viability of Keynesian-based policies.

Nor does fractured-elite theory emphasize the distinctiveness of the powerful external economic shocks that led to a new round of inflation in early 1973, which exploded to 8.7 percent by the end of the year and to 12.3 percent by the end of 1974. The fractured-elite account acknowledges that this new inflation was due in good part to the oil shock caused by the Arab oil embargo in October 1973, which is recast as "the culmination of what can now be seen as the excessive consumption of a critical natural resource without regard for the consequences." Despite the external source of the problem, the fractured-elite analysis nonetheless argues that Keynesianism had "stopped working" and "began to fail" because at the same time unemployment rose from 4.9 percent in January 1973, to as high as 9.0 percent in May 1975. Contrary to this claim, a moderate Keynesian economist, Charles Schultze, who was based at The Brookings Institution, provided the corporate moderates serving as CED trustees with an astute analysis of the economy's problems from 1973 to early 1975 at a special CED conference in May 1975. In addition to his position at Brookings, Schultze also had been an advisor to several CED study groups beginning in 1968 and later served on its Research Advisory Board.

According to Schultze, the sudden downturn in the economy was due to a sharp decline in consumer demand and had little or nothing to do with the earlier demand-pull inflation or Nixon's earlier economic policies. Instead, he claimed, the economy suffered three post-1972 inflationary shocks that acted like new taxes on consumers, and thereby decreased consumer purchasing power. To begin with, farm prices rose sharply due to bad harvests around the world; this problem was exacerbated in the United States by the sale of grain and soybean reserves to the Soviet Union in 1972 and 1973 for strategic reasons, which strained American reserves in the process. The increases in farm prices took $6.5 billion (in 2012 dollars) out of consumers' pockets. Then the costs of non-petroleum raw materials went up as well, which cost consumers another several billion dollars.

The third and biggest shock came from the six-month Arab oil embargo, which is emphasized in the fractured-elite analysis to the exclusion of the two earlier shocks. It quadrupled the price of oil and sent $36 billion of consumer purchasing power to oil-producing countries, only $5 billion of which came back to commercial and investment banks in the United States for loans and investments. In addition, the resulting inflationary spiral pushed individuals and corporations into higher tax brackets, removing another $55–60 billion from consumption and investment, which is another important issue that is not discussed in the fractured-elite account. Due to the major decline in demand, employers began to lay off workers, which of course increased the unemployment rate. This analysis is supported by later studies of this time period, although the effect of lifting the temporary Nixon price controls, which lasted in a gradually weakened form from late 1971 into 1973, has to be factored into the equation. It is noteworthy, but not an issue that can be pursued in this article, that the three external shock waves, when combined with the effects of Nixon's decision to close the gold window, generated volatility in currency values and new political regimes in many countries as well as the aforementioned inflation.

Once again contrary to fractured-elite theory, it seems unlikely that the problems facing the economy were a mystery to Schultze and the other Keynesian economists at The Brookings Institution, who were highly visible and vocal at the time. Put simply, the economy was suffering from cost-push inflation, which requires different policy responses than does demand-pull inflation because of the reduction in consumer demand it creates. Keynesian advisors therefore thought it was a bad idea for the Federal Reserve Board to fight inflation by raising interest rates under these circumstances, but the corporate community and the Nixon and Ford administrations decided otherwise.

Still, several mainstream Keynesian economists, including Schultze, even after he was appointed as the chair of the Council of Economic Advisors by President Jimmy Carter in 1977, continued to advocate tax reductions for low-income workers (perhaps through lower payroll taxes) and increased government spending. They thought such remedies were possible because there was no general underlying dynamic within the economy itself that was driving inflation at that point. By 1975, however, most corporate moderates had joined with the ultraconservatives in rejecting fiscal policy options because issues having to do with defending and increasing their power in the face of union demands were more salient to them. Nevertheless, the corporate leaders' emphasis on high interest rates and cuts in social spending did not keep them from successfully lobbying for large permanent tax cuts for higher-income individuals and corporations during the Carter years, which marked a complete triumph for the corporate community.

Contrary to fractured-elite theory, hardliners among the corporate moderates were gradually abandoning their version of Keynesianism between 1969 and 1972 for three intertwined reasons. First, as already noted, the hardliners were determined to defeat unions because they perceived

their wage demands as the reason for the inflation that developed in the late 1960s. In effect, they were arguing that unions, especially in construction, were taking advantage of tight labor markets to win exorbitant wage hikes that exceeded the growth in productivity, and thereby causing cost-push inflation. At that point the cost-of-living adjustments built into many union contracts also became completely unacceptable to them. In making their analysis, they were playing down the demand-pull inflation of the late 1960s and denying that unionized workers were for the most part playing catch-up. They therefore increasingly turned to their version of monetary theory as the main rationale for the policies they preferred, which in effect advocated high interest rates and rising unemployment in order to defeat unions.

The hardliners' concern about the increasing costs of their new factories led them to form the Construction Users Anti-Inflation Roundtable in 1969 in order to hold down wage increases in the construction industry; the new group's efforts played a role in shaping the Nixon Administration's labor and inflation policies in relation to the construction industry. This organization, in turn, was the nucleus of the Business Roundtable, which was established in 1972 and became operative over the course of the next two years. It had a primary focus on labor issues, a fact that is obscured in the fractured-elite analysis because of its incorrect emphasis on the corporate moderates' concern with regulation by the EPA and OSHA, which did not develop until three or four years later and was greatly overblown. This new policy-discussion organization was created through a merger of the Construction Users Anti-Inflation Roundtable and the Labor Law Reform Group, both of which were expressly concerned with weakening unions.

The Business Roundtable's founding statement presented an analysis of the situation it thought corporations faced. More exactly, it laid out "two narratives," one focused on the supposed negative effects of inflation on everyone, the other on the "labor gains at the expense of capital" throughout the entire postwar era. Since construction costs were rising in the late 1960s, in a context in which prices presumably could not be easily increased due to increasing international competition, the Business Roundtable claimed there was a profit squeeze for those large industrial corporations that were rapidly building new factories to maintain market share and enhance profits in a booming economy. Right or wrong, the two narratives added up to a rationale for undercutting labor unions. . . .

The idea of "core inflation," which excludes sudden changes in agricultural and energy prices from the inflation equation, was introduced in 1975 in a paper published by The Brookings Institution.

Detailed analyses of national income data for the postwar era as a whole reveal only a slight upward trend in labor's share, and as so often, different assumptions lead to different results. For example, if executive salaries are included in the same category with profits, the size of the labor share is reduced. This is due to the fact that executive compensation increased at a faster rate than average wages from the early 1950s to the early 1960s, flattened for a few years, and then rose even more rapidly after 1968, which is also when corporate moderates began to complain very loudly about undeserved gains by blue-collar workers.

Rising executive compensation to one side, the definition of the labor share that best encompasses non-executive workers for large companies actually showed a decline in the first half of the 1960s, which was overlooked by the corporate moderates as they wrote about a golden age for record-setting profits. But the labor share rose rapidly in the second half of the decade, which was all that mattered as far as the Business Roundtable's grievances concerning their need for continuing increases in profits. The fact that profits had started to recover in 1971 (later stalled by the mid-1970s recession) was not considered good news because as of 1972 they were still below the unusually high level of 1965–1966.

Aside from the corporate leaders' concern over the share of national income going to their profits, an increasing number of them were also motivated by a desire to put an end to any government inclination to develop permanent wage-price controls, which had been tried during the Kennedy and Johnson administrations despite corporate (and union) resistance. Wage-price controls administered by government boards were an ongoing concern for the new hardliners because in 1970 the most centrist of the corporate moderates had advocated a temporary version of such boards in a CED report on controlling inflation. (This concern on the part of the hardliners was then heightened by the temporary wage-price controls the Nixon Administration created in the summer of 1971, with the strong urging of many corporate moderates.) This issue receives no consideration in the fractured-elite analysis. The CED report making this surprising recommendation also said that lower interest rates, higher taxes, and higher federal expenditures were needed to deal with "the urgent problems of our cities, education, poverty and welfare, health care, and the environment." In other words, at least for a brief time, the more centrist trustees were arguing for a very different direction than the one advocated by more conservative CED trustees; this difference was reflected in the large number of disagreements that were added to the report, as well as six dissenting votes by hardliners who opposed its publication altogether.

Finally, there was a third anti-union prong to the approach taken by the members of the Business Roundtable, on which the fractured-elite analysis is once again wanting. They were determined to make sure that inflation was controlled only by higher interest rates set by the Federal Reserve Board, not by raising taxes on the well-to-do while at the same time reducing government subsidies and tax breaks that benefited corporations, as liberal Keynesians advocated. Furthermore, by 1971–1972 the centrists within the corporate community were losing whatever interest they once had in spending more money on social problems, except through the methods they had come to champion, food stamps and the Earned Income Tax Credit, which do not interfere with low-wage labor markets and in effect subsidize agricultural interests and companies that pay low wages. According to a corporate-dominance perspective, the shift in policy preferences by corporate moderates was made possible by the decline in turmoil in inner cities and the society at large beginning in 1971. The only policy option left to control inflation was the one virtually all corporate moderates now favored—higher interest rates imposed by the Fed. Ultraconservatives in the corporate community and members of the conservative voting coalition in Congress eagerly embraced this option because they had preferred it all along.

The fractured-elite account misses these crucial changes because of its emphasis on the results of a self-administered questionnaire filled out in 1971. It showed that 57 percent of the 120 chief executives and owners that returned the questionnaire could be classified as liberal or moderate Keynesians based on their answers to questions about the need for balanced budgets, the value of a guaranteed annual income, and moderately redistributive reforms such as closing tax loopholes and raising the inheritance tax. The fractured-elite analysis therefore concludes that the "postwar moderate consensus remained solid" in the early 1970s. But responses to hypothetical questions on a self-administered questionnaire by a sample of chief executives in the industrial sector ("only slightly more than 50%" responded), the nonindustrial sector (79 percent of whom responded), and owners worth over $100 million (31 percent of whom responded) do not reveal what the main power wielders in the corporate community were actually doing at the time. As a result of these mistaken emphases, and in spite of its earlier focus on the Construction Users Anti-Inflation Roundtable and the Business Roundtable, the fractured-elite analysis ends up claiming that the accelerating rightward slant during the 1970s was due to a "counteroffensive" by the ultraconservatives. It therefore discusses the rise of the Heritage Foundation, the American Enterprise Institute, and the foundations that supported them, which are minor and beside the point from a corporate-dominance perspective. The fractured-elite account then goes completely wrong when it concludes that "As traditional conservatives mobilized, especially those associated with the Far Right, large corporations began to slowly follow in their path." It thereby loses sight of the fact that the hardliners among the corporate moderates were adopting new policy stances several years before right-wing think tanks and foundations were having any policy impact.

Nor did events of the early to mid-1970s make the conservative coalition any more ultraconservative than it already was; a further move to the right came later with the arrival of southern Republicans into Congress in the late 1970s and 1980s. Not only was the conservative coalition as ultraconservative from 1972 through 1976 as it had been in the past, but it also came together for more votes and was highly successful. On some issues the corporate community and the conservatives in Congress simply relied on vetoes by President Gerald Ford to block liberal-labor proposals. . . .

Corporate Networks and Bank Centrality

As briefly noted in the Introduction, the fractured-elite account claims that the members of boards of directors of large commercial banks were a third source of moderation in the postwar era because they were sources of information and normative consensus, and had "the ability to see issues from multiple perspectives." Crucially, they were able to disseminate their information, normative consensus, and multiple perspectives because of "their centrality in the social networks created by ties among the leaders of the largest American corporations." However, due to the decline in commercial banking caused by the rise of insurance and finance companies as direct lenders, along with a steep rise in lending by shadow banks (non-regulated banks), the commercial banks lost their central position in the network. They also suffered failures and mergers. The replacement of banks at the center of the corporate network mattered because "No group of firms replaced the banks as the glue that held the system together." Making matters worse, the merger movement of the mid-1980s led to increased CEO turnover and less continuity at the top of large corporations.

The literature on the impact of corporate networks on various outcome variables suggests that director interlocks between two corporations can facilitate the flow of information from corporation to corporation and thereby aid in, or make possible, the adoption of new corporate practices, such as lucrative retirement packages for top executives, by-laws to ward off takeover bids, and a multi-division form of organization, and one study found a positive correlation between bank representation on a corporation's board and the amount of external financing the corporation used. The literature also shows that interlocked corporations are more likely to have members on government trade advisory committees. Along the same lines, corporations that have similar numbers and types of interlocks, although not necessarily with each other, have similar patterns of political campaign contributions or give common testimony to Congress. There is evidence that corporate leaders who sit on two or more corporate boards together frequently make similar campaign contributions, which does not necessarily mean that one corporation is influencing another corporation. This literature on the effects of various types of interlocks is large and complex, but there is no evidence in it that the members of bank boards per se have any unique role in the creation of the general public policies that are of concern to the fractured-elite and corporate-dominance theories.

Moreover, the most systematic study of the political consciousness of corporate directors concluded that directors with multiple directorships are just as conservative, and maybe more conservative, than those who sit on only one corporate board: "Contrary to the hypotheses on inner-group consciousness, it is neither more uniform nor more liberal than that of other class members. Indeed, the core members of the inner group—the triple-director executives—hold a more conservative general ideology than peripheral members." Nor is there any evidence that tempers this conclusion in a book-length study of the role of multiple directors. It reports that such directors may have a "more developed and nuanced understanding of the political environment and how it is most productively influenced"; they also may be more willing to compromise, but this does not mean that their political consciousness is any less conservative. Thus, they are perhaps better described as individuals who take the lead in adjusting corporate policy stances; they moved in a centrist direction in the face of the civil rights and anti-war movements, but in a more conservative direction in the 1970s. As for any evidence that fits with the idea of greater moderation, it is linked to involvement in policy-discussion groups. Thus, multiple directorships, whether they include membership on a bank board or not, may not matter as far as the dissemination of a moderate-conservative corporate perspective. What the multiple directors seem to share is the connections and visibility that make them more likely to become members of policy-discussion groups and receive appointments to government.

Over and beyond the issue of corporate interlocks and their impact, there is a bigger question: is the policy-planning network the source of the general policy positions that are adopted by members of the corporate community?

Corporate Policy and the Policy-Planning Network

Due to the emphasis that the fractured-elite perspective puts on bank boards as the sites for their members to develop policy consensus, it places less emphasis on the policy-planning network than does corporate-dominance theory. True, it frequently mentions the Business Council, the Business Roundtable, the CED, and other policy-discussion venues, and discusses the breadth of vision and multiple directorships possessed by their leaders. However, these organizations are never linked into a network that includes numerous corporate directors and is funded by corporations and foundations, and that conveys its policy positions to government through testimony to Congress, lobbying, and the appointments of its leaders and advisors to government positions as cabinet officers or members of White House and departmental advisory committees. In addition, the roles that corporate-dominance theory long ago attributed to the policy-discussion groups seem to have considerable overlap with the roles fractured-elite theory assigns to banks as "mediating mechanisms."

Although the policy-planning network is a more likely site for general policy discussions than bank-board networks, the fractured-elite argument overlooks a way in which the CEOs and other corporate leaders who serve as bank directors may have differentially contributed to policy formation in the late 1970s and early 1980s. Forty-eight percent of the people who were trustees of two or more of 12 prominent organizations in the policy-planning network in 1980 were also directors of one of the ten largest banks, compared to 19 percent in 1973 and 33 percent in 1990. These results support the idea that corporate leaders who serve as bank directors may have had a special role in policy planning at an important juncture in the late 1970s and early 1980s, but they more fully support corporate-dominance theory because that special role was played out in the policy-planning network, not the corporate network. These claims for the greater importance of the policy-planning network also have been supported by case studies mentioned in previous sections, and by other case studies that could have been mentioned for the Progressive Era (e.g., workmen's compensation insurance and the creation of the Federal Trade Commission) and the New Deal (e.g., the formulation of the National Industrial Recovery Act and the Agricultural Adjustment Act).

The claims for the greater importance of the policy-planning network are further supported in the next section with evidence for its continuing importance from 1990 to 2010 on several major policy issues. This further evidence is especially critical because the fractured-elite analysis claims that bank boards were not sources of policy cohesion during this time period. Thus, a strong degree of policy unity, albeit with the usual conservative and ultra-conservative tendencies still apparent, would show that the corporate community developed and conveyed its policy preferences through the policy-planning network during a period that fractured-elite theory sees as a time of increasing corporate fragmentation and ineffectiveness.

Case-Study Evidence for Corporate-Moderate Unity and Effectiveness, 1990 to 2010

According to fractured-elite theory, in the 1970s the "American corporate elite began to abandon its earlier commitment to a position of responsibility for the well-being of the larger society, focusing instead on its own, short-term interests." By the end of the 1980s, "the three forces that had contributed to the moderation of the postwar corporate elite—the state, organized labor, and the financial community—were no longer playing this role." As a result, the corporate elite was fragmented and ineffectual.

The first problem with this claim is that the Business Roundtable supported a tax increase in 1990 that was difficult for President George H. W. Bush to accept because he had promised during the 1988 presidential campaign that he would not raise taxes. When he reluctantly agreed to raise the gas tax by a few cents, reduce the accelerated depreciation rate for corporations for three years, and raise the top marginal tax rate on individual incomes from 28 to 31 percent as part of a budget compromise with Congressional Democrats, ultraconservatives pilloried him. This episode is dealt with as follows in the fractured-elite account: "As late as 1990, then, even after the corporate elite had become weakened by the takeover wave it had faced during the 1980s, corporate leaders were still calling for tax increases when they believed that the deficit had become uncomfortably large." From a corporate-dominance perspective, this comment does not do justice to what happened. The strong statement put forth by the Business Roundtable demonstrates that it remained able to come together despite the merger wave of the mid-1980s and the decline in bank centrality. It still could unify and deliver what proved to be a successful message.

According to the fractured-elite perspective, the fragmentation and irrelevance of the corporate elite was all but complete by the mid-1990s, by which time it had lost much of its ability "to generate either a consensus of ideas or a similarity of behavior." This conclusion is contradicted by the successful uphill battle that a united corporate community carried out between 1991 and 1994 to pass the North American Free Trade Agreement (NAFTA). This legislation was strongly opposed by the liberal-labor alliance, even though it had supported the expansion of free trade in past decades. In its view, "free trade" by this point was mostly about moving jobs to low-wage countries, which had replaced the South as the corporate community's safe haven from unions.

Detailed studies clearly demonstrate that the Business Roundtable led the way in creating the wide-ranging USA*NAFTA coalition of businesses, which appointed "captains" in 30 states to organize corporate leaders to visit Senators and members of the House. At the same time, the key corporate leaders on this issue, including many of the state captains, were members of official trade advisory committees housed within the Department of Commerce. In addition, statistical analyses showed that several company-level organizational factors, such as size, business sector, and number of foreign subsidiaries, had an impact on a corporation's degree of involvement in the issue. However, being part of the policy-planning network had an impact that was independent of the organizational level of analysis: "When controlling for foreign subsidiaries, PAC contributions, and labor intensity, [Dreiling] found that network variables remained statistically significant and explained greater variation in the odds of leadership than did the organizational interests measures." For example, involvement in the policy-planning network increased the likelihood that a corporate leader would testify before Congress in favor of the expansion of trade.

This quantitative finding is complemented by a detailed account of the individuals, corporations, and policy organizations that introduced and supported the legislation. It is also supported by an interview-based case study of the issue by the publisher-editor of *Harper's Magazine*, who gave his book the incendiary title, *The Selling of 'Free Trade:' NAFTA, Washington, and the Subversion of American Democracy*, to highlight the lengths to which the corporate leaders went to pass the legislation. The bill eventually passed because most Republicans and the remaining white Southern Democrats voted together in one of the last hurrahs for the conservative coalition before the Republicans finished their takeover of most Southern congressional seats in the next few years. It was a clear victory over the liberal-labor alliance.

Instead of facing the challenge presented by the findings on NAFTA, the fractured-elite argument discusses the failed Clinton health-care plan. According to its analysis,

the reform lost for many reasons, including the all-out opposition of ultraconservatives and small business, but the weakness of the corporate elite was crucial: "Ultimately, however, what prevented constructive reform from occurring was the ineffectuality of the corporate elite." But the corporate moderates were not ineffectual; they were not fully focused on the issues at the outset and were already headed in another direction. Based on her work as a consultant to the White House Health Care Task Force, as well as "the many discussions and presentations I made to business leaders from June 1993 through December 1994," sociologist Linda Bergthold provides an alternative analysis that builds on her earlier theoretical work on health issues as well as her direct observations.

Although there were self-interested divisions between companies that would save money through the reforms in financing health care and those that would end up paying more, even most of the businesses that stood to benefit ended up opposing an employer mandate. This anti-reform unity was based at least in part "on the grounds of ideological opposition to government mandates of any kind," as the fractured-elite account also concludes. But there were power issues at stake as well. For the corporate community in general, there were "tensions between the economic self-interest of firms (e.g., wouldn't it be cheaper to simply pay for but not manage health benefits?) and the fear of loss of control over benefits to government [that] could not be resolved," and the ultraconservatives were resolutely opposed under any circumstances. Moreover, the Clinton plan in effect eliminated a substantial number of the positions held by the human resources directors and the benefits managers who were advising their CEOs.

Just as important at that juncture, the corporate moderates were mostly concerned with restructuring the health-care delivery system. On this issue "reform of the marketplace [for health care] was proceeding headlong before Clinton focused the national spotlight on health reform," and it proceeded even faster while the Clinton plan was being discussed. As a result, and as acknowledged in the fractured-elite account, health-care costs were leveling off in 1993 and remained flat as a percentage of GDP until 1998. Thus, the corporate moderates felt no great urgency in 1994 to enact a plan about which most of them had qualms.

Based on this analysis, it seems unlikely that corporate moderates would have gone along with health care reform, even if they had been consulted as to their preferences on key issues before the plan was developed (which they weren't) and even if they had been treated respectfully by the executive director of the White House Task Force when they were able to meet with him at their own request (which they weren't). As Bergthold puts it, "we should never have expected any public support for reform from business anyway." Another sociologist, Beth Mintz, comes to a very similar conclusion. She takes exception with those who claim the large corporations were divided, or dominated by the views of major insurance companies, both of which are considered to be factors in the fractured-elite analysis. Instead, she concludes "The defection of big business can be viewed as a unified action, based not on the ability of a narrow, self-interested segment to dominate the decision-making process, but on the uncertainty that the Clinton proposal generated for the big business community." Even more strongly, sociologist Jill Quadagno, building on the wider range of studies and original sources that were available 10 years after the Clinton initiative failed, concludes "it had lost the support of all major business groups" by as early as mid-fall 1993, including the Business Roundtable, the Chamber of Commerce, and the NAM.

As part of the claim that the corporate moderates were ineffective in dealing with the Clinton health-care plan, the fractured-elite perspective contrasts the supposed lack of unity within the Business Roundtable with the unity displayed by small business, as manifested in the form of the National Federation of Independent Business (NFIB). But such a claim overlooks, and therefore never confronts, the evidence that the NFIB is an ultraconservative lobbying organization, closely tied to the Republican Party. Furthermore, it meets none of the qualifications for being any sort of business or trade association. It actually began as a small business itself, established in Northern California in 1943 by a former Chamber of Commerce employee. The founder was in effect a political entrepreneur who made profits on membership fees while lobbying for his conservative policy preferences. The NFIB's small-business members were (from at least the 1940s through the 1990s) signed up by traveling sales representatives who worked on a commission basis. Unlike voluntary business associations, there were no general meetings or votes for officers (and still aren't), and membership turnover is large each year.

Business owners that join the NFIB receive membership stickers for their store windows, a newsletter with suggestions for small businesses, and periodic surveys on a wide range of issues. The surveys are slanted to evoke conservative responses, the results of which are compiled at state and national headquarters and mailed to state and national legislators as "mandates" from small-business owners. Comparisons of the results of these surveys, which typically are returned by only about 20 percent of the members, with those from national surveys suggest that the ultraconservative claims made on the basis of the mandates are not representative of small business owners, who mostly share the attitudes of their ethnic group and/or local community.

As a more recent analysis confirmed, surveys of small-business owners show that NFIB's opposition to any government intervention in the marketplace is not consistent with the opinions of many small-business owners.

The NFIB switched to a nonprofit status in the late 1960s, with another former Chamber of Commerce employee as its new president. Located in Virginia since 1992, by that time the NFIB had 700 employees and annual revenues of over $58 million. NFIB files obtained by the Democratic National Committee support the earlier claim that the NFIB is very selective in making assertions to Congress about what small-business owners prefer in terms of policy. In the July/August 1995, issue of its magazine, *Independent Business*, it reported that 85 percent of its members opposed employer-mandated health care in 1993; however, it never publicized the fact that its July 1989 survey found that 60 percent of its respondents agreed that "government must play a more direct role in health care to bring health-care costs under control." Information provided as part of the fractured-elite analysis of the health-care issue also supports the claim that the NFIB presented an inaccurate picture of what small-business owners believed and wanted in the early stages of the battle over the Clinton reform plan. It reports that a Dun & Bradstreet survey found "there was a virtual tie among small companies in the extent to which they favored 'national health insurance,' with 38 percent saying yes, 39 percent saying no, and 23 percent responding 'don't know'."

One pair of political scientists reported that in the 1990s the NFIB was the organized interest group that "has the closest working relationship with the Republican leadership in Congress today," and then presented its staff links to the Republicans. But a survey of small-business owners with 100 or fewer employees in 2008 reported that one-third were Republicans, one-third Democrats, and 29 percent neither. Nevertheless, the NFIB gave 90 percent of its campaign donations to Republicans between 1989 and 2008; even here, the analysis does not go far enough because it did not determine if the rest of the money went to the dwindling number of ultraconservative white Southern Democrats that lingered in Congress into the late 1990s. The evidence is clear that the NFIB represents the ultraconservatives among small-business owners, which creates a problem for the fractured-elite claim about the unity of small business on government health insurance, or any other issue.

Health care aside, the fractured-elite evidence for the supposed ineffectiveness of the corporate moderates does not include any legislative issues for the rest of the 1990s. Instead, the argument is based on the low visibility of the CED and the alleged ineffectiveness of the

Business Roundtable in lobbying Congress. In the case of the CED, the fractured-elite account points to commentary in the *Congressional Record* in 1997, which simply demonstrates that many members of Congress did not know anything about the CED at that time. This fact is irrelevant because it already had been established in an account cited in the fractured-elite book that the CED was in decline by 1976 and had become at best a source of long-range policy suggestions for the Business Roundtable by 1978. As the president of the CED in the late 1970s later succinctly put it in a telephone interview, the CED chair and his corporate colleagues had created a "niche" for CED between the Business Roundtable and the American Enterprise Institute. If the CED had been relegated to a niche by 1978, it cannot come as news, or as evidence of anything, that it was unknown to many members of Congress 20 years later. (In early 2015, the CED became a quasi-independent policy center within the much bigger and older Conference Board; it is now named "The Committee for Economic Development of the Conference Board.")

To demonstrate the alleged ineffectiveness of the Business Roundtable in the late 1990s, the fractured-elite theory relies on a Fortune article entitled "The Fallen Giant." The article is based on a Fortune poll of about 2,200 "Washington insiders," who were asked to rank the most powerful business lobbies in Washington. The Business Roundtable ranked 33rd, well below the American Trucking Association, the National Retail Federation, the NFIB, the NAM, and the Chamber of Commerce. Aside from the fact that the Business Roundtable usually is not perceived as a lobbying organization, and is not classified as such by corporate-dominance theory, it is not at all evident that the votes of 2,200 Washington observers of unknown reliability and access should be taken seriously as to the power of an organization.

At that time, moreover, the Business Roundtable had organized an American Leads on Trade coalition (ALOT) to convince Congress to renew the president's "fast track" authority for negotiating new agreements to expand trade with other countries. This successful coalition then became the basis for the even larger corporate coalition USA*ENGAGE, which led a successful corporate lobbying effort to grant China the status called Permanent National Trade Relations. This status removed any constraint on the Chinese dictatorship's internal and external policies that might have been created by the need for a yearly renewal of normal trade relations. It also removed any corporate hesitation in off-shoring production to China. Well after the status was granted, some economists estimated that the agreement led to the loss of over two million manufacturing jobs in the United States during its first seven years.

As in the case of the NAFTA legislation, sociologists Michael Dreiling and Derek Darves-Bornoz carried out detailed quantitative studies to compare the relative strength of several variables in predicting corporate involvement. This time, however, their analyses employed a dyadic method, quadratic assignment procedure, which is better at assessing the strength of relationships than other methods. These studies once again found that organizationallevel variables, such as company size and large PAC donations, predicted greater involvement in temporary trade alliances, testimony before Congress, and participation in governmental trade advisory committees. But being part of the policy-planning network had a larger impact in terms of involvement in all three outcome variables, especially if a corporate dyad shared membership in the Business Roundtable.

This network-based evidence is supplemented by information in a detailed report by a public-interest watchdog group, Public Citizen, on the legislative battle itself. The report focused on campaign donations and lobbying by members of the corporate coalition. For example, members of the Business Roundtable alone "made $68.2 million in PAC, soft money and individual donations to Members of Congress and the Democratic and Republican parties between January 1999 and May 2000," the month in which the Congressional vote was held, much of it aimed at 71 swing districts that likely would be crucial in securing the legislation. These representatives were alternately threatened with reprisals by named and unnamed sources in the business press and offered help with campaign finances by means of fundraising receptions. By comparison, organized labor raised $31 million overall for the campaign.

Instead of considering the effort to grant the status of permanent national trade relationship to China, the fractured-elite perspective focuses on what it sees as another sign of weakness for the Business Roundtable. It did not call for a tax hike in 2003 despite the fact that "the deficit quickly reached record levels" due to the Bush tax cuts of 2001 and the wars in Afghanistan and Iraq. The fractured-elite critique calls the organization's silence on the issue "an illustration of the extent to which the group was unwilling to take a potentially unpopular position." However, this critique does not focus on a more basic fact in terms of the theory's emphasis on fragmentation—the corporate leaders, ranging from the Business Roundtable to the NAM to the Chamber of Commerce, were united in supporting the tax cuts in 2001 and continued to be supportive of them over the next several years. This unity may be a sign of shortsightedness, or even due to mere "loyalty to the president," but neither possibility is evidence that the corporate community was fractured on a tax issue any more than it was fractured on the issue of trade with China.

Furthermore, it is questionable that the corporate moderates should have called for a tax increase in 2003 in light of events in the 1990s and the state of the economy in the first several years of the twenty-first century. After all, the disappearance of budget deficits in the late 1990s revealed that the concern with large deficits and a growing federal debt missed the economic mark. The deficit fell very rapidly in the Clinton era primarily due to the stock-market boom. As a result, there were government projections that the federal debt would be gone within a decade, an unlikely possibility just a few years before. This news gave presidential candidate George W. Bush the opportunity to call for tax cuts for all Americans. The proposal for a tax cut was supported in Congressional testimony by the chair of the Federal Reserve Board, who warned that the disappearance of the debt might make it more difficult for the Fed to influence interest rates through the purchase or sale of Treasury bonds; he also raised the specter that the government might be "forced to buy up private assets, such as corporate bonds or shares of stock" in order to earn interest on the looming surplus.

By the time the tax cuts were starting to take effect, there was yet another reason to let the deficit and the debt grow again: the sharp decline in the economy after the stock-market boom collapsed. In that regard, the fractured-elite view notes that there were reasonable objections to focusing on the deficit at that moment, and that the concern with deficit reduction might be ideological in any case. It also notes that Republicans who expressed no concern about the deficit in 2003 did an "about-face once Barack Obama took office," which suggests that the antipathy was to spending tax dollars on what the power elite saw as the wrong kind of government spending. Nevertheless, the fact that the Business Roundtable did not call for a tax hike is described in the fractured-elite account as "a retreat from responsibility on the issue of taxes," a retreat that is "emblematic of the decline of the American corporate elite." Based on this brief summary of the booms and busts of the economy between 1994 and 2004, it is difficult for corporate-dominance theory to give credibility to the idea that the decision by the Business Roundtable not to call for a tax increase in 2003 or 2004 demonstrates fragmentation or an inability to rise above the narrow interests of the corporations.

The corporate community also demonstrated complete unity in 2008 when it organized a multimillion-dollar campaign of lobbying and media advertising in anticipation of a Congressional vote in 2009 on the Employee Free Choice Act. If the act had passed, it would have given union organizers the right to by-pass representation elections (which corporate officials often successfully delay for many months at a time) if a majority of a company's employees signed a card stating that they wanted to join the union. Working through lobbying coalitions, the corporate leaders argued that the legislation would take away workers' right to vote for or against unionization in a secret ballot. The bill never came to a vote because 41 Republican senators said they would support a filibuster, and three Democrats indicated they would not support the bill.

The Affordable Care Act

By 2007 the moderate conservatives were strong and united supporters of the basic tenets that were incorporated into the Affordable Care Act (ACA). The Act passed in 2010 despite the opposition of the Chamber of Commerce and the ultraconservative front group called the National Federation of Independent Business. The corporate moderates supported this legislation in principle because it was based on an individual mandate, an employer mandate, and maximum use of private-sector health insurance. All of these features were part of a proposal in 1993 by moderate Republicans in the Senate that was offered as an alternative to the Clinton Plan. As Quadagno concluded after detailed research, "The ACA's key provisions, the employer mandate and the individual mandate, were Republican policy ideas, and its fundamental principles were nearly identical to the Health Equity and Access Reform Today Act of 1993 (HEART), a bill promoted by Republican senators to deflect support for President Bill Clinton's Health Security plan."

Corporate moderates first supported these three principles in the early 1970s, as seen in a report by the CED, but they had been wary of the employer mandate in the context of the Clinton reform plan. As to the issue of an individual mandate, it had been offered anew by the ultraconservative Heritage Foundation in 1989, and accepted by most ultraconservatives in the 1990s, but by the early 2000's they were opposed. As for the corporate community of the twenty-first century, leaders within it began in 2007 to advocate for the individual mandate and the other two key provisions in the 1993 Republican proposal as a necessary part of the kind of health-care reform it was willing to support.

In February 2007, several major corporations joined with AARP and the Service Employees International Union (SEIU) to form a coalition for health-care reform. In May 2007, the CEO of Safeway organized the Coalition to Advance Health Care Reform, which included

36 other companies. The Business Roundtable endorsed the individual mandate a month later and said that it is the responsibility of all Americans to obtain insurance. The same year, the national trade organization for the medical devices industry came out for the individual mandate.

As part of the process of developing its health-care plan, the Obama Administration negotiated a deal in August 2009, with the prescription drug industry, which was represented by its trade association, PhRMA. The large pharmaceutical companies agree to provide discounts of $80 billion over a ten-year period for Medicare recipients in exchange for the greatly expanded market for their medications that would be created. The pharmaceutical companies then spent an estimated $150 million in lobbying and media coverage in support of the legislation.

Despite the Obama Administration's efforts to accommodate the corporate moderates on all their major concerns, a coalition of health insurance companies, America's Health Insurance Plans, which stated its support for an individual mandate shortly after Obama's election, ended up lobbying against the plan. This opposition developed because of liberal and labor support for a new provision, "the public option," which would have made it possible for the government to offer insurance programs in competition with the private sector. The insurance industry made clear that it would fiercely oppose the legislation if it included the public option, and the idea was dropped late in the process. As a result, liberals and organized labor, which originally strongly favored a single-payer system, did not work hard to pass the bill, with the exception of the SEIU.

Fractured-elite theory provides a similar account of the health-insurance initiatives by the Business Roundtable, AARP, and the SEIU in 2007 and 2008, and further notes that representatives from the Business Roundtable and other business groups met shortly after the 2008 elections. They emerged from their discussion with the conclusion that "the possibility of change was far greater at this point than during the Clinton Administration." The fractured-elite analysis then states that the corporate elite was "involved in all stages of the process" that led to the ACA. But it ends with the unexpected conclusion that the corporate elite's role "was far less central than it had been during the debate of the Clinton plan," and that "the corporate elite essentially sat on the sidelines." Whatever the merits of this puzzling claim may prove to be when new archival evidence is examined in detail, the facts remain that (1) the act was based on principles that were created and insisted upon by the moderate conservatives in the corporate community; (2) these corporate

moderates called for health-insurance reform in the run-up to the 2008 election; (3) corporate moderates were involved in the legislative process; and (4) corporate moderates did not try to block the bill. The success of the ACA, in conjunction with the failure of the Clinton health-care plan in 1994, which the corporate moderates opposed, provides strong evidence against the hypothesis that the corporate moderates were fragmented and ineffectual on the health-care issue when they could support a plan that was acceptable to all corporate moderates.

More generally, every piece of legislation discussed in this section for the years 1990 to 2010 contradicts the idea that the corporate moderates became increasingly fragmented and ineffectual in the late 1980s. Although corporate-level networks have changed in some ways during the past several decades, the core of the corporate moderates' policy-planning network has been stable since the early 1970s.

Conclusion

From a corporate-dominance vantage point, the fractured-elite analysis is based on a questionable historical analysis, a failure to take seriously the network and case-study evidence for the importance of the overall policy-planning network, a selective and poorly presented handful of brief commentaries related to domestic public policy between 1990 and 2010, and an over-reliance on opinion surveys, journalistic accounts, and changes in the interlock patterns within corporate networks over a twenty-year period. Since it is certain that the power elite completely opposes unions, actively works to hold down wages through a variety of stratagems, and fights for decreases in the progressivity of income taxes, it is difficult to imagine that the ongoing decline in union density since 1954, the stagnation of average real wages since the 1970s, the general decline since the 1960s in taxes on the corporate rich and their corporations, and the defeat of several legislative initiatives put forth by an increasingly hobbled liberal-labor alliance could have happened without the power elite's united and ongoing efforts.

Note

1. The theory is called "class-dominance theory" in books and articles that bring the social upper class into the picture.

G. WILLIAM DOMHOFF is a research professor at the University of California, Santa Cruz.

Mark S. Mizruchi    **NO**

The Fracturing of the American Corporate Elite

Like many Americans, Mark Mizruchi had grown increasingly distressed by the state of our politics. He was unhappy with the gridlock in Washington, the inability to accomplish even the most routine tasks of government, and the intransigence of those who have managed to hold the nation hostage to their extreme views. In trying to understand the problem's roots, Mizruchi came to see the issue as a lack of national leadership from a group that had previously played a major and constructive role in developing solutions to new problems and keeping American politics mostly centric: the leaders of large American corporations. His goal in *The Fracturing of the American Corporate Elite,* new this month, is to explain how this relatively cohesive group emerged, what sustained it, how it declined, and the consequences of its demise. In the book excerpt . . . , he outlines his argument.

I argue that the leaders of the largest American corporations, to whom I refer as the American corporate elite, once played an important role in addressing, if not resolving, the needs of the larger society. Since the 1970s, the members of this group have largely abandoned their concern with issues beyond those of their individual firms. This abandonment, I suggest, is one of the primary causes of the economic, political, and social disarray that American society has experienced in the twenty-first century. In earlier decades, the United States had a corporate elite that, however imperfect, was willing to see beyond the short-term interests of the firms that its members directed. Today this is no longer the case. The corporate elite that exists today is a disorganized, largely ineffectual group. Paradoxically, I argue, individual American corporations have more political power in the early twenty-first century than at any time since the 1920s. As a group, they are fragmented, however. Unlike their predecessors in earlier decades, they are either unwilling or unable to mount any systematic approach to addressing even the problems of their own community, let alone those of the larger society.

In this book I examine the rise and fall of the American corporate elite, from its pinnacle in the 1945–1973

period, through its period of turmoil and transition in the 1970s and 1980s, to its present state, in which the group is only a shadow of its former self. I argue that the decline of this elite is a significant source of the current crisis of American democracy and a major cause of the predicament in which the twenty-first-century United States finds itself.

In making this claim, I do not want to imply that the corporate elite of the postwar period was uniformly altruistic or public spirited. On the contrary, business leaders during that age were strongly protective of their interests, as they have been in every historical era. Nor am I suggesting that postwar America was a society that we should attempt to emulate in every respect. Social and cultural norms have become far less oppressive since that time. Our society today is far more tolerant and accepting of difference than it was half a century ago. Innovation, especially in the area of information technology, has improved people's lives in many, albeit not all, respects. Consumer products in general are more plentiful and less expensive than in earlier years. There is no returning to the past, nor should this be an ideal to pursue. Yet for all its problems, the postwar United States had a number of qualities that are lacking today: an expanding economy with a high level of upward mobility, declining inequality, a relatively high level of security, a well-functioning political system, and a widespread belief that problems were solvable. And underpinning these forces was a corporate elite that provided a degree of leadership and vision that are not in evidence today.

In the postwar period, a small segment of leaders emerged in the American business community. This was not the first time that American business leaders had organized. In the early 1900s, a group of business leaders formed the National Civic Federation, in which they developed a series of suggestions for dealing with some of the deleterious consequences of the rise of corporate capitalism at the turn of the twentieth century. The postwar effort to address major national concerns was equally serious. The leaders of this group sat atop the largest firms and held positions in multiple organizations, which allowed them to see the world from a relatively cosmopolitan perspective. This breadth led these elites to exhibit a moderate approach to politics that included limited acceptance of both labor unions and government regulation. They participated actively in policy-making organizations, such as the CED [Committee for Economic Development], and they played a significant role in formulating ideas that were later adopted as national policy, in both Republican and Democratic administrations. These people were not liberals. Like the heads of smaller firms, they too were largely opposed to organized labor and had major reservations about government intervention in the economy. The heads of the leading firms tended to hold a more pragmatic approach toward strategy, however. They also believed that it was in their long-term interest to have a well-functioning society.

Three forces, I argue, contributed to the moderate, pragmatic approach adopted by the postwar corporate elite: a relatively active and highly legitimate state, a well-organized and relatively powerful labor movement, and the financial community, which served as a source of interfirm consensus. The state provided regulation of the economy through its taxing and spending policies, its provision of welfare expenditures (which helped it create effective demand for the products of American industry), and its regulation of business with agencies such as the Federal Trade Commission and the Securities and Exchange Commission. Because of the enormous success that the American economy experienced during the postwar period, a Keynesian consensus emerged among national political leaders and economic policy makers. The corporate elite largely accepted this consensus. The labor movement provided a series of constraints on firms' actions as well as benefits for the firms. The unions' industry-wide presence in core sectors of the economy helped maintain

a relatively stable price structure, which prevented destructive competition. Union leaders also worked with corporations to ensure that more radical elements within their ranks were kept at bay. Management assisted in this effort by agreeing to provide relatively high wages and benefits in exchange for labor peace, an agreement that has been referred to as the postwar "capital-labor accord." The banks, meanwhile, because of their concern with the economy as a whole, played a role in mediating disputes across sectors. Bank boards of directors became meeting places for the chief executives of leading nonfinancial corporations, which helped to generate and maintain a broad consensus on issues of business-wide concern. The banks also occasionally played a role in disciplining individual capitalists who engaged in erratic or deviant behavior.

This situation prevailed from the mid-1940s until the early 1970s. Although this period was characterized by significant social turmoil, it was also a time of sustained economic growth, the expansion of the middle class, and an increasing level of economic equality. The relative strength and legitimacy of both organized labor and the state was not only a consequence of the moderate orientation of the corporate elite. These institutions, along with the financial community, also acted as constraints on business, compelling them to maintain their accommodationist perspective. Corporate leaders fought with unions and government during this period, sometimes fiercely, but they accepted the existence and permanence of these institutions, deciding it was better to work with them than to mount a full-scale assault. This approach was reflected in the attitudes of the corporate elite. By 1971, a majority of top corporate executives expressed support for both Keynesian deficit spending and the idea that the government should step in to provide full employment if the private economy was incapable of doing so.

This system began to unravel during the 1970s. High government spending levels, the emergence of foreign competition, and the energy crisis of 1973 created an unprecedented combination of high inflation and unemployment, which called into question the Keynesian economic orthodoxy of the time. The aftermath of Vietnam and Watergate created a legitimacy crisis among major American institutions, including business. The emergence of new regulatory agencies, most notably the Environmental Protection Agency and the Occupational Safety and Health Administration, which were instituted over the opposition of many corporations, turned many businesses against regulation.

As a result of these crises, corporate elites saw business as embattled, and vulnerable. In response, they mounted a counteroffensive, a full-scale mobilization in which corporations, large and small, found an increasingly unified voice. Business organizations, including the newly formed Business Roundtable, began to attack government regulation. They also became increasingly aggressive in fighting unions. By the time of Ronald Reagan's election as president, labor was already in significant retreat, and after Reagan's inauguration in 1981, regulations were more loosely enforced.

As we moved into the 1980s, however, a paradox became evident. Corporate interests had been extremely successful in weakening the labor movement and thwarting government regulation. In winning this war, however, it became apparent that organized collective action within the business community was no longer necessary. As a result, the corporate elite began to fragment. This fragmentation was hastened by the decline of commercial banks, a group whose boards of directors had served as meeting places for the heads of the leading nonfinancial

corporations. As the banks dropped from the center of the corporate network, the cohesiveness of the elite began to decline as well. Companies began to go their own way, increasingly pursuing relatively minor firm and industry-specific issues, as exemplified by the Tax Reform Act of 1986, in which a plethora of individual and small groups of firms lobbied separately for specific provisions to the law. By the late 1980s, the relatively cohesive, relatively pragmatic character of the American corporate elite had begun to disappear. The corporate elite had, ironically, been "killed" by its own success.

Mark S. Mizruchi is Robert Cooley Angell Collegiate Professor of Sociology, Barger Family Professor of Organizational Studies, professor of business administration at the University of Michigan and author of numerous scholarly books and articles.

EXPLORING THE ISSUE

Is Government Dominated by Big Business?

Critical Thinking and Reflection

1. Give an example of corporations influencing the federal government to pass or repeal policies they favored or opposed.
2. Can you identify policies that were passed against the opposition of the corporate sector? Can you identify what made that action possible?
3. What regulations or other policies have been used to limit the power of corporations to control or influence the federal government? How effective have they been? What more could be done?
4. What do recent elections reveal about the influence of big business over the government? The Koch brothers' money has been a major support for the Tea Party. What is the difference between the political support by big business and the support by wealthy individuals?
5. How is political influence exercised?
6. Discuss and critique the theory of political power that underlies the "Occupy" movement and the conflict between the 99 percent and the 1 percent.

Is There Common Ground?

No one denies that big business has a lot of power and can get their way in many areas including their influence over government. There is agreement that the political system is not a level playing field. The key issue in this debate is the extent of the influence of corporate power over the making and administering of government policies on issues that concern them. The dominant view is that neither the public nor mobilized noncorporate interests can effectively counterpose corporate interests. But EPA was created in 1970 to regulate business and other sources of pollution. NEPA was passed over the objections of business. Wall Street opposed the reforms recently imposed upon them. So everyone agrees that big business has too much power but does not have absolute power. Those are broad boundaries, so there is much room to debate how much power big business has over the federal government.

Additional Resources

Two political scientists who argue that big business dominates America in a lifetime of publications are G. William Domhoff and Thomas R. Dye. Domhoff has published the seventh edition of his book *Who Rules America?*

(McGraw-Hill, 2014). In an earlier book, *Changing the Powers That Be: How the Left Can Stop Losing and Win* (Rowman & Littlefield, 2003), he focused on how to fight this corporate power. In like manner Dye has published the tenth edition of his text, *Politics in America* (Pearson, 2012). Other works supporting this view are Michael Parenti, *Democracy for the Few* (Thomson-Wadsworth, 2008); Melissa L. Rossi, *What Every American Should Know About Who's Really Running America* (Plume Books, 2007); Martin Gilens and Benjamin I. Page, *Testing Theories of American Politics: Elites, Interest Groups, and Average Citizens* (American Political Science Association, 2014).

Several authors advance the thesis that American corporations also seek to some degree to rule the world, including David C. Korten, *When Corporations Rule the World*, 2nd ed. (Kumarian Press, 2001); and Peter Alexis Gourevich and James J. Shinn, *Political Power and Corporate Control: The New Global Politics of Corporate Governance* (Princeton University Press, 2005).

For some pluralist arguments, see Stephen E. Frantzich, *Citizen Democracy: Political Activists in a Cynical Age*, 3rd ed. (Rowman & Littlefield, 2008); Feliz Kolb, *Protest and Opportunities: The Political Outcomes of Social Movements* (Campus Verlag, 2007); David S. Meyers et al., eds., *Routing the Opposition: Social Movements, Public Policy, and Democracy* (University of Minnesota Press, 2005).

Internet References . . .

Sociology—Study Sociology Online

http://edu.learnsoc.org/

Sociology Web Resources

www.mhhe.com/socscience/sociology/resources
/index.htm

Sociosite

www.topsite.com/goto/sociosite.net

Socioweb

www.topsite.com/goto/socioweb.com

Selected, Edited, and with Issue Framing Material by:
Kurt Finsterbusch, *University of Maryland, College Park*

ISSUE

Does Capitalism Have Serious Defects?

YES: Jerry Z. Muller, from "Capitalism and Inequality," *Foreign Affairs* (2013)

NO: Chris Berg, from "Why Capitalism Is Awesome," *Cato Policy Report* (2013)

Learning Outcomes

After reading this issue, you will be able to:

- Learn how scholars deal with extremely broad and complex phenomena such as "capitalism" and "democracy" and how the actors in these systems impact each other.

- Learn how scholars use historical cases to support very general hypotheses. Understand the resulting imprecision and thus the likelihood of disagreement over the interpretations of the results.

- Understand that a variable or factor can have one set of consequences in one period of time and another set of consequences in another period of time because many conditions have changed.

- Understand that the meaning of concepts can change over time. Democracy when most politics were local is different from democracy in massive federal regimes. Capitalism was small scale in the nineteenth century except for railroads and steel, but is very large scale today. The two forms of capitalism behave very differently.

- Discern differences between the interests of various sectors of corporate America and understand the processes that coordinate their political actions. (Direct collusion is illegal.)

ISSUE SUMMARY

YES: Jerry Z. Muller, professor of history at the Catholic University of America and author of *The Mind and the Market: Capitalism in Western Thought*, reports on how capitalism inevitably increases inequality because competition results in winners and losers. It is productive but it also increases commodification which erodes cultural values. It is a force for both good and bad.

NO: Chris Berg, a research fellow with the Institute of Public Affairs in Melbourne, Australia, and author of *In Defence of Freedom of Speech*, provides an enthusiastic defence of capitalism because it stimulates millions of innovations that improve millions of items that benefit us.

One of the long-standing findings of the social sciences is the connection between capitalism, economic development, and democracy. Capitalism is a major force for economic growth. Then economic growth creates the need for skilled and professional workers and thus the expansion of education and the growth of the middle class. Over time the educated and the middle class pressure for rights, and eventually the right to participate in the selection of leaders and to influence government policies. Economic growth over the long run also tends to create government support for freer markets and individual and organizational initiatives, which can eventually increase opposition to despots. Directly and indirectly, therefore, economic growth is a major cause of democracy.

But is this how economic growth impacts modern developed nations today? Economic growth also has produced powerful multinational corporations with concentrated economic power, and these powerful corporations are a threat to democracy. Corporations finance politicians' campaigns, lobby Congress, arrange to participate in the writing of legislation, and use their resources in many legal and even illegal ways to influence government to serve their interests or to oppose actions that would hurt their interests. The social sciences are united in this view of the alignment of power in America and many other nations. There is a debate, however, about whether this situation is a case of corporate control or only corporate influence. The latter allows other interests, including the public good, to also have influence over the government and thus make it more democratic, that is, rule by the people. Muller emphasizes the current negative effects of capitalism such as increasing inequality and eroding cultural values by increasing commodification. Berg praises capitalism because it strongly stimulates innovations which greatly benefit our lives.

YES

Jerry Z. Muller

Capitalism and Inequality

What the Right and the Left Get Wrong

Recent political debate in the United States and other advanced capitalist democracies has been dominated by two issues: the rise of economic inequality and the scale of government intervention to address it. As the 2012 U.S. presidential election and the battles over the "fiscal cliff" have demonstrated, the central focus of the left today is on increasing government taxing and spending, primarily to reverse the growing stratification of society, whereas the central focus of the right is on decreasing taxing and spending, primarily to ensure economic dynamism. Each side minimizes the concerns of the other, and each seems to believe that its desired policies are sufficient to ensure prosperity and social stability. Both are wrong.

Inequality is indeed increasing almost everywhere in the postindustrial capitalist world. But despite what many on the left think, this is not the result of politics, nor is politics likely to reverse it, for the problem is more deeply rooted and intractable than generally recognized. Inequality is an inevitable product of capitalist activity, and expanding equality of opportunity only increases it—because some individuals and communities are simply better able than others to exploit the opportunities for development and advancement that capitalism affords. Despite what many on the right think, however, this is a problem for everybody, not just those who are doing poorly or those who are ideologically committed to egalitarianism—because if left unaddressed, rising inequality and economic insecurity can erode social order and generate a populist backlash against the capitalist system at large.

Over the last few centuries, the spread of capitalism has generated a phenomenal leap in human progress, leading to both previously unimaginable increases in material living standards and the unprecedented cultivation of all kinds of human potential. Capitalism's intrinsic dynamism, however, produces insecurity along with benefits, and so its advance has always met resistance. Much of the

political and institutional history of capitalist societies, in fact, has been the record of attempts to ease or cushion that insecurity, and it was only the creation of the modern welfare state in the middle of the twentieth century that finally enabled capitalism and democracy to coexist in relative harmony.

In recent decades, developments in technology, finance, and international trade have generated new waves and forms of insecurity for leading capitalist economies, making life increasingly unequal and chancier for not only the lower and working classes but much of the middle class as well. The right has largely ignored the problem, while the left has sought to eliminate it through government action, regardless of the costs. Neither approach is viable in the long run. Contemporary capitalist polities need to accept that inequality and insecurity will continue to be the inevitable result of market operations and find ways to shield citizens from their consequences—while somehow still preserving the dynamism that produces capitalism's vast economic and cultural benefits in the first place.

Commodification and Cultivation

Capitalism is a system of economic and social relations marked by private property, the exchange of goods and services by free individuals, and the use of market mechanisms to control the production and distribution of those goods and services. Some of its elements have existed in human societies for ages, but it was only in the seventeenth and eighteenth centuries, in parts of Europe and its offshoots in North America, that they all came together in force. Throughout history, most households had consumed most of the things that they produced and produced most of what they consumed. Only at this point did a majority of the population in some countries begin to buy most of the things they consumed and do so with the proceeds gained from selling most of what they produced.

The growth of market-oriented households and what came to be called "commercial society" had profound implications for practically every aspect of human activity. Prior to capitalism, life was governed by traditional institutions that subordinated the choices and destinies of individuals to various communal, political, and religious structures. These institutions kept change to a minimum, blocking people from making much progress but also protecting them from many of life's vicissitudes. The advent of capitalism gave individuals more control over and responsibility for their own lives than ever before—which proved both liberating and terrifying, allowing for both progress and regression.

Commodification—the transformation of activities performed for private use into activities performed for sale on the open market—allowed people to use their time more efficiently, specializing in producing what they were relatively good at and buying other things from other people. New forms of commerce and manufacturing used the division of labor to produce common household items cheaply and also made a range of new goods available. The result, as the historian Jan de Vries has noted, was what contemporaries called "an awakening of the appetites of the mind"—an expansion of subjective wants and a new subjective perception of needs. This ongoing expansion of wants has been chastised by critics of capitalism from Rousseau to Marcuse as imprisoning humans in a cage of unnatural desires. But it has also been praised by defenders of the market from Voltaire onward for broadening the range of human possibility. Developing and fulfilling higher wants and needs, in this view, is the essence of civilization.

Because we tend to think of commodities as tangible physical objects, we often overlook the extent to which the creation and increasingly cheap distribution of new cultural commodities have expanded what one might call the means of self-cultivation. For the history of capitalism is also the history of the extension of communication, information, and entertainment—things to think with, and about.

Among the earliest modern commodities were printed books (in the first instance, typically the Bible), and their shrinking price and increased availability were far more historically momentous than, say, the spread of the internal combustion engine. So, too, with the spread of newsprint, which made possible the newspaper and the magazine. Those gave rise, in turn, to new markets for information and to the business of gathering and distributing news. In the eighteenth century, it took months for news from India to reach London; today, it takes moments. Books and news have made possible an expansion of not only our awareness but also our imagination, our ability to empathize with others and imagine living in new ways ourselves. Capitalism and commodification have thus facilitated both humanitarianism and new forms of self-invention.

Over the last century, the means of cultivation were expanded by the invention of recorded sound, film, and television, and with the rise of the Internet and home computing, the costs of acquiring knowledge and culture have fallen dramatically. For those so inclined, the expansion of the means of cultivation makes possible an almost unimaginable enlargement of one's range of knowledge.

Family Matters

If capitalism has opened up ever more opportunities for the development of human potential, however, not everyone has been able to take full advantage of those opportunities or progress. . . . Formal or informal barriers to equality of opportunity, for example, have historically blocked various sectors of the population—such as women, minorities, and the poor—from benefiting fully from all capitalism offers. But over time, in the advanced capitalist world, those barriers have gradually been lowered or removed, so that now opportunity is more equally available than ever before. The inequality that exists today, therefore, derives less from the unequal availability of opportunity than it does from the unequal ability to exploit opportunity. And that unequal ability, in turn, stems from differences in the inherent human potential that individuals begin with and in the ways that families and communities enable and encourage that human potential to flourish.

The role of the family in shaping individuals' ability and inclination to make use of the means of cultivation that capitalism offers is hard to overstate. The household is not only a site of consumption and of biological reproduction. It is also the main setting in which children are socialized, civilized, and educated, in which habits are developed that influence their subsequent fates as people and as market actors. To use the language of contemporary economics, the family is a workshop in which human capital is produced.

Over time, the family has shaped capitalism by creating new demands for new commodities. It has also been repeatedly reshaped by capitalism because new commodities and new means of production have led family members to spend their time in new ways. As new consumer goods became available at ever-cheaper prices during the eighteenth century, families devoted more of their time to market-oriented activities, with positive effects on their ability to consume. . . .

Dynamism and Insecurity

For most of history, the prime source of human insecurity was nature. In such societies, as Marx noted, the economic system was oriented toward stability—and stagnancy. Capitalist societies, by contrast, have been oriented toward innovation and dynamism, to the creation of new knowledge, new products, and new modes of production and distribution. All of this has shifted the locus of insecurity from nature to the economy. . . .

The dynamism and insecurity created by nineteenth-century industrial capitalism led to the creation of new institutions for the reduction of insecurity, including the limited liability corporation, to reduce investor risks; labor unions, to further worker interests; mutual-aid societies, to provide loans and burial insurance; and commercial life insurance. In the middle decades of the twentieth century, in response to the mass unemployment and deprivation produced by the Great Depression (and the political success of communism and fascism, which convinced many democrats that too much insecurity was a threat to capitalist democracy itself), Western democracies embraced the welfare state. Different nations created different combinations of specific programs, but the new welfare states had a good deal in common, including old-age and unemployment insurance and various measures to support families.

The expansion of the welfare state in the decades after World War II took place at a time when the capitalist economies of the West were growing rapidly. The success of the industrial economy made it possible to siphon off profits and wages to government purposes through taxation. The demographics of the postwar era, in which the breadwinner-homemaker model of the family predominated, helped also, as moderately high birthrates created a favorable ratio of active workers to dependents. Educational opportunities expanded, as elite universities increasingly admitted students on the basis of their academic achievements and potential, and more and more people attended institutions of higher education. And barriers to full participation in society for women and minorities began to fall as well. The result of all of this was a temporary equilibrium during which the advanced capitalist countries experienced strong economic growth, high employment, and relative socioeconomic equality.

Life in the Postindustrial Economy

For humanity in general, the late twentieth and early twenty-first centuries have been a period of remarkable progress, due in no small part to the spread of capitalism around the globe. Economic liberalization in China, India, Brazil, Indonesia, and other countries in the developing world has allowed hundreds of millions of people to escape grinding poverty and move into the middle class. Consumers in more advanced capitalist countries, such as the United States, meanwhile, have experienced a radical reduction in the price of many commodities, from clothes to televisions, and the availability of a river of new goods that have transformed their lives.

Most remarkable, perhaps, have been changes to the means of self-cultivation. As the economist Tyler Cowen notes, much of the fruit of recent developments "is in our minds and in our laptops and not so much in the revenue-generating sector of the economy." As a result, "much of the value of the internet is experienced at the personal level and so will never show up in the productivity numbers." Many of the great musical performances of the twentieth century, in every genre, are available on YouTube for free. Many of the great films of the twentieth century, once confined to occasional showings at art houses in a few metropolitan areas, can be viewed by anybody at any time for a small monthly charge. Soon, the great university libraries will be available online to the entire world, and other unprecedented opportunities for personal development will follow.

All this progress, however, has been shadowed by capitalism's perennial features of inequality and insecurity. In 1973, the sociologist Daniel Bell noted that in the advanced capitalist world, knowledge, science, and technology were driving a transformation to what he termed "postindustrial society." Just as manufacturing had previously displaced agriculture as the major source of employment, he argued, so the service sector was now displacing manufacturing. In a postindustrial, knowledge-based economy, the production of manufactured goods depended more on technological inputs than on the skills of the workers who actually built and assembled the products. That meant a relative decline in the need for and economic value of skilled and semiskilled factory workers—just as there had previously been a decline in the need for and value of agricultural laborers. In such an economy, the skills in demand included scientific and technical knowledge and the ability to work with information. The revolution in information technology that has swept through the economy in recent decades, meanwhile, has only exacerbated these trends.

One crucial impact of the rise of the postindustrial economy has been on the status and roles of men and women. Men's relative advantage in the preindustrial and industrial economies rested in large part on their greater physical strength—something now ever less in demand. Women, in contrast, whether by biological disposition or socialization, have had a relative advantage in human skills and emotional intelligence, which have become increasingly more important in an economy more oriented to human services than to the production of material objects. The portion of the economy in which women could participate has expanded, and their labor has become more valuable—meaning that time spent at home now comes at the expense of more lucrative possibilities in the paid work force.

This has led to the growing replacement of male breadwinner-female homemaker households by dual-income households. Both advocates and critics of the move of women into the paid economy have tended to overemphasize the role played in this shift by the ideological struggles of feminism, while underrating the role played by changes in the nature of capitalist production. The redeployment of female labor from the household has been made possible in part by the existence of new commodities that cut down on necessary household labor time (such as washing machines, dryers, dishwashers, water heaters, vacuum cleaners, microwave ovens). The greater time devoted to market activity, in turn, has given rise to new demand for household-oriented consumer goods that require less labor (such as packaged and prepared food) and the expansion of restaurant and fast-food eating. And it has led to the commodification of care, as the young, the elderly, and the infirm are increasingly looked after not by relatives but by paid minders.

The trend for women to receive more education and greater professional attainments has been accompanied by changing social norms in the choice of marriage partners. In the age of the breadwinner-homemaker marriage, women tended to place a premium on earning capacity in their choice of partners. Men, in turn, valued the homemaking capacities of potential spouses more than their vocational attainments. It was not unusual for men and women to marry partners of roughly the same intelligence, but women tended to marry men of higher levels of education and economic achievement. As the economy has passed from an industrial economy to a postindustrial service-and-information economy, women have joined men in attaining recognition through paid work, and the industrious couple today is more likely to be made of peers, with more equal levels of education and more comparable levels of economic achievement—a process termed "assortative mating."

Inequality on the Rise

These postindustrial social trends have had a significant impact on inequality. If family income doubles at each step of the economic ladder, then the total incomes of those families higher up the ladder are bound to increase faster than the total incomes of those further down. But for a substantial portion of households at the lower end of the ladder, there has been no doubling at all—for as the relative pay of women has grown and the relative pay of less-educated, working-class men has declined, the latter have been viewed as less and less marriageable. Often, the limitations of human capital that make such men less employable also make them less desirable as companions, and the character traits of men who are chronically unemployed sometimes deteriorate as well. With less to bring to the table, such men are regarded as less necessary—in part because women can now count on provisions from the welfare state as an additional independent source of income, however meager.

In the United States, among the most striking developments of recent decades has been the stratification of marriage patterns among the various classes and ethnic groups of society. When divorce laws were loosened in the 1960s, there was a rise in divorce rates among all classes. But by the 1980s, a new pattern had emerged: divorce declined among the more educated portions of the populace, while rates among the less-educated portions continued to rise. In addition, the more educated and more well-to-do were more likely to wed, while the less educated were less likely to do so. Given the family's role as an incubator of human capital, such trends have had important spillover effects on inequality. Abundant research shows that children raised by two parents in an ongoing union are more likely to develop the self-discipline and self-confidence that make for success in life, whereas children—and particularly boys—reared in single-parent households (or, worse, households with a mother who has a series of temporary relationships) have a greater risk of adverse outcomes.

All of this has been taking place during a period of growing equality of access to education and increasing stratification of marketplace rewards, both of which have increased the importance of human capital. One element of human capital is cognitive ability: quickness of mind, the ability to infer and apply patterns drawn from experience, and the ability to deal with mental complexity. Another is character and social skills: self-discipline, persistence, responsibility. And a third is actual knowledge. All of these are becoming increasingly crucial for success in the postindustrial marketplace. As the economist Brink Lindsey notes in his recent book *Human Capitalism,* between 1973 and 2001, average annual growth in real income was only 0.3 percent for people in the bottom fifth of the U.S. income distribution, compared with 0.8 percent for people in the middle fifth and 1.8 percent for those in the top fifth. Somewhat similar patterns also prevail in many other advanced economies.

Globalization has not caused this pattern of increasingly unequal returns to human capital but reinforced it. The economist Michael Spence has distinguished between "tradable" goods and services, which can be easily imported and exported, and "untradable" ones, which cannot. Increasingly, tradable goods and services are imported to advanced capitalist societies from less advanced capitalist societies, where labor costs are lower. As manufactured goods and routine services are outsourced, the wages of the relatively unskilled and uneducated in advanced capitalist societies decline further, unless these people are somehow able to find remunerative employment in the untradable sector.

The Impact of Modern Finance

Rising inequality, meanwhile, has been compounded by rising insecurity and anxiety for people higher up on the economic ladder. One trend contributing to this problem has been the financialization of the economy, above all in the United States, creating what was characterized as "money manager capitalism" by the economist Hyman Minsky and has been called "agency capitalism" by the financial expert Alfred Rappaport.

As late as the 1980s, finance was an essential but limited element of the U.S. economy. The trade in equities (the stock market) was made up of individual investors, large or small, putting their own money in stocks of companies they believed to have good long-term prospects. Investment capital was also available from the major Wall Street investment banks and their foreign counterparts, which were private partnerships in which the partners' own money was on the line. All of this began to change as larger pools of capital became available for investment and came to be deployed by professional money managers rather [than] the owners of the capital themselves.

One source of such new capital was pension funds. In the postwar decades, when major American industries emerged from World War II as oligopolies with limited competition and large, expanding markets at home and abroad, their profits and future prospects allowed them to offer employees defined-benefit pension plans, with the risks involved assumed by the companies themselves. From the 1970s on, however, as the U.S. economy became

more competitive, corporate profits became more uncertain, and companies (as well as various public-sector organizations) attempted to shift the risk by putting their pension funds into the hands of professional money managers, who were expected to generate significant profits. Retirement income for employees now depended not on the profits of their employers but on the fate of their pension funds.

Another source of new capital was university and other nonprofit organizations' endowments, which grew initially thanks to donations but were increasingly expected to grow further based on their investment performance. And still another source of new capital came from individuals and governments in the developing world, where rapid economic growth, combined with a high propensity to save and a desire for relatively secure investment prospects, led to large flows of money into the U.S. financial system.

Spurred in part by these new opportunities, the traditional Wall Street investment banks transformed themselves into publicly traded corporations—that is to say, they, too, began to invest not just with their own funds but also with other people's money—and tied the bonuses of their partners and employees to annual profits. All of this created a highly competitive financial system dominated by investment managers working with large pools of capital, paid based on their supposed ability to outperform their peers. The structure of incentives in this environment led fund managers to try to maximize short-term returns, and this pressure trickled down to corporate executives. The shrunken time horizon created a temptation to boost immediate profits at the expense of longer-term investments, whether in research and development or in improving the skills of the company's work force. For both managers and employees, the result has been a constant churning that increases the likelihood of job losses and economic insecurity.

An advanced capitalist economy does indeed require an extensive financial sector. Part of this is a simple extension of the division of labor: outsourcing decisions about investing to professionals allows the rest of the population the mental space to pursue things they do better or care more about. The increasing complexity of capitalist economies means that entrepreneurs and corporate executives need help in deciding when and how to raise funds. And private equity firms that have an ownership interest in growing the real value of the firms in which they invest play a key role in fostering economic growth. These matters, which properly occupy financiers, have important consequences, and handling them requires intelligence, diligence, and drive, so it is neither surprising nor undesirable that specialists in this area are highly paid. But whatever its benefits and continued social value, the financialization of society has nevertheless had some unfortunate consequences, both in increasing inequality by raising the top of the economic ladder (thanks to the extraordinary rewards financial managers receive) and in increasing insecurity among those lower down (thanks to the intense focus on short-term economic performance to the exclusion of other concerns). . . .

What Is to Be Done?

Capitalism today continues to produce remarkable benefits and continually greater opportunities for self-cultivation and personal development. Now as ever, however, those upsides are coming with downsides, particularly increasing inequality and insecurity. As Marx and Engels accurately noted, what distinguishes capitalism from other social and economic systems is its "constant revolutionizing of production, uninterrupted disturbance of all social conditions, [and] everlasting uncertainty and agitation." . . .

The challenge for government policy in the advanced capitalist world is thus how to maintain a rate of economic dynamism that will provide increasing benefits for all while still managing to pay for the social welfare programs required to make citizens' lives bearable under conditions of increasing inequality and insecurity. Different countries will approach this challenge in different ways, since their priorities, traditions, size, and demographic and economic characteristics vary. (It is among the illusions of the age that when it comes to government policy, nations can borrow at will from one another.) But a useful starting point might be the rejection of both the politics of privilege and the politics of resentment and the adoption of a clear-eyed view of what capitalism actually involves, as opposed to the idealization of its worshipers and the demonization of its critics.

JERRY Z. MULLER is professor of history at the Catholic University of America and author of several books including *The Mind and the Market: Capitalism in Western Thought*, *The Other God That Failed: Hans Freyer and the Deradicalization of German Conservatism*, and *Conservatism: An Anthology of Social and Political Thought from David Hume to the Present.*

Chris Berg  **NO**

Why Capitalism Is Awesome

Each year the glossy business magazine *FastCompany* releases a list of what it considers to be the "World's 50 Most Innovative Companies." This list is populated much as you would expect.

In 2012 the leader was Apple, followed by Facebook, Google, and Amazon.com. Spot a theme? In the top 10, there are only two companies that are not primarily digital companies. One, Life Technologies, works in genetic engineering. (The other—try not to laugh—is the Occupy Movement. *FastCompany* describes them as "Transparent. Tech savvy. Design savvy. Local and global. Nimble.") Not only are most of them digital firms, but they're all flashy and unique, and they're almost all household names.

Everybody from *Forbes* to *BusinessWeek* hands out most innovative company awards. They're all pretty similar and predictable. But these lists have a perverse effect. They suggest that the great success of capitalism and the market economy is inventing cutting edge technology and that if we want to observe capitalist progress, we should be looking for sleek design and popular fashion. Innovation, the media tells us, is inventing cures for cancer, solar panels, and social networking.

But the true genius of the market economy isn't that it produces prominent, highly publicized goods to inspire retail queues, or the medical breakthroughs that make the nightly news. No, the genius of capitalism is found in the tiny things—the things that nobody notices.

A market economy is characterized by an infinite succession of imperceptible, iterative changes and adjustments. Free market economists have long talked about the unplanned and uncoordinated nature of capitalist innovation. They've neglected to emphasize just how invisible it is.

One exception is the great Adam Smith. In his *Wealth of Nations*, the example he used to illustrate the division of labor was a pin factory. He described carefully the complex process by which a pin is made. Producing the head of the pin "requires two to three distinct operations." To place the head on the wire is a "peculiar business." Then the pins have to be whitened. The production of a pin, Smith concluded, is an 18-step task.

Smith was making an argument about specialization, but just as important was his choice of example. It would be hard to think of something less impressive, less consequential than a pin. Smith wanted his contemporaries to think about the economy not by observing it from the lofty heights of the palace or the lecture hall, but by seeing it from the bottom up—to recognise how a market economy is the aggregate of millions of little tasks. It's a lesson many have not yet learned. We should try to recognise the subtleties of the apparently mundane.

Capitalism Means Efficiency

Ikea's Billy bookshelf is a common, almost disposable, piece of household furniture that has been produced continuously since 1979. It looks exactly the same as it did more than three decades ago. But it's much cheaper. The standard model—more than six feet tall—costs $59.99. And from an engineering perspective the Billy bookshelf is hugely different from its ancestors.

In those 30 years the Billy has changed minutely but importantly. The structure of the back wall has changed over and over, as the company has tried to reduce the weight of the back (weight costs money) but increase its strength. Even the studs that hold up the removable book shelves have undergone dramatic changes. The studs were until recently simple metal cylinders. Now they are sophisticated shapes, tapering into a cup at one end on which the shelf rests. The brackets that hold the frame together are also complex pieces of engineering.

Ikea is a massive company. Tiny changes—even to metal studs—are magnified when those products are produced in bulk. There is no doubt somebody, somewhere in the Ikea product design hierarchy whose singular focus has been reducing the weight and increasing the strength of those studs. They went to sleep thinking about studs and metals and the trade-offs between strength and weight. Their seemingly inconsequential work helps keep

Ikea's prices down and its profits high. With each minute change to the shape of the Billy's metal studs they earn their salary many times over.

Being massive, however, Ikea has an advantage: it is able to hire specialists whose job is solely to obsess about simple things like studs. Ikea is well-known for its more prominent innovations—for instance, flat-packing, which can reduce to one-sixth the cost of shipping—and the extremely low staffing of its retail stores.

For big-box retailers, innovation is about efficiency, not invention. Extremely resilient supply chains may not win glossy innovation awards but they are the source of much of our modern prosperity. But Ikea is big and famous. So let me suggest another icon of capitalist innovation and dynamism: pizza.

Capitalism Tastes Better, Cheaper

Pizza is one of our most mundane and simple foods. It would be the last place most people would look for innovation and engineering. It is, at its most basic, a thin bread topped by tomatoes and cheese—a food of the poor of Naples exported, which is endlessly interpreted by the rest of the world.

Forty-one percent of Americans eat pizza at least once a week, whether purchased frozen and reheated in home ovens, delivered, taken away, or cooked from scratch at home. All of these choices are more complicated than they seem. Keeping a pizza crisp long out of the oven so that it can be delivered, or making sure it will crisp up in a variable home oven after having been frozen for weeks is anything but simple.

Moisture is the enemy. For frozen pizzas, this means that toppings have to be precooked precisely to avoid some ingredients being burned while others are still heating through. Frozen pizza takes a lot of abuse—it is partially thawed each time it is transferred from manufacturer to supermarket to home freezer. So the dough has to be precisely regulated to manage its water content. Cheese freezes poorly, and consumers expect it to melt evenly across the base, so manufacturers obsess about cheese's pH range and its water and salt content. And of course all these decisions are made with an eye on the customer's budget and the manufacturer's profitability. The consumers of family sized frozen pizzas tend to be extremely price sensitive. The opportunities for innovation in processes, equipment, automation, and chemistry are virtually endless.

It gets even more complicated when we factor in changing consumer tastes. The modern pizza customer doesn't just want cheese, tomato, and pepperoni. As food tastes grow more sophisticated they look for more sophisticated flavors, even in frozen pizza. It's one thing to master how cheddar or mozzarella melts. Dealing with more flavorful brie or smoked Gouda is another thing entirely. Like Ikea's stud specialist, there are hundreds of people across the world obsessed with how frozen cheese melts in a home oven. These sorts of complications are replicated across every ingredient in this simple product. (How does one adapt an automated pepperoni dispenser to dispense feta instead?)

Customers demand aesthetic qualities too. Frozen products have to look authentic. Customers like their pizza crusts to have slight burn marks, even if home ovens won't naturally produce them. So manufacturers experiment with all sorts of heating techniques to replicate the visual result of a wood fired oven.

Takeout pizza seems easier but has almost as many complexities. Some large pizza chains are slowly integrating the sort of sauce and topping applicators used by frozen goods manufacturers. Cheese is costly and hard to spread evenly. The pizza chain Dominos uses a proprietary "auto-cheese," which takes standardized blocks of cheese and, with a push of a button, shreds them evenly across a base.

Moisture problems are even more endemic in takeout pizza. The cooked pizza has to survive, hot and crispy and undamaged, for some time before it is consumed. If the box is closed, the steam from the hot pizza seeps through the bread, making it soft and unappealing. But an open box will lose heat too quickly. Engineers have struck a balance. Vents in the box and plastic tripods in the centre of the pizza encourage airflow. Deliverers carry the pizzas in large insulated sleeves to keep the heat in but reduce risk of steam damage.

We could easily replicate this analysis for almost every processed or manufactured food in the typical supermarket. Then we could reflect on the complexity of serving food, not in a home kitchen, but on an airplane flying more than 600 miles per hour and 37,000 feet in the air, cooked in a tiny galley for hundreds of people at a time.

Some of the most extraordinary logistical accomplishments of the modern world are entirely unnoticed. Some—like airline food—we actively disparage, without recognizing the true effort behind them.

Capitalism Is About Innovation, as Well as Invention

One of the great essays in the free market tradition is Leonard Read's "I, Pencil." Read was the founder of the influential American think tank the Foundation for

Economic Education. In his essay, he adopts the perspective of an ordinary wooden lead pencil and purports to write his genealogy. He began as a cedar tree from North California or Oregon, was chopped down and harvested and shipped on a train to a mill in San Leandro, California, and there cut down into "small, pencil-length slats less than one-fourth of an inch in thickness."

Read's point: "Not a single person on the face of this earth" knows how to make a pencil on their own. The construction of a pencil is entirely dispersed among "millions of human beings," from the Italians who mine pumice for the eraser to the coffee manufacturers who supply their drinks to the cedar loggers in Oregon.

Read was vividly illustrating a famous point of Friedrich Hayek's—these separate people manage, through nothing but the price system, to make something extraordinarily complex. None of the pumice miners intend to make a pencil. They simply want to trade their labor for wages. Adam Smith's invisible hand does the rest.

Read published his essay in 1958. The chemical formula for the eraser, known as the "plug," has changed repeatedly over the half century since. The production is highly automated, and the supply lines are tighter. Chemicals are added to keep the eraser from splitting. Synthetic rubber production in 2012 is much different than it was in 1958. These tiny plugs look pretty much the same but have evolved in a dozen different ways.

"I, Pencil" magnificently captures the complexity of markets, but it doesn't quite capture their dynamism. The millions of people involved in pencil production aren't merely performing their market-allocated tasks but are trying to find new ways to make their tiny segment easier, cheaper, and more profitable. The pencil market—as far from a cutting-edge firm like Facebook as you could imagine—is still full of entrepreneurs trying to break apart established business models to shave costs and rationalize supply chains. In 1991 a gross of 144 simple, Chinese-made wood pencils sold on the wholesale market for $6.91. In 2004 that price had dropped to $4.48.

And this is before we consider the variety of pencils available to consumers—not just wooden ones of different shapes, sizes, colors, and densities, but mechanical pencils, jumbo sized children's pencils, rectangular carpenters' pencils (rectangular pencils can't roll away) and on, and on, and on.

It is to capitalism's great disadvantage that there's nothing inherently exciting about pencils. Humans like novelty. We like invention. We like high-technology breakthroughs that will change the world.

I, Pork

The most insightful book about capitalism published in the last decade isn't a treatise on economics or philosophy but an art project. In *Pig 05049*, the Dutch artist Christien Meindertsma starkly shows photographs of the 185 separate products that are made from a single pig.

Every part of a slaughtered pig is sold and repurposed. Obviously, we're familiar with pork and ham but how many people realise that pig bones are converted into a glue that holds sandpaper together? Or that pig fat is a constituent part of paint, helping its spread and giving it a glossy sheen? Pig parts are found in everything from yogurt to train brakes to photography paper to matches—even in bullets.

One response to Meindertsma's book is to see it as simply a modern-day reworking of Leonard Read's pencil. But it's more than that. *Pig 05049* reveals what a market economy tries to obscure: the deep complexities of individual products.

That single pig was stripped down and shipped to factories and markets across the world. It went into matches and copper and crayons and floor wax. These products are as mundane as can be imagined—what consumer spends more than a moment's thought on which crayon to purchase, let alone how those crayons are produced? But as Meindertsma points out, the distinctive smell of many crayons comes from fatty acids, which in turn come from pig bone fat, used as a hardening agent.

Pig 05049 was published in 2007. The oleochemical industry—that is, the industry that derives chemicals from natural oils and fats—is one of the most innovative in the world. Like any industry experiencing rapid technological and scientific change, it is restructuring as well, moving production from Western Europe and the United States to China, Malaysia, and Indonesia.

Six years is a long time in a competitive marketplace. As simple as they seem, those crayons are changing: costs of production have been shaved down, raw materials are being utilized more efficiently, and supply lines are being tightened. Amazon now lists 2,259 separate products in the children's drawing crayon category alone.

Government Doesn't Understand Innovation

If *FastCompany* has a warped view about the nature of innovation in a market economy, it is not alone. Governments do, too.

The Australian federal government has its very own minister for innovation, and his Department of Industry,

Innovation, Science, Research and Tertiary Education doles out grants for inventions and startups. Its Commercialisation Australia program sponsors inventors who "have transformed an innovative idea into reality." Innovation Australia funds grant-seekers to turn their "ground-breaking ideas into commercial products." This is the invention fetish—the idea that technological progress occurs when dreamers have great ideas. All society needs to do is subsidize dreams into reality.

But ideas are the easy part. Getting things done is hard. Setting up a business, paring down costs, acquiring and retaining market share: those are the fields in a market economy where firms win or lose. The brilliance of the market economy is found in small innovations made to polish and enhance existing products and services.

Invention is a wonderful thing. But we should not pretend that it is invention that has made us rich.

We have higher living standards than our ancestors because of the little things. We ought to be more aware of the continuous, slow, and imperceptible creative destruction of the market economy, the refiners who are always imperceptibly bettering our frozen pizzas, our bookshelves, our pencils, and our crayons.

CHRIS BERG is a research fellow with the Institute of Public Affairs in Melbourne, Australia, and author of *In Defence of Freedom of Speech*. He authored *The Growth of Australia's Regulatory State*, and edited *The National Curriculum: A Critique* (2011).

EXPLORING THE ISSUE

Does Capitalism Have Serious Defects?

Critical Thinking and Reflection

1. Provide a definition of capitalism that distinguishes it from socialism, communism, collectivism, and a mixed economy. What aspects of the economy are capitalistic and what aspects are socialistic? (Remember that I teach at the University of Maryland, which is socialism because the public owns the means of production. I would argue that the University of Maryland is good socialism.)
2. How does capitalism supposedly undermine democracy? How does it supposedly help create democracies?
3. Why does capitalism need to be restrained by the government or is it better for capitalism to not be regulated?
4. If the corporations run the country, they have to work together in an organized way to be successful. How are they organized? Many corporations have contrary interests. How and when do they push in unison? Why do we assume that they stand united?
5. How does capitalism cause such great inequality?
6. What would you say are the three greatest positive impacts that capitalism has on society?
7. How does capitalism affect values and culture?
8. Do organizations that oppose corporate interests feel that they succeed sometimes against the corporations? If they do, how do you explain this?

Is There Common Ground?

The foremost issue in understanding our society is the structure of power. There is common agreement that power is very unevenly distributed in America and this power inequality has been increasing over time. When that inequality gets too large, it can effectively destroy democracy because the votes of most of the people do not really count when they are contrary to the desires of the economic powers. The candidates are selected (funded) by the capitalist class that also controls them when in office. The debate is over whether the inequality in America has reached that point or not. Another issue is whether the economic benefits of capitalism are much greater than the negative impacts of capitalism on values, character, and culture. Everyone agrees that there are both positive and negative effects of capitalism. The debate is over which are greater.

Additional Resources

In 1962, Milton Friedman convincingly demonstrated that economic freedom is a key precondition for political freedom in his classic book *Capitalism and Freedom* (University of Chicago Press). His thesis became the major argument for the virtues of capitalism. He maintains that capitalism's defects are few and minimal. Other works

that support Friedman's view include Azar Gat, *Victorious and Vulnerable: Why Democracy Won in the 20th Century and How It Is Still Imperiled* (Rowman & Littlefield, 2010); Alasdair Roberts, *The Logic of Discipline: Global Capitalism and the Architecture of Government* (Oxford University Press, 2010); Colin Cremin, *Capitalism's New Clothes: Enterprise, Ethics and Enjoyment in Times of Crisis* (Pluto Press, 2011); Peter L. Berger, *The Capitalist Revolution: Fifty Propositions About Prosperity, Equality, and Liberty* [a classic] (Basic Books, 1986); Andrew Bernstein, *The Capitalist Manifesto: The Historic, Economic and Philosophic Case for Laissez-Faire* (University Press of America, 2005); Dhanjoo N. Ghista, *Socio-Economic Democracy and the World Government: Collective Capitalism, Depovertization, Human Rights, Template for Sustainable Peace* (World Scientific, 2004); Michael G. Heller, *Capitalism, Institutions, and Economic Development* (Routledge, 2009); Dennis C. Mueller, *Capitalism and Democracy: Challenges and Responses in an Increasingly Interdependent World* (Edward Elgar Publishing, 2003); Arthur Seldon, ed., *The Virtues of Capitalism* (Liberty Fund, 2004); and Edward W. Younkins, *Champions of a Free Society: Ideas of Capitalism's Philosophers and Economists* (Lexington Books, 2008). The works that are critical of capitalism's impact on society include Henry A. Giroux, *Zombie Politics and Culture in the Age of Casino Capitalism* (Peter Lang, 2011); Brian C. Anderson, *Democratic Capitalism and Its Discontents* (ISI Books, 2007); Yves Smith,

ECONned: How Unenlightened Self Interest Undermined Democracy and Corrupted Capitalism (Palgrave Macmillan, 2010); Noreena Hertz, *The Silent Takeover: Global Capitalism and the Death of Democracy* (Heinemann, 2001); Michael Parenti, *Democracy for the Few* (Thompson-Wadsworth, 2008); Alex Callinicos, *An Anti-Capitalist Manifesto* (Polity Press, 2003); Mark A. Martinez, *The Myth of the Free Market: The Role of the State in a Capitalist Economy* (Kumarian Press, 2009); and Robert Reich's *Super-Capitalism: The Transformation of Business, Democracy, and Everyday Life* (Alfred A. Knopf, 2007). Jacob S. Hacker examines a prosperous United States where citizens increasingly feel politically powerless in *Great Risk Shift: The Assault on American Jobs, Families, Health Care and Retirement—And How You Can Fight Back* (Oxford University Press, 2006). A major response to the above critics of capitalism is Martin Wolf's "The Morality of the Market," *Foreign Policy* (September/October 2003), in which he tries to refute the allegation that the global economy undermines democracy. Three works that study the connection of capitalism and democracy more neutrally are Tony Porter and Karsten Ronit, eds., *The Challenges of Global Business Authority: Democratic Renewal, Stalemate, or Decay?* (State University of New York Press, 2010); Amiya Kumar Bagchi, *Perilous Passage: Mankind and the Global Ascendancy of Capital* (Rowman & Littlefield, 2005), and Peter Nolan, *Capitalism and Freedom: The Contradictory Character of Globalisation* (Anthem Press, 2007). Two works that see very positive effects of capitalism if it were modified in certain ways are Sandra A. Waddock, SEE *Change: Making the Transition to a Sustainable Enterprise Economy* (Greenleaf Publishing, 2011) and R. P. Bootle, *The Trouble with Markets: Saving Capitalism from Itself* (Nicholas B. Realey Publishing, 2011). Several authors propose alternative economic systems to capitalism which will better support democracy, including Allen Engler, *Economic Democracy: The Working-Class Alternative to Capitalism* (Fernwood Publishing, 2010); Chris Wyatt, *The Defetishized Society: New Economic Democracy as a Libertarian Alternative to Capitalism* (Continuum, 2011); Peer Hull Kristensen and Kari Lilja, eds., *Nordic Capitalisms and Globalization: New Forms of Economic Organization and Welfare Institutions* (Oxford University Press, 2011); and Costas Panayotakis, *Remaking Scarcity: From Capitalist Inefficiency to Economic Democracy* (Pluto, 2011).

Internet References . . .

Sociology—Study Sociology Online

http://edu.learnsoc.org/

Sociology Web Resources

www.mhhe.com/socscience/sociology/resources/index.htm

Sociosite

www.topsite.com/goto/sociosite.net

Socioweb

www.topsite.com/goto/socioweb.com

Selected, Edited, and with Issue Framing Material by:
Kurt Finsterbusch, *University of Maryland, College Park*

ISSUE

Does Government Need to Be Restrained?

YES: Chris Edwards, from "Forget Too Big to Fail . . . The Federal Government Is Too Big to Work, *Washington Examiner* (2015)

NO: Richard Eskow, from "We Need a Bold Left to Challenge Government Downsizing," Campaign for America's Future (2015)

Learning Outcomes

After reading this issue, you will be able to:

- Identify why government generally performs badly and needs to be restrained.
- Understand why many believe that intervention is necessary to address many problems and why many others believe that almost always the government will cause more harm than good.
- Identify a number of specific problems that seem to require government interventions.
- Identify a number of specific adverse consequences that government interventions could cause.
- Conduct a simple qualitative risk assessment of government interventions in a capitalist economy. This method would list possible positive and negative consequences of a specific potential government intervention and estimate whether each of the possible consequences is very likely, likely, 50/50, unlikely, or very unlikely. On the basis of the results, draw your conclusion as to whether the government should intervene or not in the case that you were considering. Perhaps this method would allow you to tentatively identify when government intervention would be good and when it would be bad.
- Evaluate the type and strength of the support that is provided for each side of this debate. Is the argument based mainly on a few stories, on ideology, on theories, on carefully selected cases, or on a large number of cases?

ISSUE SUMMARY

YES: Chris Edwards editor of Cato Institute's DownsizingGovernment.org, argues that the federal government runs badly. It is wasteful and inept. It does too much and does not have strong incentives for efficiency and effectiveness. Its problems include top-down planning and bloated bureaucracy. Cut it back.

NO: Richard Eskow, writer, a former Wall Street executive and a radio journalist, argues that the government must not be cut back because its services are badly needed. The anti-government side does want increases to the military budget, but the domestic side generates more jobs and growth.

The expression "That government is best which governs least" sums up a deeply rooted attitude of many Americans. From early presidents Thomas Jefferson and Andrew Jackson to some of America's most recent leaders, Ronald Reagan, George Bush, Bill Clinton, and George W. Bush, American politicians have often echoed the popular view

that there are certain areas of life best left to the private actions of citizens.

One such area is the economic sphere, where people make their living by buying, selling, and producing goods and services. The tendency of most Americans is to regard direct government involvement in the economic sphere as both unnecessary and dangerous. The purest expression of this view is the economic theory of laissez-faire, a French term meaning "let be" or "let alone." The seminal formulation of laissez-faire theory was the work of eighteenth-century Scottish philosopher Adam Smith, whose treatise *The Wealth of Nations* appeared in 1776. Smith's thesis was that each individual, pursuing his or her own selfish interests in a competitive market, will be "led by an invisible hand to promote an end which was no part of his intention." In other words, when people single-mindedly seek profit, they actually serve the community, because sellers must keep prices down and quality up if they are to meet the competition of other sellers.

Laissez-faire economics was much honored (in theory, if not always in practice) during the nineteenth and early twentieth centuries. But as the nineteenth century drew to a close, the Populist Party sprang up. The Populists denounced eastern bankers, Wall Street stock manipulators, and rich "moneyed interests," and they called for government ownership of railroads, a progressive income tax, and other forms of state intervention. The Populist Party died out early in the twentieth century, but the Populist message was not forgotten. In fact, it was given new life after 1929, when the stock market collapsed and the United States was plunged into the worst economic depression in its history.

By 1932, a quarter of the nation's workforce was unemployed, and most Americans were finding it hard to believe that the "invisible hand" would set things right. Some Americans totally repudiated the idea of a free market and embraced socialism, the belief that the state (or "the community") should run all major industries. Most stopped short of supporting socialism, but they were now prepared to welcome some forms of state intervention in the economy. President Franklin D. Roosevelt, elected in 1932, spoke to this mood when he pledged a "New Deal" to the American people. "New Deal" has come to stand for a variety of programs that were enacted during the first eight years of Roosevelt's presidency, including business and banking regulations, government pension programs, federal aid to the disabled, unemployment compensation, and government-sponsored work programs. Side by side with the "invisible hand" of the marketplace was now the very visible hand of an activist government.

Government intervention in the economic sphere increased during World War II as the government fixed prices, rationed goods, and put millions to work in government-subsidized war industries. After the war the government's role in the economy declined dramatically, but the government continued to be fairly active during the 1950s. During the late 1960s and early 1970s, however, the role of the government in the economy increased greatly. It launched a variety of new welfare and regulatory programs: the multibillion dollar War on Poverty; new civil rights and affirmative action mandates; and new laws protecting consumers, workers, disabled people, and the environment. These, in turn, led to a proliferation of new government agencies and bureaus, as well as shelves and shelves of published regulations. Critics of government involvement like Edwards call attention not only to its direct costs but also to its effect on business activity and individual freedom. The government's defenders conceded that it was expensive, but they insisted that government is necessary to protect Americans against pollution, discrimination, dangerous products, and other effects of the modern marketplace and provide the services that many depend upon.

YES ↵

Chris Edwards

Forget Too Big to Fail . . . The Federal Government Is Too Big to Work

Americans have a sour view of the federal government. Just one-third of people think Washington is competent. The public thinks half of taxes collected are wasted. More people say "government" is the nation's most important problem than say that honor goes to the economy, immigration or terrorism.

And Americans are right. The federal government is wasteful and inept, which is a huge problem because it controls so many aspects of our lives. Federal spending consumes more than a fifth of the nation's income, and federal regulations infiltrate a multitude of state, local and private activities.

In recent years, big scandals have erupted at the Department of Veterans Affairs, Internal Revenue Service, Secret Service and other agencies. Federal auditors routinely uncover waste, fraud and abuse, and revelations about special-interest giveaways in Congress are commonplace.

But such problems are nothing new. In 1932, legal scholar James Beck explored wasteful federal spending in *Our Wonderland of Bureaucracy,* lambasting subsidies for shipping and sugar firms, and labeling farm subsidies a "stupendous failure" and "inexcusable legislative folly." Federal efforts to run businesses were "costly failures" of "extraordinary ineptitude." And regulations that were supposed to help rail customers instead increased costs. The problem with the government, Beck concluded, was that the "remedy may often be worse than the disease."

Failure has always plagued the federal government, and in recent years, that failure has multiplied as the government has grown too big to be adequately managed or overseen. While politicians usually blame federal bungling on the other party, the reality is that the only way to reduce endemic failure is to downsize the government.

Top-Down Planning

To understand the government, let's look first at markets. Their driving force is voluntary exchange. Buyers and sellers pursuing their own interests engage in billions of transactions, which are mutually beneficial and thus create value. Markets generate cooperation between disparate people, and they thrive on diversity.

Government does not work like that. Rather than voluntary exchange, it relies on top-down planning and coercion. As a result, it does not know whether its actions generate value. Because it imposes policies by decree, there is no sure way to know that they make sense.

The federal government imposes more than 3,000 new regulations each year, and spends trillions of dollars on more than 2,300 subsidy and benefit programs. These are funded by compulsory taxation, not customer revenue. Without voluntary agreement behind its actions, the government is flying blind on its decision-making, and so it makes a lot of mistakes.

It is true that in markets, businesses also make plenty of mistakes. But when they do, they are punished with financial losses and bankruptcy. A remarkable 10 percent of all American firms go out of business each year. So the market fixes its own mistakes, and it reallocates resources to better uses. By contrast, there is no built-in mechanism to prune waste in government, so the mistakes compound year after year and create rising economic damage.

Another failure created by the top-down nature of government is that its policies create winners and losers. For example, with the Affordable Care Act, consider that in markets, individuals choose their own levels of goods and service to consume. Markets cater to diversity. But government imposes one-size-fits-all schemes, which invariably make many people worse for wear. This suppression of individual choice in favor of top-down directives destroys value, and it is a key reason we should keep government limited.

People often assume that government has an advantage in tackling society's problems because it is a powerful institution that can use coercion. Actually, the fact that it can mandate actions and has a compulsory revenue stream is a huge weakness that leads it astray. Endemic government failure is baked into the cake because its misguided actions are not self-limiting the way that marketplace actions are.

Lack of Knowledge

When the government subsidizes and regulates, it throws a wrench into market pricing, the key mechanism that makes economies work. Prices allow millions of individuals and businesses to coordinate their activities. They communicate data about changes in resources, tastes and technology, and they create incentives for people to produce and consume efficiently.

Whenever the government distorts prices, it can produce a range of unintended negative consequences. Minimum wage laws are intended to help workers, but they raise the cost of hiring low-skill workers, so businesses hire fewer of them. Farm price supports are intended to help farmers, but they prompt farmers to over-produce subsidized crops and under-produce other, more valuable, crops.

Interventions create a range of side-effects. When farmers increase production of subsidized crops, they bid up land prices and bring less fertile lands into production. Those lands may require more intensive fertilizer and irrigation use, which can generate environmental problems. As land prices rise, it becomes harder for young farmers to break into the business.

Here are other examples of harmful side-effects caused by federal subsidies and regulations:

- Unemployment insurance induces more unemployment.
- Subsidized flood insurance induces people to live in riskier flood-prone areas.
- Irrigation subsidies cause over-consumption of water, which exacerbates droughts.
- Subsidized loans for housing and college induce people to borrow too much.
- Traditional welfare encourages people to work less.
- Ethanol subsidies reduce the cropland available for food and increase food prices.
- Trade restrictions designed to aid some industries harm others.
- Business subsidies undermine incentives for companies to innovate.
- Endangered species laws prompt landowners to rid their land of endangered species.
- Foreign aid empowers foreign dictators and stalls reforms.
- Disability benefits encourage people who could work to drop out of the labor force.

- Social Security and Medicare discourage saving for retirement.
- Health mandates raise insurance costs and induce firms to drop coverage.
- Drug prohibition spawns organized crime and violence.
- Fuel efficiency standards result in more people buying small cars and more road deaths.

Many policymakers mistakenly see the economy as a simple machine that can be easily manipulated. But they do not have enough knowledge to plan our complex economy successfully, and people are not as easily manipulated as the government thinks.

Economist Adam Smith famously observed: "The man of system . . . seems to imagine that he can arrange the different members of a great society with as much ease as the hand arranges the different pieces upon a chess board. He does not consider that the pieces upon the chess board have no other principle of motion besides that which the hand impresses upon them; but that, in the great chess board of human society, every single piece has a principle of motion of its own, altogether different from that which the legislature might choose to impress upon it."

More than two centuries after Smith, governments are still full of "men of system." They assume mistakenly that by regulating and subsidizing they can reorganize society to fit their vision. The result is failure after failure. One of actor Clint Eastwood's most famous lines is, "A man's got to know his limitations." The government should too.

Misaligned Political Incentives

In a romantic view of democracy, legislators always act with the interests of the public in mind. They grapple with policy issues, work toward a broad consensus and pass legislation that has strong support. They reevaluate existing programs and regulations, and prune the low-value and harmful ones.

Unfortunately, that is not how Washington works. Congress often enacts ill-conceived laws that do not have broad public support. Many programs perform poorly year after year, but receive growing budgets. Programs are almost never terminated because legislators will not admit that their favored programs do not work. Many failed programs are described at Cato's www.DownsizingGovernment.org.

The fundamental incentive steering political behavior is re-election. So members cater to voters in their districts, which is often a good thing. But it is also a source of policy failure because members focus on gaining benefits for their states at the expense of the nation. Many programs are enacted that have higher costs than benefits because minorities of members vigorously push them for parochial reasons.

Logrolling compounds the inefficiency. Lawmakers can bundle many low-value items—none of which has broad support—into an omnibus bill and gain enough votes to pass it. Logrolling has always been a key cause of wasteful spending. In 1836, for example, Virginia Rep. John Patton criticized a rivers and harbors bill as a "species of logrolling most disreputable and corrupting." That description matches the way the unpopular Affordable Care Act was rammed through Congress in 2010.

It is true that some legislators rise above parochial politics and pursue other goals. But those other goals often reflect personal beliefs that are untethered from reality. So the problem is that policymakers have no guide steering them toward making value-added decisions for the nation. Voters can help correct some of the worst abuses and mistakes. But most people are too busy with their lives to focus on the details of policy and the behind-the-scenes machinations on Capitol Hill.

Government failures are often caused by Congress intervening where it should not. The activist orientation of many members is reinforced by the environment in Washington. Special-interest groups dominate policy discussions. Most witnesses to congressional hearings favor the expansion of programs. Most visitors to member offices plead for special benefits. To lawmakers, the benefits of government action are often immediate and visible, while the costs are usually more distant and abstract.

Congress uses various techniques to hide the costs of programs. One technique is the use of borrowing, which makes a portion of spending seem "free" to taxpayers. Another technique is employer withholding of income and payroll taxes, which Congress mandates to reduce the psychic pain of paying taxes. With the use of these and other methods of hiding costs, lawmakers are emboldened to pursue additional low-value spending.

The amount of federal duplication and program overlap is remarkable. The government has 47 job training programs in nine different agencies. It has 15 programs for financial literacy. It has 15 agencies overseeing food safety, 20 programs for the homeless, 80 for economic development, 82 for teacher quality and 80 programs for helping poor people with transportation.

Legislators are entrepreneurs, and they gain prestige by creating new programs. They do not admit when their favored programs fail because their reputations and pride are on the line. Besides, trying to trim obsolete programs

creates enemies, so few members focus on that. The consequence is that, over time, the government carries a growing burden of programs and regulations that weigh down the nation's productivity and reduce our freedom.

Misaligned Bureaucratic Incentives

Narratives about executive branch employees usually fall along two lines. They are either hard-working "public servants" who are skilled and politically neutral experts, or they are slothful and inept "bureaucrats" whose mismanagement is behind government failures. Which portrayal is more accurate?

Actually, the personal characteristics of federal employees is less important than the incentives they face. Federal employees face a range of incentives that generate failure:

- **Absence of profits:** Unlike businesses, federal agencies do not have the straightforward and powerful goal of earning profits. So agencies have little reason to restrain costs, improve the quality of their services, or increase their management effectiveness.
- **Absence of losses:** Unlike in the private sector, poorly-performing federal activities do not go bankrupt. There are no automatic correctives to programs that have rising costs and falling quality. In the private sector, businesses are forced by markets to abandon activities that no longer make sense.
- **Output measurement and transparency:** Business output can be measured by profits, revenue and other metrics. But government output is difficult to measure, and the missions of agencies are often vague and multifaceted. That makes it hard for Congress and the public to judge agency performance and hold officials accountable for results.
- **Rigid compensation:** Federal employee pay is based on standardized scales generally tied to longevity, not performance. The rigid pay structure makes it hard to encourage improved efforts or to reward outstanding achievements. The pay structure also reduces morale among the best workers because they see the poor workers being rewarded equally. Furthermore, the best workers have the most incentive to leave, while the poor workers will stay, decade after decade.
- **Lack of firing:** Disciplining federal workers is difficult because of strong civil service and union protections. Just 0.5 percent of federal civilian workers are fired each year, which is just one-sixth

of the private-sector firing rate. The firing rate is just 0.1 percent in the federal senior executive service, which is just one-twentieth of the firing rate of corporate CEOs.

- **Bureaucratic layering:** American businesses have become leaner in recent decades, with flatter managements. By contrast, the number of layers of federal management has greatly increased. Paul Light of the Brookings Institution found that the number of layers in the typical agency has jumped from seven to 18 since the 1960s. He argues that today's "over-layered chain of command" in the government is a major cause of failure. Overlaying stifles information flow and makes it harder to hold people accountable.
- **Political appointees:** At the top of the executive branch is a layer of about 3,000 full-time political appointees. Administrations come into office eager to launch new initiatives, but they are less interested in managing what is already there. Political appointees may think that they know all the answers, so they repeat mistakes. The average tenure of federal political appointees is short—just two and half years—and so they shy away from tackling longer-term, structural reforms. Another problem, as we sadly witnessed during Hurricane Katrina, is that many appointees are political partisans who lack management or technical experience.

Can these problems be fixed? Many presidents have tried, beginning with Theodore Roosevelt and his Keep Commission of 1905. Roosevelt declared, "There is every reason why our executive government machinery should be at least as well-planned, economical and efficient as the best machinery of the great business organizations, which at present is not the case." Roosevelt was expressing Progressive-era optimism in government. But, as we now know, such optimism was misguided.

President William Howard Taft appointed a Committee on Economy and Efficiency in 1910. Then there was President Franklin Roosevelt's Brownlow Commission in the 1930s, President Harry Truman's and Dwight Eisenhower's Hoover Commissions in the 1940s and 1950s, President Ronald Reagan's Grace Commission in the 1980s and Vice President Al Gore's "reinventing government" project in the 1990s. Presidents George W. Bush and Barack Obama also took a crack at improving federal management.

But these efforts are just tinkering around the edges. Some indicators show that federal performance has gotten worse in recent years, not better. Management reforms cannot solve fundamental structural problems, such as the lack of incentives for cost control in government. The government will always fall far short of private markets in efficiency, value generation and innovation.

Huge Size and Scope

Federal government has failed since the beginning. A federal effort to run Indian trading posts begun in the 1790s, for example, was beset with waste and inefficiency. Federal failure is a much worse problem today because the government has grown so much.

Its huge size is overwhelming the ability of lawmakers to allocate spending efficiently and to make needed reforms. Consider that the federal budget of about $4 trillion is 100 times larger than the average state government budget of about $40 billion. The federal government has many more employees, programs, contractors and subsidy recipients to keep track of than any state government. So even if federal legislators spent their time diligently scrutinizing programs, the job is simply too large for them to do effectively.

The federal government is not just large in size, it is sprawling in scope. In addition to handling core functions such as national defense, the government, as noted, runs more than 2,300 subsidy and benefit programs. It has spread its tentacles into many state, local and private activities, such as education, energy, welfare, housing and urban transit.

Congress has neither the time nor expertise to oversee all these activities efficiently. Members are spread too thin, which is evident from the fact that they routinely miss all or parts of congressional hearings. Congress grabs for itself vast powers over non-federal activities, but then members do not have the time properly to monitor how their interventions are working.

Numerous agency failures have erupted into major scandals recently, and each time the White House has claimed to have been unaware of the developing problem. Its lack of awareness is another failure. Numerous foreign policy developments have also caught the White House by surprise. The government is involved in so many activities that warnings about brewing failures are not percolating up to the president's desk until it is too late.

Meanwhile, members of Congress spend their time fundraising, securing benefits for their districts and giving speeches, but little time actually learning about policy. Members usually blame government failures on the executive branch, but they often fail in their own oversight roles. When the Secret Service and the VA scandals erupted in 2014, we found out that both of the problems had been developing for years, but went unaddressed by Congress and the executive branch.

The government is doing too much and doing little well. It is like a conglomerate corporation involved in so many activities that executives are distracted from their core business. Markets force bloated corporations to refocus and shed their low-value activities, but no mechanism forces the federal government to do so.

The more programs the government has, the more likely they will work at cross purposes. Some federal programs keep food prices high, while others subsidize food for people with low incomes. Some programs encourage people to live in risky flood areas, while others try to reduce flood risks. The government promotes breastfeeding, but it also subsidizes baby formula. Many programs subsidize healthcare and infrastructure, but regulations raise the costs of those activities.

Ironically, even as Congress has created programs to supposedly help the public, the public has not grown fonder of the government. Instead, people have become more alienated. Pew Research Center finds that the share of people who trust government plunged from more than 70 percent in the early 1960s to about 30 percent by 1980, even though that period was one of government expansion. Trust edged upward slightly during the 1980s and 1990s when domestic spending was being trimmed, but it has fallen since 2000 as the government has grown again.

As the government has grown larger, leaders have become overloaded. They do not have enough time to understand programs, to oversee them, or to fix them. The more programs there are, the harder it is to allocate resources efficiently, and the more likely it is that programs will work at cross purposes. Within departments, red tape has multiplied, information is getting bottled up under layers of management and decision-making is becoming more difficult because more people are involved. The government is failing more, and the public is getting more disgusted.

How to Fix It

The federal government and the private sector both fail. The difference is that the government fails more and fixes less. But America desperately needs better governance to meet today's challenges in areas such as foreign policy, the global economy and our aging population.

The solution is to stop centralizing power in Washington, and to begin shifting activities back to the states. State and local governments suffer failures, but their failures are not thrust onto the whole nation. When policies fail in some states, other states can learn the lessons and pursue different strategies. States compete with each other for people and investment, which creates continuous pressure to reform.

Polls show that Americans support moving power out of Washington. Large majorities of people prefer state over federal control of education, housing, transportation, welfare, health insurance and other activities. People think that state and local governments provide more competent service than the federal government. And when asked which level of government gives them the best value for their taxes, two-thirds of people say state and local governments and just one-third say the federal government.

In sum, political and bureaucratic incentives and the huge size of the federal government cause endemic failure. The causes of failure are structural, and they will not be solved by appointing more competent officials or putting a different party in charge. Americans are deeply unhappy with the way that Washington works, and everyone agrees that we need better governance. The only way to achieve it is to greatly cut the federal government's size and scope.

CHRIS EDWARDS is editor of Cato Institute's Downsizing-Government.org and the director of tax policy studies at Cato. He is a top expert on federal and state tax and budget issues. He is the author of *Downsizing the Federal Government* and coauthor of Global Tax Revolution.

Richard Eskow  **NO**

We Need a Bold Left to Challenge Government Downsizing

Has the American left lost sight of the big picture? While liberals have been fighting line-item battles against the Republican right, government itself has been changing—and slowly disappearing.

Are we winning some battles (not so many, come to think of it) but losing the war?

We need an active, independent left willing to challenge the push for smaller government.

Discretionary spending has fallen dramatically—too dramatically—in recent decades, primarily as the result of lower, post – Cold War military budgets. But the promised post – Cold War "peace dividend" has failed to materialize. We've seen neither better public services nor wider prosperity. The military budget is still bloated, and only the wealthy and corporations are better off than they were four or five decades ago.

We need an active, independent left willing to challenge the push for smaller government. A well-managed government can revitalize the economy, even as it makes our world a better place to live. Many Americans seem to understand that instinctively. Where, then, is the movement that will make that argument?

Our nation needs a new vision—one that proposes using government resources to meet newer and broader challenges, instead of downsizing them to ease the tax burdens of the wealthy and corporations.

Disappearing Government

A recent report from the Congressional Budget Office (CBO) shows that discretionary Federal spending was 13.1 percent of the economy (gross domestic product, or GDP) in 1968, and was consistently above 10 percent between 1965 and 1972. Yet today it is 6.8 percent of GDP, little more than half its 50-year high.

It also shows that the reduction is largely attributable to lower military spending, which fell from a high of 9.1 percent of GDP in 1968 (that included Vietnam's costs, as well as the Cold War's) to 3.5 percent in 2014.

We could have invested this "peace savings" in more productive government activities. Instead, government itself was downsized—with very little debate.

The Home Front

Non-defense spending has declined too. It's currently 3.4 percent of GDP. That's down from its 1965 level of 3.8 percent, and is dramatically lower than its 1980 level of 5.0 percent. Those figures are even more striking when we consider the fact that some forms of military spending are included in the "non-defense" portion of the budget.

The Department of Homeland Security, for example, is considered a "non-defense" expenditure. That's a military-related "domestic" expense which didn't even exist in the 20th century. The president has requested approximately $48 billion for the Homeland Security in his new budget, an increase of 9.1 percent.

The proposed $165 billion budget for Veterans' Affairs isn't allocated to the Department of Defense, either. Additional defense-related expenditures can be found in other departments, including Energy and Justice.

Strip away all of these miscategorized expenditures and we're likely to find that our government's non-military spending—which according to these figures is near its 50-year low—is even lower than the numbers would have us believe.

Following the Money

Where did those savings go? They were, in effect, given to corporations and the wealthy as tax breaks.

The CBO's data shows that corporate income taxes fell dramatically as spending declined. So did inheritance and gift taxes.

Here are the figures: Corporate income tax revenues were 3.6 of GDP in 1965, rising to 4.1 percent in 1967.

But they fell to 1.9 percent in 2014, less than half of their 50-year high. And today inheritance taxes and gift taxes are one-fourth of what they were in 1965.

The Limits of the Debate

Instead of benefiting the privileged, some of those savings could have been used to fund domestic programs to improve the lives of millions of Americans.

That would have had another benefit: Studies have shown that non-military government spending is more cost-effective in creating jobs than military spending. So a shift from military to domestic spending would tend to boost both employment and middle-class wage growth, two areas where our economic picture has declined since the early decades shown in the chart above.

That's a compelling big-picture argument. Unfortunately, nobody seems to be making it.

President Obama's latest budget proposal shows the limit of our current debate. He has proposed increasing military and non-military (discretionary) spending by roughly the same amounts, which means that defense spending under the president's plan would still exceed domestic spending ($561 billion vs. $530 billion—and that smaller domestic figure includes significant military expenditures, as explained above).

Why should that be the *liberal* side of the debate? A vibrant, independent left would propose *reductions* in military spending—and steeper increases in domestic spending. After all, we are the sole remaining superpower. By broad consensus, our greatest national security threat is terrorism conducted by non-state actors. Why, then, are we still greenlighting costly high-tech weapon systems?

And why are we expected to spend $355 billion in the next 10 years (according to the CBO), and as much as $1 trillion over 30 years (as estimated by the Center for Nonproliferation Studies), to maintain and rebuild our nuclear arsenal? (See also the Arms Control Association.)

That makes no sense.

A Left That's Willing to Think Big

What would a revitalized left propose to do about the declining size of government? First, it would point out that government has an important role to play, both in our lives and in our economy. That should be a source of pride, not a cause for shame.

A revitalized left would point out that our military spending is still out of control. It would challenge our obsession with invasive spying technology—technology that enriches NSA contractors, but threatens our freedoms and distracts us from the human-intensive efforts which genuinely make us safer.

But, even as it argues for military cuts, this new strong left would point out that well-managed domestic spending is a force for good. It educates our children and preserves our health. It can rebuild our bridges, highways, and transportation systems. It can protect our planet and support research which creates the scientific breakthroughs of the future. It can develop technologies like the Internet that transform our world and our economy.

And as it's doing all these things, it can also create millions of additional jobs while strengthening wages for the middle class.

No Apologies

What about that portion of the government's budget that falls under mandatory spending? The left could explain why we must expand Social Security, not cut it, promoting the well-crafted proposals that would finance that expansion. Those proposals are popular with the American people, and no wonder: Now that other forms of retirement security have been eroded, Social Security is the most cost-effective vehicle we have for replacing what's been lost.

A bold left could argue for limiting the role of profit-making corporations in medical care. That would reduce our overall health care costs while lowering the cost of Medicare, our second-largest mandatory spending program. At the same time it could propose covering everyone under a single-payer system, since Medicare is already more cost-effective than private insurance. The resulting savings would give our economy a much-needed boost, while providing Americans with better health care.

Discretionary spending has declined dramatically over the last 50 years. But it was at its highest during some of our best years of growth and middle-class prosperity. That's neither a coincidence nor an accident.

We've accepted the downsizing of government without a struggle, and that needs to change. That means reclaiming the voice and spirit of a strong and vital left, without fear or apology.

RICHARD ESKOW is a writer, a former Wall Street executive, and a radio journalist. He has experience in health insurance and economics, occupational health, risk management, finance, and IT.

EXPLORING THE ISSUE

Does Government Need to Be Restrained?

Critical Thinking and Reflection

1. Why do commentators think that the government is too big and should be cut back?
2. What role does the government already play in the economy and how successful has it been?
3. Would you say that the removal or weakening of government regulations was a primary cause of the recent financial crisis?
4. What actions of government are badly needed and what actions could we do without?
5. If American businesses have the dominant influence over the government, they would have the regulations that would help them and not have the regulations that would hinder them. Is that the way things are? If not, why?
6. In 2011 a GOP candidate publicly declared that he would eliminate three departments if elected president because that would appeal to many voters. Can you explain this appeal?

Is There Common Ground?

As with most good debates, the issue of the rightness of government actions is difficult to decide. Part of the difficulty is that it involves the trade-off of values that are in conflict in real situations, and part of the difficulty is that it involves uncertain estimations of the future consequences of policy changes. Both experts and interested parties can differ greatly on value trade-offs and estimations of impacts. Government regulations and other interventions cost money for both administration and compliance. Nevertheless, Eskow argues that certain government actions will provide benefits that greatly exceed the costs, and Edwards argues the contrary view, that the costs will be far greater than Eskow expects and probably will have net negative results. Part of the strength of Edwards' argument is that regulations often fail to do what they are designed to do. Part of the strength of Eskow's argument is that there are many observable problems that need to be addressed, and for some of these government action seems to be the only viable option. Possibly the best solution is to intervene as little as possible. This avoids the extreme positions that all interventions are bad or that beneficial interventions can address almost all problems. Of course, the debate would continue over where the tipping point is between good and bad interventions.

Additional Resources

One aspect of the issue is that less government means more power to business and business does not have a good reputation right now. Most commentators view business as harming the environment, exporting jobs, charging high prices (especially drug companies), not paying their share of taxes, acting illegally behind the screens their lawyers make, etc. They create the need for government interventions and regulations. Since they will not do what is right, they must be made to do what is right. For support of this view that is critical of corporations, see Thomas Piketty, *Capital in the Twenty-First Century* (Harvard University Press 2014); Frank Partnoy, *Infectious Greed: How Deceit and Risk Corrupted the Financial Markets* (PublicAffairs, 2009); Paul Mattick, *Business as Usual: The Economic Crisis and the Failure of Capitalism* (Reaktion Books, 2011); Robert H. Parks, *The End of Capitalism: Destructive Forces of an Economy Out of Control* (Prometheus Books, 2011); R. P. Bootle, *The Trouble with Markets: Saving Capitalism from Itself* (Nicholas Brealey Publishing, 2011); John Bellamy Foster, *The Ecological Rift: Capitalism's War on the Earth* (Monthly Review Press, 2010). Some commentators, however, defend businesses in a competitive capitalistic market like Peter Wehner and Arthur C. Brooks, *Wealth and Justice: The Morality of Democratic Capitalism* (AEI Press, 2011), and Andrew Bernstein, *Capitalism Unbound: The Incontestable Moral Case for Individual Rights* (University Press of America, 2010). Government also is frequently criticized. See Jay Cost, *A Republic No More: Big Government and the Rise of American Political Corruption* (Encounter Books, 2015); Janine R. Wedel, *Unaccountable: How Elite Power Brokers Corrupt Our Finances, Freedom, and Security* (Pegasus Books, 2014); Peter H. Schuck, *Why Government Fails So Often: and How It Can Do Better* (Princeton University Press, 2014); Sue Llewellyn, Stephen Brooke, and Ann Mahon, *Trust and Confidence in Government and Services* (Routledge, 2013); and H. Kent Baker and John F. Nofsinger, eds., *Socially Responsible Finance and Investing* (John Wiley, 2012).

Internet References . . .

Sociology—Study Sociology Online

http://edu.learnsoc.org/

Sociology Web Resources

www.mhhe.com/socscience/sociology/resources
/index.htm

Sociosite

www.topsite.com/goto/sociosite.net

Socioweb

www.topsite.com/goto/socioweb.com

Selected, Edited, and with Issue Framing Material by:
Kurt Finsterbusch, *University of Maryland, College Park*

ISSUE

Was Welfare Reform the Right Approach to Poverty?

YES: Josh Sager, from "The Flaw in Conservative Anti-Welfare Arguments," *The Progressive Cynic* (2013)

NO: George F. Will, from "The Harm Incurred by a Mushrooming Welfare State," *The Washington Post* (2015)

Learning Outcomes

After reading this issue, you will be able to:

- Understand labor force changes since the 1950s and the changing role of welfare (Aid to Families with Dependent Children [AFDC]) up to the Welfare Reform Act of 1996.
- Understand the basic changes that the new welfare law made. Know the main differences between AFDC and TANF (Temporary Assistance for Needy Families).
- Understand what was wrong with AFDC that made both Republicans and Democrats want to abolish it and replace it with a very different welfare system.
- Evaluate how successful the new welfare bill was in creating widespread welfare-to-work transitions.
- Understand the problems that are occurring in administering the new welfare law and assess how it needs to be improved.

ISSUE SUMMARY

YES: Josh Sager, health policy intern at Community Catalyst, argues that most people on welfare want what all Americans want which is a job, the ability to provide for a family, and have pride in what they do. He denies the view of the right that they are lazy and enjoy being dependent and would get jobs when their welfare is taken away. Rather he advocates addressing the underlying causes of poverty.

NO: George F. Will, an American newspaper columnist with the *Washington Post* and political commentator with Fox News, points out the negative results of welfare. He blasts the American government for classifying large numbers of Americans as "needy." He gets his statistics from Nicholas Eberstadt, who documents the massive expansion of the welfare state and its erosion of recipients' character.

In his 1984 book *Losing Ground: American Social Policy, 1950–1980* (Basic Books), policy analyst Charles Murray recommended abolishing Aid to Families with Dependent Children (AFDC), the program at the heart of the welfare debate. At the time of the book's publication, this suggestion struck many as simply a dramatic way for Murray to make some of his anti-welfare points. However, 14 years later this idea became the dominant idea in Congress. In 1996, President Bill Clinton signed into law the Work Opportunity Reconciliation Act and fulfilled his 1992 campaign pledge to end welfare as we know it. Murray's thesis that welfare hurt the poor had become widely accepted. In "What to Do About Welfare," *Commentary* (December 1994), Murray argues that welfare contributes to dependency, illegitimacy, and the number of absent fathers, which in turn can have terrible effects on the children involved. He states that workfare, enforced child support, and the abolition of welfare would greatly reduce these problems. One reason why Congress ended AFDC was the emergence of a widespread backlash against welfare recipients. Much of the backlash, however, was misguided. It often rested on the assumptions that welfare is generous and that most people on welfare are professional loafers. In fact, over the previous two decades, payments to families with dependent children eroded considerably relative to the cost of living. Average monthly benefits went from $238 in 1978 to $154 in 2006. Furthermore, most women with dependent children on welfare had intermittent periods of work, were elderly, or were disabled. Petty fraud may be common because welfare payments are insufficient to live on in many cities, but welfare queens who cheat the system for spectacular sums are so rare that they should not be part of any serious debate on welfare issues. The majority of people on welfare are those whose condition would become desperate if payments were cut off. Although many believe that women on welfare commonly bear children in order to increase their benefits, there is no conclusive evidence to support this idea.

Not all objections to AFDC can be easily dismissed, however. There does seem to be evidence that in some cases AFDC reduces work incentives and increases the likelihood of family breakups. But there is also a positive side to AFDC: it helped many needy people get back on their feet. When all things are considered together, therefore, it is not clear that welfare, meaning AFDC, was bad enough to be abolished. But it was abolished on July 1, 1997, when the Work Opportunity Reconciliation Act went into effect. Now the question is whether the new policy is better than the old policy.

All of the above is ancient history but the basic issues remain the same. There are many people today who are in desperate need and many others who struggle to keep afloat. Should they be helped? But how can they be helped without making them dependent and undermining their character? It is ironic that the character issue does not come up when the upper middle class and the rich receive far more benefits from the government than the welfare recipients. I must admit that I do but no one questions my character.

In the readings that follow, Josh Sager presents a fair summary of the case for the benefits of welfare reform. On the other side, George Will is outraged by the massive increase in welfare because "Expanding dependency requires erasing Americans' traditional distinction between the deserving and the undeserving poor." Welfare is out of hand and must be cut back. Currently there are widespread negative feelings against welfare and Will forcefully gives voice to them.

YES

Josh Sager

The Flaw in Conservative Anti-Welfare Arguments

Last week, the GOP-controlled House of Representatives voted to cut food stamps by $4 billion a year, for 10 years (adding up to a total cut of $40 billion). These cuts are estimated to eliminate SNAP benefits for millions of Americans, many of whom are in desperate need of help. While it is unlikely that these cuts will be passed into law because the Democrats control the Senate and are unlikely to sign onto such cuts, this vote does tell us a lot about the GOP's view on welfare.

After the House vote on the farm bill, Majority Leader Eric Cantor (arguably the most powerful person in the House), said the following:

> "This bill is designed to give people a hand when they need it most. Most people don't choose to be on food stamps. Most people want a job. Most people want to go out and be productive so that they can earn a living, so that they can support a family, so that they can have hope for a more prosperous future. They want what we want."

Cantor's quote illustrates a perfect example of the central misassumption that many in the right wing make about welfare: They believe that poor people who take welfare are just lazy and, if we could only get them off of the teat, they would magically no longer need welfare money because they would just go get well-paying jobs.

It is true that most people would be ecstatic to have a well-paying job and not need to rely upon welfare. That said, taking away these people's welfare does nothing to fix the underlying causes of their need to take welfare, nor does it magically create jobs with which they can earn enough money to be self-sufficient. Because of this, kicking people off of welfare without addressing the underlying causes to their poverty only serves to cut the lifelines of these needy people and make a shallow rhetorical point for the right wing ideologues.

Currently, the US is in an economic slump and there are more people looking for work than jobs which pay a living wage—this necessitates that some people will be jobless and others will be working jobs which do not pay enough for them to survive unassisted.

In the face of the current economic situation, kicking people off of welfare may feel good rhetorically to some groups, but it is terrible policy. Welfare money allows poor people to survive (not necessarily comfortably) and bolsters the economy as a whole through increasing the buying power of the American people. Every dollar cut out of welfare equals a dollar taken directly out of the economy (more if you consider the fact that the SNAP program has a multiplier effect of 1.79) and a dollar that some poor person must find a way to make in order to ensure that their children don't go hungry.

Unless we solve the structural and economic roots of poverty, there are simply no legitimate bootstraps with which the poor can pull themselves up by once their welfare money is repurposed to fund more wars or tax cuts for the wealthy (which, ironically enough, is truly wasteful welfare for the rich and defense contractors).

Welfare Cuts, Desperation, and Crime

In a way, the right wing idea that poor people who are kicked off of welfare will take personal responsibility is correct—albeit not the kind of responsibility that the right wing is talking about.

Desperate people who are unable to make money legally often turn to illegal means in order to provide enough resources to let their families survive; we see this both in situations of long-term poverty as well as in natural disasters (when people will "rob" stores in order to get water and food in the aftermath of a disaster).

Illegal, high profit, industries like drug production and dealing take over in areas of economic depression (ex. the meth epidemic in poor Midwestern areas) because people need to feed their families and drugs are seen as one of the only ways for a person to make a living.

It is important for me to make clear that I am not saying that only poor people deal drugs or that all welfare recipients are potential dealers—that said, the fact remains that a person with a starving family and no other way out will often choose to break the law rather than let their family suffer.

Currently, welfare helps plug the gaps in many Americans' income, thus preventing many people from being forced into illicit industries or watching their kids go hungry. If we start eviscerating SNAP and throwing people off of welfare programs, we will force some of these people into high-risk, high-reward illegal industries. Not only will this cause an increase of criminal conduct, but it will perpetuate the terrible cycle of poverty, crime, and imprisonment.

When poor people are forced to commit crimes for survival, they often end up arrested and imprisoned. Once these people have a criminal record, they are even less able to secure legal employment and are forced even further into an illegal lifestyle. This cycle reverberates through generations and stifles opportunity for those who are trapped in it.

Conclusion

Rather than ignoring the problems that created the need for welfare, cutting welfare programs and paying for the effects of these cuts in the long run, the USA needs to do the exact opposite—we must increase welfare payouts/ time limits until we can address the root causes of poverty, and start breaking the cycle of criminality.

It is true that increasing the benefits of welfare programs costs money but there is plenty of waste to cut that would allow us to do so in a budget-neutral manner. For example, extremely profitable petrochemical corporations receive $41 billion dollars in subsidies a year (nearly half a trillion dollars every decade), despite the fact that such subsidies are absolutely pointless. We should cut this wasteful corporate welfare and repurpose it for a truly necessary form of welfare that will help millions of Americans. Such a shift would improve the living standards of many needy Americans and would serve to increase the total amount of money in the demand-side of the economy (leading to more jobs to provide services and an uplifting effect on the entire system).

Welfare is simply a tourniquet—keeping people alive until the bleeding is stopped—and we need to address the causes of poverty. These causes are massively complex, including everything from automation and outsourcing, to wealth inequality and a lack of demand. Put simply (in a space-necessitated oversimplification), we need to use stimulus to increase the number of jobs in the marketplace, promote a more equitable distribution of benefits for work between workers and executives, and use education to ensure that our workforce is able to compete in a global economy. If we can increase the numbers of well-paying jobs, we can eventually reduce welfare, not by kicking needy people off but through making it so that fewer people need help.

People who commit non-violent crimes because they have no other options need to be given opportunities to find legitimate employment, not jail cells. Those guilty of non-violent drug and property crimes should be given restitution and community service, during which they should also receive job training and education assistance. If we can give criminals legal employment options and stop crippling them with the stigma attached to a criminal record, we can start turning them into productive members of society and help their children escape the cycle of criminality and poverty.

Josh Sager is a health policy intern at Community Catalyst and publishes the blog, TheProgressiveCynic.com.

George F. Will    **NO**

The Harm Incurred by a Mushrooming Welfare State

America's national character will have to be changed if progressives are going to implement their agenda. So, changing social norms *is* the progressive agenda. To understand how far this has advanced, and how difficult it will be to reverse the inculcation of dependency, consider the data Nicholas Eberstadt deploys in *National Affairs* quarterly:

> America's welfare state transfers more than 14 percent of gross domestic product to recipients, with more than a third of Americans taking "need-based" payments. In our wealthy society, the government officially treats an unprecedented portion of the population as "needy."

Transfers of benefits to individuals through social welfare programs have increased from less than 1 federal dollar in 4 (24 percent) in 1963 to almost 3 out of 5 (59 percent) in 2013. In that half-century, entitlement payments were, Eberstadt says, America's "fastest growing source of personal income," growing twice as fast as all other real per capita personal income. It is probable that this year a majority of Americans will seek and receive payments.

This is not primarily because of Social Security and Medicare transfers to an aging population. Rather, the growth is overwhelmingly in means-tested entitlements. More than twice as many households receive "anti-poverty" benefits than receive Social Security or Medicare. Between 1983 and 2012, the population increased by almost 83 million—and people accepting means-tested benefits increased by 67 million. So, for every 100-person increase in the population there was an 80-person increase in the recipients of means-tested payments. Food stamp recipients increased from 19 million to 51 million—more than the combined populations of 24 states.

What has changed? Not the portion of the estimated population below the poverty line (15.2 percent in 1983; 15 percent in 2012). Rather, poverty programs have become untethered from the official designation of poverty: In 2012, more than half the recipients were not classified as poor but accepted being treated as needy. Expanding dependency requires erasing Americans' traditional distinction between the deserving and the undeserving poor. This distinction was rooted in this nation's exceptional sense that poverty is not the unalterable accident of birth and is related to traditions of generosity arising from immigrant and settler experiences.

Eberstadt's essay, "American Exceptionalism and the Entitlement State," argues that this state is extinguishing the former. America "arrived late to the 20th century's entitlement party." The welfare state's European pedigree traces from post-1945 Britain, back through Sweden's interwar "social democracy," to Bismarck's late-19th-century social insurance. European welfare states reflected European beliefs about poverty: Rigid class structures rooted in a feudal past meant meager opportunities for upward mobility based on merit. People were thought to be stuck in neediness through no fault of their own, and welfare states would reconcile people to intractable social structures.

Eberstadt notes that the structure of U.S. government spending "has been completely overturned within living memory," resulting in the "remolding of daily life for ordinary Americans under the shadow of the entitlement state." In two generations, the American family budget has been recast: In 1963, entitlement transfers were less than $1 out of every $15; by 2012, they were more than $1 out of every $6.

Causation works both ways between the rapid increase in family disintegration (from 1964 to 2012, the percentage of children born to unmarried women increased from 7 to 41) and the fact that, Eberstadt says, for many women, children and even working-age men, "the entitlement state is now the breadwinner of the household." In the past 50 years, the fraction of civilian men ages 25 to 34 who were neither working nor looking for work approximately quadrupled.

Eberstadt believes that the entitlement state poses "character challenges" because it powerfully promotes certain habits, including habits of mind. These include corruption. Since 1970, Americans have become healthier, work has become less physically stressful, the workplace has become safer—and claims from Social Security Disability Insurance have increased almost sixfold. Such claims (including fraudulent ones) are gateways to a plethora of other payments.

Daniel Patrick Moynihan, a lifelong New Deal liberal and accomplished social scientist, warned that "the issue of welfare is not what it costs those who provide it but what it costs those who receive it." As a growing portion of the population succumbs to the entitlement state's ever-expanding menu of temptations, the costs, Eberstadt concludes, include a transformation of the nation's "political culture, sensibilities, and tradition," the weakening of America's distinctive "conceptions of self-reliance, personal responsibility, and self-advancement," and perhaps a "rending of the national fabric." As a result, "America today does not look exceptional at all."

GEORGE F. WILL is an American newspaper columnist with the *Washington Post* and *Newsweek* and political commentator with Fox News.

EXPLORING THE ISSUE

Was Welfare Reform the Right Approach to Poverty?

Critical Thinking and Reflection

1. How can welfare actually hurt the people that it helps?
2. How has the bill that abolished AFDC created a program that avoids the problems and failures of its predecessor?
3. Is there a legitimate place for the old style of welfare?
4. A welfare hand up can make the recipient dependent but can also help him or her to become independent. What factors make the difference?
5. To what extent is the welfare problem a cultural or values problem?
6. Does our country provide the opportunities that encourage and enable the poor to get out of their poverty?
7. Are the welfare aspects of the United States harmful or helpful?

Is There Common Ground?

There was considerable national agreement that the old welfare system had to be changed so that it would encourage people to find jobs and achieve self-sufficiency. Much success has been gained regarding this goal so far, but some analysts point out that numerous problems still remain. Sager focuses on the positive results of the welfare system and Will focuses on how welfare concerns have led to vast expansion of welfare transfers and this weakens America. One of the reforms under TANF was the welfare-to-work initiative, which required work of at least 20 hours per week in exchange for time-limited financial assistance. It also listed 12 authorized activities that could meet this requirement. According to reports, within 3 years millions of Americans had moved from being dependent on welfare to being self-sufficient. At the same time welfare rolls declined significantly. The peak in the number of families receiving cash payments was in 1994 at 5.1 million families. In 2013 that number was 1.7 million families. In 2003, welfare was reformed again with the goal of protecting children and strengthening families as well as providing assistance to individuals and families in achieving financial independence from the government.

Additional Resources

Michael B. Katz, in *The Undeserving Poor: From the War on Poverty to the War on Welfare* (Pantheon Books, 1989), traces the evolution of welfare policies in the United States from the 1960s through the 1980s. Charles Noble, in *Welfare as*

We Knew It: A Political History of the American Welfare State (Oxford University Press, 1997), traces the evolution of welfare policies into the late 1990s and argues that the structure of the political economy has greatly limited the welfare state. Joel F. Handler, in *Blame Welfare, Ignore Poverty and Inequality* (Cambridge University Press, 2007), carries the historical analysis of welfare in the United States close to the present. For discussions of welfare reform, see Jeff Grogger and Lynn A. Karoly, *Welfare Reform: Effects of a Decade of Change* (Harvard University Press, 2005); Ron Haskins, *Work Over Welfare: The Inside Story of the 1996 Welfare Reform Law* (Brookings Institution Press, 2006); Mary Reintsma, *The Political Economy of Welfare Reform in the United States* (Edward Elgar, 2007); Harrell R. Rodgers Jr., *American Poverty in a New Era of Reform* (M. E. Sharpe, 2006); Scott W. Allard, *Out of Reach: Place, Poverty, and the New American Welfare State* (Yale University Press, 2009); Frank Ridzi, *Selling Welfare Reform: Work-First and the New Common Sense of Employment* (New York University Press, 2009); and Justin Feldman, *Effects of Welfare Reform in Terms of Costs and Mortality: Data Analysis* (Harvard Kennedy School, Shorenstein Center on Media, Politics and Public Policy, January 26, 2015).

Four works that suggest how welfare should be handled under current conditions are David Snow, *What's Wrong with Benevolence: Happiness, Private Property, and the Limits of Enlightenment* (Encounter Books, 2011); Lawrence M. Mead, *From Prophecy to Charity: How to Help the Poor* (AEI Press, 2011); Andrew R. Feldman, *What Works in Work-First Welfare: Designing and Managing Employment Programs in New York City* (W. E. Upjohn Institute for Employment Research, 2011); and Matthew D. Adler, *Well-Being and*

Fair Distribution: Beyond Cost-Benefit Analysis (Oxford University Press, 2011). A great deal of information can be obtained from the reauthorization hearings in the House Committee on Education and the Workforce, *Welfare Reform: Reauthorization of Work and Child Care* (March 15, 2005).

Most assessments of the 1996 welfare reform are positive. Three works that explore the negative consequences of this bill are Marci Ybarra, *Welfare Reform Has Negative Impact for the Extremely Poor*, (NASW News November 2012); Jane Henrici, ed., *Doing Without: Women and Work after Welfare Reform* (University of Arizona Press, 2006), and Kathleen M. Shaw, et al., *Putting Poor People to Work: How the Work-First Idea Eroded College Access for the Poor* (Russell Sage Foundation, 2006).

Internet References . . .

Sociology—Study Sociology Online

http://edu.learnsoc.org/

Sociology Web Resources

www.mhhe.com/socscience/sociology/resources
/index.htm

Sociosite

www.topsite.com/goto/sociosite.net

Socioweb

www.topsite.com/goto/socioweb.com

Selected, Edited, and with Issue Framing Material by:
Kurt Finsterbusch, *University of Maryland, College Park*

ISSUE

Is the Progressive Vision the Answer for Improving the U.S. School System?

YES: Ruth Conniff, from "A Progressive Vision for Education," *The Progressive* (2014/2015)

NO: Russ Walsh, from "Fix Society, and the Schools Will Follow," *The Progressive* (2014)

Learning Outcomes

After reading this issue, you will be able to:

- Identify many weaknesses in the current 1–12 school system.
- Criticize the current emphasis on the rewarding and sanctioning of schools on the basis of testing as in No Child Left Behind and the recent Every Student Succeeds Act.
- Discuss the types of teachers and teaching styles that can produce students who are ready for the new world of the twenty-first century.
- Describe the type of student culture needed for school success.
- Discuss some excellent examples of really good schools.

ISSUE SUMMARY

YES: Ruth Conniff, editor and chief of *The Progressive*, criticizes No Child Left Behind for its excessive testing and teaching to the tests. She promotes a superior model of education which seeks to truly engage students and promote critical thinking. It gives teachers more control and thus treats them as professionals. This has worked in middle-class schools and she advocates its use in poor areas.

NO: Russ Walsh, author, teacher, and coordinator of college reading at Rider University in Pennsylvania, reports on the book *Fear and Learning in America: Bad Data, Good Teachers, and the Attack on Public Education*, by John Kuhn. It blasts most school reform efforts as covers for corporate takeovers of the schools behind the rhetoric of reform.

The quality of American public schooling has been criticized for several decades. Secretary of Education Richard Riley said in 1994 that some American schools are so bad that they "should never be called schools at all." The average school year in the United States is 180 days, whereas Japanese children attend school 240 days of the year. American schoolchildren score lower than the children of many other Western countries on certain standardized achievement tests. In 1983, the National Commission on Excellence in Education published *A Nation at Risk*, which argued that American education was a failure.

Critics of *A Nation at Risk* maintain that the report produced very little evidence to support its thesis, but the public accepted it anyway. Currently, much of the public still thinks that the American school system is failing and needs to be fixed. The solution that the Bush administration instituted in 2002 with overwhelming bipartisan support in Congress was the No Child Left Behind Act (NCLB).

The main feature of NCLB is standards-based education. High standards and measurable goals are set and monitored by the states. All government-run schools receiving federal funding are required to administer a state-wide standardized test. The students' scores determine the performance score of the schools and progress is expected annually. If schools fall below their goals then increasingly radical steps are taken to fix the problems. Five failing years result in plans to restructure the entire school. Common options include closing the school, turning the school into a charter school, hiring a private company to run the school, or asking the state office of education to run the school directly. This is a tough standard and drew much criticism for being unreasonable. The main criticism, however, is its focus on testing. Test results lead to rewards or sanctions so teachers teach to the tests, with poor educational results.

On December 10, 2015 Congress passed the Every Student Succeds Act which is an effort to improve the NCLB. It retains the program of testing Math and English and demanding improving scores especially for schools with low scores. It confers much more power to the states and local school districts for methods for implementing the tests and instituting sanctions. It tries to preserve the spirit of the NCLB but change its implementation.

Since NCLB two major reform efforts have arisen. First is the further promotion of charter schools which many educators, including Russ Walsh and John Kuhn, view as the corporate takeover of public schools. Second is the critical thinking reform that is advocated by Ruth Conniff. It is interesting to note that the critical thinking reform is supported by what is happening in Europe. The research on countries on top of the educational rankings find them to have educational systems that are almost the inverse of the American system. Their students do well on measures of higher-order problem solving in math, reading, and science. They choose their teachers from among their most talented graduates, train them extensively, create opportunities for them to collaborate with their peers within and across schools to improve their practice, provide them the external supports that they need to do their work well, and underwrite all these efforts with a strong welfare state. In this system external monitoring is unimportant. Their system is very professional and America's is amateurish.

Ruth Conniff agrees that American schools are bad. The children are bored, never excited about discovery and accomplishment, and leave school uneducated in a deep sense and unprepared for rapidly changing technologies and job demands. She wants teachers to be highly trained and given authority to help students to develop their creativity and critical thinking. Ideally, teachers should be coaches and mentors, not lecturers or tutors. Russ Walsh and John Kuhn attack the flaws in the current education system, especially the corporate education reform movement, and advocate changes in the broader society which would make it possible to fix the schools. They also propose six specific changes including abandoning the property value basis for funding schools.

YES

Ruth Conniff

A Progressive Vision for Education

In 1997, a group of schools across New York State banded together to oppose high-stakes testing and promote a richer model of education, based on engaging students, critical thinking, and supporting teachers as professionals. This approach, long favored by upper-middle-class parents for their own children, has been on the wane for low-income kids.

The twenty-eight New York Performance Standards Consortium schools have developed an assessment system based on quality teaching and a student-centered learning environment. They have drawn increasing interest both because their results are impressive and because the public is becoming aware that the high-stakes testing approach to education is not working.

I spoke with Consortium executive director Ann Cook and Consortium teacher, author, and professor of education Phyllis Tashlik about their vision of a progressive model for education reform.

"What we are doing is unique," says Cook. "It's all built on collaboration, whereas everything else that's going on now is built on the idea that if you have teachers competing with each other somehow you're going to wind up with a better system, which is completely false."

To run their alternative curriculum, the Consortium schools opt out of the New York Regents test—a commercially produced exam that is required of most New York State public schools.

Test-prep at traditional schools is "excessive and obsessive," says Tashlik.

"We've always said assessment should grow out of what goes on in the classroom—instead, what goes on in the classroom is now growing out of assessment. It's a whole perversion of what education actually is all about," Tashlik adds. "It's hard in that environment for any kind of innovation or student-centered work or in-depth work to flourish."

"So-called reformers—look, where are their kids going to school? They are sending their kids to places like Sidwell Friends and the Chicago Lab School, where they wouldn't consider having testing every year," says Cook.

At the Consortium schools, students are asked to consider multiple viewpoints, not just memorize facts. The tone is respectful and supportive.

"In our schools, teachers feel they have control over their environment; they are respected for the experience that they have. It's almost like doctors, who are respected for their clinical experience," says Tashlik. "They don't advise patients just based on research."

"We are focusing on the whole idea of teachers as professionals," she adds.

"There are very intense discussions. Very often visitors come in and after they observe the classroom, they say, 'Gifted, right?' " says Cook. "What they are responding to here are these kids who don't fit the profile of kids who they think should be able to discuss things like credit default swaps. The only way they can get their hands around it is to say, 'Oh, they must be gifted.' "

In fact, the Consortium schools serve a higher proportion of special ed students than the traditional New York public schools. Many have transferred from places where they were not successful. Many are English-language learners.

"If you are helping kids really grapple with things that interest them, like 'Did Martin Luther King make the movement, or did the movement make King?' or, 'Should women in France be denied the right to wear head scarves?' or a science issue around climate change, it's more likely you'll have more success getting kids involved," says Cook.

Eric Foner, professor of history at Columbia, has read the Consortium students' papers. "One thing he points out is it's clear these students have exposure to different points of view, and can juggle multiple perspectives," says Cook. "And a lot of his freshmen at Columbia, from posh private schools, don't do that easily—it's hard for them."

The trend in education reform is moving away from creative and critical thinking.

"If you don't have kids discussing and debating ideas, having an opportunity to have civil debate and discourse, you are not going to get anywhere," says Tashlik. "That's one of the things we lack in this country right now. And that has major implications for where this country is going."

Tashlik and Cook worry that preschool programs serving low-income kids are abandoning the sand table and the block corner to become test-prep factories.

"What kids from high-poverty areas really need is the opportunity to figure out how to share, to use materials in different ways, to solve problems, have books read to them, draw—all sorts of things the Malias and Sashas of this world have as almost their entitlement," says Cook.

Skill-and-drill preschool programs are producing younger and younger delinquents, Tashlik and Cook point out.

"What happens is this: Kids come from poor areas into preschool, and someone decides what we need to do is teach them, not have them develop social and emotional skills," says Cook. "You have formal lessons, and the kids are not ready. They have behavior problems, and

before you know it, you have kids as young as five or six hauled into the principal's office. You set up the whole school to a prison pipeline."

"We are seeing kids as young as five or six taken out of schools in handcuffs," says Tashlik.

Not surprisingly, the schools in New York City with the highest suspension rate of kids in kindergarten through third grade are all in poor neighborhoods. "What these schools are using as a reading program is the most didactic, least open-ended program," says Cook.

"There's so much money behind denigrating teachers. So much money behind charters and vouchers and computer-based education.

"I can't imagine how much money is going into corporate pockets on all of this," says Cook. "Yet there is so much evidence that none of it works. It's like climate change. It makes you wonder, what does it take to convince people?"

RUTH CONNIFF is an American progressive journalist who serves as editor-in-chief of *The Progressive* and has written for *The Nation* and *The New York Times*.

Russ Walsh  **NO**

Fix Society, and the Schools Will Follow

In his first book, *Test-and-Punish* (Park Place Publications, 2013), John Kuhn told the story of how Texas released the "test and punish" monster on public education and how, as in a 1950s science fiction movie, that monster came to threaten the entire country.

Now, in his latest book, Kuhn gives us the next chapter. Using personal narrative, sound research, and righteous indignation, he lays waste to the corporate education reform movement in America.

What I love about Kuhn's writing is that his well-told stories and carefully cited sources give way at times to bursts of passionate advocacy that have the reader, at least this life-long educator, primed to storm the beaches of the Gates Foundation or the halls of Teach for America if necessary, to do what is right by children, teachers, parents, and public education.

I have had the opportunity to hear Kuhn speak, and his writing voice leaps off the page at you, just as his speaking voice jumps out at you in an auditorium.

Kuhn first came to prominence for a speech he gave at a Save Our Schools rally in Texas a few years ago that went viral on YouTube. That speech is included in this, his second book. Fans of Kuhn, the public speaker, are sure to be fans of Kuhn, the author.

Kuhn's bona fides as a critic of the education reform movement are impeccable. After two years working as a missionary in Peru, Kuhn returned to his native Texas and became a teacher of Spanish, eventually working as an assistant principal, principal, and superintendent in rural Texas. His book is punctuated by anecdotes from his time as a teacher and administrator—and the students and parents he encountered along the way.

Part of Kuhn's appeal is the way he describes his failures and turns a harsh eye on himself for not doing a better job. This is not a tale of the hero teacher who parachutes into a failing school to save the day—a mainstay of the education reform narrative—but rather of the lifelong teacher, working hard day-to-day and doing the best job he can while trying to balance work, family, and community. Kuhn says that he is confident that the lifelong

educator, plugging along, has a more lasting impact on students and the community than the fly-by hero teacher who is burnt out and gone in a few years.

The fear that Kuhn refers to in the book's title is the fear generated by "a generation of liars and saboteurs, reckless mishandlers of evidence who worried first about their agendas and last about the Socratic pursuit of the truth."

This fear began in 1983 with the release of *A Nation at Risk*, the landmark study that Kuhn says started the country down the "failing schools" path, which has reached its nadir with the current corporate education reform agenda. Kuhn says the most potent fear exploited by the *Risk* authors was the fear of declining American influence in the world. This fear gave the education reformers an issue they could sell.

While Kuhn was working as a missionary in Peru, he writes, he came upon an open-air market in the rural Andes. A man standing on a box armed with a bullhorn was selling "magic soap." This soap, the backwater entrepreneur declared, "could cure all your ailments," including rheumatism, cancer, and AIDS.

Kuhn accuses the corporate education reform movement of using fear to sell the American public "magic soap." The ingredients in the reform soap include overreliance on standardized tests and "sketchy metrics and magical education solutions like value-added measures of teacher effectiveness." By selling the public magic soap, the corporate education reformers seek to distract attention from the issues they have no intention of addressing, such as poverty and inequality, he writes.

Here is how Kuhn says it in one of those bursts of passion I enjoy so much: "I believe fervently that Michelle Rhee and an army of like-minded bad-schools philosophizers will one day look around and see piles where their painstakingly built sandcastles of reform once stood, and they will know the tragic fame of Ozymandias. Billion-dollar data-sorting systems will be mothballed because of their reckless top-down construction. Value-added algorithms will be tossed in a bin marked 'History's Dumb Ideas.' The mantra 'no-excuses' will retain the significance of 'Where's the beef?' And teachers will still be teaching, succeeding, and failing all over the country, much as they would have done if Michelle Rhee had gone into the foreign service and Bill Gates had invested his considerable wealth and commendable humanitarian ambition in improving law enforcement practices or poultry production."

Kuhn says we must set our sights higher if we truly want to close the much-discussed achievement gap between racial minorities and white students. First, we must recognize that the achievement gap is merely a symptom of the "opportunity gap." The opportunity gap includes all the issues related to poverty, inequality, and segregation that our society faces. That is the glaring reality the education reformers want you to ignore. No amount of testing and measuring, school closures, and teacher firings will close the opportunity gap, and without closing that gap we will never have a meaningful impact on the achievement gap.

The answer to better outcomes in school is not better teachers or digital learning or Common Core or school choice. It is a better, fairer, more just society.

"The enemy, then, of academic achievement in poor America is not the failing teacher," Kuhn writes. "It is the failing citizen." As a citizenry, we are letting teachers take the blame for the failure of all Americans to accept our joint responsibility to needy children. The gross inequity in our society is the greatest barrier to learning for children, and no amount of magic soap will wash away the stain of that inequity in America today.

While he fears for public education in the face of the corporate reformers' poisonous prescription, which includes overtesting, abandoning, and privatizing our schools, Kuhn ends the book on a hopeful note and with a new prescription.

What do we need to do?

1. Implement Universal Pre-K for Poor Children: Research has shown the debilitating impact poverty has on young children's cognitive development. The United States must spend more now on early childhood education.
2. Remove Property Worth as a Factor in School Funding: The funding of schools must be tied to the actual cost of educating a child, not to the property values in the neighborhood where the child lives. As long as funding is tied to property values, inequity will persist.
3. Enlist Better Gatekeepers in Educator Prep Programs: By carefully vetting the quality of students entering into teacher preparation programs and carefully monitoring alternative training programs, we can squeeze the pipeline of teacher supply, drive up salaries, and attract the best and brightest to the profession.
4. Use Testing for Diagnostic, Not Punitive Purposes: Skilled teachers and administrators can learn from the data supplied by a reasoned testing program, but "high-stakes" testing turns the "enterprise of teaching children into a bloodthirsty race."
5. Reject Any Accountability Measure that Doesn't Mathematically Factor Context: By leaving poverty and inequity out of accountability, "we have deliberately shut off the spotlights" that might otherwise illuminate the real problems schools face.
6. Amplify Teachers' and Students' Voices in Policy: Teachers should drive the design of an evaluation system that holds them accountable, and students should have a seat at the table as well.

For Kuhn, all the dire warnings in *A Nation at Risk* have proven baseless. The country still hasn't been, as that report said, "overtaken by competitors throughout the world." The fear that has been used to sell education reform was unwarranted. Schooling in America is not perfect, but if reform is to happen, Kuhn says, "reform should be done *by* educators, not *to* them," (emphasis mine.)

I recommend this book highly to all those who labor in the field of education and to anyone looking for a clear-eyed, passionate spokesperson who understands what is happening to the teaching profession and to public education in 2014.

RUSS WALSH is an author, teacher, and coordinator of college reading at Rider University in Pennsylvania and prolific publisher on social media.

EXPLORING THE ISSUE

Is the Progressive Vision the Answer for Improving the U.S. School System?

Critical Thinking and Reflection

1. Why are there constant, frequent, and fervent cries for school reforms and yet it always seems to need to be reformed again? Why do the reforms not work most of the time?
2. Do you see a way to improve NCLB or should it be abandoned?
3. Why do American students score lower on standard tests than most European students?
4. Explain why American teachers and teaching methods are inferior to European teachers and methods.
5. How can students be made more creative and capable of complex thinking?
6. Is there a school model which you think is the best?

Is There Common Ground?

The main common ground is an agreement that NCLB is a failure. Its promoters strongly sought to push school systems to improve and do it with a complex set of rewards and sanctions. The problem is that new policies have multiple consequences and some of the unintended consequences are quite negative. NCLB has improved many schools, as demonstrated by improving test scores. But critics point to the resulting problem of teaching to the test and focusing on the poorer students to the neglect of the better students. No one wants these and other negative impacts but they seem to be unavoidable. Experts at least agree that something needs to be done.

Both Conniff and Walsh Kuhn agree that NCLB is a failure. It does not inspire learning, nor teach creativity and complex thinking. A higher grade of teachers is needed to work in a less structured and restricting framework. Europe supplies some useful models.

Additional Resources

NCLB is the current major education policy and has been extensively examined. Important books on NCLB include Joanne M. Carris, *Ghosts of No Child Left Behind* (P. Lang, 2011); John E. Chubb, *Learning from No Child Left Behind: How and Why the Nation's Most Important but Controversial Education Law Should Be Renewed* (Hoover Institution Press, 2009); Todd Alan Price and Elizabeth Peterson, eds., *The Myth and Reality of No Child Left Behind: Public Education and High Stakes Assessment* (University Press of America, 2009); and Michael A. Rebell and Jessica R. Wolff, eds., *NCLB at*

the *Crossroads: Reexamining the Federal Effort to Close the Achievement Gap* (Teachers College, Columbia University, 2009). Richard Rothstein, "The Corruption of School Accountability," *The School Administrator* (June 2008), critiques NCLB as relying on flawed numerical measures to evaluate performance, but this causes an emphasis on drill, teaching to the test, and manipulating data.

For the history of education reform, see William J. Reese, *America's Public Schools: From the Common School to "No Child Left Behind"* (Johns Hopkins University Press, 2011). For more general treatments of accountability in education, see Kathryn A. McDermott, *High-Stakes Reform: The Politics of Educational Accountability* (Georgetown University Press, 2011); Keven Carey and Mark Schneider, eds., *Accountability in American Higher Education* (Palgrave Macmillan, 2010); Theodore Hershberg and Claire Robertson-Kraft, eds., *A Grand Bargain for Education Reform: New Rewards and Supports for New Accountability* (Harvard University Press, 2009); and Sherman Dorn, *Accountability Frankenstein: Understanding and Taming the Monster* (Information Age Publishing, 2007). Covering some other crucial related issues are these recommended articles: David Mathews, "The Public and the Public Schools: The Coproduction of Education," *Phi Delta Kappan* (April 2008); Paul D. Houston, "The Seven Deadly Sins of No Child Left Behind," *Phi Delta Kappan* (June 2007); and John Chubb and Diane Ravitch, "The Future of No Child Left Behind: End It? Or Mend It?" *Education Next* (Summer 2009).

Works that look beyond NCLB include Jal Mehta, Robert B. Schwartz, and Frederick M. Hess, eds., *The Futures of School Reform* (Cambridge: Harvard Education Press, 2012); Jal Mehta, *The Allure of Order: High Hopes, Dashed*

Expectations and the Troubled Quest to Remake American Schooling (New York: Oxford University Press, 2013); Ron Nash, *Shake-Up Call: The Need to Transform K-12 Classroom Methodology* (Rowman & Littlefield Education, 2013), Patricia Anne Duncan Parrish, *Getting It Right: Dynamic School Renewal* (Rowman & Littlefield, 2014); Glenn H. Reynolds, *The New School: How the Information Age Will Save American* *Education from Itself* (Encounter Books, 2014); Vicki Abeles, *Beyond Measure: Rescuing an Overscheduled, Underestimated Generation* (Simon and Schuster, 2015); David C. Berliner, *50 Myths and Lies That Threaten America's Public Schools* (Teachers College Press, 2014); and Joseph P. McDonald, *American School Reform: What Works, What Fails, and Why* (University of Chicago Press, 2014).

Internet References . . .

Sociology—Study Sociology Online

http://edu.learnsoc.org/

Sociology Web Resources

www.mhhe.com/socscience/sociology
/resources/index.htm

Sociosite

www.topsite.com/goto/sociosite.net

Socioweb

www.topsite.com/goto/socioweb.com

Selected, Edited, and with Issue Framing Material by:
Kurt Finsterbusch, *University of Maryland, College Park*

ISSUE

Will the Fourth Industrial Revolution Bring About a Wonderful World?

YES: **Danny Crichton**, from "Fear Not the Robot: Automation Will Continue to Raise Our Quality of Life," *National Review* (2015)

NO: **Katherine Mangu-Ward**, from "Will They Take Our Jobs?" *Reason* (2015)

Learning Outcomes

After reading this issue, you will be able to:

- Understand and appreciate some of the amazing new technologies that will revolutionize our economy and our lives.
- Understand why some people are fearful about the impacts of robotization.
- Explore the way that impacts fan out throughout the economy and society.
- Have a general understanding of what promising technological research might achieve in the future and how these might affect societies.
- Know the potential achievements that 3D printing and other innovations in production could make possible.

ISSUE SUMMARY

YES: Danny Crichton sees new technologies greatly increasing production and therefore consumption. Technologies will improve our lives. Digitally run robots are and will produce much faster than humans can and bring us into a wonderful world.

NO: Katherine Mangu-Ward sees technology as both good and bad. She is worried that the robots will take away many of our jobs and make most people unneeded in the labor force. What will happen? The results could pull our society apart.

As a sociologist I feel that I am on relatively firm ground discussing the other issues in this book. I am not on firm ground discussing the issue of the potential impacts of evolving technologies. Probably the most challenging new technology is biotechnology, and who knows how it should or should not be used? Already America is debating the use of drugs to enhance athletic performance. Athletes and body builders want to use them to build muscle, strength, and/or endurance, but much of the public do not approve. They have been outlawed from competitive sports, and athletes that use them have been publicly discredited. Soon, however, parents will be able to pay for genetic engineering to make their children good athletes and perhaps even great athletes. Will that also be illegal? This is only the tip of the iceberg. Thousands of difficult questions will arise as the technology for designing babies will become more and more powerful. Stem cell research is currently a divisive issue. Are we blocking the development of technologies that can save thousands of lives by severely limiting stem cell research?

The technologies that this issue focuses on are not as controversial as genetic engineering because they do not change people but only the equipment that serves people. Wait a minute. Perhaps they will change people. Fire changed people. The light bulb changed people. Cars, trains, airplanes, radios, TVs, computers, the Internet, etc., changed people. How will the evolving new industrial revolution with 3D printing, chips in everything, and abundant robots affect our lives and our character?

The classic expression of this issue is in the stories and legends of a very learned sixteenth-century German doctor named Faust. According to legend, he sold his soul to the devil in exchange for knowledge and magical power. The first printed version of the legend was by Johann Spiess, which was later used by Christopher Marlow as the basis for his famous play, *Dr. Faustus* (1593). Spiess and Marlow presented Faust as a scoundrel who deserved damnation. Some of the other representations of Faust made him a heroic figure who strived for knowledge and power for good. This theme was continued by the most famous Faust legend of all, written by Johann Wolfgang von Goethe in both a poem and a play. In the beginning, Faust's bargain with the devil was for a moment of perfect happiness or contentment. The devil, however, could not deliver this to Faust. More elements are added to the story, including women's love. In the end, Faust finds a moment of perfect contentment and happiness in helping others and dies because of the wager. But Goethe gives the story a Hollywood ending and Faust, the hero, goes to heaven.

Many of the issues in the current technologies debates are found in the Faust legends. Both are focused on the search for knowledge and its use. Is the knowledge-seeking Faust a scoundrel or a saint? Will his knowledge be used for selfish or altruistic purposes? Is mankind better off with the new technologies already here or on the horizon? I am sure that we will use the new technologies in beneficial ways, but someone will find evil uses of them. Who thought that computers would be used so effectively for crime? Crime by computers causes more loss of money than street crime. Nevertheless, let's hope that the new technologies will improve our lives with minimal negative effects.

YES ⬅

Danny Crichton

Fear Not the Robot: Automation Will Continue to Raise Our Quality of Life

EVERY few years, we experience a wave of concern over the rise of robots and its effect on jobs. Automation, we hear, will rid the economy of human labor, replacing the inefficient flesh-and-blood employee with amazingly powerful computers. Yet the robot takeover has so far not occurred—human workers seem to be surviving and even thriving alongside all the machines.

Another one of these surges of concern is upon us, fueled by books such as Tyler Cowen's *Average Is Over* and Martin Ford's *Rise of the Robots*, as well as a spate of articles arguing that this time, the computer revolution really is different. And when we wade through the headlines, this time actually does look different.

Google's autonomous car has already traveled nearly a million miles on California and Nevada roads. Elon Musk, the founder of the electric-car company Tesla Motors, recently predicted that autonomous cars could enter the market as soon as this year, potentially wiping out the taxi and trucking industries in one fell swoop.

Robots are getting better not only at understanding road conditions but also at "reading" their human operators. IBM's computer system Watson, which famously defeated its human opponents in the television game show *Jeopardy*, has continued to rapidly improve and is now answering complex queries about such subjects as medicine. Apple's Siri voice interface for the iPhone has also improved. Silicon Valley seems close to building a starship *Enterprise*–like voice-based computer, threatening hundreds of thousands of jobs in customer-support call centers.

Added to the usual worries about computers' replacing workers is a new concern: Who will own these robots? Will a small stratum of people (capitalists, of course) control them and extract exorbitant rents from the rest of us? If you thought inequality was a problem before, the critics warn, wait until you see what happens next.

Technological change always brings out these negative voices, because we don't have answers for many important questions. We don't know where new jobs are going to come from or even whether there will be work to do at all in 50 years. Yet in light of the history of technological innovation, such fears are unfounded.

Far from exclusively benefiting elites, automation has allowed people of modest means to buy products that were once luxury items available only to the most deep-pocketed consumers. Robotics have caused tremendous social change and will probably continue to do so, but their long-term effect may well be to decrease inequality rather than increase it. Indeed, robotics and automation have perhaps done more to improve quality of life than has any other economic force in history. We need to keep this in mind as we assess the massive, world-changing potential of the next round of technical innovations.

THANKS to *Star Wars*, many of us have images of robots as humanoid figures walking around the desert, but the reality is that robots are often built into the products we use every day. Consider the Keurig coffeemaker. We place a special cup in the machine, hit a button, and the built-in computer handles the rest, leaving us a steaming hot cup of coffee, with minimal human involvement in the brewing process. The device has become a mainstay in office break rooms, and Keurig has sold millions of units around the world. Yet baristas haven't disappeared from the work force. Despite the popularity of automated coffee machines, Starbucks continues to increase its earnings and expand to new locations, with about 1,500 new stores opening just last year.

We often think of robotics as a zero-sum economic game in which humans and machines are locked in a tug-of-war. The Keurig coffeemaker shows that the zero-sum calculus can be flat wrong. Similarly, accountants did not disappear after the arrival of Excel and QuickBooks; in fact, accounting majors have been some of the most in-demand college graduates in recent years.

Home appliances are particularly good examples of how automation increases convenience, since they are among the most common robots we use daily. Cooking is simplified by microwaves that have all kinds of automation built in, such as buttons that heat our food to the perfect temperature. Cleaning our homes takes less and less effort as well, with devices such as iRobot's Roomba, which can automatically sweep the floors.

Perhaps no robots have had a greater effect on quality of life than the washing machine and the dishwasher. In the mid-20th century, when women no longer had to do laundry or wash dishes by hand, they suddenly had considerably more time for themselves. The devices saved hundreds of millions of hours of household labor per year. Some scholars argue that the laundry machine did more to increase female participation in the economy than any other change in the last century.

While many of these conveniences began as luxury goods, history shows us that automation tends to permeate the economy quickly. Yesterday's computers cost millions of dollars and took up whole floors of office buildings, and printers cost tens of thousands of dollars. Today, we can carry a supercomputer in our pocket and purchase a desktop printer for less than a hundred dollars.

Those who fear that robotics will increase inequality overlook the great consumer demand for these products, and the supply-and-demand interplay and competition that force prices ever downward. Based on its autonomous-driving technology, Google could become a monopoly that owns all cars, but it's more likely that all car manufacturers will incorporate this technology into their models.

There is little reason to think that this trend of democratization will stop, and it may even be accelerating. Soon 3-D printers will allow us to "print" millions of different objects, from mugs to the coasters they sit on. Such printers cost thousands of dollars today, but their prices have fallen dramatically over the past few years, and they will probably be in wide use by the end of the decade. Further, 3-D printers will probably increase the pace of innovation across many fields, as they make it cheaper to quickly make product prototypes and sell early models, allowing more inventors to get in the game and make their work available to the public.

When technology allows consumers to produce average-quality goods at home, companies must offer higher-quality products to compete. The greeting-card industry, for instance, faced extinction with the advent of desktop printing, but it started producing specialized designs that home printers cannot (yet) match. The market expanded to encompass a greater range of consumer tastes.

To be fair, patents and other intellectual-property protections ensure that the inventors of technologies are well rewarded for their efforts. Hewlett-Packard has made millions off its printer ink, much as Keurig and Whirlpool have made millions off their products. But economies of scale are no more likely to drive out competition tomorrow than they are today.

BUT we shouldn't tout the benefits to the individual consumer of all these conveniences without taking a wider look at automation and its overall effect on the economy. Greater efficiency through robots allows us to produce more in less time, but these changes can force some workers to change their occupations.

The most important factor in improving quality of life is productivity growth. Productivity is simply the quantity of goods and services we can produce given limited resources, particularly our time.

If we want to improve our standard of living, there are only two options available. One way is to increase our work hours and thus the amount that we produce. But human productivity rarely grows linearly in proportion to hours worked, nor do we necessarily want to spend more time at work. The other option is to increase productivity per hour. We do this when we expand access to education and job training, increasing the productivity of individual workers. We do this also by enhancing human industry through the use of tools, which includes automation and robotics. When we use a microwave to produce a meal in five minutes rather than an hour, we have increased our food-preparation productivity more than tenfold. Multiply such improvements across all devices throughout the economy, and the massive efficiency gains we've made in the last hundred years look unsurprising.

Automation in the economy doesn't strike randomly; it takes hold when market forces determine that physical capital (a robot) is cheaper than human capital (a worker). America's entire manufacturing sector used to be heavily dependent on human labor, but today's highly efficient factories produce more goods than ever before while employing far fewer people, because of robotics.

It's not only a line worker in a factory or a burger flipper who might be replaced by a robot. Many white-collar workers are also at risk. The rules of the market affect everyone. Investors have poured millions of dollars, for instance, into computer startups targeting the legal industry, because lawyers read boilerplate contracts at hours billable well into the triple digits.

Creative destruction is as old as history, but the pace today is accelerating, with millions of workers potentially affected by automation in a matter of years instead of decades. Professions created just a few decades ago are now being eliminated, and entire job categories can rise and fall within a single generation.

There are no simple solutions. Increased efficiency rewards all of us with lower prices for higher-quality goods and services, but certain groups of workers could suffer deep losses. It's possible that education itself will become more automated, which would allow more workers to take classes and improve their skills to compete in the marketplace. English teaching robots already exist in Japan and South Korea, and more subjects may soon be offered by such automated programs. Workers must constantly improve their productivity to increase their value. This is fundamentally good for the economy, because it means that the average hourly value of a human worker is increasing over time.

We are all going to have to improve our skills to be competitive in this economy, but this transition shouldn't distract us from the economic bounty that awaits on the other side of the revolution in robotics.

WHILE the issue of employment garners the most attention from commentators, robotics' socially transformative effects deserve our scrutiny as well. Perhaps no technology has more potential to improve our quality of life than the autonomous car. We will be able to relax during our commutes, reducing our stress and improving our health. Autonomous cars could almost instantaneously deliver a greater number of goods and services, such as meals, household supplies, and home-maintenance services, giving us more leisure time. Perhaps most significant, many fewer accidents would be caused by drunk driving or distraction while driving.

If autonomous cars become popular, we could greatly reduce the land space devoted to roads and parking. City governments could dedicate vast tracts of land to a variety of new uses, such as parks or housing.

Finally, and perhaps most futuristically, we will have to adapt to having more robots in nearly all aspects of our daily life. Siri and Watson are just the first steps toward fully personalized digital assistants, and future generations of these sorts of products will lead to all kinds of new social interactions and situations, affecting human relationships in ways we can't yet predict.

There is no question that our economy will undergo vast changes in the next few years. Critics are right to warn that many jobs will be made redundant, and that automation might increase inequality, at least in the short term. But we've survived—and thrived—through waves of automation for centuries, and the productivity gains show that we should be championing these improvements, not hoping they stop soon. The best has been, and always will be, just around the corner. Let R2-D2 show the way.

DANNY CRICHTON is a doctoral student in public policy at Harvard's John F. Kennedy School of Government and a writer for TechCrunch.

Katherine Mangu-Ward

Will They Take Our Jobs?

MIT economist Andrew McAfee on driverless cars, wireless fishermen, and the second machine age

Massachusetts Institute of Technology economist Andrew McAfee hasn't been replaced by a robot just yet. The following interview was conducted between two humans. Neither of the humans needed to bother to remember what was said, however: We recorded the conversation on an iPhone app, essentially outsourcing memory to a computer. Pre-interview research was conducted with the aid of Google—no humans required there either, just well-crafted algorithms pointing in the direction of McAfee's blog, popular TED Talks about automation and unemployment, and Amazon author pages. But the resulting MP3 file? It was transcribed by a human intern. Accuracy was important, and commercially available voice-to-text programs just aren't good enough yet. Which is a bit disappointing. Especially for the intern.

The rapidly shifting interplay between tasks that humans still do and tasks we delegate to our automated servants should feel like a familiar progression. In the first machine age—the Industrial Revolution—we replaced human brawn with steam power. But in so doing, we wound up creating more demand for labor: We needed people to tend to the increasingly complex machines, and to staff entire new industries that arose once humans were freed from the burden of lifting heavy stuff.

We continue to contract out our need for brawn to machines, say McAfee and his co-author Erik Brynjolfsson, but we have also started replacing human brains with processing power. In their 2014 book, *The Second Machine Age*, the economists describe a new world driven by the relentless doubling of computer processing capacity, known as Moore's Law. McAfee, who has a Ph.D. from Harvard Business School, cheerily anticipates a fresh profusion of consumer goods from this machine age, similar to the glut produced by the last one. But he says he's no Candide—like many, he predicts that this time there will be no compensating boom in demand for human labor and he's worried about the social and economic effects of widespread unemployment. Is he right? Are things really different this time around?

In January, Managing Editor Katherine Mangu-Ward spoke with McAfee about the economics of the robot revolution.

Reason: You rode in the Google driverless car. Tell me about it.

Andrew McAfee: The experience went from terrifying to passionately interesting to boring in the space of one ride.

Reason: Why was that?

McAfee: When the guy who was driving the car hit the big red button and took his hands off the wheel on the highway, that was a white-fingernail moment,

Reason: Is there literally a big cartoon red button?

McAfee: There's honestly a big cartoon red button on the dashboard.

Reason: That's delightful. So he hits the button—

McAfee: —and takes his hands and feet off the controls, and we're going at highway speeds in a completely self-guided car. That was a little scary. Very quickly that passed, and then it became super interesting, because I felt like an astronaut. I'm having this really uncommon experience, and after a while, it sunk in that I was in a car that was obeying all relevant statutes, not weaving, not seizing opportunities in the right-hand lane, going down the road at 55 miles per hour. I mean this as the highest compliment: It was a godawful boring ride.

Reason: What are some places in everyday life where people may be undervaluing the extent to which the robots or machines have already taken our jobs or taken over our lives?

McAfee: I won't say "taken our jobs," because I still have one. A lot of these changes don't keep screaming at you. They happen kind of gradually. They're bit by bit, but then you look up and you're living your life pretty differently than you did a few years ago.

For me, professionally, if I could sit down and look at what I was doing a decade ago or 15 years ago, I think it'd be night-and-day different. When I sit down to start writing something or to learn something, I basically have 30 tabs open on my browser. I'm searching for a little stat, or I pull up a number from the St. Louis Fed that's got this great data repository. I don't go to the library; I don't fire off requests to research librarians. I use a research assistant for some things, but not for "hunt down this fact for me," simply because it's easier and quicker for me to do it myself. When you've got the world's knowledge at your fingertips all the time and you're supposed to be doing knowledge work, it really does change the way things happen.

Reason: And how do you think that applies—if it does—to people who are doing a different kind of job? There are some guys in **reason's** office right now assembling a million new desk chairs. It looks like their jobs aren't very different. Am I wrong?

McAfee: I think that part of their job is probably not very different, but how they got their day's schedule, how they communicate with the head office, how they alert them that the job is done, the extent to which they're monitored—maybe their truck has a GPS device in it so headquarters knows where they are—I think those things are actually pretty big changes.

In long-haul trucking, for example, the industry has actually transformed itself, and trucking companies started owning trucks again instead of giving them to subcontractors, mainly because they could monitor the drivers so carefully that they didn't have to rely on the fact that people take better care of their own equipment.

Let me give you one from my nonprofessional life. I moved to New York City for the first half of 2015. Let's assume that I didn't have any friends here.

Reason: Should we make such a sad assumption?

McAfee: (Laughs) No, luckily I've got a lot of people to hang out with and to show me around. But let's say I didn't have any of that but I was still interested in finding a good cafe to go hang out at, at exploring different parts of the city, at getting around efficiently.

I would do that by trial and error before. I'd make a ton of mistakes. I personally would find it really stressful, because I hate being lost and I hate feeling stupid.

Those problems are basically gone for me. I've got an app called City Mapper on my phone. I'm pretty sure it was free. All I ever do is say, "I'm here in the Upper East Side, I'm going to meet a friend for dinner down here in the West Village. How do I get there?"

And it says, "OK, you walk over to Lex and 63rd, hop on the F train, you'll take it six stops, and get off here." If incredibly detailed information about how to navigate a very unfamiliar city, so I can get around about as well as somebody who's lived here a long time.

Reason: Tell me what this has to do with the fisherman in Kerala.

McAfee: That is probably my all-time favorite and most heartening solid piece of research about what's going on. A guy named Robert Jensen got to observe the economic lives of some systems-level fishermen in Kerala, India, before and after they got mobile phones for the very first time ever.

These folks were living in an I.T. vacuum. They'd go out every day and do their fishing, and they'd come back in and have to pick which local market to go to, to try to sell their fish. And you can imagine all the inefficiencies that would result because you couldn't match supply with demand carefully. Some days they would do great. Some days they would do lousy. Some days they would have to throw their fish away because nobody would pay them anything for it. It was a terrible situation.

In a really beautifully designed study, Jensen got to watch what happened before and after cell phone towers went in at different points along the coast. So he had a bunch of different experiments, and he saw the same thing over and over and over again. Markets start to behave predictably and rationally immediately after the new technology becomes available. The first thing these people did was all go and buy a phone, because none of them are stupid, and they would use it to call ahead and say, "What's the price at this market? Should I go over here?" And you just watch the markets regularize and clear in a way they could never do before.

This is an example of what happens, what's happening over and over and over around the world, as these new technologies diffuse. We are greatly improving the lives of people in a lot of ways.

Reason: The current education system is almost hilariously unsuited to this universe that you have just described. Tell me why everything is bad and how you can fix it.

McAfee: I think there are a lot of really extraordinarily hard-working people in education, and I don't presume for a second to have all the fixes. But one thing that our primary education system is doing a really good job of is preparing the kinds of workers that we needed 50 years ago in the height of the industrial era. They acquire a suite of skills: They can read, they can write, they can do math at some level. And more fundamentally, they're encouraged to follow instructions and to be obedient. You sit in the same place. You go through this orderly process. People in the front of the room talk to you. It's great training for industrial-era white-collar and blue-collar workers. It's pretty lousy training for the kind of thinking and the kind of people and workers that we're going to need as we move deeper into the second machine age.

Reason: So what's better?

McAfee: I was a Montessori kid, and I'm incredibly grateful I was a Montessori kid, because my earliest education bore no relationship to that system I just described. It taught me the world was an interesting place and my job was to go poke at it.

Reason: You've said that entrepreneurship is something we should encourage in American kids and welcome in our immigrants. Why that, specifically?

McAfee: I haven't seen a computer that could convince investors to put together a business plan or really spot an opportunity and figure out how to go after it. That still does feel to me like a human skill. But as we mentioned in the book, entrepreneurship, and in particular tech entrepreneurship, has been driven by immigrants to a wild degree, and the people who want to come to this country very often are the kind of tenacious, ambitious, hard-to-satisfy ones. These are exactly the kinds of folks that you want to come in if you're interested in entrepreneurship. So especially at the level of skilled immigration, I find that kind of the biggest policy no-brainer out there. Even at the low-skill levels, we're not displacing tons of native workers from jobs.

Reason: "Income inequality," "coming apart," "two Americas." There are lots of names for the ways that rich people and poor people are economically separating, particularly in the labor market. You call it "the spread."

McAfee: There used to be a bunch of economic measures that all went up and down together, luckily primarily up. They did it in lockstep. They were really tightly coupled. And then, in recent years, we start to see these measures head in different directions and gaps opening up between them.

For example, one of the graphs we draw has four lines on it for the entire postwar period: GDP per capita, labor productivity, raw number of jobs, and median family or median household [income]. For decades after the end of the war, they were all going up, and they were all going up just super, super close together. Around 1980, the average median family income line starts to tail off. More recently, the job growth line starts to tail off. And the job growth line starts to tail off before even the great recession kicked in. Job growth was fairly anemic all throughout the 2000s.

We call that phenomenon "the great decoupling." It's an example of this spread. You see it in returns to labor vs. capital. You see it in these four lines. You see it when we look at wealth and income measures. Thomas Piketty certainly sees it [in *Capital in the Twenty-First Century*]. He just looks at a couple aspects of it and labels them inequality, but these are all manifestations of a pretty common phenomenon.

Reason: People get very emotional about this topic. You can see that in the response to the Piketty book, and you can see it in lots of other peoples' writing, including Tyler Cowen's *The Great Stagnation* and Charles Murray's *Coming Apart*. So before we get to your solutions, give me your "So what?" Why does everyone care quite so much, given that the vast majority of people are doing better, there's just a differential in the gains that seems to be opening up.

McAfee: Let's be careful about that. We are all doing better as consumers—as people who want access to goods and services, and who want more of them, who want higher variety, higher quality, lower prices, all those things. The bounty that comes out of capitalist systems, and in particular technologically driven ones, is just stupefying. It's pretty unbelievable, and I find that unambiguously good news.

The challenge comes when I look at things like the median American household income. Even after we adjust for inflation and for changes in family size, it's not that it's growing more slowly than it used to, it's actually lower than it was 50 years ago. For me, that's a decent answer to the "So what?" question, because the fact that it's real income means that it represents our best attempts to take into account the fact that flatscreen TVs cost less than they used to, that it is your actual purchasing power. It's not a precipitous decline, it's not that the middle class is starving in the streets, but it is a slow, steady decline.

That's part of the "So what?" answer. Another part is that there are some important categories of stuff that are not getting a lot cheaper over time. Higher education, health care, housing. Now, we can have a really active debate about why they're following different trajectories and whether we should head more toward libertarian-style market solutions for that. That's a really important, valid debate. It's a bit of a separate question from the fact that are these things getting more or less affordable to the American family at the 50th percentile, and in a lot of cases they're becoming less affordable.

It's also becoming more clear as we get the evidence that social mobility is not where we think it is. The economic circumstances of your birth seem to play a really large role in this country in determining your economic life trajectory, even more so than they do in a lot of these European social democracies that we like to disparage. The low mobility is also part of an answer to "So what?"

Charles Murray has documented that among lower-middle-class Americans, there's been, over the past half-century, a really alarming rise in a bunch of social ills: in drug use, in dropping out of the labor force, in not staying married, in children raised in single-parent homes, in incarceration rates. What's interesting to me is that all those go along with a really sharp decline in work, just being engaged in a job. Those social ills are almost nonexistent in upper-middle-class Americans, and those upper-middle-class Americans have been working pretty steadily through this period as well. Murray would disagree with the following: My very simple narrative there is that work is a really good thing to have as technology encroaches and takes away some of the classic lower-middle-class job opportunities. I think we see some social ills coming out of that.

And then the last part of the answer is that there's some pretty alarming data that among the lower rungs of the education and income ladder, health outcomes are heading in the wrong direction. Average life span, for some demographic groups, is actually going down recently in America after decades of pretty impressive gains.

I put all those things together, and I don't find it easy to be blasé about the spread.

Reason: You've said nice things about work for work's own sake. But actually, people hate work, don't they? Most people hate their jobs, at least some of the time. So why do you want them to keep working?

McAfee: Among people who have looked pretty hard at this, there's a really broad consensus that when work—I

won't say jobs—when work goes away from the community, relatively few good things happen and lots of bad things happen. And again, that list, that litany that Murray put together, is pretty telling to me. I don't want to pretend that if everybody had a job, all those things would magically go away, but I do believe that part of the **reason** that these ills creep in is idleness and not having the sense of purpose and dignity that comes along with the job. I don't think those are just empty things.

Reason: So if work has these good effects, and we're concerned about culture and economies coming apart, and meanwhile McDonald's is automating order-taking and burger-flipping and Google is automating driving, then . . . what?

McAfee: I want to be clear: I don't demonize McDonald's and Google and all these other companies for trying to use technology and use automation. They're trying to keep their costs low. They're a business. They're not a social welfare organization. And they're doing it because they think they deliver better goods and services to all of us. So I'm not saying that companies should take one for the team somehow and just start bringing on lots of labor willy-nilly for the good of the community or the good of society.

But all these companies acting in their own interests are generating, I think, less labor demand than was the case previously. For about 200 years, we had this wonderful phenomenon where, as the capitalist engine progressed, it needed a ton of labor at all different levels of skill, and instead of dropping out, instead of mass unemployment, instead of mass starvation, we had the rise of a large stable prosperous middle class in country after country.

It feels to me like this time might finally be different. The data that I talked about are not just blips; they look like trends. And when I look at tech progress, I don't see it changing course.

Now, what do we do about it? I think we try as hard as possible to prove me wrong and to make this time just like all the other times, where even though there was a lot of tech progress, the average worker wound up with a better job and a higher wage.

Reason: And how do we do that?

McAfee: In the book we tried to concentrate on the really uncontroversial parts of the Econ 101 playbook. And you've got to go a long way outside of the mainstream economics profession before you'll find someone who'll say that the government should not be involved in building out infrastructure or primary education or basic research, because the private sector tends to undervalue and therefore underfund that kind of stuff. So our playbook consists of things like education reform and immigration reform and increased focus on entrepreneurship and doubling down on infrastructure and revitalizing basic research. To me, that's our best chance to create an economic environment that would let the happy pattern repeat itself and bring labor demand back. There's no way that labor demand is going to come without a lot more economic growth. Great. Let's do what we can to get the economic growth.

Reason: In the next, say, five to 10 years, what are the first jobs to go?

McAfee: One of the quickest ones to me looks like different flavors of customer service reps, where they're using their language skills. They're using their pattern-matching skills. Our technologies are really, really good at both of those right now. They're going to get worlds better over the next five to 10 years, so people doing that kind of knowledge work, I think, are going to face some unemployment headwinds.

Depending on the regulatory environment, I think a highly functional, autonomous vehicle is easily in that timeframe, so we have a lot of people who drive for a living now who are going to be confronted by automation.

I think if a piece of technology is not already the world's best medical diagnostician, it easily will be in five or 10 years. Now, I don't know if, again, there are going to be regulatory policy changes that would allow that technology to diffuse. But if that happens, we've got a lot of people who diagnose us for a living who are going to be confronted by technology that does it better.

What then happens in these different fields is not that the employment goes down to absolutely zero. It's that it goes down to a pretty small number of very competent, pretty high-level people supported by a ton of automation.

Reason: That's something that has happened in lots of other places already, right?

McAfee: Yeah. Longshoremen are the classic job where that happened in the 20th century, but the happy phenomenon is that other industries sprang up that, again, needed labor at all different skill levels. I'm encouraged by things like Uber and Airbnb and the rental economy that's giving average people a chance to earn some money. That's great. I hope it continues.

Reason: There's this vogue for famous technophiles to freak out about artificial intelligence [A.I.]. We've got a statement from the Future of Life Institute signed by Stephen Hawking and Elon Musk, saying basically, "Everyone panic, the robots are going to kill us all." Are they right?

McAfee: This is just not high on my list of concerns at all. The best I ever heard it explained is that we are multiple Watson and Crick moments away from anything like a Terminator or a Matrix scenario.

I could be wrong about that. I could easily be wrong. In which case, oops. Because the interesting point they make is, "Look, even if it's a very low probability of that, and even if it's kind of a long way off in the future, we're talking about an existential risk." OK. It's easy to look at some of the recent advances and extrapolate them forward and say, "Holy Toledo."

Reason: What do you think is the most "Holy Toledo"-inducing advance recently?

McAfee: The most telling demonstration for me was when the guys at Deep Mind Technologies told their system to learn to play classic '80s-vintage Atari video games. They didn't tell them the rules of the games, they didn't tell them what controls they had, they didn't try to tell them what was good or what was bad or advanced or "shoot that tank, but don't shoot that thing over there." All they said was to the system, "Your job is to maximize that number up there, which is called the score. Knock yourself out." For the majority of the games that they included, the system is now the world's best player.

Reason: How did it do on Pong!

McAfee: You would never score a point against it on Pong.

Reason: That's disappointing. That's a lot of time wasted by a lot of teenagers.

McAfee: Yeah. It's the world's best Battlezone player, and I played a lot of Battlezone. I'm not getting those hours back. (Laughs)

Reason: What technologies are people currently undervaluing and what tech are people currently overvaluing?

McAfee: I think we're simultaneously overconcerned about A.I. progress in an existential sense and underconcerned about it in an economic sense. Because I do think that these advances are going to pretty quickly enter the business world, and I think they're going to accentuate all these phenomena that we talk about in our book.

I personally think 3-D printing is extraordinarily cool, and it's going to help with our innovation work and our prototyping and stuff like that. There are people who believe it's going to massively disrupt office supply chains and the manufacturing industry and everything all around the world in some realistic timeframe. I don't see that.

Reason: So you're telling me that the future of, "Computer, please make me a ray gun" is further off than I was hoping?

McAfee: That's actually going to—if you want to invest the time to put one of these things in your house and learn to use it and acquire the plans, you can print out your gun. People have done that. What I don't think is that all the gun manufacturers should say, "Oh man, all of our big centralized factories are now completely worthless."

Reason: What is the "to be sure" paragraph you wish you had put in the book?

McAfee: Ask me that question in a few more years. Maybe the job market's going to spontaneously tighten back up and the middle class is going to get on a healthy trajectory again and this whole book is going to stand as another example of "Ha ha ha, see how terrible that timing was."

Reason: Right.

McAfee: And I guess when the Terminator comes and knocks on my door, I'll say, "Gosh, I wish I'd been a little more guarded about the prospects for artificial intelligence."

Reason: I think the Terminator's going to let you live, because you're convincing all of us to lower our defenses.

McAfee: That's true. I could be the quisling for the Terminators, right? I'll be their intermediary.

KATHERINE MANGU-WARD is managing editor of *Reason*, with considerable experience as a journalist and commentator on radio and TV.

EXPLORING THE ISSUE

Will the Fourth Industrial Revolution Bring About a Wonderful World?

Critical Thinking and Reflection

1. What are the potential benefits of the new technologies for humans?
2. How might robots change the way that I live at home?
3. What role should society play via government in decisions about how these new technologies be used?
4. Should religions have a say or even a final say in the use of new technologies such as designing by biotechnology what qualities babies should be genetically engineered to have?
5. What is the potential of new digital technologies to produce abundantly and generate worldwide affluence?
6. Will digital production require special regulations?

Is There Common Ground?

The best argument for using new technologies is their greater benefits in more production or solved problems. The main arguments against them are the costs and the danger of negative unanticipated consequences. The latter are sometimes hard to measure or to notice. For robots it is the jobs that are displaced. For biotechnology it is the mistakes that might happen. For digital advances it is their possible misuse. Everyone would like the benefits to exceed the costs. The debate is over the estimate of those factors in the future and how much weight to give each factor when they differ in nature. Is it acceptable for one life to be lost if several millions are gained in additional production and consumption? A special problem is that different people are generally affected by the benefits and the costs. Usually the corporations get the benefits and the general public gets the costs. If the corporations also paid all the costs then they could figure out whether the new technology is worth the costs. The articles in this issue deal with both the costs and benefits of new technologies. They differ considerably on how severe the negative impacts are expected to be.

Additional Resources

By and large America has positive attitudes toward technological developments. But it is also true that America has a history of doomsday prophets. Many of them are religious and preach about the coming tribulation, but many others talk about the destruction of our society and way of life because of disruptive technological changes. In some sense, this is an old debate, as the Faust legend indicates. Nevertheless, it is only recently that science has brought us to the doorstep of rapid and dramatic changes so it is time to revive the Faustian debate.

Among the commentaries on the new technological age and its risks are Nick Beckstead et al., *Unprecedented Technological Risks* (Future of Humanity Institute, September 2014); Martin Ford, *Rise of the Robots: Technology and the Threat of a Jobless Future* (Basic Books, 2015); Benjamin Wittes and Gabriella Blum, *The Future of Violence: Robots and germs, Hackers and Drones—Confronting a New Age of Threat* (Basic Books, 2015); Ian Morris, *War! What Is It Good For?: Conflict and the Progress of Civilization from Primates to Robots* (Farrar, Straus and Giroux, 20014); Ann Rogers and John Hill, *Unmanned: Drone Warfare and Global Security* (Pluto Press, 2014); Ronald J. Deibert, *Black Code: Inside the Battle for Cyberspace* (McClelland and Stewart, 2013); and C. A. Bowers, *The False Promises of the Digital Revolution* (Peter Lang Publishing, 2014). Most articles on 3-D printing are journalistic or online articles. Three major works are Neil A. Gershenfeld, *Fab: The Coming Revolution on Your Desktop—From Personal Computers to Personal Fabrication* (New York: Basic Books, 2005); William E. Halal, *Technology's Promise: Expert Knowledge on the Transformation of Business and Society* (New York: Palgrave Macmillan, 2008); and Rutger van Santen, Djan Khoe, and Bram Vermeer,

2030: Technology That Will Change the World (New York: Oxford University Press, 2010). Works that are opposed to bioengineering include Marcus Wohlsen, *Biopunk: DIY* *Scientists Hack the Software of Life* (Current, 2011); and Craig Holdrege, *Beyond Biotechnology: The Barren Promise of Genetic Engineering* (University of Kentucky Press, 2010).

Internet References . . .

Sociology—Study Sociology Online

http://edu.learnsoc.org/

Sociology Web Resources

www.mhhe.com/socscience/sociology/resources/index.htm

Sociosite

www.topsite.com/goto/sociosite.net

Socioweb

www.topsite.com/goto/socioweb.com

Unit 5

UNIT

Crime and Social Control

*A*ll societies label certain hurtful actions as crimes and punish those who commit them. Other harmful actions, however, are not defined as crimes, and the perpetrators are not punished. Today the definition of crime and the appropriate treatment of criminals is widely debated. Many view the legal system, police practices, and high incarceration rates as needing major reforms.

ISSUE

Selected, Edited, and with Issue Framing Material by:
Kurt Finsterbusch, *University of Maryland, College Park*

Are the Police in America to Be Condemned?

YES: Nancy A. Heitzeg, from "'Broken Windows,' Broken Lives and the Ruse of 'Public Order' Policing," *Truthout* (2015)

NO: Nick Wing, from "If Most Police Officers Are 'Good Cops,' These Are Even Better," *Huffington Post* (2015)

Learning Outcomes

After reading this issue, you will be able to:

- Have a knowledge about some of the awful actions of police who have murdered unarmed black men.
- Understand the "broken windows" theory of policing policy.
- Understand some of the consequences of the "broken windows" policy.
- Relate crime rate data to recommendations for changes in criminal justice policies such as rehabilitation and new policing policies.
- Develop some ideas about necessary changes in police practices.

ISSUE SUMMARY

YES: Nancy A. Heitzeg, a professor of sociology and director of the critical studies of race/ethnicity program at St. Catherine University, presents and refutes the theory behind the "broken windows" approach to policing which is tough on crime and produces high imprisonment rates. She also presents several cases of police killing unarmed blacks and argues that the police need to be better controlled.

NO: Nick Wing, Senior Viral Editor at *The Huffington Post,* emphasizes that most cops are good cops and act responsibly. He presents many reports by policemen and police chiefs which tell very positive stories about policemen to balance the very negative stories in the media.

The first obligation of government is law and order. Without this life would be nasty, brutish, and short. The other institutions of society would not work, there would be little economic exchange, and everyone would be desperately poor. Law and order undergirds everything that we have in society. The judicial system provides that law and order. Laws are passed and enforced by police, courts, judges, attorneys, and prisons. Currently the police are in the news because many events show some policemen using unnecessary force, even killing unarmed citizens. Citizens are rightly demanding justice but most murderous policemen go free or have very light penalties. How

should these cases be handled? The police have a hard job and they should be the guardians of the community. The people and the government should stand behind them. But that support seems to have gone too far so that the police are allowed to get away with murder or other brutal acts. In such situations the public response often goes too far. Hopefully sane heads will prevail.

The police are not the main restraint against criminal actions. We are. The fact of the matter is that most people do not commit crimes because we do not want to. We have been trained by parents, teachers, ministers, comrades, and role models to be good people. The result of these influences is that we have consciences or, as Freud said, superegos.

We may exceed the speed limit or take a few supplies from our employer but the things that we would not do number in the thousands. Effective societies depend on our good behavior. But what is truly strange is that crime can have positive effects. According to Durkheim, witnessing a crime (in person or on TV) is likely to strengthen our morals by stimulating moral outrage. For some people, however, the prevalence of violence can normalize violence and make people more likely to use violence. Crime and police behavior are highly charged and complex issues today and the two articles presented here explore both facts and values. Heitzeg explains the broken windows theory, which claims that broken windows or other signs that the neighborhood is running down invite social abandonment, which leads to more crime. Therefore, quick prosecution of petty crimes in a neighborhood will tend to keep out more serious crimes. This policy has led to the tough on crime policy which locks up too many people for too long and with little emphasis on rehabilitation.

The readings that follow focus on the behavior of policemen. Heitzeg emphasizes the stories of overactive policemen and high imprisonment in accord with the "broken windows" perspective. He also presents several cases of policemen killing unarmed blacks. Wing tells positive stories of police behavior and their close work with communities. Most policemen are good cops so he tries to balance the negative reports that the police are receiving in the media.

YES ↩

Nancy A. Heitzeg

"Broken Windows," Broken Lives and the Ruse of "Public Order" Policing

Author's note: As we approach the one year anniversary of Eric Garner's death, New York City reached a settlement with his family, agreeing to pay $5.9 million to resolve a wrongful-death claim. The settlement is the latest in a long series of civil pay-outs (over $1 billion) made by the city to victims of NYPD.

But that has largely been the only accounting. While still under investigation, the officers involved in Garner's death will likely face no legal consequences. A Grand Jury has already declined to indict them. In fact, those who filmed the police action that killed Garner—Ramsey Orta and Tanisha Allen—have singularly received more police scrutiny than the killers themselves.

The Mayor, elected on a progressive wave, has co-signed continued NYPD repression—budgeting for 1300 new officers and standing in support of both broken windows and the chokehold. This, despite growing protests over police killings in NYC and across the nation. As of this writing, that number approaches 600, a rate of more than 3 dead per day.

The death of Eric Garner, which preceded that of Mike Brown by a month, reinvigorated a national call to end police violence against Black Lives. It continues apace, perhaps has even accelerated. And so we demand again in the name of Eric Garner and so many more:

"It Stops Today."

The murder of Eric Garner at the hands of NYPD brings to light again the never-ending unanswered questions. Unchecked police killings of mostly Black Men—one every 28 hours. Rampant racial profiling, most recently high-lighted in *Floyd v City of New York*. Excessive use of force, even in the handling of non-violent crime. Deadly restraint tactics, such as the choke-hold that killed Michael Stewart, killed Anthony Baez, and was supposedly banned in NYC despite being the on-going subject of more than 1000 civilian complaints.

Lurking behind all these atrocities is the flawed theory and fatal practice that makes it all possible: "Broken Windows" and public order policing. Widely promoted but rarely publicly critiqued, in light of Eric Garner, let's take a closer look.

Broken Windows: Flawed Theory and Practice

Broken Windows theory and the subsequent proliferation of "public ordering/quality of life/order maintenance" policing emerges from the seminal 1982 article, "Broken Windows: The Police and Neighborhood Safety" (George L. Kelling and James Q. Wilson, *Atlantic Monthly*). The theory basically claims that "disorder" leads to community withdrawal, loss of informal social control, and then, to more serious crime. One unattended broken window leads to more "physical disorder," then to "social disorder" in the form of public drunkenness, panhandlers, the homeless, taggers, public urinators, squee-gee men, and more, and finally in "criminal invasions" of neighborhoods that seem abandoned, unkempt or out of control. Perhaps, most importantly, the theory posits too that policing can prevent this, that a rigorous/repressive approach—sometimes "zero tolerance"—to public order crimes is necessary in order to curtail serious violent and property crimes.

Broken Windows has always been theoretically problematic. (See "Assessing "Broken Windows": A Brief Critique" by Randall G. Shelden and "Street Stops and Broken Windows: Terry, Race and Disorder in New York City" by Jeffery Fagan and Garth Davies for excellent overviews.) It emerges from the tradition of criminology which searches vainly for individual and environmental causes of crime while ignoring the vast array of well-documented structural contributors such as poverty, unemployment, lack of quality education, and racism. Further, broken windows relies heavily on long discredited classical deterrence theory and the notion that participation in crime represents an individualized "rational choice" that can be averted by the threat of punishment, or policing.

This certainly did not dampen the appeal of this theory for those who saw the opportunity it offered for expanded police patrol and resources. Nor did it prevent police departments—most notably NYPD under the former and now current again Police Commissioner William Bratton—from rushing to implementation of this "theory" that was supported by neither logic nor data. Teamed up with then Mayor Rudy Giuliani, Bratton claimed to have "re-captured" the subways from fare dodgers and the homeless, and then turned attention to the streets armed with both zero tolerance tactics to search for drugs and guns, and a new form of crime mapping called "Compstat," a computer system that provides data for each precinct on arrests, complaints and other information about crime. In tandem, the two claimed credit for the decrease in New York City crime, using dubious data, but plenty of PR.

It should be noted that despite the claims that public order policing tactics had a direct impact on crime rates in NYC and elsewhere, there is little to no evidence to support this. Beyond this, the flawed and continued fixation with the ostensible connections between police practices and the reality of crime is misguided—there isn't one. Crime rates operate independently of police and criminal justice system practices, rising and falling according to larger social conditions. Don't take it from me—two of the top researchers on the police, David Bayley and Lawrence Sherman state it simply:

"The police do not prevent crime. This is one of the best kept secrets of modern life."

What is widely known, is this: the police have the power to destroy and disrupt community, to harass individuals and entire groups of people without legal cause,

injure, maim and kill with impunity and little fear of recourse. All in the name of law and order.

Broken Windows makes that even easier, and in NYC, the result was, not a police induced decrease in crime, but rather an increase in police killings of citizens and civilian lawsuits/complaints.

Broken Windows: Racial Profiling and Gentrification in an Era of "Color-Blindness"

The reality of public order policing in NYC and elsewhere has been "harassment" policing, which has targeted communities of color and the poor. The rise of Broken Windows theory and related police practices neatly coincides with the War on the Poor, extensive criminalization of poverty/homelessness, Black motherhood, appearance and the use of public space, the escalation of the War on Drugs and attendant mass incarceration. It too provides a convenient "color-blind" cover for warrant-less pretextual stops of "suspicious" people (read Black), mass arrests for minor offenses, and sweeps of entire communities. "Disorder" became the new proxy for race, and public order policing maintains the literal and figurative boundaries of whiteness. This certainly became clear via stop/frisk data revealed in *Floyd v City of New York*: over 86 percent of the stops were of Black or Latino individuals. Still Bratton's successor, Ray Kelly, argued that Blacks were "understopped," despite the fact that nearly 90 percent of the people stopped were released without the officer finding any basis for a summons or arrest.

Money matters here too, as it always does, and public order policing offers a major tool in reclaiming space for economic interests vested in gentrification. In the Giuliani-Bratton 1990s, public order policing was the central tactic in the so-called "clean-up" of Times Square, pushing out the "disorderly" regulars to the city margins to make the space "safe" for the Disneys, the well-to-do and white, and out of town tourists. This trend continues unabated in NYC and elsewhere. Bratton, of course, took his tactics to Los Angeles, where the "Safer Cities Initiative" displaced thousands of low income people of color in service of the gentrification of Skid Row. Observers note:

> Longtime residents and community organizers see what is happening on Skid Row as an extreme example of what is happening in cities across the United States: as predominantly white middle- and upper-middle-class people find urban centers increasingly desirable places to live, gentrification displaces lower-income communities of color.

Policing strategies such as "broken windows" are often used to facilitate gentrification, resulting not only in displacement but increased incarceration of poor people of color.

Expect more of the same. Less 100 days after his return as Police Commissioner, Bratton was meeting with real estate elites and retired US Army General Stanley McChrystal, touting a slideshow comparing crime rates with local real estate values, and encouraging still more collusion between the police and the military in support of 'poor doors', in pursuit of panhandlers, jaywalkers, food vendors or teenagers dancing on a train for money.

Coming soon too to a town near you.

Whose "Quality of Life"?

Broken Windows theory and the public order police tactics that have sprung from it have proven to be disastrous for communities of color. Under the color-blind guise of "safety" and "quality of life," white well-off property owners are protected from "disorder," spared the horror of having to refuse a panhandler or step over a drunk on the street. Meanwhile those deemed to be indicative of "disorder" themselves are displaced, endlessly policed, surveilled, brutalized, arrested just for being alive.

Eric Garner is dead because of public order policing. Murdered for Standing While Black and Suspected—of what? Selling loose cigarettes for 50 cents each. Can the general public finally come out of the brain-washed fog of fear to see how absurd, how obscene this actually is?

From the Malcolm X Grassroots Movement Statement on the Murder of Eric Garner by the NYPD:

> The 'broken windows' philosophy of policing, which purports that focusing resources on the most minor violations will somehow prevent larger ones, has consistently resulted in our rights being violated. We demand the criminal indictment and termination of the officers who unnecessarily attacked and killed Eric Garner. We also demand that the NYPD end the era of broken windows and militarized policing which has brought tragedy and mistrust of the police to many of our communities. We send our deepest condolences to the family of Eric Garner and support their struggle for justice in this case.

Broken Windows theory and public order policing is built and perpetuated on nothing but a ruse and many lies—it is profiling and apartheid, called by another name. Let the last words of Eric Garner mean more than just his last breath:

"It Stops Today."

NANCY A. HEITZEG is a professor of sociology at St Catherine's University where she is director of the Critical Studies of Race and Ethnicities program. She has published extensively on issues of race, class, gender, and social control; and she is co-founder and co-editor of the Critical Injustice series on the Critical Mass Progress blog. Heitzeg's most recent book is *The School to Prison Pipeline: Education, Discipline, and Double Standards* (Praeger, 2015).

Nick Wing    **NO**

If Most Police Officers Are 'Good Cops,' These Are Even Better

As protesters around the nation continue to call for police reform, they are regularly reminded of an important fact: While some officers abuse their power, the majority are "good cops." For every officer who visits harm on someone or violates the public's trust, there are countless others who follow the rules and who want nothing more than to protect, serve and return home safe at the end of their shift.

It's a point that many activists are aware of. Just as corrupt and racist officers don't represent American law enforcement as a whole, so are the minority of radical protesters who have called for violence against the police *not* representative of the demonstrators who have gathered again and again since the grand jury decisions not to indict officers in the deaths of Michael Brown and Eric Garner.

If bad cops are those who abuse their power, what does it take to be a good cop? Some of those same peaceful demonstrators have suggested the following: professional conduct; good relationships with the community; and the humility, or simply the pragmatism, to admit that calls for accountability, transparency and improved training are not indictments of every police officer, but rather objective critiques of a law enforcement system that has substantial flaws.

Part of what makes reform so difficult is the insular culture that reportedly exists in many police departments. Numerous former officers have described a "blue wall of silence" that compels them to place loyalty and secrecy above all else. This often keeps police from reporting misconduct among their colleagues, due to the risk of retaliation. There is little room for officers, no matter how good they might be themselves, to speak out about individual bad actors or the larger structural issues that enable them.

But not everyone in law enforcement has taken such a rigid stance. Below are a number of police officials who have denounced the idea that cops and protesters need to have a "them or us" mentality. These officers have shown a willingness at least to listen to the criticism and calls for reform, and their approach shows that cooperation and meaningful dialogue are possible as people on both sides of the line work toward solutions. Of course, the fact that there are so few officers publicly expressing this viewpoint also speaks volumes about the complexity of the issue.

Police Chief Chris Magnus, Richmond, California

In December, Magnus joined protesters—including some of his fellow officers—and held a sign that read "#Black-LivesMatter," which has become a rallying cry for activists who want to see an end to racial profiling and police discrimination.

The gesture drew immediate backlash from the law enforcement community, with the Richmond Police Officers Association accusing the chief of politicking in uniform, a violation of state law. But Magnus told the *San Francisco Chronicle* that while he understood the issue is divisive, he didn't see the statement on the sign as political. "I looked at it for a minute and realized this is actually pretty innocuous," he said. "When did it become a political act to acknowledge that 'black lives matter' and show respect for the very real concerns of our minority communities?"

"It was intended to be a humane statement," Magnus continued.

The chief, who has been credited with reforming his department's use of force and significantly reducing crime rates since he came to Richmond in 2006, later received support from dozens of community activists at a city council meeting.

Police Chief Steve Anderson, Nashville, Tennessee

In November, when Nashville police greeted protesters with hot chocolate and an open line of communication instead of handcuffs and tear gas, a member of the community took umbrage, listing his grievances in an open letter to Anderson. In response, Anderson posted a letter of his own addressing each one of the citizen's concerns. In his letter, Anderson urged the individual to keep an open mind and be "respectful of all people," even if their views challenged his own:

> It is only when we go outside that comfort zone, and subject ourselves to the discomfort of considering thoughts we don't agree with, that we can make an informed judgment on any matter. We can still disagree and maintain our opinions, but we can now do so knowing that the issue has been given consideration from all four sides. Or, if we truly give fair consideration to all points of view, we may need to swallow our pride and amend our original thoughts.

You can read Anderson's full response at http://www .tennessean.com/story/news/local/davidson/2014/12/26 /nashville-police-chief-shares-message-responds-to -questions/20914171/.

Police Officer Adhyl Polanco, New York City

Polanco, who in the past has publicly criticized the department he works for, appeared on the news show "Democracy Now!" in December to denounce a decision by hundreds of his colleagues to turn their backs on New York City Mayor Bill de Blasio while he was speaking at the funeral of Rafael Ramos. Ramos was one of the two officers gunned down in the line of duty as they sat in their patrol car in Brooklyn last month. Polanco characterized the display as divisive and disrespectful of the calls for peace and unity that had been made by Ramos' family and other activists.

"How come we cannot honor what they are calling for?" said Polanco. "Mayor de Blasio came to the police department that had a lot of issues before he got to this police department. Mayor de Blasio came with the attitude that 'I can fix this police department.' But this police department has a culture that is going to make whoever tries to change that culture, like, impossible, including the mayor."

Later in the interview, Polanco offered a response to Patrick Lynch, the head of a top NYPD union who'd recently objected to de Blasio's comments about his own son, whose mother is black. The mayor spoke about telling his son to be cautious when dealing with police, and Lynch claimed de Blasio's words had helped incite anti-police violence that led to the two officers' deaths.

"How can a parent who has a black child, how can a parent who has seen millions of kids been stopped by stop and frisk—and you know the statistic of that—how can the parents of black kids see kids get killed by police over and over, how can parents that see kids be summoned illegally, being arrested in their own building for trespassing, and . . . the treatment they get from the police department—not from all officers, because not all officers are the same—how can you not responsibly have that conversation with your son?" said Polanco. "I have to have the conversation, and I'm a police officer."

Polanco also spoke out about his own rough treatment by police during times when he was off-duty. He said officers have thrown him up against a wall and frisked him. His comments were similar to those made by a number of other black NYPD officers, some retired and some still serving, in a December Reuters story. In that article, all but one of 25 officers said they'd been a victim of racial profiling while out of uniform. Most chose to speak anonymously.

Police Chief Cameron McLay, Pittsburgh

At a First Night parade earlier this month, members of a local activist group known as WHAT'S UP?! Pittsburgh photographed McLay holding up a protest sign. The photo promptly made the rounds on social media.

> Here's a New Years resolution we can get behind. Pittsburgh's Police Chief McLay resolves to challenge racism at work.

> We're going to hold you to that Chief . . . and support you every step of the way.

Thanks WHATS UP for this photo and for some great organizing.

The president of a local police union was quick to interpret the photograph as a direct affront to the entire force. "The chief is calling us racists," the officer told a reporter. "He believes the Pittsburgh Police Department is racist. This has angered a lot of officers."

In a letter to the Bureau of Police, McLay said he was sorry if he'd offended anyone in the department. He was, he wrote, simply making a call for awareness.

The sign indicated my willingness to challenge racial problems in the workplace. I am so committed. If there are problems in the [Pittsburgh Bureau of Police] related to racial injustice, I will take action to fix them.

To me, the term "white silence" simply means that we must be willing to speak up to address issues of racial injustice, poverty, etc. In my heart, I believe we all must come together as community to address real world problems; and I am willing to be a voice to bring community together.

I saw no indictment of police or anyone else in this sign, but I do apologize to any of you who felt I was not supporting you; that was not my intent.

The reality of U.S. policing is that our enforcement efforts have a disparate impact on communities of color. This is a statistical fact. You know, as well as I, the social factors driving this reality. The gross disparity in wealth and opportunity is evident in our city. Frustration and disorder are certain to follow. The predominant patterns of our city's increased violence involves black victims as well as actors. If we are to address this violence, we must work together with our communities of color.

Pittsburgh Mayor Bill Peduto has since offered support for McLay and his message.

The Sanford Police Department

In 2012, neighborhood watch coordinator George Zimmerman killed 17-year-old Trayvon Martin in Sanford, Florida, inflaming local and national tensions. Years later, the country is grappling with different cases but many of the same underlying issues. In November, activists in Sanford held a peaceful march following the decision not to indict Darren Wilson, then a Ferguson, Missouri, police officer, in the shooting death of Michael Brown. A number of Sanford police officers led the group through town. Sanford Police Chief Cecil Smith also met with organizers before the demonstration and offered his support.

"We're changing who we are. The community is starting to change their perception of law enforcement here in Sanford," he told WKMG.

Smith has also said that his department has stressed communication and cooperation with the community since Martin's death, and that this approach has helped to repair the relationship between local police and the public.

Police Chief Scott Thomson, Camden, New Jersey

Thomson appeared on CBS' "Face the Nation" in December to discuss his city's new approach to policing, which was completely revamped about two years ago and has since led to a significant reduction in crime. In the interview, Thomson highlighted the importance of engaging with the community and forging relationships through one-on-one contact.

"We did this without militarizing neighborhoods, without polarizing the community," Thomson said. "We established a culture from very, very early on that the relationship that would bind us with our people was one based on building community first and enforcing the law second."

Thomson also spoke about the need for the law enforcement community to listen to the public in order to regain the sort of trust that's required for police to be effective.

"It's a critical moment for law enforcement for us to not circle our wagons, to get defensive, but to keep our ears and our minds open and move forward in a way that has a collective, universal agreement of how the justice system should operate," he said.

Similarly, in the aftermath of Brown's death and subsequent protests in Ferguson, which were met with a heavily militarized police response, Thomson spoke about the broader problems laid bare by the clashes.

"Ferguson serves as a reminder to all of government the certainty of disaster when the people you serve no longer view you with legitimacy," he said. "The best remedy to prevent this is to maintain a constant, sincere dialogue and inclusion of the public you serve."

Police Sgt. Bret Barnum, Portland, Oregon

When 12-year-old Devonte Hart held up a sign for "Free Hugs" at a November protest in Portland, he probably wasn't expecting a police officer to take him up on the offer. When Barnum saw Devonte crying, however, he called the boy over to ask what was wrong. Devonte reportedly explained his concerns about police brutality and injustice, which turned into a bigger conversation about activism, school and life. After the talk, the sergeant and the boy shared a moment of humanity that immediately spread around the world.

Freelance photographer Johnny Nguyen captured the image . . . which has since been shared hundreds of thousands of times across social media. Nguyen told *The Huffington Post* that he interpreted the hug, as well as the photo's viral popularity, as a sign that there's hope for real change to be made as a result of this debate.

"We all have hurt in our heart, but we have to turn that hurt into hope, hope for humanity," he said. "We need to find a way to come together and find a common ground and find peace."

It's since been pointed out that while the photograph may offer a feeling of hope, the hug between Barnum and Devonte didn't banish systemic racism from the world, nor did it suddenly create a nationwide culture of police accountability. Critics have argued that the significance so quickly assigned to this image suggests that many people are eager to simplify and sugarcoat the difficult issue of race in America.

Others questioned Barnum's sincerity after discovering that he'd "liked" a colleague's post on Facebook that carried a pro-Darren Wilson message. Barnum later said he was showing support for the police profession, not the actions of Wilson, but the controversy illustrates how emotionally fraught the past several months have been, for officers and activists alike. But regardless of Barnum's sincerity or the true significance of the photo, one thing is undoubtedly true: We could all benefit from more "free hugs," especially between police and the civilians they serve.

SEPTA Police Chief Thomas J. Nestel III, Philadelphia

Nestel, who oversees the Southeastern Pennsylvania Transportation Authority, has been an outspoken supporter of the protests that have taken place around Philadelphia over the past few months. Nestel is highly active on social media, and in November tweeted a number of updates from a demonstration in which he participated following a grand jury decision not to indict Darren Wilson in the death of Michael Brown.

"Protestors have arrived at City Hall," he wrote as he accompanied marchers on their way downtown. "Peaceful protestors + Professional police = Successful democracy. Well done Philadelphia!"

Citing the importance of civil liberties and fostering trust between law enforcement and civilians, Nestel has also endorsed a plan to outfit his officers with body cameras.

"I think the police and the community are on the same page on this. I think body cameras will strengthen the bond between communities and the police," Nestel told Philly Mag. "The police officers who are using them are completely sold."

NICK WING is a graduate of Colorado College where he majored in political science and journalism. He is the Washington based Senior Viral Editor, writer, and researcher at *The Huffington Post*.

EXPLORING THE ISSUE

Are the Police in America to Be Condemned?

Critical Thinking and Reflection

1. Why do we know so much more today about overly brutal actions of the police?
2. How much does racial bias factor into recent police behavior?
3. How would you try to fix some of the current problems with police behavior?
4. What are the positive things you can say about police behavior today?
5. Why do police who are probably guilty of murdering unarmed people seem to get away unpunished?

Is There Common Ground?

Both authors are deeply concerned about how police perform their duties and how crime can be minimized. There are differences in judgments, however, about how aggressive police should be toward petty crimes and how they should conduct themselves in apprehending possible criminals. No one wants events like the ones that are dominating the news to happen. The questions that drive both authors are what policies should govern the police and how should police police? All are concerned that the police have good relations with the community and that the community supports the police. In many places that relationship is strong and this keeps crime down.

Additional Resources

There has always been considerable research on policing but recent works take into account the recent horrific events that have captured considerable media attention. See Lori Beth Way and Ryan Patten, *Hunting for Dirtbags: Why Cops Overpolice the Poor and Racial Minorities* (Northeastern University Press, 2013); Douglas A. Kelly, *Accountability by Camera: Online Video's Effects on Police-Civilian Interactions* (LFB Scholarly Publishing, 2014); Sankar Sen, *Enforcing*

Police Accountability Through Civilian Oversight (Sage, 2010); Samuel Walker, *The New World of Police Accountability* (Sage, 2014), L. Scott Silverii, *Cop Culture: Why Good Cops Go Bad* (CRC Press, 2014); Malcolm D. Holmes, *Race and Police Brutality* (State University of New York Press, 2008); Charles R. Epp, *Pulled Over: How Police Stops Define Race and Citizenship* (University of Chicago Press, 2014); and Christine M. H. Orthmann, *Management and Supervision in Law Enforcement* (Cengage Learning, 2016).

Most works on crime deal mainly with theft, drugs, and violence, and the injury and fear that they cause. See Danielle Lively Neal, *Social Capital and Urban Crime* (LFB Scholarly Publishing, 2011); Marcus Felson and Rachel L. Boba, *Crime and Everyday Life* (Sage, 2010); and Elizabeth Kandel Englander, *Understanding Violence* (Lawrence Erlbaum, 2007). Three works on gangs, which are often connected with violent street crime, are William J. Mitchell, ed., *Code of the Street: Violent Youths and Gangs* (Nova Science, 2011); Robert J. Franzese, Herbert C. Covey, and Scott Menard, *Youth Gangs* (Charles C. Thomas, 2006); and Jay T. Soordhas, ed., *Gangs: Violence, Crime and Antigang Initiatives* (Nova Science, 2009). Finally, there is a new type of crime that is increasingly troublesome: digital crime and terrorism. This is thoroughly examined by Robert W. Taylor, et al., in *Digital Crime and Digital Terrorism* (Pearson/Prentice Hall, 2006).

Internet References . . .

Sociology—Study Sociology Online

http://edu.learnsoc.org/

Sociology Web Resources

www.mhhe.com/socscience/sociology/resources
/index.htm

Sociosite

www.topsite.com/goto/sociosite.net

Socioweb

www.topsite.com/goto/socioweb.com

Selected, Edited, and with Issue Framing Material by:
Kurt Finsterbusch, *University of Maryland, College Park*

ISSUE

Is American Justice Too Severe?

YES: Eric Holder, from "Bold Steps to Reform and Strengthen America's Criminal Justice System," *Vital Speeches of the Day* (2013)

NO: Zaid Jilani, from "Who Are the Biggest Killers in America? The Numbers Will Shock You," *AlterNet* (2015)

Learning Outcomes
After reading this issue, you will be able to:
• Understand how and why the judicial system tends to back up the policemen in confrontations with the public and with defendants.
• Identify possible solutions to the current problems of the police.
• Understand the laws and enforcement practices that have put so many people in prison.
• Be able to compare the imprisonment rates for street crimes and white-collar crimes.
• Analyze how the media impacts the behavior of the police and of the communities.

ISSUE SUMMARY

YES: Eric Holder judges the current judicial system as broken and needing a major overhaul. The prison system needs to continue to punish and deter but also to rehabilitate. Their populations should be reduced, which requires revised judicial laws and policies. "Too many Americans go to too many prisons for far too long, and for no truly good law enforcement reason." His reforms must also make communities safer.

NO: Zaid Jilani is an *AlterNet* staff writer who makes a good case that the really dangerous criminals are not the poor but the rich and powerful. They make decisions that kill hundreds of thousands of people, while murderers kill about 15,000 a year. For example, medical malpractice kills about 225,000 people a year. They also swindle, defraud, and cheat people out of $486 billion a year versus all property crimes mounting to $17.6 billion a year. These facts point out the real failure of the criminal justice system.

There are many things wrong with the American justice system. Holder points to racial biases in the justice process and overly zealous policing of petty crimes. According to Holder the American justice system is too severe. Jilani points to the very weak effort to stop and prosecute white-collar crimes, so he calls for stronger policing of these crimes. Since the operation of the whole criminal justice system has been called into question it would be useful to take one issue and examine it in some detail to demonstrate the complexity of the issue of judicial reform. We choose to examine the issue of drugs.

One problem with the judicial system that is getting a lot of attention today is the dysfunctional laws against drug use. Laws that were appropriate to the crime would be functional but the laws are overly punitive to the drugs used mostly by blacks while the laws against drugs used mostly by whites are much less severe. Many experts now propose the decriminalization of drugs. They argue that the strict enforcement of drug laws damages American society because it drives people to violence and crime and that the drug laws have a racist element associated with them. People arrested for drug offenses overburden the court system, thus rendering it ineffective. Moreover, they contend that the criminalization of drugs fuels organized crime, allows children to be pulled into the drug business, and makes illegal drugs more dangerous because they are manufactured without government standards or regulations. Hence, drugs may be adulterated or of unidentified potency. Decriminalization advocates also argue that decriminalization would take the profits out of drug sales, thereby decreasing the value of and demand for drugs. In addition, the costs resulting from law enforcement are far greater than the benefits of criminalization.

Some decriminalization advocates argue that the federal government's prohibition stance on drugs is an immoral and impossible objective. To achieve a drug-free society is self-defeating and a misnomer because drugs, including alcohol, have always been a part of human culture. Furthermore, prohibition efforts indicate a disregard for the private freedom of individuals because they assume that individuals are incapable of making their own choices. Drug proponents assert that their personal sovereignty should be respected over any government agenda, including the war on drugs. Less restrictive laws, they argue, would take the emphasis off of law enforcement policies and allow more effort to be put toward education, prevention, and treatment. Also, it is felt that most of the negative impacts of drug prohibition would disappear.

Of course, there is another side to the drug issue. Opponents of drug decriminalization maintain that less restrictive drug laws are not the solution to drug problems and that it is a very dangerous idea. Less restrictive laws, they assert, will drastically increase drug use. This upsurge in drug use will come at an incredibly high price: American society will be overrun with drug-related accidents, lost worker productivity, and hospital emergency rooms filled with drug-related emergencies. Drug treatment efforts would be futile because users would have no legal incentive to stop taking drugs. Also, users may prefer drugs rather than rehabilitation, and education programs may be ineffective in dissuading children from using drugs.

Advocates of less restrictive laws maintain that drug abuse is a victimless crime in which the only person being hurt is the drug user. Opponents argue that this notion is ludicrous and dangerous because drug use has dire repercussions for all of society. Drugs can destroy the minds and bodies of many people. Also, regulations to control drug use have a legitimate social aim to protect society and its citizens from the harm of drugs. We conclude that reform is very complicated. In the following selections, Holder advocates a major overhaul and reduction of the criminal justice system and Jilani advocates a major enlargement of the judicial system to adequately prosecute white-collar crimes.

YES

Eric Holder

Bold Steps to Reform and Strengthen America's Criminal Justice System

The course we are on is far from sustainable. And it is our time—and our duty—to identify those areas we can improve in order to better advance the cause of justice for all Americans.

Thank you, Bob Carlson, for those kind words—and for your exemplary service as Chair of the American Bar Association's House of Delegates. It's a pleasure to be with you this morning. And it's a privilege to join so many friends, colleagues, and leaders—including US Attorney for the Northern District of California Melinda Haag—here in San Francisco for the ABA's 2013 Annual Meeting.

I'd like to thank your Delegates for all that they've done to bring us together this week—and for their dedication to serving as faithful stewards of the greatest legal system the world has ever known. From its earliest days, our Republic has been bound together by this system, and by the values that define it. These values—equality, opportunity, and justice under law—were first codified in the US Constitution. And they were renewed and reclaimed—nearly a century later—by this organization's earliest members.

With the founding of the ABA in 1878, America's leading legal minds came together—for the first time—to revolutionize their profession. In the decades that followed, they created new standards for training and professional conduct. And they established the law as a clear and focused vocation at the heart of our country's identity.

Throughout history, Americans of all backgrounds and walks of life have turned to our legal system to settle disputes, but also to hold accountable those who have done wrong—and even to answer fundamental questions about who we are and who we aspire to be. On issues of slavery and segregation; voting and violence; and equal rights and equal justice—generations of principled lawyers have engaged directly in the work of building a more perfect Union. Today, under the leadership of my good friend, President Laurel Bellows, this organization is fighting against budget cuts that undermine the ability of our courts to administer justice. You're standing with me—and with my colleagues across the Obama Administration—in calling for Congressional action on common-sense measures to prevent and reduce gun violence. And you're advancing our global fight against the heinous crime of human trafficking.

In so many ways, today's ABA is reminding us that, although our laws must be continually updated, our shared dedication to the cause of justice—and the ideals set forth by our Constitution—must remain constant. It is this sense of dedication that brings me to San Francisco today—to enlist your partnership in forging a more just society. To ask for your leadership in reclaiming, once more, the values we hold dear. And to draw upon the ABA's legacy of achievement in calling on every member of our profession to question that which is accepted truth; to challenge that which is unjust; to break free of a tired status quo; and to take bold steps to reform and strengthen America's criminal justice system—in concrete and fundamental ways.

It's time—in fact, it's well past time—to address persistent needs and unwarranted disparities by considering a fundamentally new approach. As a prosecutor; a judge; an attorney in private practice; and now, as our nation's Attorney General, I've seen the criminal justice system firsthand, from nearly every angle. While I have the utmost faith in—and dedication to—America's legal system, we must face the reality that, as it stands, our system is in too many respects broken. The course we are on is far from sustainable. And it is our time—and our duty—to identify those areas we can improve in order to better advance the cause of justice for all Americans.

Even as most crime rates decline, we need to examine new law enforcement strategies—and better allocate resources—to keep pace with today's continuing threats as violence spikes in some of our greatest cities. As studies show that 6 in 10 American children are exposed to violence at some point in their lives—and nearly one in four college women experience some form of sexual assault by their senior year—we need fresh solutions for assisting victims and empowering survivors. As the so-called "war on drugs" enters its fifth decade, we need to ask whether it, and the approaches that comprise it, have been truly effective—and build on the Administration's efforts, led by the Office of National Drug Control Policy, to usher in a new approach. And with an outsized, unnecessarily large prison population, we need to ensure that incarceration is used to punish, deter, and rehabilitate—not merely to warehouse and forget.

Today, a vicious cycle of poverty, criminality, and incarceration traps too many Americans and weakens too many communities. And many aspects of our criminal justice system may actually exacerbate these problems, rather than alleviate them.

It's clear—as we come together today—that too many Americans go to too many prisons for far too long, and for no truly good law enforcement reason. It's clear, at a basic level, that 20th-century criminal justice solutions are not adequate to overcome our 21st-century challenges. And it is well past time to implement common sense changes that will foster safer communities from coast to coast.

These are issues the President and I have been talking about for as long as I've known him—issues he's felt strongly about ever since his days as a community organizer on the South Side of Chicago. He's worked hard over the years to protect our communities, to keep violent criminals off our streets, and to make sure those who break the law are held accountable. And he's also made it part of his mission to reduce the disparities in our criminal justice system. In Illinois, he passed legislation that addressed racial profiling and trained police departments on how they could avoid racial bias. And in 2010, this Administration successfully advocated for the reduction of the unjust 100-to-1 sentencing disparity between crack and powder cocaine.

That's the balance the President and I have tried to strike—because it's important to safeguard our communities and stay true to our values. And we've made progress. But as you heard the President say a few weeks ago when he spoke about the Trayvon Martin case, he also believes—as I do—that our work is far from finished.

That's why, over the next several months, the President will continue to reach out to Members of Congress from both parties—as well as governors, mayors, and other leaders—to build on the great work being done across the country to reduce violent crime and reform our

criminal justice system. We need to keep taking steps to make sure people feel safe and secure in their homes and communities. And part of that means doing something about the lives being harmed, not helped, by a criminal justice system that doesn't serve the American people as well as it should.

At the beginning of this year, I launched a targeted Justice Department review of the federal system—to identify obstacles, inefficiencies, and inequities, and to address ineffective policies. Today, I am pleased to announce the results of this review—which include a series of significant actions that the Department has undertaken to better protect the American people from crime; to increase support for those who become victims; and to ensure public safety by improving our criminal justice system as a whole. We have studied state systems and been impressed by the policy shifts some have made.

I hope other state systems will follow our lead and implement changes as well. The changes I announce today underscore this Administration's strong commitment to common sense criminal justice reform. And our efforts must begin with law enforcement.

Particularly in these challenging times—when budgets are tight, federal sequestration has imposed untenable and irresponsible cuts, and leaders across government are being asked to do more with less—coordination between America's federal, state, local, and tribal law enforcement agencies has never been more important. It's imperative that we maximize our resources by focusing on protecting national security; combating violent crime; fighting against financial fraud; and safeguarding the most vulnerable members of our society.

This means that federal prosecutors cannot—and should not—bring every case or charge every defendant who stands accused of violating federal law. Some issues are best handled at the state or local level. And that's why I have today directed the US Attorney community to develop specific, locally-tailored guidelines—consistent with our national priorities—for determining when federal charges should be filed, and when they should not.

I've also issued guidance to ensure that every case we bring serves a substantial federal interest and complements the work of our law enforcement partners. I have directed all US Attorneys to create—and to update—comprehensive antiviolence strategies for badly afflicted areas within their districts. And I've encouraged them to convene regular law enforcement forums with state and local partners to refine these plans, foster greater efficiency, and facilitate more open communication and cooperation.

By targeting the most serious offenses, prosecuting the most dangerous criminals, directing assistance to crime "hot spots," and pursuing new ways to promote public safety, deterrence, efficiency, and fairness—we in the federal government can become both smarter and tougher on crime. By providing leadership to all levels of law enforcement—and bringing intelligence-driven strategies to bear—we can bolster the efforts of local leaders, US Attorneys, and others in the fight against violent crime.

Beyond this work, through the Community Oriented Policing Services—or "COPS"—Office, the Justice Department is helping police departments keep officers on the beat while enhancing training and technical support. Over the last four years, we have allocated more than $1.5 billion through the COPS Hiring Program to save or create over 8,000 jobs in local law enforcement. In the coming weeks, we will announce a new round of COPS grants—totaling more than $110 million—to support the hiring of military veterans and school resource officers throughout the country.

In addition, through our landmark Defending Childhood Initiative and the National Forum on Youth Violence Prevention, we're rallying federal leaders, state officials, private organizations, and community groups to better understand, address, and prevent young people's exposure to violence. We have assembled a new Task Force to respond to the extreme levels of violence faced by far too many American Indian and Alaska Native children. Next month, we will launch a national public awareness campaign—and convene a Youth Violence Prevention Summit—to call for comprehensive solutions. And, through the Department's Civil Rights Division and other components, we'll continue to work with allies— like the Department of Education and others throughout the federal government and beyond—to confront the "school-to-prison pipeline" and those zero-tolerance school discipline policies that do not promote safety, and that transform too many educational institutions from doorways of opportunity into gateways to the criminal justice system. A minor school disciplinary offense should put a student in the principal's office and not a police precinct.

We'll also continue offering resources and support to survivors of sexual assault, domestic violence, and dating violence. Earlier this summer, I announced a new Justice Department initiative—known as Vision 21—which offers an unprecedented snapshot of the current state of victim services. It calls for sweeping, evidence-based changes to bring these services into the 21st century, and to empower all survivors by closing research gaps and developing new ways to reach those who need our assistance the most.

This work shows tremendous promise. I'm hopeful that it will help to bring assistance and healing to more and more crime victims across the country. But it is only the beginning.

More broadly, through the Department's Access to Justice Initiative, the Civil Rights Division, and a range of grant programs, this Administration is bringing stakeholders together—and providing direct support—to address the inequalities that unfold every day in America's courtrooms, and to fulfill the Supreme Court's historic decision in *Gideon v. Wainwright*. Fifty years ago last March, this landmark ruling affirmed that every defendant charged with a serious crime has the right to an attorney, even if he or she cannot afford one. Yet America's indigent defense systems continue to exist in a state of crisis, and the promise of Gideon is not being met. To address this crisis, Congress must not only end the forced budget cuts that have decimated public defenders nationwide—they must expand existing indigent defense programs, provide access to counsel for more juvenile defendants, and increase funding for federal public defender offices. And every legal professional, every member of this audience, must answer the ABA's call to contribute to this cause through pro bono service—and help realize the promise of equal justice for all.

As we come together this morning, this same promise must lead us all to acknowledge that—although incarceration has a significant role to play in our justice system— widespread incarceration at the federal, state, and local levels is both ineffective and unsustainable. It imposes a significant economic burden—totaling $80 billion in 2010 alone—and it comes with human and moral costs that are impossible to calculate.

As a nation, we are coldly efficient in our incarceration efforts. While the entire US population has increased by about a third since 1980, the federal prison population has grown at an astonishing rate—by almost 800 percent. It's still growing—despite the fact that federal prisons are operating at nearly 40 percent above capacity. Even though this country comprises just 5 percent of the world's population, we incarcerate almost a quarter of the world's prisoners. More than 219,000 federal inmates are currently behind bars. Almost half of them are serving time for drug-related crimes, and many have substance use disorders. Nine to 10 million more people cycle through America's local jails each year. And roughly 40 percent of former federal prisoners—and more than 60 percent of former state prisoners—are rearrested or have their supervision revoked within three years after their release, at great cost to American taxpayers and often for technical or minor violations of the terms of their release.

As a society, we pay much too high a price whenever our system fails to deliver outcomes that deter and punish crime, keep us safe, and ensure that those who have paid their debts have the chance to become productive citizens. Right now, unwarranted disparities are far too common. As President Obama said last month, it's time to ask tough questions about how we can strengthen our communities, support young people, and address the fact that young black and Latino men are disproportionately likely to become involved in our criminal justice system—as victims as well as perpetrators.

We also must confront the reality that—once they're in that system—people of color often face harsher punishments than their peers. One deeply troubling report, released in February, indicates that—in recent years—black male offenders have received sentences nearly 20 percent longer than those imposed on white males convicted of similar crimes. This isn't just unacceptable—it is shameful. It's unworthy of our great country, and our great legal tradition. And in response, I have today directed a group of US Attorneys to examine sentencing disparities, and to develop recommendations on how we can address them.

In this area and many others—in ways both large and small—we, as a country, must resolve to do better. The President and I agree that it's time to take a pragmatic approach. And that's why I am proud to announce today that the Justice Department will take a series of significant actions to recalibrate America's federal criminal justice system.

We will start by fundamentally rethinking the notion of mandatory minimum sentences for drug-related crimes. Some statutes that mandate inflexible sentences—regardless of the individual conduct at issue in a particular case—reduce the discretion available to prosecutors, judges, and juries. Because they oftentimes generate unfairly long sentences, they breed disrespect for the system. When applied indiscriminately, they do not serve public safety. They—and some of the enforcement priorities we have set—have had a destabilizing effect on particular communities, largely poor and of color. And, applied inappropriately, they are ultimately counterproductive.

This is why I have today mandated a modification of the Justice Department's charging policies so that certain low-level, nonviolent drug offenders who have no ties to large-scale organizations, gangs, or cartels will no longer be charged with offenses that impose draconian mandatory minimum sentences. They now will be charged with offenses for which the accompanying sentences are better suited to their individual conduct, rather than excessive prison terms more appropriate for violent criminals or drug kingpins. By reserving the most severe penalties for serious, high-level, or violent drug traffickers, we can better promote public safety, deterrence, and rehabilitation—while making our expenditures smarter and more

productive. We've seen that this approach has bipartisan support in Congress—where a number of leaders, including Senators Dick Durbin, Patrick Leahy, Mike Lee, and Rand Paul have introduced what I think is promising legislation aimed at giving federal judges more discretion in applying mandatory minimums to certain drug offenders. Such legislation will ultimately save our country billions of dollars while keeping us safe. And the President and I look forward to working with members of both parties to refine and advance these proposals.

Secondly, the Department has now updated its framework for considering compassionate release for inmates facing extraordinary or compelling circumstances—and who pose no threat to the public. In late April, the Bureau of Prisons expanded the criteria which will be considered for inmates seeking compassionate release for medical reasons. Today, I can announce additional expansions to our policy—including revised criteria for elderly inmates who did not commit violent crimes and who have served significant portions of their sentences. Of course, as our primary responsibility, we must ensure that the American public is protected from anyone who may pose a danger to the community. But considering the applications of nonviolent offenders—through a careful review process that ultimately allows judges to consider whether release is warranted—is the fair thing to do. And it is the smart thing to do as well, because it will enable us to use our limited resources to house those who pose the greatest threat.

Finally, my colleagues and I are taking steps to identify and share best practices for enhancing the use of diversion programs—such as drug treatment and community service initiatives—that can serve as effective alternatives to incarceration.

Our US Attorneys are leading the way in this regard—working alongside the judiciary to meet safety imperatives while avoiding incarceration in certain cases. In South Dakota, a joint federal-tribal program has helped to prevent at-risk young people from getting involved in the federal prison system—thereby improving lives, saving taxpayer resources, and keeping communities safer. This is exactly the kind of proven innovation that federal policymakers, and state and tribal leaders, should emulate. And it's why the Justice Department is working—through a program called the Justice Reinvestment Initiative—to bring state leaders, local stakeholders, private partners, and federal officials together to comprehensively reform corrections and criminal justice practices.

In recent years, no fewer than 17 states—supported by the Department, and led by governors and legislators of both parties—have directed funding away from prison construction and toward evidence-based programs and services, like treatment and supervision, that are designed to reduce recidivism. In Kentucky, for example, new legislation has reserved prison beds for the most serious offenders and refocused resources on community supervision and evidence-based alternative programs. As a result, the state is projected to reduce its prison population by more than 3,000 over the next 10 years—saving more than $400 million.

In Texas, investments in drug treatment for nonviolent offenders and changes to parole policies brought about a reduction in the prison population of more than 5,000 inmates last year alone. The same year, similar efforts helped Arkansas reduce its prison population by more than 1,400. From Georgia, North Carolina, and Ohio, to Pennsylvania, Hawaii, and far beyond—reinvestment and serious reform are improving public safety and saving precious resources. Let me be clear: these measures have not compromised public safety. In fact, many states have seen drops in recidivism rates at the same time their prison populations were declining. The policy changes that have led to these welcome results must be studied and emulated. While our federal prison system has continued to slowly expand, significant state-level reductions have led to three consecutive years of decline in America's overall prison population—including, in 2012, the largest drop ever experienced in a single year.

Clearly, these strategies can work. They've attracted overwhelming, bipartisan support in "red states" as well as "blue states." And it's past time for others to take notice.

I am also announcing today that I have directed every US Attorney to designate a Prevention and Reentry Coordinator in his or her district—to ensure that this work is, and will remain, a top priority throughout the country. And my colleagues and I will keep working closely with state leaders, agency partners, including members of the Federal Interagency Reentry Council—and groups like the American Bar Association—to extend these efforts.

In recent years, with the Department's support, the ABA has catalogued tens of thousands of statutes and regulations that impose unwise and counterproductive collateral consequences—with regard to housing or employment, for example—on people who have been convicted of crimes. I have asked state attorneys general and a variety of federal leaders to review their own agencies' regulations. And today I can announce that I've directed all Department of Justice components, going forward, to consider whether any proposed regulation or guidance may impose unnecessary collateral consequences on those seeking to rejoin their communities.

The bottom line is that, while the aggressive enforcement of federal criminal statutes remains necessary, we cannot simply prosecute or incarcerate our way to becoming a safer nation. To be effective, federal efforts must also focus on prevention and reentry. We must never stop being tough on crime. But we must also be smart and efficient when battling crime and the conditions and the individual choices that breed it.

Ultimately, this is about much more than fairness for those who are released from prison. It's a matter of public safety and public good. It makes plain economic sense. It's about who we are as a people. And it has the potential to positively impact the lives of every man, woman, and child—in every neighborhood and city—in the United States. After all, whenever a recidivist crime is committed, innocent people are victimized. Communities are less safe. Burdens on law enforcement are increased. And already-strained resources are depleted even further.

Today—together—we must declare that we will no longer settle for such an unjust and unsustainable status quo. To do so would be to betray our history, our shared commitment to justice, and the founding principles of our nation. Instead, we must recommit ourselves—as a country—to tackling the most difficult questions, and the most costly problems, no matter how complex or intractable they may appear. We must pledge—as legal professionals—to lend our talents, our training, and our diverse perspectives to advancing this critical work. And we must resolve—as a people—to take a firm stand against violence; against victimization; against inequality—and for justice.

This is our chance—to bring America's criminal justice system in line with our most sacred values.

This is our opportunity—to define this time, our time, as one of progress and innovation.

This is our promise—to forge a more just society.

And this is our solemn obligation, as stewards of the law, and servants of those whom it protects and empowers: to open a frank and constructive dialogue about the need to reform a broken system. To fight for the sweeping, systemic changes we need. And to uphold our dearest values, as the ABA always has, by calling on our peers and colleagues not merely to serve their clients, or win their cases—but to ensure that—in every case, in every circumstance, and in every community—justice is done.

This, after all, is the cause that has been our common pursuit for more than two centuries, the ideal that has guided the ABA since its inception, and the goal that will drive additional actions by President Obama—and leaders throughout his Administration—in the months ahead. Of course, we recognize—as you do—that the reforms I've announced today, and others that we must consider, explore, and implement in the coming years, will not take hold overnight. There will be setbacks and false starts. We will encounter resistance and opposition.

But if we keep faith in one another, and in the principles we've always held dear; if we stay true to the ABA's history as a driver of positive change; and if we keep moving forward together—knowing that the need for this work will outlast us, but determined to make the difference that we seek—then I know we can all be confident in where these efforts will lead us. I look forward to everything that we will undoubtedly achieve. And I will always be proud to stand alongside you in building the brighter, more just, and more prosperous future that all of our citizens deserve.

Thank you.

ERIC HOLDER served as the attorney general of the United States from 2009 to 2015. He has also served as judge of the Superior Court of the District of Columbia and as United States Attorney of the District of Columbia.

Zaid Jilani  **NO**

Who Are the Biggest Killers in America? The Numbers Will Shock You

The richest Americans not only steal more wealth through white-collar crime, but their crimes also lead to more deaths.

The criminal justice reform movement has shined a light on the inhumane conditions in our prisons, and the horrific killings of unarmed people by the police. This movement has done important work in demonstrating the needless brutality involved in our system, particularly as it is directed against marginalized groups: the poor and racial minorities.

Recently, I examined the economic backgrounds of those killed by police this year. I found that between January and May 2015, 95 percent of police killings occurred in neighborhoods with average incomes under $100,000. There were no killings in neighborhoods with incomes of $200,000 or above.

I received many responses to this article, but one of the most common was that the wealthy simply don't commit as much street crime. In other words, the rich behave themselves, so the police don't bother them.

There is truth to this argument in one dimension: street crime. It has long been consensus among sociologists and economists that high levels of poverty and inequality are associated with various street crimes such as homicide and assault.

However, this doesn't actually mean that the poor and middle class are harming more people, or stealing more of their property, or destroying more of their wealth. It is a little-known fact that the richest Americans not only steal more wealth through white-collar crime, but their crimes also lead to the deaths of more people. Yet despite the destructiveness of rich criminals, our criminal justice system does not respond in the same way it tackles crimes by poorer Americans.

How the Rich Commit Crime

Jeffrey Reiman is a criminologist, sociologist and philosopher based at American University. In 1979, Reiman published the first edition of the book, *The Rich Get Richer, The Poor Get Prison*. The book had a simple but counterintuitive thesis: the rich are actually committing society's most destructive crimes in terms of both financial damage and loss of human lives, but our criminal justice system is harshest toward the poorest Americans, whose crimes inflict the least damage.

As time rolled on, and mass incarceration of mostly poor and working-class people skyrocketed while prosecution of white-collar crimes dialed down, Reiman's thesis has gained steam. With his co-researchers, he has released new editions of the book with updated statistics regularly, the most recent edition in 2013.

Although much of his statistical work is somewhat outdated in 2015, the wider narrative is as relevant today as it was when his book was originally published.

He begins his explanation of the difference between deadly white-collar crime and far less deadly street crime in the second paragraph:

> "If it takes you an hour to read this chapter, by the time you reach the last page, two of your fellow citizens will have been murdered. During that same time, more than six Americans will die as a result of unhealthy or unsafe conditions in the workplace. Although these work-related deaths were due to human actions, they are not called murders. Why not? Doesn't a crime by any other name still cause misery and suffering? What's in a name?"

That is the crux of the issue: we refer to street crime as crime, and tackle it with the most blunt police state instruments, but we don't respond the same way to the kinds of crimes elites commit through indifference or hunger for greater profits.

Using data ranging from 1992 to 2006, Reiman estimates there are 55,325 "occupation-related deaths" per year—this includes deaths caused by unsafe work conditions, needless exposure to disease and other forms of death that would be a direct result of employer negligence, but does not amount to the total number of negligent workplace deaths, which is difficult to compute.

Compare this to deaths from common street crime, referred to as homicides; in 2006, this number was around 15,000. Reiman writes that the "risk to occupational disease and death falls only on members of the labor force, whereas the risk of crime falls on the whole population, from infants to the elderly. Because the civilian labor force is about half (50.8 percent) of the total population . . . to get a true picture of the relative threat posed by occupational diseases compared with that posed by [what we refer to as] crimes, we should multiply the crime statistics by half."

If you do that, even discounting bad luck and errors on the part of the employee, you'd be comparing tens of thousands of occupational deaths to around 7,500 homicides. That would mean your job—through the negligence of your employer—is seven times more likely to kill you than common street crime is. Reiman concludes that this means "workers are more likely to stay alive and healthy in the face of the danger from the underworld than from the workworld."

The primary difference between the deaths that occur in the "workworld" vs. the "underworld" is simply the perspective our society—which is tilted towards the worldview of the rich—gives them. A poor mugger killing you after a fight over your wallet is considered a grave crime, whereas a worker being killed because their employer didn't spend the money necessary to give them proper safety is considered routine.

This is something that is immediately obvious if you look at how these crimes are punished. According to PBS Frontline, the average time served for a homicide is 71 months (nearly six years in prison). The Occupational Safety and Health Administration as well as various state agencies are in charge of holding companies accountable that violate safety regulations, including in circumstances where these violations lead to death. But it is rare for management or owners to be held personally responsible for any deaths.

Take this recent case from Columbus, Ohio. OSHA fined a cabinet maker $50,000 after finding 21 safety violations that were "discovered after the Jan. 13 death of employee Tom Hegg. Hegg died of acute exposure to wood dust after 15 years with the company."

It's often said you can't put a price on a human life, but our regulatory agencies do exactly that.

Reiman lists numerous other ways the rich get away with killing Americans yet face a less severe response from the government. One is through botched medical operations, which a July 2000 *Journal of the American Medical Association* article estimated results in 225,000 deaths a year, making them the third largest cause of death in the United States, overall.

These deaths include 88,000 to 100,000 deaths from healthcare-associated infections and as many as 16,000 deaths from unnecessary surgical operations (which is slightly higher than those killed by homicides). Even discounting the baseline of human error, rather than being a grave cause of concern among the media and political class, the issue is regularly minimized as one of egregious lawsuits making the incomes of very-rich doctors unnecessarily low. Cries for "tort reform" were a feature of the Republican Party's assault on Democratic health reform efforts.

These are just a few of the ways the rich and corporate America kill people in America. There are many others that deserve to be discussed, such as spreading deadly pollution, making unsafe consumer products, pricing out Americans from affordable health care, and other dire threats to our well-being.

But for the sake of space, let's move on to monetary costs.

The image of the bank robber holding up a bank has been glamorized in many Hollywood films such as *The Town*, where Ben Affleck's character works with other poor residents of South Boston trying to make enough money to escape their lives. But it's worth pointing out that such street crime doesn't actually cost Americans that much overall.

Reiman notes that the FBI's 2007 estimate for the amount of wealth stolen in all property crimes topped out at $17.6 billion. That sounds like a lot, until you compare it to white-collar and financial crimes.

When you put together acts such as insurance fraud, telemarketing fraud, industrial espionage, credit card fraud, and other major financial crimes, you find that white-collar crimes cost the economy around $486 billion annually. That's about 28 times as much as what common street crime costs us.

Sometimes these white-collar crimes cost us more than other times. The crime spree on Wall Street that led to the global Great Recession was estimated to have thrown

64 million additional people into extreme poverty—meaning they were forced to live on less than $1.25 a day—by the World Bank. There were many collateral effects from this Wall Street crime wave, so many it would be difficult to list them all.

Changing the Way We Respond

How did the government respond? The Great Recession was partly caused, after all, by massive fraud by financial institutions. But as actual crime grew more pervasive and destructive, the federal government's prosecution of those crimes declined[.]

This raises a stark question: why do we punish crimes by the poor so severely and yet let the richest Americans off the hook? The crimes committed by the rich not only cause more monetary damage but kill far more people than ordinary street crime, yet the former are treated with kid gloves while the latter are treated with long prison sentences or even executions.

Our criminal justice system may be less about punishing the unjust than just another reflection of the power inequities we have in the United States.

ZAID JILANI attended the University of Georgia, where he helped found its first progressive newspaper. He is a frequent writer for several progressive media outlets, including *Salon, Think Progress, The Huffington Post,* and *The Nation*. He is a blogger and campaigner for the Progressive Change Campaign Committee.

EXPLORING THE ISSUE

Is American Justice Too Severe?

Critical Thinking and Reflection

1. Why are the authorities very likely to back up the police who seem to treat suspects too violently?
2. What should reformers like Holder do to correct the problems of police brutality and racism?
3. What should reformers like Jilani do to see that white-collar criminals get the justice that they deserve?
4. How can the prison population be reduced without endangering the public?

Is There Common Ground?

Everyone agrees that the judicial system needs to be reformed. It has to be made fairer. Currently there is gross racial bias in penalties, treatment of suspects, and surveillance. Police have been trained to be less biased but the training did not work well enough. Too many people are put into jail and for too long. There are too many wrongful convictions. Too many confessions and testimonies are false. But what should be done? General principles like greater fairness would be widely supported, but any major changes would be difficult to get consensus on.

To show the complexity of changes in the criminal justice system we will return to America's drug problem. Drugs have ruined many lives. Everyone agrees that something should be done about it. But what? The answer is easy, outlaw drug use. That is what we did, but everyone agrees the result was not what we were hoping for. Now we are not sure whether outlawing drugs was the right action to take, but other options also have bad consequences. Some assert that utilizing the criminal justice system to maintain the illegal nature of drugs is necessary to keep society free of the detrimental effects of drugs. Loosening drug laws is unwise and dangerous. But criminalizing drugs has created the illegal drug trade which has created drug cartels, a massive increase in crime, and the extremely high imprisonment rates without reducing the drug trade. But are the effects of legalizing drugs any better? Would that greatly expand drug use and its ill effects? It is hard to say. The legalization of alcohol and tobacco does not make problems associated with them disappear (alcohol and tobacco have extremely high addiction rates as well as a myriad of other problems associated with their use). The counter argument is that many European countries, such as the Netherlands and Switzerland, have a system of legalized drugs, and most have far lower addiction rates and lower incidences of drug-related violence and crime than the United States. A further issue is the loss of many of our civil liberties. Adults should decide for themselves what they will ingest. The law says that the government takes that right away. Is that the American way?

Additional Resources

There are many works on justice systems, policing, prisons, and reforms. Some of these are George Kelling, "Don't Blame My 'Broken Windows' Theory for Poor Policing," *Politico Magazine*, August 11, 2015; Tracy L. Meares, "Rightful Policing," U.S. Department of Justice, Office of Justice Programs, National Institute of Justice, 2015; Sue Rahr, "From Warriors to Guardians: Recommitting American Police Culture to Democratic Ideals," U.S. Department of Justice, Office of Justice Programs, National Institute of Justice, 2015; Malcolm K. Sparrow, "Measuring Performance in a Modern Police Organization," U.S. Department of Justice, Office of Justice Programs, National Institute of Justice, 2015; Anthony W. Batts et al., "Policing and Wrongful Convictions," U.S. Department of Justice, Office of Justice Programs, National Institute of Justice, 2014; Karen Bullock, *Citizens, Community and Crime Control* (Palgrave Macmillan, 2014); Edward F. Davies, III et al., *Social Media and Police Leadership* (National Institute of Justice, 2014); Fassin Didier, *Enforcing Order: An Ethnography of Urban Policing* (Polity Press, 2013); Alfonso Gonzales, *Reform Without Justice* (Oxford University Press, 2014); Charles H. Ramsey, *The Challenge of Policing in a Democratic Society: A Personal Journey Toward Understanding* (National Institute of Justice, 2014); Lori Beth Way and Ryan Patten, *Hunting for Dirtbags: Why Cops Overpolice the Poor and Racial Minorities* (Northeastern University Press, 2013); Sankar Sen, *Enforcing Police Accountability Through Civilian Oversight* (Sage, 2010); Samuel Walker, *The New World of Police Accountability* (Sage, 2014); Christine M. H. Orthmann, *Management and Supervision in Law Enforcement* (Cengage Learning, 2016); Joe Domanick, *Blue: The LAPD and the Battle to Redeem American Policing* (Simon & Schuster, 2015); Samuel Walker, *The New World of Police Accountability* (Sage, 2014); Andrew Silke, ed., *Prisons,* *Terrorism and Extremism: Critical Issues in Management, Radicalisation and Reform* (Routledge, 2014); Francis T. Cullen, *Correctional Theory: Context and Consequences* (Sage, 2012); and Amy Levad, *Restorative Justice: Theories and Practices of Moral Imagination* (LFB Scholarly Pub., 2012).

Internet References . . .

Sociology—Study Sociology Online

http://edu.learnsoc.org/

Sociology Web Resources

www.mhhe.com/socscience/sociology/resources/index.htm

Sociosite

www.topsite.com/goto/sociosite.net

Socioweb

www.topsite.com/goto/socioweb.com

Selected, Edited, and with Issue Framing Material by:
Kurt Finsterbusch, *University of Maryland, College Park*

ISSUE

Is the United States in Significant Danger of Large-Scale Terrorist Attacks?

YES: James R. Clapper, from "Statement for the Record: Worldwide Threat Assessment of the US Intelligence Community," Senate Intelligence Committee (2015)

NO: Washington's Blog, from "There Are Far Fewer Terror Attacks Now Than in the 1970s," *Washington's Blog* (2015)

Learning Outcomes

After reading this issue, you will be able to:

- Understand the reasons why a WMD terrorist act in the United States is an unlikely event.
- Understand the official estimation of why others believe that a WMD terrorist event in the United States is likely.
- Identify important factors that you should examine more closely to gain more confidence in your judgment about the likelihood of a WMD terrorist event. For example, you might examine further how easy it is for terrorists to obtain nuclear materials.
- Identify the actions that America can take to reduce the likelihood of a major terrorist event.
- Attempt to figure out how what you learned should affect your life.

ISSUE SUMMARY

YES: James R. Clapper, director of national intelligence, gave this statement to Congress in 2015. It covers all types of terrorism from cyber terrorism to WMD and organized crime terrorism.

NO: Washington's Blog points out that terrorists' attacks have become practically nonexistent since 2003 (shootings by psychos are not included in these statistics). Its point is that the threat of terrorism in the United States has been greatly exaggerated.

Clapper presents a high-level report on all kinds of terrorism but since the terrorist attacks of September 11, 2001, America's focus has been on terrorism by weapons of mass destruction (WMD). America has a history of terrorist attacks, but until fairly recently they have been shootings of fewer than 50 people or destroying an airplane in the air. Their purpose was generally to make a political statement so an excessive event involving several or many thousands of victims would turn the public against the terrorists and their cause rather than turn the public toward their cause. The new breed of terrorists, however, wants to kill as many people as possible and strike fear into the hearts of the public. For that purpose WMD weapons are perfect if the terrorist group has the capacity to effectively use such devises. As a result the literature on terrorism is now focusing on WMD. Fear of WMD is the main reason why America has considerably beefed up its security agencies. Fortunately, they have been able to deter WMD attacks up to this writing. Nuclear terrorism is our worst fear and the most likely event would be the releasing of a dirty bomb (one loaded radioactive material) in an urban/civilian setting. Indeed, the arrest of a U.S. man that was suspected of having a dirty bomb indicates that such plans may indeed be in the works between ISIS, Al-Qaeda, and other terrorist cells. When this horror is combined with the availability of elements of nuclear-related material in places like the states of the former Soviet Union, Pakistan, India, Iraq, Iran, North Korea, and many other states, one can envision a variety of sobering scenarios.

Hollywood feeds these views with such fiuch as *The Sum of All Fears* and *The Peacemaker,* in which nuclear terrorism is portrayed as all too easy to carry out and likely to occur. It is difficult in such environments to separate fact from fiction and to ascertain objectively the probabilities of such events. So many factors go into a successful initiative in this area. One must find a committed cadre of terrorists, sufficient financial backing, technological know-how, intense security and secrecy, the means of delivery, and many other variables, including luck. In truth, such acts may have already been advanced and thwarted by governments, security services, or terrorist mistakes and incompetence. We do not know, and we may never know.

Regional and ethnic conflicts of a particularly savage nature in places like Chechnya, Kashmir, Colombia, and Afghanistan help to fuel fears that adequately financed zealots will see in nuclear weapons a swift and catastrophic answer to their demands and angers. Osama bin Laden's contribution to worldwide terrorism has been the success of money over security and the realization that particularly destructive acts with high levels of coordination can be "successful." This will undoubtedly encourage others

with similar ambitions against real or perceived enemies. So far ISIS uses terror locally rather than internationally (possibly the downing of a commercial airliner in Egypt may change this view of ISIS).

Conversely, many argue that fear of the terrorist threat has left us imagining that which is not likely. They point to a myriad of roadblocks to terrorist groups' obtaining all of the elements necessary for a nuclear or dirty bomb. They cite technological impediments, monetary issues, lack of sophistication, and inability to deliver. They also cite governments' universal desire to prevent such actions. Even critics of former Iraqi leader Saddam Hussein have argued that were he to develop such weapons, he would not deliver them to terrorist groups, nor would he use them except in the most dire of circumstances, such as his own regime's survival. They argue that the threat is overblown and, in some cases, merely used to justify increased security and the restriction of civil liberties.

The following selections debate terrorism from two different angles: Clapper presents an official assessment of the potential danger to the United States of all kinds of terrorism including WMD but also cyber terrorism and criminal terrorism. On WMD, Clapper seems most concerned about Iran (the fear possibly removed by the recent agreement) and North Korea. China and Russia have immense WMD capacity but are likely to act responsibly. Washington's Blog argues that terrorists do not have the capacity to launch WMD attacks so our fears are unfounded.

YES

James R. Clapper

Statement for the Record: Worldwide Threat Assessment of the US Intelligence Community

Introduction

Chairman McCain, Ranking Member Reed, Members of the Committee, thank you for the invitation to offer the United States Intelligence Community's 2015 assessment of threats to US national security. My statement reflects the collective insights of the Intelligence Community's extraordinary men and women, whom I am privileged and honored to lead. We in the Intelligence Community are committed every day to provide the nuanced, multi-disciplinary intelligence that policymakers, warfighters, and domestic law enforcement personnel need to protect American lives and America's interests anywhere in the world. Information available as of February 13, 2015 was used in the preparation of this assessment.

Global Threats

Cyber

Strategic Assessment
Cyber threats to US national and economic security are increasing in frequency, scale, sophistication, and severity of impact. The ranges of cyber threat actors, methods of attack, targeted systems, and victims are also expanding. Overall, the unclassified information and communication technology (ICT) networks that support US Government, military, commercial, and social activities remain vulnerable to espionage and/or disruption. However, the likelihood of a catastrophic attack from any particular actor is remote at this time. Rather than a "Cyber Armageddon" scenario that debilitates the entire US infrastructure, we envision something different. We foresee an ongoing series of low-to-moderate level cyber attacks from a variety of sources over time, which will impose cumulative costs on US economic competitiveness and national security.

- A growing number of computer forensic studies by industry experts strongly suggest that several nations—including Iran and North Korea—have undertaken offensive cyber operations against private sector targets to support their economic and foreign policy objectives, at times concurrent with political crises.

Risk. Despite ever-improving network defenses, the diverse possibilities for remote hacking intrusions, supply chain operations to insert compromised hardware or software, and malevolent activities by human insiders will hold nearly all ICT systems at risk for years to come. In short, the cyber threat cannot be eliminated; rather, cyber risk must be managed. Moreover, the risk calculus employed by some private sector entities does not adequately account for foreign cyber threats or the systemic interdependencies between different critical infrastructure sectors.

Costs. During 2014, we saw an increase in the scale and scope of reporting on malevolent cyber activity that can be measured by the amount of corporate data stolen or deleted, personally identifiable information (PII) compromised, or remediation costs incurred by US victims. For example:

- After the 2012–13 distributed denial of service (DDOS) attacks on the US financial sector, JPMorgan Chase (JPMorgan) announced plans for annual cyber security expenditures of $250 million by the end of 2014. After the company suffered a hacking intrusion in 2014, JPMorgan's CEO said he would probably double JPMorgan's annual computer security budget within the next five years.
- The 2014 data breach at Home Depot exposed information from 56 million credit/debit cards and 53 million customer email addresses. Home Depot estimated the cost of the breach to be $62 million.

Clapper, James R. Statement for the Record Worldwide Threat Assessment of the US Intelligence Community, Office of the Director of National Intelligence, February 2015.

- In 2014, unauthorized computer intrusions were detected on the networks of the Office of Personnel Management (OPM) as well as its contractors, US Investigations Services (USIS) and KeyPoint Government Solutions. The two contractors were involved in processing sensitive PII related to national security clearances for Federal Government employees.
- In August 2014, the US company, Community Health Systems, informed the Securities and Exchange Commission that it believed hackers "originating from China" had stolen PII on 4.5 million individuals.

Attribution. Although cyber operators can infiltrate or disrupt targeted ICT networks, most can no longer assume that their activities will remain undetected. Nor can they assume that if detected, they will be able to conceal their identities. Governmental and private sector security professionals have made significant advances in detecting and attributing cyber intrusions.

- In May 2014, the US Department of Justice indicted five officers from China's Peoples' Liberation Army on charges of hacking US companies.
- In December 2014, computer security experts reported that members of an Iranian organization were responsible for computer operations targeting US military, transportation, public utility, and other critical infrastructure networks.

Deterrence. Numerous actors remain undeterred from conducting economic cyber espionage or perpetrating cyber attacks. The absence of universally accepted and enforceable norms of behavior in cyberspace has contributed to this situation. The motivation to conduct cyber attacks and cyber espionage will probably remain strong because of the relative ease of these operations and the gains they bring to the perpetrators. The result is a cyber environment in which multiple actors continue to test their adversaries' technical capabilities, political resolve, and thresholds. The muted response by most victims to cyber attacks has created a permissive environment in which low-level attacks can be used as a coercive tool short of war, with relatively low risk of retaliation. Additionally, even when a cyber attack can be attributed to a specific actor, the forensic attribution often requires a significant amount of time to complete. Long delays between the cyber attack and determination of attribution likewise reinforce a permissive environment.

Threat Actors
Politically motivated cyber attacks are now a growing reality, and foreign actors are reconnoitering and developing access to US critical infrastructure systems, which might be quickly exploited for disruption if an adversary's intent became hostile. In addition, those conducting cyber espionage are targeting US government, military, and commercial networks on a daily basis. These threats come from a range of actors, including: (1) nation states with highly sophisticated cyber programs (such as Russia or China), (2) nations with lesser technical capabilities but possibly more disruptive intent (such as Iran or North Korea), (3) profit-motivated criminals, and (4) ideologically motivated hackers or extremists. Distinguishing between state and non-state actors within the same country is often difficult—especially when those varied actors actively collaborate, tacitly cooperate, condone criminal activity that only harms foreign victims, or utilize similar cyber tools.

Russia. Russia's Ministry of Defense is establishing its own cyber command, which—according to senior Russian military officials—will be responsible for conducting offensive cyber activities, including propaganda operations and inserting malware into enemy command and control systems. Russia's armed forces are also establishing a specialized branch for computer network operations.

- Computer security studies assert that unspecified Russian cyber actors are developing means to access industrial control systems (ICS) remotely. These systems manage critical infrastructures such as electric power grids, urban mass-transit systems, air-traffic control, and oil and gas distribution networks. These unspecified Russian actors have successfully compromised the product supply chains of three ICS vendors so that customers download exploitative malware directly from the vendors' websites along with routine software updates, according to private sector cyber security experts.

China. Chinese economic espionage against US companies remains a significant issue. The "advanced persistent threat" activities continue despite detailed private sector reports, public indictments, and US demarches, according to a computer security study. China is an advanced cyber actor; however, Chinese hackers often use less sophisticated cyber tools to access targets. Improved cyber defenses would require hackers to use more sophisticated skills and make China's economic espionage more costly and difficult to conduct.

Iran. Iran very likely values its cyber program as one of many tools for carrying out asymmetric but proportional retaliation against political foes, as well as a sophisticated means of collecting intelligence. Iranian actors have been implicated in the 2012–13 DDOS attacks against US financial institutions and in the February 2014 cyber attack on the Las Vegas Sands casino company.

North Korea. North Korea is another state actor that uses its cyber capabilities for political objectives. The North Korean Government was responsible for the November 2014 cyber attack on Sony Pictures Entertainment (SPE), which stole corporate information and introduced hard drive erasing malware into the company's network infrastructure, according to the FBI. The attack coincided with the planned release of a SPE feature film satire that depicted the planned assassination of the North Korean president.

Terrorists. Terrorist groups will continue to experiment with hacking, which could serve as the foundation for developing more advanced capabilities. Terrorist sympathizers will probably conduct low-level cyber attacks on behalf of terrorist groups and attract attention of the media, which might exaggerate the capabilities and threat posed by these actors.

Integrity of Information

Most of the public discussion regarding cyber threats has focused on the confidentiality and availability of information; cyber espionage undermines confidentiality, whereas denial-of-service operations and data-deletion attacks undermine availability. In the future, however, we might also see more cyber operations that will change or manipulate electronic information in order to compromise its integrity (i.e. accuracy and reliability) instead of deleting it or disrupting access to it. Decisionmaking by senior government officials (civilian and military), corporate executives, investors, or others will be impaired if they cannot trust the information they are receiving.

- Successful cyber operations targeting the integrity of information would need to overcome any institutionalized checks and balances designed to prevent the manipulation of data, for example, market monitoring and clearing functions in the financial sector

Counterintelligence

We assess that the leading state intelligence threats to US interests in 2015 will continue to be Russia and China, based on their capabilities, intent, and broad operational scopes. Other states in South Asia, the Near East, and East Asia will pose increasingly sophisticated local and regional intelligence threats to US interests. For example, Iran's intelligence and security services continue to view the United States as a primary threat and have

stated publicly that they monitor and counter US activities in the region.

Penetrating the US national decisionmaking apparatus and Intelligence Community will remain primary objectives for foreign intelligence entities. Additionally, the targeting of national security information and proprietary information from US companies and research institutions dealing with defense, energy, finance, dual-use technology, and other areas will be a persistent threat to US interests.

Non-state entities, including transnational organized criminals and terrorists, will continue to employ human, technical, and cyber intelligence capabilities that present a significant counterintelligence challenge. Like state intelligence services, these non-state entities recruit sources and perform physical and technical surveillance to facilitate their illegal activities and avoid detection and capture.

The internationalization of critical US supply chains and service infrastructure, including for the ICT, civil infrastructure, and national security sectors, increases the potential for subversion. This threat includes individuals, small groups of "hacktivists," commercial firms, and state intelligence services.

Trusted insiders who disclose sensitive US Government information without authorization will remain a significant threat in 2015. The technical sophistication and availability of information technology that can be used for nefarious purposes exacerbates this threat.

Terrorism

Sunni violent extremists are gaining momentum and the number of Sunni violent extremist groups, members, and safe havens is greater than at any other point in history. These groups challenge local and regional governance and threaten US allies, partners, and interests. The threat to key US allies and partners will probably increase, but the extent of the increase will depend on the level of success that Sunni violent extremists achieve in seizing and holding territory, whether or not attacks on local regimes and calls for retaliation against the West are accepted by their key audiences, and the durability of the US-led coalition in Iraq and Syria.

Sunni violent extremists have taken advantage of fragile or unstable Muslim-majority countries to make territorial advances, seen in Syria and Iraq, and will probably continue to do so. They also contribute to regime instability and internal conflict by engaging in high levels of violence. Most will be unable to seize and hold territory on a large scale, however, as long as local, regional, and international support and resources are available and dedicated to halting their progress. The increase in the number of Sunni violent extremist groups also will probably be balanced by a lack of cohesion and authoritative leadership. Although the January 2015 attacks against Charlie Hebdo in Paris is a reminder of the threat to the West, most groups place a higher priority on local concerns than on attacking the so-called far enemy—the United States and the West—as advocated by core al-Qa'ida.

Differences in ideology and tactics will foster competition among some of these groups, particularly if a unifying figure or group does not emerge. In some cases, groups—even if hostile to each other—will ally against common enemies. For example, some Sunni violent extremists will probably gain support from like-minded insurgent or anti-regime groups or within disaffected or disenfranchised communities because they share the goal of radical regime change.

Although most homegrown violent extremists (HVEs) will probably continue to aspire to travel overseas, particularly to Syria and Iraq, they will probably remain the most likely Sunni violent extremist threat to the US homeland because of their immediate and direct access. Some might have been inspired by calls by the Islamic State of Iraq and the Levant (ISIL) in late September for individual jihadists in the West to retaliate for US-led airstrikes on ISIL. Attacks by lone actors are among the most difficult to warn about because they offer few or no signatures.

If ISIL were to substantially increase the priority it places on attacking the West rather than fighting to maintain and expand territorial control, then the group's access to radicalized Westerners who have fought in Syria and Iraq would provide a pool of operatives who potentially have access to the United States and other Western countries. Since the conflict began in 2011, more than 20,000 foreign fighters—at least 3,400 of whom are Westerners—have gone to Syria from more than 90 countries.

Weapons of Mass Destruction and Proliferation

Nation-states' efforts to develop or acquire weapons of mass destruction (WMD), their delivery systems, or their underlying technologies constitute a major threat to the security of the United States, its deployed troops, and allies. Syrian regime use of chemical weapons against the opposition further demonstrates that the threat of WMD is real. The time when only a few states had access to the most dangerous technologies is past. Biological and chemical materials and technologies, almost always dual-use, move easily in the globalized economy, as do personnel with the scientific expertise to design and use them. The latest discoveries in the life sciences also diffuse rapidly around the globe.

Iran Preserving Nuclear Weapons Option

We continue to assess that Iran's overarching strategic goals of enhancing its security, prestige, and regional influence have led it to pursue capabilities to meet its civilian goals and give it the ability to build missile-deliverable nuclear weapons, if it chooses to do so. We do not know whether Iran will eventually decide to build nuclear weapons.

We also continue to assess that Iran does not face any insurmountable technical barriers to producing a nuclear weapon, making Iran's political will the central issue. However, Iranian implementation of the Joint Plan of Action (JPOA) has at least temporarily inhibited further progress in its uranium enrichment and plutonium production capabilities and effectively eliminated Iran's stockpile of 20 percent enriched uranium. The agreement has also enhanced the transparency of Iran's nuclear activities, mainly through improved International Atomic Energy Agency (IAEA) access and earlier warning of any effort to make material for nuclear weapons using its safeguarded facilities.

We judge that Tehran would choose ballistic missiles as its preferred method of delivering nuclear weapons, if it builds them. Iran's ballistic missiles are inherently capable of delivering WMD, and Tehran already has the largest inventory of ballistic missiles in the Middle East. Iran's progress on space launch vehicles—along with its desire to deter the United States and its allies—provides Tehran with the means and motivation to develop longer-range missiles, including intercontinental ballistic missiles (ICBMs).

North Korea Developing WMD-Applicable Capabilities

North Korea's nuclear weapons and missile programs pose a serious threat to the United States and to the security environment in East Asia. North Korea's export of ballistic missiles and associated materials to several countries, including Iran and Syria, and its assistance to Syria's construction of a nuclear reactor, destroyed in 2007, illustrate its willingness to proliferate dangerous technologies.

In 2013, following North Korea's third nuclear test, Pyongyang announced its intention to "refurbish and restart" its nuclear facilities, to include the uranium enrichment facility at Yongbyon, and to restart its graphite-moderated plutonium production reactor that was shut down in 2007. We assess that North Korea has followed through on its announcement by expanding its Yongbyon enrichment facility and restarting the reactor.

North Korea has also expanded the size and sophistication of its ballistic missile forces, ranging from close-range ballistic missiles to ICBMs, while continuing to conduct test launches. In 2014, North Korea launched an unprecedented number of ballistic missiles.

Pyongyang is committed to developing a long-range, nuclear-armed missile that is capable of posing a direct threat to the United States and has publicly displayed its KN08 road-mobile ICBM twice. We assess that North Korea has already taken initial steps toward fielding this system, although the system has not been flight-tested.

Because of deficiencies in their conventional military forces, North Korean leaders are focused on developing missile and WMD capabilities, particularly building nuclear weapons. Although North Korean state media regularly carries official statements on North Korea's justification for building nuclear weapons and threatening to use them as a defensive or retaliatory measure, we do not know the details of Pyongyang's nuclear doctrine or employment concepts. We have long assessed that, in Pyongyang's view, its nuclear capabilities are intended for deterrence, international prestige, and coercive diplomacy.

China's Expanding Nuclear Forces

The People's Liberation Army's (PLA's) Second Artillery Force continues to modernize its nuclear missile force by adding more survivable road-mobile systems and enhancing its silo-based systems. This new generation of missiles is intended to ensure the viability of China's strategic deterrent by providing a second strike capability. In addition, the PLA Navy continues to develop the JL-2 submarine-launched ballistic missile (SLBM) and might produce additional JIN-class nuclear-powered ballistic missile submarines. The JIN-class submarines, armed with JL-2 SLBMs, will give the PLA Navy its first long-range, sea-based nuclear capability. We assess that the Navy will soon conduct its first nuclear deterrence patrols.

Russia's New Intermediate-Range Cruise Missile

Russia has developed a new cruise missile that the United States has declared to be in violation of the Intermediate-Range Nuclear Forces (INF) Treaty. In 2013, Sergei Ivanov, a senior Russian administration official, commented in an interview how the world had changed since the time the INF Treaty was signed 1987 and noted that Russia was "developing appropriate weapons systems" in light of the proliferation of intermediate- and shorter-range ballistic missile technologies around the world. Similarly, as far back as 2007, Ivanov publicly announced that Russia had tested a ground-launched cruise missile for its Iskander weapon system, whose range complied with the INF Treaty "for now." The development of a cruise missile that is inconsistent with INF, combined with these statements about INF, calls into question Russia's commitment to this treaty.

WMD Security in Syria

In June 2014, Syria's declared CW stockpile was removed for destruction by the international community. The most hazardous chemical agents were destroyed aboard the MV CAPE RAY as of August 2014. The United States and its allies continue to work closely with the Organization for the Prohibition of Chemical Weapons (OPCW) to verify the completeness and accuracy of Syria's Chemical Weapons Convention (CWC) declaration. We judge that Syria, despite signing the treaty, has used chemicals as a means of warfare since accession to the CWC in 2013. Furthermore, the OPCW continues to investigate allegations of chlorine use in Syria.

Space and Counterspace

Threats to US space systems and services will increase during 2015 and beyond as potential adversaries pursue disruptive and destructive counterspace capabilities. Chinese and Russian military leaders understand the unique information advantages afforded by space systems and services and are developing capabilities to deny access in a conflict. Chinese military writings highlight the need to interfere with, damage, and destroy reconnaissance, navigation, and communication satellites. China has satellite jamming capabilities and is pursuing antisatellite systems. In July 2014, China conducted a non-destructive antisatellite missile test. China conducted a previous destructive test of the system in 2007, which created long-lived space debris. Russia's 2010 Military Doctrine emphasizes space defense as a vital component of its national defense. Russian leaders openly assert that the Russian armed forces have antisatellite weapons and conduct antisatellite research. Russia has satellite jammers and is pursuing antisatellite systems.

Transnational Organized Crime

Transnational Organized Crime (TOC) is a global, persistent threat to our communities at home and our interests abroad. Savvy, profit-driven criminal networks traffic in drugs, persons, wildlife, and weapons; corrode security and governance; undermine legitimate economic activity and the rule of law; cost economies important revenue; and undercut US development efforts.

Drug Trafficking

Drug trafficking will remain a major TOC threat to the United States. Mexico is the largest foreign producer of US-bound marijuana, methamphetamines, and heroin, and the conduit for the overwhelming majority of US-bound cocaine from South America. The drug trade also undermines US interests abroad, eroding stability in parts of Africa and Latin America; Afghanistan accounts for 80 percent of the world's opium production. Weak Central American states will continue to be the primary transit area for the majority of US-bound cocaine. The Caribbean is becoming an increasingly important secondary transit area for US- and European-bound cocaine. In 2013, the world's capacity to produce heroin reached the second highest level in nearly 20 years, increasing the likelihood that the drug will remain accessible and inexpensive in consumer markets in the United States, where heroin-related deaths have surged since 2007. New psychoactive substances (NPS), including synthetic cannabinoids and synthetic cathinones, pose an emerging and rapidly growing global public health threat. Since 2009, US law enforcement officials have encountered more than 240 synthetic compounds. Worldwide, 348 new psychoactive substances had been identified, exceeding the number of 234 illicit substances under international controls.

Criminals Profiting from Global Instability
Transnational criminal organizations will continue to exploit opportunities in ongoing conflicts to destabilize societies, economies, and governance. Regional unrest, population displacements, endemic corruption, and political turmoil will provide openings that criminals will exploit for profit and to improve their standing relative to other power brokers.

Corruption
Corruption facilitates transnational organized crime and vice versa. Both phenomena exacerbate other threats to local, regional, and international security. Corruption exists at some level in all countries; however, the symbiotic relationship between government officials and TOC networks is particularly pernicious in some countries. One example is Russia, where the nexus among organized crime, state actors, and business blurs the distinction between state policy and private gain.

Human Trafficking
Human trafficking remains both a human rights concern and a challenge to international security. Trafficking in persons has become a lucrative source of revenue—estimated to produce tens of billions of dollars annually. Human traffickers leverage corrupt officials, porous borders, and lax enforcement to ply their illicit trade. This exploitation of human lives for profit continues to occur in every country in the world—undermining the rule of law and corroding legitimate institutions of government and commerce.

Wildlife Trafficking
Illicit trade in wildlife, timber, and marine resources endangers the environment, threatens rule of law and border security in fragile regions, and destabilizes communities that depend on wildlife for biodiversity and ecotourism. Increased demand for ivory and rhino horn in Asia has triggered unprecedented increases in poaching in Africa. Criminal elements, often in collusion with corrupt government officials or security forces, are involved in poaching and movement of ivory and rhino horn across Africa. Poaching presents significant security challenges for militaries and police forces in African nations, which often are outgunned by poachers and their allies. Illegal, unreported, and unregulated fishing threatens food security and the preservation of marine resources. It often occurs concurrently with forced labor in the fishing industry.

Theft of Cultural Properties, Artifacts, and Antiquities
Although the theft and trafficking of cultural heritage and art are traditions as old as the cultures they represent, transnational organized criminals are acquiring, transporting, and selling valuable cultural property and art more swiftly, easily, and stealthily. These criminals operate on a global scale without regard for laws, borders, nationalities or the significance of the treasures they smuggle.

Economics and Natural Resources

The global economy continues to adjust to and recover from the global financial crisis that began in 2008; economic growth since that period is lagging behind that of the previous decade. Resumption of sustained growth has been elusive for many of the world's largest economies, particularly in European countries and Japan. The prospect of diminished or forestalled recoveries in these developed economies as well as disappointing growth in key developing countries has contributed to a readjustment of energy and commodity markets.

Energy and Commodities
Energy prices experienced sharp declines during the second half of 2014. Diminishing global growth prospects, OPEC's decision to maintain its output levels, rapid increases in unconventional oil production in Canada and the United States, and the partial resumption of some previously sidelined output in Libya and elsewhere helped drive down prices by more than half since July, the first substantial decline since 2008–09. Lower-priced oil and gas will give a boost to the global economy, with benefits enjoyed by importers more than outweighing the costs to exporters.

Macroeconomic Stability

Extraordinary monetary policy or "quantitative easing" has helped revive growth in the United States since the global financial crisis. However, this recovery and the prospect of higher returns in the United States will probably continue to draw investment capital from the rest of the world, where weak growth has left interest rates depressed.

Global output improved slightly in 2014 but continued to lag the growth rates seen before 2008. Since 2008, the worldwide GDP growth rate has averaged about 3.2 percent, well below its 20-year, pre-GFC average of 3.9 percent. Looking ahead, prospects for slowing economic growth in Europe and China do not bode well for the global economic environment.

Economic growth has been inconsistent among developed and developing economies alike. Outside of the largest economies—the United States, the EU, and China—economic growth largely stagnated worldwide in 2014, slowing to 2.1 percent. As a result, the difference in growth rates of developing countries and developed countries continued to narrow—to 2.6 percentage points. This gap, smallest in more than a decade, underscores the continued weakness in emerging markets, whose previously much-higher average growth rates helped drive global growth.

Human Security

Critical Trends Converging

Several trends are converging that will probably increase the frequency of shocks to human security in 2015. Emerging infectious diseases and deficiencies in international state preparedness to address them remain a threat, exemplified by the epidemic spread of the Ebola virus in West Africa. Extremes in weather combined with public policies that affect food and water supplies will probably exacerbate humanitarian crises. Many states and international institutions will look to the United States in 2015 for leadership to address human security issues, particularly environment and global health, as well as those caused by poor or abusive governance.

Global trends in governance are negative and portend growing instability. Poor and abusive governance threatens the security and rights of individuals and civil society in many countries throughout the world. The overall risk for mass atrocities—driven in part by increasing social mobilization, violent conflict, and a diminishing quality of governance—is growing. Incidents of religious persecution also are on the rise. Legal restrictions on NGOs and the press, particularly those that expose government shortcomings or lobby for reforms, will probably continue.

Infectious Disease Continues to Threaten Human Security Worldwide

Infectious diseases are among the foremost health security threats. A more crowded and interconnected world is increasing the opportunities for human and animal diseases to emerge and spread globally. This has been demonstrated by the emergence of Ebola in West Africa on an unprecedented scale. In addition, military conflicts and displacement of populations with loss of basic infrastructure can lead to spread of disease. Climate change can also lead to changes in the distribution of vectors for diseases.

- The Ebola outbreak, which began in late 2013 in a remote area of Guinea, quickly spread into neighboring Liberia and Sierra Leone and then into dense urban transportation hubs, where it began spreading out of control. Gaps in disease surveillance and reporting, limited health care resources, and other factors contributed to the outpacing of the international community's response in West Africa. Isolated Ebola cases appeared outside of the most affected countries—notably in Spain and the United States—and the disease will almost certainly continue in 2015 to threaten regional economic stability, security, and governance.

- Antimicrobial drug resistance is increasingly threatening global health security. Seventy percent of known bacteria have acquired resistance to at least one antibiotic that is used to treat infections, threatening a return to the pre-antibiotic era. Multidrug-resistant tuberculosis has emerged in China, India, Russia, and elsewhere. During the next twenty years, antimicrobial drug-resistant pathogens will probably continue to increase in number and geographic scope, worsening health outcomes, straining public health budgets, and harming US interests throughout the world.

- MERS, a novel virus from the same family as SARS, emerged in 2012 in Saudi Arabia. Isolated cases migrated to Southeast Asia, Europe, and the United States. Cases of highly pathogenic influenza are also continuing to appear in different regions of the world. HIV/AIDS and malaria, although trending downward, remain global health priorities. In 2013, 2.1 million people were newly infected with HIV and 584,000 were killed by malaria, according to the World Health Organization. Diarrheal diseases like cholera continue to take the lives of 800,000 children annually.

- The world's population remains vulnerable to infectious diseases because anticipating which pathogen might spread from animals to humans or if a human virus will take a more virulent form is nearly impossible. For example, if a highly pathogenic avian influenza virus like H7N9 were to become easily transmissible among humans, the outcome could be far more disruptive than the great influenza pandemic of 1918. It could lead to global economic losses, the unseating of governments, and disturbance of geopolitical alliances.

Extreme Weather Exacerbating Risks to Global Food and Water Security

Extreme weather, climate change, and public policies that affect food and water supplies will probably create or exacerbate humanitarian crises and instability risks. Globally averaged surface temperature rose approximately 0.8 degrees Celsius (about 1.4 degrees Fahrenheit) from 1951 to 2014; 2014 was warmest on earth since record-keeping began. This rise in temperature has probably caused an increase in the intensity and frequency of both heavy precipitation and prolonged heat waves and has changed the spread of certain diseases. This trend will probably continue. Demographic and development trends that concentrate people in cities—often along coasts—will compound and amplify the impact of extreme weather and climate change on populations. Countries whose key systems—food, water, energy, shelter, transportation, and medical—are resilient will be better able to avoid significant economic and human losses from extreme weather.

- Global food supplies will probably be adequate for 2015 but are becoming increasingly fragile in Africa, the Middle East, and South Asia. The risks of worsening food insecurity in regions of strategic importance to the United States will increase because of threats to local food availability, lower purchasing power, and counterproductive government policies. Price shocks will result if extreme weather or disease patterns significantly reduce food production in multiple areas of the world, especially in key exporting countries.
- Risks to freshwater supplies—due to shortages, poor quality, floods, and climate change—are growing. These problems hinder the ability of countries to produce food and generate energy, potentially undermining global food markets and hobbling economic growth. Combined with demographic and economic development pressures, such problems will particularly hinder the efforts of North Africa, the Middle East, and South Asia to cope with their water problems. Lack of adequate water might be a destabilizing factor in countries that lack the management mechanisms,

financial resources, political will, or technical ability to solve their internal water problems.
- Some states are heavily dependent on river water controlled by upstream nations. When upstream water infrastructure development threatens downstream access to water, states might attempt to exert pressure on their neighbors to preserve their water interests. Such pressure might be applied in international forums and also includes pressing investors, nongovernmental organizations, and donor countries to support or halt water infrastructure projects. Some countries will almost certainly construct and support major water projects. Over the longer term, wealthier developing countries will also probably face increasing water-related social disruptions. Developing countries, however, are almost certainly capable of addressing water problems without risk of state failure. Terrorist organizations might also increasingly seek to control or degrade water infrastructure to gain revenue or influence populations.

Increase in Global Instability Risk

Global political instability risks will remain high in 2015 and beyond. Mass atrocities, sectarian or religious violence, and curtailed NGO activities will all continue to increase these risks. Declining economic conditions are contributing to risk of instability or internal conflict.

- Roughly half of the world's countries not already experiencing or recovering from instability are in the "most risk" and "significant risk" categories for regime-threatening and violent instability through 2015.
- Overall international will and capability to prevent or mitigate mass atrocities will probably diminish in 2015 owing to reductions in government budgets and spending.
- In 2014, about two dozen countries increased restrictions on NGOs. Approximately another dozen also plan to do so in 2015, according to the International Center for Nonprofit Law.

JAMES R. CLAPPER has held a number of top positions in the Intelligence community, including Director of the Defense Intelligence Agency, and Under Secretary of Defense for Intelligence. He is currently the Director of National Intelligence. When in 2013 he denied under oath to a Congressional committee that the NSA collects data on millions of Americans, his veracity was called into question.

Washington's Blog    **NO**

There Are Far Fewer Terror Attacks Now Than in the 1970s

Putting the Terror Threat in Perspective

The terror threat is greatly exaggerated. After all, the type of counter-terror experts who frequently appear on the mainstream news are motivated to hype the terror threat, because it drums up business for them.

The same is true for government employees. As former FBI assistant director Thomas Fuentes put it last week:

> If you're submitting budget proposals for a law enforcement agency, for an intelligence agency, you're not going to submit the proposal that "We won the war on terror and everything's great," cuz the first thing that's gonna happen is your budget's gonna be cut in half.
>
> You know, it's my opposite of Jesse Jackson's "Keep Hope Alive"—it's "Keep Fear Alive." Keep it alive.

Fearmongering also serves political goals. For example, FBI agents and CIA intelligence officials, a top constitutional and military law expert, *Time* magazine, the *Washington Post* and others have all said that U.S. government officials "were trying to create an atmosphere of fear in which the American people would give them more power." Indeed, the former Secretary of Homeland Security Tom Ridge *admitted* that he was pressured to raise terror alerts to help Bush win reelection. Former U.S. National Security Adviser Zbigniew Brzezinski—also a top foreign policy advisor to President Obama—told the Senate that the war on terror is a "a mythical historical narrative."

Indeed, the government justifies its geopolitical goals—including seizing more power at home, and overthrowing oil-rich countries—by hyping the terror menace. So the government wants you to be scared out of your pants by the risk of terrorism. No wonder national security employees see a terrorist under every bush.

But terrorism has actually *dramatically declined* in the United States. Daniel Benjamin—the Coordinator for Counterterrorism at the United States Department of State from 2009 to 2012—noted last month (at 10:22):

> *The total number of deaths from terrorism in recent years has been extremely small in the West. And* ***the threat itself has been considerably reduced.*** *Given all the headlines people don't have that perception; but if you look at the statistics that is the case.*

Indeed, the *Washington Post* noted in 2013 that the number of terror attacks in the U.S. has *plummeted* since the 1970s[.]

Indeed, you're now much more likely to be killed by brain-eating parasites, texting while driving, toddlers, lightning, falling out of bed, alcoholism, food poisoning, a financial crash, obesity, medical errors or "autoerotic asphyxiation" than by terrorists.

Obviously, a huge number of innocent Americans—3,000—were killed on 9/11 . . . a *single* terror attack.

However, 9/11—like the Boston Bombing (and the Paris terror attack)—happened because mass surveillance *replaced* traditional anti-terror measures. Similarly, Cheney and company were criminally negligent.

And the "War on Terror" has been counter-productive, and only *increased* the terrorism problem.

If we had stuck with tried-and-true anti-terror techniques, high-fatality events like 9/11 would *never* have happened.

Washington's Blog strives to provide real-time, well-researched, and actionable information.

EXPLORING THE ISSUE

Is the United States in Significant Danger of Large-Scale Terrorist Attacks?

Critical Thinking and Reflection

1. Why would anyone want to nuclear bomb America?
2. What can be done to minimize the desire of people to terrorize us?
3. How much expansion of police powers should we accept to increase our security? How much more should we bar people from entering the United States to increase our security?
4. What more can we do to protect ourselves?

Is There Common Ground?

There are many arguments to support the contention that WMDs are hard to obtain, difficult to move and assemble, and even harder to deliver. There is also ample evidence to suggest that most, if not all, of the U.S. government's work is in one way or another designed to thwart such actions because of the enormous consequences were such acts to be carried out. These facts should make Americans rest easier and allay fears if only for reasons of probability.

However, Washington's Blog's optimistic statement should not reduce the level of funding and support for the intelligence agencies' efforts to deter terrorism. Since September 11, it is clear that the world has entered a new phase of terrorist action. It is dangerous, therefore, for a nation to believe that because something is difficult it is unlikely to take place or that a lack of terrorist events is a good reason to let our guard down. Clapper's factual report gives plenty of reasons to stay alert though the greatest dangers seem to be abroad.

What everyone agrees on is that terrorism and especially WMD terrorism is a major concern for this country, and that almost everything possible should be done to prevent such an attack. Also, most people agree that if states are to err, perhaps they should err on the side of caution and preventive action rather than on reliance on the statistical probability that WMD terrorism is unlikely. We may never see a WMD terrorist act in this century, but it is statistically likely that the reason for this will not be lack of effort on the part of motivated terrorist groups. Most people also agree that we must not panic. However, when the time comes we probably will panic. Extraordinary leadership may lead us to a different response, but I would not bet on it.

Additional Resources

Some important research and commentary on WMD terrorism can be found in Gary LaFree et al., *Putting Terrorism in Context: Lessons from the Global Terrorism Database* (Routledge, Taylor & Francis Group, 2015); Brian Michael Jenkins, *Will Terrorists Go Nuclear?* (Prometheus Books, 2008); Todd Masse, *Nuclear Jihad: A Clear and Present Danger?* (Potomac Books, 2011); Jack Caravelli, *Nuclear Insecurity: Understanding the Threat from Rogue Nations and Terrorists* (Praeger Security International, 2008); Benjamin Cole, *The Changing Face of Terrorism: How Real Is the Threat from Biological, Chemical, and Nuclear Weapons?* (I. B. Tauris, 2011); and John E. Mueller, *Atomic Obsession: Nuclear Alarmism from Hiroshima to al-Qaeda* (Oxford University Press, 2010).

Some recent general works on terrorism include Sandra Walklate and Gabe Mythen, *Contradictions of Terrorism: Security, Risk and Resilience* (Routledge, 2015); Anat Berko, *The Smarter Bomb: Women and Children as Suicide Bombers* (Rowman & Littlefield, 2012); Eli Berman, *Radical, Religious, and Violent: the New Economics of Terrorism* (MIT Press, 2009); Basia Spalek, ed., *Counter-Terrorism: Community-Based Approaches to Preventing Terror Crime* (Palgrave Macmillan, 2012); Frank Shanty, ed., *Counterterrorism: From the Cold War to the War on Terror* (Praeger, 2012); Jonathan Barker, *The No-Nonsense Guide to Global Terrorism*, 2nd ed. (New Internationalist, 2008); Cornelia Beyer, *Violent Globalisms: Conflict in Response to Empire* (Ashgate, 2008); Peter R. Neumann, *Old and New Terrorism: Late Modernity, Globalization and the Transformation of Political Violence* (Polity, 2009); Paul J. Smith, *The Terrorism Ahead: Confronting Transnational Violence in the Twenty-First Century* (M. E. Sharpe, 2008); Peter Lentini, *Neojihadism: Towards a New*

Understanding of Terrorism and Extremism? (Edward Elgar, 2013); Gershon Shafir et al., *Lessons and Legacies of the War on Terror: From Moral Panic to Permanent War* (Routledge, 2013); and Lisa Stampnitzky, *Disciplining Terror: How Experts Invented "Terrorism"* (Cambridge University Press, 2013).

For information on how to respond to a nuclear terrorist event, see *Responding to a Radiological or Nuclear Terrorism Incident: A Guide for Decision Makers* (National Council on Radiation Protection and Measurements, 2010).

Internet References . . .

Sociology—Study Sociology Online

http://edu.learnsoc.org/

Sociology Web Resources

www.mhhe.com/socscience/sociology
/resources/index.htm

Sociosite

www.topsite.com/goto/sociosite.net

Socioweb

www.topsite.com/goto/socioweb.com

Unit 6

UNIT

The Future: Population/ Environment/Society

*T*he leading issues for the beginning of the twenty-first century include global warming, environmental decline, immigration, and globalization. The state of the environment and the effects of globalization produce strong arguments concerning what can be harmful or beneficial. Technology has increased enormously in the last 100 years, as have world-wide population growth, consumption, and new forms of pollution that threaten to undermine the world's fragile ecological support system. Although all nations have a stake in the health of the planet, many believe that none are doing enough to protect its health. Will technology itself be the key to controlling or accommodating the increase in population and consumption, along with the resulting increase in waste production? Perhaps so, but new policies will also be needed. What about global leadership and globalization? What role should the United States have in the world? Should it be the world hegemonic power or would it do better by sharing power?

Selected, Edited, and with Issue Framing Material by:
Kurt Finsterbusch, *University of Maryland, College Park*

ISSUE

Does Immigration Benefit the Economy?

YES: Robert Lynch and Patrick Oakford, from "The Economic Effects of Granting Legal Status and Citizenship to Undocumented Immigrants," Center for American Progress (2013)

NO: Association for Mature American Citizens, from "How Much Does Illegal Immigration Cost You?" The Heritage Foundation (2015)

Learning Outcomes

After reading this issue, you will be able to:

- With effort understand the economic arguments on which the different sides are based.
- Sort out where the two articles agree and where they disagree.
- Understand how terrorism has radically changed the debate on immigration.
- Understand how the country could benefit from immigration but certain groups could lose benefits due to the immigration.
- Understand that most immigrants have mostly positive values like the importance of strong family ties, hard work, ambition to better themselves, etc.
- Know that illegal immigration raises other issues and greater public resentment.

ISSUE SUMMARY

YES: Robert Lynch, Everett E. Nuttle Professor and chair of the Department of Economics at Washington College, and Patrick Oakford, research assistant at the Center for American Progress, show that legal status and a road to citizenship for the unauthorized will bring about significant economic gains in terms of economic growth, earnings, tax revenues, and jobs and the sooner we provide legal status and citizenship, the greater the economic benefits will be for the nation. The main reason is that the immigrants will produce and earn significantly more than they cost and the results will ripple throughout the economy.

NO: The Association for Mature American Citizens argues that "Unlawful immigration and amnesty for current unlawful immigrants can pose large fiscal costs for U.S. taxpayers." The benefits would include Social Security, Medicare, welfare, education, police, and other services. Each such household would receive benefits that would exceed various payments to government of $14,387.

Immigrants move to the United States for various reasons: to flee tyranny and terrorism, to escape war, or to join relatives who have already settled. Above all, they immigrate because in their eyes America is an island of affluence in a global sea of poverty; here they will earn many times what they could only hope to earn in their native countries. One hotly debated question is,

What will these new immigrants do to the United States or for it?

Opposition to immigration comes from several sources. One is prejudice based on race, ethnicity, religion, or some other characteristic. Second, more legitimate in the view of many, is worry that immigrants are diluting the host country's language and other aspects of its national culture.

Security concerns are a third source of opposition to immigration.

Some critics of immigration argue that crime is higher among immigrant populations, and in recent years the possibility of immigrants being terrorists has increased this worry for some. Economic concerns are a fourth source of opposition to immigrants and are the focus of this debate. One economic argument is that immigrants work for low wages, thereby undercutting the wages of native-born workers. Also, they are seen as taking jobs away from American workers. Another charge is that immigrants are an economic burden, requiring far more in terms of welfare, medical care, education, and other services than the migrants return to their host country in terms of productivity and taxes.

These charges are met by counter-arguments that depict immigrants as providing needed workers and filling jobs that American workers do not want anyway. Finally, it can be argued that they give a boost to their new country's economy. In fact, several countries including the United States were largely developed by immigrants. Sometimes such influxes have gone fairly smoothly.

At other times, they have met significant opposition within the country of destination. Such is the case currently, with the global tide of refugees and immigrants, both legal and illegal, facing increasing resistance. Certainly, the fact that immigrants attacked the World Trade Center and the Pentagon on September 11, 2001, made many Americans favor the reduction of immigration.

But if we would have a better economy if we continued to allow immigration on a generous scale, they would be worth the risk.

Since 1965, the number of immigrants has changed markedly. Legal immigration has grown almost 300 percent from a yearly average of 330,000 in the 1960s to an annual average of 978,000 in the 1990s and just over 1 million during 2000–2007. Illegal (undocumented, unauthorized) immigrants probably add over 1 million to this total. Perhaps 11 million such immigrants are currently in the United States, with approximately 80 percent of them from Central America, especially Mexico. The presence of so many undocumented immigrants has become a major political issue in the United States.

American attitudes are strongest against illegal immigration, but are also hostile to legal immigration. Polls find that most Americans favor decreasing all immigration. When Americans are asked what bothers them about illegal immigration, they talk about its impacts on wages, job availability, and the cost of social and educational services. In other words, they are concerned about economic issues. Taking up this concern, Lynch and Oakford examine the economic impact of immigrants on the United States and find that the country benefits. The Association for Mature American Citizens disagrees, finding that immigration has negative economic effects.

YES ↵

Robert Lynch and Patrick Oakford

The Economic Effects of Granting Legal Status and Citizenship to Undocumented Immigrants

[T]he debate over immigration reform has important legal, moral, social, and political dimensions. Providing or denying legal status or citizenship to the undocumented has implications for getting immigrants in compliance with the law, affects whether or not immigrant families can stay in their country of choice, and determines whether they have the opportunity to become full and equal members of American society.

But legal status and citizenship are also about the economic health of the nation as a whole. As our study demonstrates, legal status and a road map to citizenship for the unauthorized will bring about significant economic gains in terms of growth, earnings, tax revenues, and jobs—all of which will not occur in the absence of immigration reform or with reform that creates a permanent sub-citizen class of residents. We also show that the timing of reform matters: The sooner we provide legal status and citizenship, the greater the economic benefits are for the nation.

The logic behind these economic gains is straightforward. As discussed below, legal status and citizenship enable undocumented immigrants to produce and earn significantly more than they do when they are on the economic sidelines. The resulting productivity and wage gains ripple through the economy because immigrants are not just workers—they are also consumers and taxpayers. They will spend their increased earnings on the purchase of food, clothing, housing, cars, and computers. That spending, in turn, will stimulate demand in the economy for more products and services, which creates jobs and expands the economy.

This paper analyzes the 10-year economic impact of immigration reform under three scenarios. The first scenario assumes that legal status and citizenship are both accorded to the undocumented in 2013. The second scenario assumes that the unauthorized are provided legal status in 2013 and are able to earn citizenship five years thereafter. The third scenario assumes that the unauthorized

are granted legal status starting in 2013 but that they are not provided a means to earn citizenship—at least within the 10-year timeframe of our analysis.

Under the first scenario—in which undocumented immigrants are granted legal status and citizenship in 2013—U.S. gross domestic product, or GDP, would grow by an additional $1.4 trillion cumulatively over the 10 years between 2013 and 2022. What's more, Americans would earn an additional $791 billion in personal income over the same time period—and the economy would create, on average, an additional 203,000 jobs per year. Within five years of the reform, unauthorized immigrants would be earning 25.1 percent more than they currently do and $659 billion more from 2013 to 2022. This means that they would also be contributing significantly more in federal, state, and local taxes. Over 10 years, that additional tax revenue would sum to $184 billion—$116 billion to the federal government and $68 billion to state and local governments.

Under the second scenario—in which undocumented immigrants are granted legal status in 2013 and citizenship five years thereafter—the 10-year cumulative increase in U.S. GDP would be $1.1 trillion, and the annual increases in the incomes of Americans would sum to $618 billion. On average over the 10 years, this immigration reform would create 159,000 jobs per year. Given the delay in acquiring citizenship relative to the first scenario, it would take 10 years instead of five for the incomes of the unauthorized to increase 25.1 percent. Over the 10-year period, they would earn $515 billion more and pay an additional $144 billion in taxes—$91 billion to the federal government and $53 billion to state and local governments.

Finally, under the third scenario—in which undocumented immigrants are granted legal status starting in 2013 but are not eligible for citizenship within 10 years—the cumulative gain in U.S. GDP between 2013 and 2022 would still be a significant—but comparatively more modest—$832 billion. The annual increases in the incomes of Americans would sum to $470 billion over the 10-year period, and the economy would add an average of 121,000 more jobs per year. The income of the unauthorized would be 15.1 percent higher within five years. Because of their increased earnings, undocumented immigrants would pay an additional $109 billion in taxes over the 10-year period—$69 billion to the federal government and $40 billion to state and local governments.

These immigration reform scenarios illustrate that unauthorized immigrants are currently earning far less than their potential, paying much less in taxes, and contributing significantly less to the U.S. economy than they potentially could. They also make clear that Americans stand to gain more from an immigration reform policy of legalization and citizenship than they do from one of legalization alone—or from no reform at all. Finally, the magnitude of potential economic gains depends significantly on how quickly reforms are implemented. The sooner that legal status and citizenship are granted to the unauthorized, the greater the gains will be for the U.S. economy.

Analyzing the Economic Effects of Legal Status and Citizenship

Numerous studies and government data sets have shown that positive economic outcomes are highly correlated with legal status and citizenship. Large and detailed government data sets—such as the U.S. Census Bureau's American Community Survey and Current Population Survey—have documented, for example, that U.S. citizens have average incomes that are 40 percent greater or more than the average incomes of noncitizen immigrants, both those here legally and the unauthorized.

Within the immigrant community, economic outcomes also vary by legal status. A study done by George Borjas and Marta Tienda found that prior to 1986 Mexican immigrant men legally in the United States earned 6 percent more than unauthorized Mexican male immigrants. Research suggests that undocumented immigrants are further "underground" today than they were in 1986—and that they experience an even wider wage gap. Katherine Donato and Blake Sisk, for example, found that between 2003 and 2009, the average hourly wage of Mexican immigrants legally in the United States was 28.3 percent greater than it was for undocumented Mexican immigrants.

In addition, a U.S. Department of Labor study—based on a carefully constructed and large longitudinal survey of the nearly 3 million unauthorized immigrants who were granted legal status and given a road map to citizenship under the Immigration Reform and Control Act of 1986—found that these previously undocumented immigrants experienced a 15.1 percent increase in their average inflation-adjusted wages within five years of gaining legal status. Studies have also reported that citizenship provides an added economic boost above and beyond the gains from legalization. Manuel Pastor and Justin Scoggins, for instance, found that even when controlling for a range of factors such as educational attainment and national origin, naturalized immigrants earned 11 percent more than legal noncitizens.

There are several reasons why legalization and citizenship both raise the incomes of immigrants and improve economic outcomes. Providing a road map to citizenship to undocumented immigrants gives them legal protections that raise their wages. It also promotes investment in the education and training of immigrants that eventually pays off in the form of higher wages and output; grants access to a broader range of higher-paying jobs; encourages labor mobility which increases the returns on the labor skills of immigrants by improving the efficiency of the labor market such that the skillsets of immigrants more closely match the jobs that they perform; and makes it more possible for immigrants to start businesses and create jobs. . . .

We estimate that the income premium of citizenship for all immigrants—both documented and undocumented—by comparing the earnings of naturalized and noncitizen immigrant populations while statistically controlling for observable differences other than citizenship that may affect income-level differences between the two groups. We find that citizenship is associated with a statistically significant boost in the incomes of immigrants.

To estimate the effect of citizenship on the earnings of unauthorized immigrants alone, we then decompose the income effect of citizenship that we estimated for all noncitizens into two components: one to estimate the percentage gain in income that the unauthorized experience as a consequence of attaining legal status and the other to estimate the percentage gain in income that they obtain from becoming naturalized citizens.

For the first component, we estimated that the unauthorized would gain a 15.1 percent increase in income from obtaining legal status. For the second component, we estimate that previously unauthorized and newly legalized immigrants would experience an additional 10 percent gain in income if they acquired citizenship.

Taking into account both components, our most likely estimate of the full effect of granting legal status and citizenship to unauthorized immigrants is an income gain of 25.1 percent. Of this boost in income, about three-fifths comes from legalization and about two-fifths is attributable to transitioning from legal status to citizenship.

10-Year Projections of the Economic Gains from Immigration Reform

Applying our 25.1 percent citizenship effect on the income of the undocumented, we project the economic gains from immigration reform under three scenarios. The first and most politically unlikely scenario—but one that is nonetheless useful for comparison purposes—assumes that legal status and citizenship are both conferred on the undocumented in 2013. The second scenario assumes that the unauthorized are provided legal status in 2013 and citizenship five years thereafter. The third scenario assumes that the unauthorized are granted legal status starting in 2013 but that they are not given a road map to citizenship.

Under the first scenario—both legal status and citizenship in 2013—U.S. GDP would grow by an additional $1.4 trillion cumulatively, and the personal income of Americans would grow an additional $791 billion over the 10 years between 2013 and 2022. Over the same time period, there would be an average of 203,000 more jobs per year.

Unauthorized immigrants would also be better off. Within five years they would be earning 25.1 percent more annually. As a consequence, over the full 10-year period, the formerly unauthorized would earn an additional $659 billion and pay at least $184 billion more in federal, state, and local taxes—$116 billion more to the federal government and $68 billion more to state and local governments.

Under the second scenario—legal status in 2013 followed by citizenship five years thereafter—the 10-year cumulative increase in the economy of the United States would be $1.1 trillion, and the annual increases in the incomes of Americans would sum to $618 billion. Over the 10 years, this immigration reform would create an average of 159,000 jobs per year. Given the delay in acquiring citizenship relative to the first scenario, it would take 10 years instead of five years for the incomes of the unauthorized to increase 25.1 percent. Over the 10-year period, they would earn $515 billion more and pay an additional $144 billion in taxes—$91 billion to the federal government and $53 billion to state and local governments.

Finally, under the third scenario—legal status only starting in 2013—the cumulative gain in U.S. GDP between 2013 and 2022 would be a more modest $832 billion. The annual increases in the incomes of residents of the United States would sum to $470 billion over the 10 years, and the economy would have an average of 121,000 more jobs per year. The income of the unauthorized would be 15.1 percent higher within five years. Over the 10-year period, they would earn $392 billion more and pay an additional $109 billion in taxes—$69 billion to the federal government and $40 billion to state and local governments.

In each of the three scenarios we have almost certainly understated the amount of additional taxes that will be paid by undocumented immigrant workers because the tax estimates include only taxes from the increased earnings of the previously undocumented. While it has been widely documented that unauthorized workers are contributing billions of dollars in federal, state, and local taxes each year, the Congressional Budget Office estimates that between 30 percent and 50 percent of the undocumented population fails to declare their income. To the extent that some of these immigrants— who are working in the underground economy—are not reporting their incomes for fear of being discovered and deported, however, legal status and citizenship is likely to push them into the legal economy, where they will be declaring their income and paying billions of dollars in taxes in addition to the amounts that we have calculated above. The reporting of this income, however, may increase business deductions for labor compensation, offsetting part of the tax gain. In addition, some currently unauthorized immigrants who have income taxes withheld may—upon attaining legal status—file returns and claim refunds or deductions and exemptions that will offset some of the tax revenue gained from the higher reporting of income.

Conclusion

The positive economic impacts on the nation and on undocumented immigrants of granting them legal status and a road map to citizenship are likely to be very large. The nation as a whole would benefit from a sizable increase in GDP and income and a modest increase in jobs. The earnings of unauthorized immigrants would rise significantly, and the taxes they would pay would increase dramatically. Given that the full benefits would phase in over a number of years, the sooner we grant legal status and provide a road map to citizenship to unauthorized immigrants, the sooner Americans will be able to reap these benefits. It is also clear that legalization and a road map to citizenship bestow greater gains on the American people and the U.S. economy than legalization alone.

ROBERT LYNCH, Everett E. Nuttle Professor and chair of the Department of Economics at Washington College, has authored numerous books and focuses on education and the economy. He is the author of numerous works. One of his research interests is in assessing the impact of public investment in early childhood education on government budgets, the economy, and crime. One of his publications in this area is *Exceptional Returns: Economic, Fiscal, and Social Benefits of Investment in Early Childhood Development* (2004).

PATRICK OAKFORD is a research assistant at the Center for American Progress and focuses his education on immigration.

Association for Mature American Citizens

How Much Does Illegal Immigration Cost You?

Executive Summary

Unlawful immigration and amnesty for current unlawful immigrants can pose large fiscal costs for U.S. taxpayers. Government provides four types of benefits and services that are relevant to this issue:

- Direct benefits. These include Social Security, Medicare, unemployment insurance, and workers' compensation.
- Means-tested welfare benefits. There are over 80 of these programs which, at a cost of nearly $900 billion per year, provide cash, food, housing, medical, and other services to roughly 100 million low-income Americans. Major programs include Medicaid, food stamps, the refundable Earned Income Tax Credit, public housing, Supplemental Security Income, and Temporary Assistance for Needy Families.
- Public education. At a cost of $12,300 per pupil per year, these services are largely free or heavily subsidized for low-income parents.
- Population-based services. Police, fire, highways, parks, and similar services, as the National Academy of Sciences determined in its study of the fiscal costs of immigration, generally have to expand as new immigrants enter a community; someone has to bear the cost of that expansion.

The cost of these governmental services is far larger than many people imagine. For example, in 2010, the average U.S. household received $31,584 in government benefits and services in these four categories.

The governmental system is highly redistributive. Well-educated households tend to be net tax contributors: The taxes they pay exceed the direct and means-tested benefits, education, and population-based services they receive. For example, in 2010, in the whole U.S. population, households with college-educated heads, on average, received $24,839 in government benefits while paying $54,089 in taxes. The average college-educated household

thus generated a fiscal surplus of $29,250 that government used to finance benefits for other households.

Other households are net tax consumers: The benefits they receive exceed the taxes they pay. These households generate a "fiscal deficit" that must be financed by taxes from other households or by government borrowing. For example, in 2010, in the U.S. population as a whole, households headed by persons without a high school degree, on average, received $46,582 in government benefits while paying only $11,469 in taxes. This generated an average fiscal deficit (benefits received minus taxes paid) of $35,113.

The high deficits of poorly educated households are important in the amnesty debate because the typical unlawful immigrant has only a 10th-grade education. Half of unlawful immigrant households are headed by an individual with less than a high school degree, and another 25 percent of household heads have only a high school degree.

Some argue that the deficit figures for poorly educated households in the general population are not relevant for immigrants. Many believe, for example, that lawful immigrants use little welfare. In reality, lawful immigrant households receive significantly more welfare, on average, than U.S.-born households. Overall, the fiscal deficits or surpluses for lawful immigrant households are the same as or higher than those for U.S.-born households with the same education level. Poorly educated households, whether immigrant or U.S.-born, receive far more in government benefits than they pay in taxes.

In contrast to lawful immigrants, unlawful immigrants at present do not have access to means-tested welfare, Social Security, or Medicare. This does not mean, however, that they do not receive government benefits and services. Children in unlawful immigrant households receive heavily subsidized public education. Many unlawful immigrants have U.S.-born children; these children are currently eligible for the full range of government welfare and medical benefits. And, of course, when unlawful immigrants live in a community, they use roads, parks, sewers, police, and fire protection; these services must expand to cover the added population or there will be "congestion" effects that lead to a decline in service quality.

In 2010, the average unlawful immigrant household received around $24,721 in government benefits and services while paying some $10,334 in taxes. This generated an average annual fiscal deficit (benefits received minus taxes paid) of around $14,387 per household. This cost had to be borne by U.S. taxpayers. Amnesty would provide unlawful households with access to over 80 means-tested welfare programs, Obamacare, Social Security, and Medicare. The fiscal deficit for each household would soar.

If enacted, amnesty would be implemented in phases. During the first or interim phase (which is likely to last 13 years), unlawful immigrants would be given lawful status but would be denied access to means-tested welfare and Obamacare. Most analysts assume that roughly half of unlawful immigrants work "off the books" and therefore do not pay income or FICA taxes. During the interim phase, these "off the books" workers would have a strong incentive to move to "on the books" employment. In addition, their wages would likely go up as they sought jobs in a more open environment. As a result, during the interim period, tax payments would rise and the average fiscal deficit among former unlawful immigrant households would fall.

After 13 years, unlawful immigrants would become eligible for means-tested welfare and Obamacare. At that point or shortly thereafter, former unlawful immigrant households would likely begin to receive government benefits at the same rate as lawful immigrant households of the same education level. As a result, government spending and fiscal deficits would increase dramatically. The final phase of amnesty is retirement. Unlawful immigrants are not currently eligible for Social Security and Medicare, but under amnesty they would become so. The cost of this change would be very large indeed.

EXPLORING THE ISSUE

Does Immigration Benefit the Economy?

Critical Thinking and Reflection

1. The simple rule of morality is the greatest good for the greatest number (utilitarianism). Apply this rule to the issue of immigration. Do you accept the outcome or would you amend the rule?
2. Who benefits from heavy immigration and who benefits from very light immigration?
3. Why is America at an impasse on immigration legislation?
4. What are the various economic impacts of immigration and in sum does it help or harm the economy?
5. When did you or your ancestors come to America? Was that immigration good for America?
6. What should be done about "illegal" immigrants living in America? What should be done about children of illegal immigrants who were born here and are U.S. citizens?

Is There Common Ground?

This nation was built by immigration. Now most Americans want to keep what we have largely to ourselves and greatly limit immigration. Now pro-immigration commentators have to justify immigration by demonstrating the benefits of immigration for America. Lynch and Oakford claim that immigration is making America stronger. Many people disagree because they fear the consequences of today's immigration.

This issue has deeply divided the country. It seems that Congress cannot agree on immigration policy and pass meaningful immigration legislation.

At the moment, there is no common ground except all sides are committed to trying to keep illegal immigrants out. Beyond that there are options but not agreement. Some want to deport the illegal immigrants in the United States. Others favor a guest-worker program that permits undocumented immigrants currently in the country to remain for several years as temporary workers but that also requires them to leave the country. Yet others support allowing unauthorized immigrants already in the country to get a work permit and eventually to apply for citizenship. A 2007 poll found 30 percent of Americans favoring the first option, 28 percent supporting the second, and 37 percent preferring the third option, with 5 percent unsure. Opinions were similarly split in the halls of Congress, so it has failed to enact a comprehensive plan. As of this writing it is on the agenda of Congress but no one seems to believe anything will pass this Congress.

Additional Resources

Several major works debate whether or not immigrants, on average, economically benefit America and whether they can be assimilated. Sources that argue that immigrants largely benefit America include Martin Ruhs and Carlos Vargas-Silvia, *The Labour Effects of Immigration* (The Migration Observatory, May 22, 2015); Jason L. Riley, *Let Them In: The Case for Open Borders* (Gotham, 2008); Darrell M. West, *Brain Gain: Rethinking U.S. Immigration Policy* (Brookings Institution Press, 2010); Joseph H. Carens, *Immigrants and the Right to Stay* (MIT Press, 2010); Benjamin Powell, ed., *The Economics of Immigration* (Oxford University Press, 2015); George J. Borjas, *Immigration Economics* (Harvard University Press, 2014); Robert E. Koulish, *Immigration and American Democracy: Subverting the Rule of Law* (Routledge, 2010). For a more even-handed discussion, see Allan M. Williams, *Migration, Risk and Uncertainty* (Routledge, 2015); Sarah Spencer, *The Migration Debate* (Policy Press, 2011); Örn B. Bodvarsson, *The Economics of Immigration: Theory and Policy* (Springer, 2009); Peter Kivisto and Thomas Faist, *Beyond the Border: The Causes and Consequences of Contemporary Immigration* (Pine Forge Press, 2010); Philip L. Martin, *Importing Poverty?: Immigration and the Changing Face of Rural America* (Yale University Press, 2009). On the issue of Mexican immigration, see Douglas S. Massey, Jorge Durand, and Nolan J. Malone, *Beyond Smoke and Mirrors: Mexican Immigration in an Era of Economic Integration* (Russell Sage Foundation, 2003), and Victor Davis Hanson, *Mexifornia: A State of Becoming*

(Encounter Books, 2003). Works that focus on attitudes toward immigrants and their rights include Peter Schrag, *Not Fit for Our Society: Nativism and Immigration* (University of California Press, 2010); Armando Navarro, *The Immigration Crisis: Nativism, Armed Vigilantism, and the Rise of a Countervailing Movement* (AltaMira Press, 2009); Michael Sobczak, *American Attitudes Toward Immigrants and Immigration Policy* (LFB Scholarly Publishing, 2010); Dorothee Schneider, *Crossing Borders: Immigration and Citizenship in the Twentieth-Century United States* (Harvard University Press, 2011); Christian Joppke, *Citizenship and Immigration*

(Polity, 2010); and Kim Voss and Irene Bloemraad, eds., *Rallying for Immigrant Rights: The Fight for Inclusion in 21st Century America* (University of California Press, 2011).

An overview of the history of U.S. immigration and policy is found in Aristide R. Zolberg, *A Nation by Design: Immigration Policy in the Fashioning of America* (Harvard University Press, 2008). A group that favors fewer immigrants is the Center for Immigration Studies at www.cis.org. Taking a positive view of immigration and immigrants is the National Immigration Forum at www.immigrationforum.org.

Internet References . . .

Sociology—Study Sociology Online

http://edu.learnsoc.org/

Sociology Web Resources

www.mhhe.com/socscience/sociology/resources
/index.htm

Sociosite

www.topsite.com/goto/sociosite.net

Socioweb

www.topsite.com/goto/socioweb.com

Selected, Edited, and with Issue Framing Material by:
Kurt Finsterbusch, *University of Maryland, College Park*

ISSUE

Is Humankind Dangerously Harming the Environment?

YES: Daniel Immerwahr, from "Growth vs. the Climate," *Dissent* (2015)

NO: Ramez Naam, from "How Innovation Could Save the Planet," *The Futurist* (2013)

Learning Outcomes

After reading this issue, you will be able to:

- Discern the trends or issues that greatly concern many environmentalists.
- Identify what has been done to address the environmental issues and estimate what still needs to be done.
- Assess the accuracy of the information on which you depend to understand environmental issues.
- Begin to explore the potential consequences of environmental problems on societies and lifestyles.
- Identify the information that you need to acquire a pretty good understanding of the environmental issues that are facing us today.

ISSUE SUMMARY

YES: Daniel Immerwahr reviews the history of environmental concern to 1980 and then the unconcern until recently. He reports the arguments of many major spokespersons for the environmental crisis view and the solutions that they propose. All of them argue that major cutbacks in resource use will be required, but a few of them believe that the quality of our lives could improve at lower consumption levels.

NO: Ramez Naam, a computer scientist, author, and former Microsoft executive, argues that innovations will deal with the serious issues of population growth, peak oil, resources depletion, climate change, and limits to growth. After reviewing some of the recent great accomplishments and some of the risks facing the planet, he shows how ideas and innovations have solved similar crises in the past and then gives reasons for being optimistic about the future.

$\mathbf{M}$uch of the literature on socioeconomic development in the 1960s was premised on the assumption of inevitable material progress for all. It largely ignored the impacts of development on the environment and presumed that the availability of raw materials would never be a problem. The common belief was that all societies would get richer because all societies were investing in new equipment and technologies that would increase productivity and wealth. Theorists recognized that some poor countries were having trouble developing, but they blamed those problems on the deficiencies of the values and attitudes of those countries and on inefficient governments and organizations.

In the late 1960s and early 1970s, an intellectual revolution occurred. Environmentalists had criticized the growth paradigm throughout the 1960s, but they were not taken very seriously at first. By the end of the 1960s, however, marine scientist Rachel Carson's book *Silent Spring* (Alfred A. Knopf, 1962) had worked its way into the public's consciousness. Carson's book traces the noticeable loss of birds to the use of pesticides. Her book made the middle and upper classes in the United States realize that pollution affects complex ecological systems in ways that put even the wealthy at risk. In 1968, Paul Ehrlich, a professor of population studies, published *The Population Bomb* (Ballantine Books), which states that overpopulation is the major problem facing mankind. This means that population has to be controlled or the human race might cause the collapse of the global ecosystems and the deaths of many humans. Ehrlich explained why he thought the devastation of the world was imminent: because the human population of the planet is about five times too large, and we're managing to support all these people at today's level of misery only by spending our capital, burning our fossil fuels, dispersing our mineral resources, and turning our fresh water into salt water. We have not only overpopulated but overstretched our environment. We are poisoning the ecological systems of the earth upon which we are ultimately dependent for all of our food, for all of our oxygen, and for all of our waste disposal. In 1973, *The Limits to Growth* (Universe) by Donella H. Meadows et al. was published. It presents a dynamic systems computer model for world economic, demographic, and environmental trends. When the computer model projected trends into the future, it predicted that the world would experience ecological collapse and population die-off unless population growth and economic activity were greatly reduced. This study was both attacked and defended, and the debate about the health of the world has been heated ever since.

Let us examine the population growth rates for the past, present, and future. At about A.D. 1, the world had about one-quarter billion people. It took about 1,650 years to double this number to one-half billion and 200 years to double the world population again to 1 billion by 1850. The next doubling took only about 80 years, and the last doubling took about 45 years (from 2 billion in 1930 to about 4 billion in 1975). The world population may double again to 8 billion sometime between 2020 and 2025. At the same time that population is growing, people are trying to get richer, which means consuming more, polluting more, and using more resources. Are all these trends threatening the carrying capacity of the planet and jeopardizing the prospects for future generations? In the following selections, Daniel Immerwahr warns that climate change presents a real and very dangerous crisis. Its impacts on the environment will be devastating and lead to much human suffering. It must be dealt with but nations are resisting appropriate actions because it is "going to hurt." Ramez Naam presents and acknowledges both the positive and negative trends in the planet but focuses on the miraculous coming results of innovations which will adequately address the environmental problems and most other problems. Environmental collapse and die-off will not occur. Ideas will save the planet.

YES ↵

Daniel Immerwahr

Growth vs. the Climate

The year 2013 was one of the ten hottest on record. So was 2010. So were 2009, 2007, 2006, 2005, 2003, 2002, and 1998. Last year, with its polar vortex and biting winter, seemed to bring relief to North America. Except it also brought temperatures of over 120°F to Australia, massive flooding to Malaysia, and the third harrowing year of drought to California. As it turns out, 2014 was the hottest single year since meteorologists started measuring in 1850.

By now, we've raised the average global temperature a little less than one degree Celsius since the beginning of the industrial revolution. The best predictions suggest that, if we go about our business as usual, we will raise it somewhere between four and six degrees by 2100. With the heat will also come side effects: fiercer and more frequent storms, droughts, acidifying oceans, melting glaciers, and the loss of species.

And the bad news is, that's not even the bad news. Although the altered climate is threatening in its own right—heat alone killed tens of thousands of Europeans in the lethal summer of 2003—the thing to really worry about is the infrastructure. Each drought, each megastorm, each scorching summer puts a strain on the complex systems that provide us with water, food, and power and that keep disease and disorder at bay. These systems can often endure a single crisis—one Sandy, one Katrina. The problem is what happens when the Sandys and Katrinas start coming back to back, piling up on each other. That's when the money runs out, the electricity goes off, and everyone starts wondering where to find water. If true catastrophe arrives, it will not come gradually—the frog in boiling water—but, as the historian Nils Gilman writes, "as a series of radical discontinuities—a series of bewildering 'oh shit' events."

Welcome to the future. Oh shit.

Those with long memories will know that this isn't the first time it felt like we were testing the earth's ability to support us. In 1968, the biologist Paul Ehrlich published *The Population Bomb*, which prophesied civilizational collapse for societies unable to rapidly bring down their birth rates. There were simply too many people, he argued, for the planet's dwindling supply of resources. Ehrlich got a vasectomy and preached birth control, though he also advocated for more extreme measures: compulsory sterilization, a ban on cars, and a tax on cribs. Internationally, he proposed "triage," aiding the countries that remained viable but writing off those, like India, that he saw as too far gone.

Remarkably, his message resounded. In 1969, a large oil spill off the coast of Santa Barbara yielded televised images of oil-drenched birds. Six months later, the massively polluted Cuyahoga River in Cleveland caught fire. The notion that humans were pressing on the limits of the natural world was becoming common sense. And as it did, Ehrlich became ubiquitous. He wrote for *Playboy* and *Penthouse*. He appeared, twenty times, as a guest on the *Tonight Show*. In 1970 alone, he delivered a hundred public lectures and appeared two hundred times on radio and television.

Looking back on the Age of Ehrlich, as it is wonderfully rendered in Paul Sabin's *The Bet*, two things stand out as surprises. The first is how seriously politicians across the spectrum took the matter. It was the Republican Richard Nixon who signed the National Environmental Policy Act on January 1, 1970—his first presidential act of the decade. The 1970s "absolutely must be the time when America pays its debt to the past by reclaiming the purity of its air, its water and our living environment," Nixon declared. "It is literally now or never."

The second surprise is how readily Ehrlich's message of self-denial was accepted. No one internalized it better than Jimmy Carter. "'More' is not necessarily 'better,'" Carter observed in his inaugural address, and he was determined to lead by example. He put solar panels up on the White House and turned the heat down. "My offices were so cold that I couldn't concentrate, and my staff was typing with gloves on," remembered First Lady Rosalynn Carter. "I pleaded with Jimmy to set the thermostats at 68 degrees but it didn't do any good." At his first meeting with the National Security Council, Carter announced, "This is the last warm meeting we'll have."

The belt-tightening and thermostat-lowering wasn't just a matter of personal restraint, of course. Carter governed in the shadow of the oil crisis. By the 1970s, oil-producing countries had discovered that they held enough power to dictate terms to the global economy. In 1973, after the United States sided with Israel in the Yom Kippur War, those countries first dramatically raised their prices and then boycotted the United States entirely, quadrupling the cost of oil. The economy came to a jarring halt. Coca-Cola announced that it would turn off its outdoor illuminated signs in fifty cities, beginning with the one in Times Square. The governor of Florida locked his car in his garage and started walking to work. The cover of *Newsweek* showed a shivering Uncle Sam, icicles dangling from his nose, staring forlornly into an empty horn of plenty. "Running Out of Everything," ran the headline.

But the country wasn't running out of everything, no matter how it seemed at the time. It was experiencing a temporary crunch. Ehrlich's prediction that growing populations would quickly outpace natural resources turned out to be wrong. He didn't count on declining birth rates (we now think that the global population will level off somewhere around nine billion). And he underestimated the abilities of markets to winnow out new resources—to encourage offshore drilling, for instance, when the stick-a-straw-in-the-ground method of extracting oil no longer sufficed. The past decades have shown industrial civilization to be more resilient, more adaptable, than Ehrlich foresaw.

They have also seen a turn away from the idea of limits. The Age of Ehrlich ended with the 1980 election, when Ronald Reagan defeated Carter in a landslide. "They tell us we must learn to live with less, and teach our children that their lives will be less full and prosperous than ours have been," complained Reagan as he announced his candidacy. "I don't believe that. And I don't believe you do either." Upon taking office, he took the solar panels down and turned the heat back up. He also set about dismantling the environmental regulations of the Nixon, Ford, and Carter years, which he regarded as impediments to the economy.

That basic logic has characterized U.S. politics since. Not every politician today has inherited Reagan's deep hostility to environmentalism, but few would dare to dissent from the central post-1980 orthodoxy: growth is sacred.

This is not, it is important to note, a partisan issue. Growth is the national creed and has been, with some wavering in the 1970s, for at least a century. It is not hard to see why. Not only has it given us long lives and staggering

wealth, it's also protected us from hard political choices. Are workers striking? Give them raises. Are developing countries being difficult? Send foreign aid. Since the late nineteenth century, the United States has boasted the world's largest economy, and its affluence has insulated it from many of the shocks that other nations have had to grimace their way through. Its dependence on growth seems to have gotten even stronger with time. Every president now inherits, upon election, two above-all-else directives: don't let terrorists attack U.S. soil, and don't interfere with growth. It's unclear which of the two ranks higher.

Growth is not just politically convenient; we're now learning its importance for the maintenance of a fair society. French economist Thomas Piketty's recent treatise *Capital in the Twenty-First Century* offers the most thorough account of the way in which growth has historically reduced inequality. For Piketty, the relationship can be boiled down to a simple formula: a society risks increasing inequality when, over the long term, its rate of return on capital exceeds its overall growth rate—or, in Piketty-speak, when $r > g$. In the past century, Piketty finds, there were two great motors of equality. The first was war, which tended to bring down the rate of return on capital. The second, and the more obvious, was growth. When an economy is growing, the power of inherited wealth is diluted. When it is not, the super-rich need only to avoid squandering their fortunes in order to remain super-rich. You lose growth, you get a plutocracy.

Not surprisingly, all of this growth-mania has influenced the terms in which global warming is addressed. In June 2013, in his most forthright speech on the topic since assuming the presidency, Barack Obama advised the country to brace itself for rising seas and "severe" storms. But when it came to the economy, the speech turned positively upbeat. "The old rules may say we can't protect our environment and promote economic growth at the same time," the president said, but "it's not an either/or; it's a both/and." There is, he underscored, "no contradiction between a sound environment and strong economic growth." For illustration, Obama pointed enthusiastically to a recent statement on climate change signed by more than 500 businesses, including General Motors, Apple, Starbucks, Microsoft, Nestlé, Nike, and Disney. "Tackling climate change is one of America's greatest economic opportunities of the 21st century," it reads. In doing so, it continues, "we will maintain our way of life and remain a true superpower in a competitive world."

These views have the whiff of the press release about them, but they are also the doctrines of serious economists. Joseph Stiglitz, a Nobel laureate and the author of one of the most-used textbooks in economics, has warned that, in ignoring global warming, the world is "writing the script for its own doomsday scenario." And yet his most recent book treats climate change as a side issue, something to be adjusted for with a few (vaguely specified) policy shifts. Nothing about the crisis seems to conflict with Stiglitz's "growth agenda," a program for "more opportunity, a higher total national income, a stronger democracy, and higher living standards for most individuals." The economist and *New York Times* writer Paul Krugman, also a Nobel laureate, sees it similarly. Global warming is the "road to catastrophe," he writes, but turning off that road won't be particularly difficult. "There's no reason we can't become richer while reducing our impact on the environment."

Said that way, of course it's true. It's perfectly possible to have an economy that greens as it grows, weaning itself off fossil fuels with time. The problem is that time is just what we don't have. The majority of the world's governments have set 2°C as an upper limit on warming by the end of the century. There's a vigorous debate about whether even that limit is too risky but, either way, staying below it will require a sudden, severe curtailment of carbon emissions in rich countries.

Reducing carbon emissions by 1 percent is difficult—it has rarely happened without a recession. A determined nation capable of swiftly and smoothly switching to renewable energy *might* be able to cut back by as much as 4 percent while still growing. But how much do we actually need to reduce emissions to meet the 2°C target? Kevin Anderson and Alice Bows-Larkin of the Tyndall Centre for Climate Change Research in Britain have crunched the numbers. To keep warming under two degrees, they argue, all rich countries would need to simultaneously cut their emissions around 8 to 10 percent a *year*, starting yesterday. Calculations such as these have led the former executive secretary of the UN Framework Convention on Climate Change to conclude that the only remaining way to stay under two degrees is to "shut down the whole global economy."

Such talk conjures up visions of government rationing. A more feasible way to cut back, however, would be to place a large tax on emissions and let the market handle the rest. William Nordhaus, the former president of the American Economics Association, regards the carbon tax as a test of conviction: any politician who does not propose raising the price of carbon, no matter how eloquently she speaks about the danger of global warming, is "not really serious." By that measure, few of our leaders are genuinely committed to the issue. They know that taxing carbon at the requisite rate is not the way to win votes.

Nor is it the way to build a movement. Protesters fare best when they promise a better world: less injustice or more abundance. But environmentalists, who tend to speak instead of limits, have had little to offer. In the 1970s, they advocated a "steady-state economy" and "zero growth." Today, it is worse. "Econocide" is a word that sometimes gets tossed around: a sharp, intentional economic depression in deference to ecological reality. "Degrowth" is also frequently heard. Neither sounds particularly attractive, though the logic behind them is clear enough. If your car is hurtling toward a brick wall, it's better to hit the brakes than to let the wall stop the car.

Enter Naomi Klein, stage left. Klein, a journalist and frequent contributor to the *Nation*, is not a lifelong environmentalist. Rather, she came to the issue sideways, as an anti-corporate activist and opponent of unfettered markets. She nonetheless has the zeal of a convert. She sits on the board of 350.org, the country's leading climate change organization. With her latest book, *This Changes Everything*, Klein has set out to write the bible for the movement.

What turned Klein's politics green was not just, as one might think, a sense of urgency concerning the fate of the planet. It was a sense of possibility. "The climate moment offers an overarching narrative in which everything from the fight for good jobs to justice for migrants to reparations for historical wrongs like slavery and colonialism can all become part of the grand project of building a nontoxic, shockproof economy." Climate action, she continues, is not only necessary to stop global warming, but promises "a future far more exciting than anything else currently on offer."

It is an extraordinary claim. Usually, we think of environmentalism as being unconnected to causes such as racial justice, fair wages, immigration reform, and global equality—or perhaps in conflict with them. But for Klein they are all linked struggles against a common enemy. At first she identifies the foe as "contemporary, hyper-globalized capitalism"—her familiar bête noire—but over the course of her book she reaches deeper. The problem, fundamentally, is "extractivism," the "nonreciprocal, dominance-based relationship with the earth, one of purely taking," that wrecks the planet and treats both humans and nature as commodities.

Klein hopes that the threat of global warming will be serious enough to, finally, rip extractivism out by its roots. She suggests that the only way to avert catastrophe is to transform our society wholesale—to win, essentially, everything that leftists have been demanding for decades, all at once. Our salvation, as she envisions it, will include some combination of a multi-trillion-dollar "Marshall Plan for the Earth," guaranteed incomes, reparations for slavery and empire, healthier food, open borders, indigenous land rights, reduced global inequality, new subways, shorter work weeks, and a social safety net extensive enough to cover the cost of in vitro fertilization for anyone wanting a child.

Klein, in other words, not only rejects the idea that combating global warming means we will have to make do with less—what she calls the "grinding logic of austerity"—but goes to the opposite extreme, describing the job ahead as some sort of progressive shopping spree. "We *can* afford to build a decent, inclusive society," she writes. Part of her logic is that a "decent" society is not necessarily an expensive one. As environmentalists have argued for decades, many of the things that make us happiest, like neighbors and nature, are cheap enough. Klein thus imagines an economy based less on goods and more on services.

Yet many of the things she calls for *do* clearly require material investments. To get them, Klein proposes a radical redistribution of resources; corporate profits, military spending, and the wealth of the 1 percent are her prime targets. In essence, it's a shoot-the-moon strategy. Tackling climate change on its own would entail harrowing cutbacks. But throw in tax hikes for corporations, huge cuts to the military, and an assault on the oligarchy and suddenly things don't look so bad. For the broad lower and middle swaths of the population, they start to look—well, they start to look a lot like growth.

This approach allows Klein to escape the bind that has trapped the movement in the past. The cartoonist Walt Kelly captured the dour spirit of 1970s environmentalism when he had his character Pogo survey a badly polluted landscape and conclude, "We have met the enemy and he is us." Not so for Klein. Her book contains little by way of self-flagellation. In it, she offhandedly describes doing all of the things that make environmentalists cringe: she moves out of the city, she drives and flies, she has a child, she eats meat.

In place of guilt, Klein offers rage—against the GOP, the military, neoliberals, imperialists, corporate-sponsored environmental groups, and extractivists of every stripe. Her true wrath, though, is reserved for the fossil-fuel industry. "Lots of companies do rotten things in the course of their business," she writes. But "with the fossil-fuel industry, wrecking the planet is their business model. It's what they do." Stopping climate change is, then, first and foremost a matter of battling energy companies. As Klein's comrade at 350.org, Bill McKibben, puts it: "We have met the enemy, and they is Shell."

Politically, this new outlook has begun to bear fruit. Last September, about a third of a million protestors converged on New York City for the People's Climate March, making it the largest climate protest there has ever been. Climate activism is no longer just a scattered coalition of scientists and woodland cranks. As it has mastered the us-versus-them cadences of street protests, it's begun to transform itself into something more substantial: a social movement.

But, in switching from "the enemy is us" to "the enemy is Shell," has it also lost something crucial? Energy companies undoubtedly have much to answer for, but they are only profitable because we buy from them. It is hard to square Klein's sense of urgency about the climate crisis with her insistence that ordinary North Americans—including just about everyone reading this article—needn't give up anything in order to address it.

A global perspective is useful here. The average person in the United States earns about $53,000 a year (it's only slightly less in Klein's home country of Canada: $52,000). Given that $34,000 is the cut-off line for the top percentile of world income, many North Americans fall easily into the global 1 percent. And, since economic activity translates roughly into greenhouse gas production, it's no surprise that the United States and Canada have among the highest per-capita carbon emissions of all the large countries, ranking just below Saudi Arabia.

Then consider the other side of things. Bangladesh contributes very little to global warming; the average carbon footprint there is about 2 percent the size of the average U.S. footprint. And yet low-lying, wet, hot, and densely populated Bangladesh promises to be one of the worst-hit countries. If warming continues on schedule, tens of millions of Bangladeshis will simply have to flee the country—to where, we don't know—in the coming years. Shouldn't North Americans, many of whom are members of the global 1 percent, take some responsibility for that? And shouldn't we stop pretending that it's going to be easy and fun?

We've made painful cuts before—but only when it appeared that wrecking the planet was going to break the bank as well. In the 1970s, predictions of future disaster were undergirded by a very real economic threat: the skyrocketing cost of oil. It's not hard to learn restraint when your energy bill has just tripled. Today, we're nowhere near running out of fossil fuels. Gasoline pumps at an obliging price and energy companies are growing ever more deft at sucking carbon from the earth's crust. If there is another oil crisis, it'll have to be self-inflicted.

Cutting back without having any pressing economic need to do so is possible, but it will require resolve. And that's the problem with promising ordinary North Americans—as Klein, Krugman, and General Motors and Starbucks are doing—that they can fight climate change while getting *more* of the things they want.

For politicians to take the necessary steps to bring warming to a halt, they will have to be convinced of two things. First, that voters want action taken. Second, that those voters are willing to bear the consequences of that action. If our representatives only hear the first message but never the second, they will rightly conclude that the thing to do is to condemn global warming but do nothing about it. Which is precisely what they are currently doing.

It would be nice to hear it straight for once. Global warming is real, it's here, and it's mind-bogglingly dangerous. How bad it gets—literally, the degree—depends on how quickly the most profligate countries rein in their emissions. Averting catastrophe will thus require places like the United States and Canada to make drastic cutbacks, bringing their consumption more closely in line with the planetary average. Such cuts can be made more or less fairly, and the richest really ought to pay the most, but the crucial thing is that they are made. Because, above all, stopping climate change means giving up on growth.

That will be hard. Not only will our standards of living almost certainly drop, but it's likely that the very quality of our society—equality, safety, and trust—will decline, too. That's not something to be giddy about, but it's still a price that those of us living in affluent countries should prepare to pay. Because however difficult it is to slow down, flooding Bangladesh cannot be an option. In other words, we can and should act. It's just going to hurt.

DANIEL IMMERWAHR is an Assistant Professor of History at Northwestern University who has written several books including *Thinking Small,* (Harvard, 2015)

Ramez Naam

How Innovation Could Save the Planet

Ideas may be our greatest natural resource, says a computer scientist and futurist. He argues that the world's most critical challenges—including population growth, peak oil, climate change, and limits to growth—could be met by encouraging innovation.

The Best of Times: Unprecedented Prosperity

There are many ways in which we are living in the most wonderful age ever. We can imagine we are heading toward a sort of science-fiction Utopia, where we are incredibly rich and incredibly prosperous, and the planet is healthy. But there are other reasons to fear that we're headed toward a dystopia of sorts.

On the positive side, life expectancy has been rising for the last 150 years, and faster since the early part of the twentieth century in the developing world than it has in the rich world. Along with that has come a massive reduction in poverty. The most fundamental empowerer of humans—education—has also soared, not just in the rich world, but throughout the world.

Another great empowerer of humanity is connectivity: Access to information and access to communication both have soared. The number of mobile phones on the planet was effectively zero in the early 1990s, and now it's in excess of 4 billion. More than three-quarters of humanity, in the span of one generation, have gotten access to connectivity that, as my friend Peter Diamandis likes to say, is greater than any president before 1995 had. A reasonably well-off person in India or in Nigeria has better access to information than Ronald Reagan did during most of his career.

With increased connectivity has come an increase in democracy. As people have gotten richer, more educated, more able to access information, and more able to communicate, they have demanded more control over the places where they live. The fraction of nations that are functional democracies is at an all-time high in this world—more than double what it was in the 1970s, with the collapse of the Soviet Union.

Economically, the world is a more equal place than it has been in decades. In the West, and especially in the United States, we hear a lot about growing inequality, but on a global scale, the opposite is true. As billions are rising out of poverty around the world, the global middle classes are catching up with the global rich.

In many ways, this is the age of the greatest human prosperity, freedom, and potential that has ever been on the face of this planet. But in other ways, we are facing some of the largest risks ever.

The Worst of Times: The Greatest Risks

At its peak, the ancient Mayan city of Tikal was a metropolis, a city of 200,000 people inside of a civilization of about 20 million people. Now, if you walk around any Mayan city, you see mounds of dirt. That's because these structures were all abandoned by about the mid-900s AD. We know now what happened: The Mayan civilization grew too large. It overpopulated. To feed themselves, they had to convert forest into farmland. They chopped down all of the forest. That, in turn, led to soil erosion. It also worsened drought, because trees, among other things, trap moisture and create a precipitation cycle.

When that happened, and was met by some normal (not human-caused) climate change, the Mayans found they didn't have enough food. They exhausted their primary energy supply, which is food. That in turn led to more violence in their society and ultimately to a complete collapse.

The greatest energy source for human civilization today is fossil fuels. Among those, none is more important than oil. In 1956, M. King Hubbert looked at production in individual oil fields and predicted that the United States would see the peak of its oil production in 1970 or so, and then drop. His prediction largely came true: Oil production went up but did peak in the 1970s, then plummeted.

Oil production has recently gone up in the United States a little bit, but it's still just barely more than half of what it was in its peak in the 1970s.

Hubbert also predicted that the global oil market would peak in about 2000, and for a long time he looked very foolish. But it now has basically plateaued. Since 2004, oil production has increased by about 4%, whereas in the 1950s it rose by about 4% every three months.

We haven't hit a peak; oil production around the world is still rising a little bit. It's certainly not declining, but we do appear to be near a plateau; supply is definitely rising more slowly than demand. Though there's plenty of oil in the ground, the oil that remains is in smaller fields, further from shore, under lower pressure, and harder to pump out.

Water is another resource that is incredibly precious to us. The predominant way in which we use water is through the food that we eat: 70% of the freshwater that humanity uses goes into agriculture.

The Ogallala Aquifer, the giant body of freshwater under the surface of the Earth in the Great Plains of the United States, is fossil water left from the melting and the retreat of glaciers in the end of the last Ice Age, 12,000–14,000 years ago. Its refill time is somewhere between 5,000 and 10,000 years from normal rainfall. Since 1960, we've drained between a third and a half of the water in this body, depending on what estimate you look at. In some areas, the water table is dropping about three feet per year.

If this was a surface lake in the United States or Canada, and people saw that happening, they'd stop it. But because it's out of sight, it's just considered a resource that we can tap. And indeed, in the north Texas area, wells are starting to fail already, and farms are being abandoned in some cases, because they can't get to the water that they once did.

Perhaps the largest risk of all is climate change. We've increased the temperature of the planet by about 2°F in the last 130 years, and that rate is accelerating. This is primarily because of the carbon dioxide we've put into the atmosphere, along with methane and nitrous oxide. CO_2 levels, now at over 390 parts per million, are the highest they've been in about 15 million years. Ice cores go back at least a million years, and we know that they're the highest they've been in that time. . . .

Over the next century, the seas are expected to rise about 3 to 6 feet. Most of that actually will not be melting glaciers; it's thermal expansion: As the ocean gets warmer, it gets a little bit bigger.

But 3 to 6 feet over a century doesn't sound like that big a deal to us, so we think of that as a distant problem. The reality is that there's a more severe problem

with climate change: its impact on the weather and on agriculture.

In 2003, Europe went through its worst heat wave since 1540. Ukraine lost 75% of its wheat crop. In 2009, China had a once-in-a-century level drought; in 2010 they had another once-in-a-century level drought. That's twice. Wells that had given water continuously since the fifteenth century ran dry. When those rains returned, when the water that was soaked up by the atmosphere came back down, it came down on Pakistan, and half of Pakistan was under water in the floods of 2010. An area larger than Germany was under water.

Warmer air carries more water. Every degree Celsius that you increase the temperature value of air, it carries 7% more water. But it doesn't carry that water uniformly. It can suck water away from one place and then deliver it in a deluge in another place. So both the droughts are up and flooding is up simultaneously, as precipitation becomes more lumpy and more concentrated.

In Russia's 2010 heat wave, 55,000 people died, 11,000 of them in Moscow alone. In 2011, the United States had the driest 10-month period ever in the American South, and Texas saw its worst wildfires ever. And 2012 was the worst drought in the United States since the Dust Bowl—the corn crop shrank by 20%. . . .

Ideas as a Resource Expander, Resource Preserver, and Waste Reducer

. . . Ideas can reduce resource use. I can give you many other examples. In the United States, the amount of energy used on farms per calorie grown has actually dropped by about half since the 1970s. That's in part because we now only use about a tenth of the energy to create synthetic nitrogen fertilizer, which is an important input.

The amount of food that you can grow per drop of water has roughly doubled since the 1980s. In wheat, it's actually more than tripled since 1960. The amount of water that we use in the United States per person has dropped by about a third since the 1970s, after rising for decades. As agriculture has gotten more efficient, we're using less water per person. So, again, ideas can reduce resource use. . . .

One more thing that ideas can do is transform waste into value. In places like Germany and Japan, people are mining landfills. Japan estimates that its landfills alone contain 10-year supplies of gold and rare-earth minerals for the world market. Alcoa estimates that the world's landfills contain a 15-year supply of aluminum. So there's tremendous value.

When we throw things away, they're not destroyed. If we "consume" things like aluminum, we're not really consuming it, we're rearranging it. We're changing where it's located. And in some cases, the concentration of these resources in our landfills is actually higher than it was in our mines. What it takes is energy and technology to get that resource back out and put it back into circulation.

Ideas for Stretching the Limits

So ideas can reduce resource use, can find substitutes for scarce resources, and can transform waste into value. In that context, what are the limits to growth?

Is there a population limit? Yes, there certainly is, but it doesn't look like we're going to hit that. Projections right now are that, by the middle of this century, world population will peak between 9 billion and 10 billion, and then start to decline. In fact, we'll be talking much more about the graying of civilization, and perhaps underpopulation—too-low birthrates on a current trend.

What about physical resources? Are there limits to physical resource use on this planet? Absolutely. It really is a finite planet. But where are those limits?

To illustrate, let's start with energy. This is the most important resource that we use, in many ways. But when we consider all the fossil fuels that humanity uses today—all the oil, coal, natural gas, and so on—it pales in comparison to a much larger resource, all around us, which is the amount of energy coming in from our Sun every day.

The amount of energy from sunlight that strikes the top of the atmosphere is about 10,000 times as much as the energy that we use from fossil fuels on a daily basis. Ten seconds of sunlight hitting the Earth is as much energy as humanity uses in an entire day; one hour of sunlight hitting the Earth provides as much energy to the planet as a whole as humanity uses from all sources combined in one year.

This is an incredibly abundant resource. It manifests in many ways. It heats the atmosphere differentially, creating winds that we can capture for wind power. It evaporates water, which leads to precipitation elsewhere, which turns into things like rivers and waterfalls, which we can capture as hydropower.

But by far the largest fraction of it—more than half—is photons hitting the surface of the Earth. Those are so abundant that, with one-third of 1% of the Earth's land area, using current technology of about 14%-efficient solar cells, we could capture enough electricity to power all of current human needs.

The problem is not the abundance of the energy; the problem is cost. Our technology is primitive. Our technology for building solar cells is similar to our technology for manufacturing computer chips. They're built on silicon wafers in clean rooms at high temperatures, and so they're very, very expensive.

But innovation has been dropping that cost tremendously. Over the last 30 years, we've gone from a watt of solar power costing $20 to about $1. That's a factor of 20. We roughly drop the cost of solar by one-half every decade, more or less. That means that, in the sunniest parts of the world today, solar is now basically at parity in cost, without subsidies, with coal and natural gas. Over the next 12–15 years, that will spread to most of the planet. That's incredibly good news for us.

Of course, we don't just use energy while the Sun is shining. We use energy at night to power our cities; we use energy in things like vehicles that have to move and that have high energy densities. Both of these need storage, and today's storage is actually a bigger challenge than capturing energy. But there's reason to believe that we can tackle the storage problem, as well.

For example, consider lithium ion batteries—the batteries that are in your laptop, your cell phone, and so on. The demand to have longer-lasting devices drove tremendous innovations in these batteries in the 1990s and the early part of the 2000s. Between 1991 and 2005, the cost of storage in lithium ion batteries dropped by about a factor of nine, and the density of storage—how much energy you can store in an ounce of battery—increased by a little over double in that time. If we do that again, we would be at the point where grid-scale storage is affordable and we can store that energy overnight. Our electric vehicles have ranges similar to the range you can get in a gasoline-powered vehicle.

This is a tall order. This represents perhaps tens of billions of dollars in R&D, but it is something that is possible and for which there is precedent.

Another approach being taken is turning energy into fuel. When you use a fuel such as gasoline, it's not really an energy source. It's an energy carrier, an energy storage system, if you will. You can store a lot of energy in a very small amount.

Today, two pioneers in genome sequencing—Craig Venter and George Church—both have founded companies to create next-generation biofuels. What they're both leveraging is that gene-sequencing cost is the fastest quantitative area of progress on the planet.

What they're trying to do is engineer microorganisms that consume CO_2, sunlight, and sugar and actually excrete fuel as a byproduct. If we could do this, maybe just 1% of the Earth's surface—or a thirtieth of what we use for agriculture—could provide all the liquid fuels that we need. We would conveniently grow algae on saltwater and waste water, so biofuel production wouldn't compete for freshwater. And the possible yields are vast if we can get there.

If we can crack energy, we can crack everything else: . . .

* Food. Can we grow enough food? Between now and 2050, we have to increase food yield by about 70%. Is that possible? I think it is. In industrialized nations, food yields are already twice what they are in the world as a whole. That's because we have irrigation, tractors, better pesticides, and so on. Given such energy and wealth, we already know that we can grow enough food to feed the planet.

Another option that's probably cheaper would be to leverage some things that nature's already produced. What most people don't know is that the yield of corn per acre and in calories is about 70% higher than the yield of wheat. Corn is a C_4 photosynthesis crop: It uses a different way of turning sunlight and CO_2 into sugars that evolved only 30 million years ago. Now, scientists around the world are working on taking these C_4 genes from crops like corn and transplanting them into wheat and rice, which could right away increase the yield of those staple grains by more than 50%.

Physical limits do exist, but they are extremely distant. We cannot grow exponentially in our physical resource use forever, but that point is still at least centuries in the future. It's something we have to address eventually, but it's not a problem that's pressing right now.

* Wealth. One thing that people don't appreciate very much is that wealth has been decoupling from physical resource use on this planet. Energy use per capita is going up, CO_2 emissions per capita have been going up a little bit, but they are both widely outstripped by the amount of wealth that we're creating. That's because we can be more efficient in everything—using less energy per unit of food grown, and so on.

This again might sound extremely counterintuitive, but let me give you one concrete example of how that happens. Compare the ENIAC—which in the 1940s was the first digital computer ever created—to an iPhone. An iPhone is billions of times smaller, uses billions of times less energy, and has billions of times more computing power than ENIAC. If you tried to create an iPhone using ENIAC technology, it would be a cube a mile on the side, and it would use more electricity than the state of California. And it wouldn't have access to the Internet, because you'd have to invent that, as well.

This is what I mean when I say ideas are the ultimate resource. The difference between an ENIAC and an iPhone is that the iPhone is embodied knowledge that allows you to do more with less resources. That phenomenon is not limited to high tech. It's everywhere around us.

So ideas are the ultimate resource. They're the only resource that accumulates over time. Our store of knowledge is actually larger than in the past, as opposed to all physical resources.

Challenges Ahead for Innovation

Today we are seeing a race between our rate of consumption and our rate of innovation, and there are multiple challenges. One challenge is the Darwinian process, survival of the fittest. In areas like green tech, there will be hundreds and even thousands of companies founded, and 99% of them will go under. That is how innovation happens. . . .

Ramez Naam is a computer scientist, author, and former Microsoft executive. He was involved in the development of widely used software products such as Microsoft Internet Explorer and Microsoft Outlook. He was the CEO of Apex Nanotechnologies, a company involved in developing nanotechnology.

EXPLORING THE ISSUE

Is Humankind Dangerously Harming the Environment?

Critical Thinking and Reflection

1. What is the evidence that food production is inadequate for the current world population and probably will become even less adequate in the next two decades?
2. What current trends are worsening world agriculture's ability to keep total food production on pace with world population and increasingly rich (more meat) diets?
3. How are the world's major biosystems declining over the past four decades: croplands, grasslands, forests, and oceans?
4. What are the likely impacts of global warming over the next half century? What are the possible but debatable impacts of global warming?

Is There Common Ground?

There is common ground in the belief that the environment is worsening in many ways. The disagreement is about how serious these problems are and whether market responses to higher prices along with technological innovations will largely take care of them. Most environmentalists, however, cannot believe these problems can be taken care of so easily. In general, conservation actions cost three times the value of the benefits they bring. This inhibits their application if market forces determine actions. Government regulations can force actions that polluters and other environmental abusers would resist. But powerful people and the corporations do a good job of preventing tough regulations and policies. So far this train of thought suggests that even if solutions are available, they may be difficult to institute, so the problems are likely to worsen.

Immerwahr warns that the world has had 30–40 years to make the needed changes and has done little. Now it must act at wartime speed or environmental crises are possible. Naam is not worried about current problems because he believes that new ideas and technologies will deal with the problems, save the planet, and bring worldwide affluence.

Additional Resources

The issue of the state of the environment and prospects for the future has been hotly debated for over 40 years, with little chance of ending soon. Two key issues define this debate. First, what are the potential impacts of global warming? Second, what are the net effects of increasing resource use and future agricultural technologies? Will they be able to supply and feed the world even as increasing millions will demand more goods and richer diets (more meat).

For works that argue that global warming and environmental damage are major world problems, see the International Panel on Climate Change, *Fifth Assessment Report: Climate Change* (2014); World Wildlife Federation Report 2014, *Living Planet Report* (2014); United Nations Environment Programme, *Global Environmental Outlook 5: Environment for the Future We Want;* U.S. Climate Change Program, U.S. Climate Assessment, *Climate Change Impacts on the United States* (2014); R. Paul and Anne H. Ehrlich, "Can a Collapse of Global Civilization Be Avoided?" *Proceedings of the Royal Society* (January 9, 2013); Planet Under Pressure March 26–29, 2012, London, *State of the Planet Declaration: International Scientific Community Issues First "State of the Planet Declaration";* Mark Hertsgaard, *Hot: Living Through the Next Fifty Years on Earth* (Houghton Mifflin Harcourt, 2011); Charles Derber, *Greed to Green: Solving Climate Change and Remaking the Economy* (Paradigm, 2010); and Jonathan A. Foley, "Can We Feed the World and Sustain the Planet"? *Scientific American* (November 2011).

An early crusader against increasing AGW (anthropomorphic global warming) was Al Gore with his early book called *The Earth in the Balance.* His more recent book is *An Inconvenient Truth: The Planetary Emergency of Global Warming and What We Can Do About It* (Rodale Press, 2006). Antagonists to the global warming thesis that human activities are a major cause of global warming include Steven Moore, "State of the Planet: Its Better Than Ever," *Washington Times* (April 26, 2015); S. Fred Singer and Dennis T. Avery, *Unstoppable Global Warming: Every 1,500 Years* (Rowman & Littlefield, 2007); Nongovernmental International Panel on Climate Change, *Climate Change Reconsidered II: Biological Impacts* (2014); The Right Climate Stuff Research Team, *Anthropogenic Global Warming Science Assessment Report* (April 2013); Roy W. Spencer, *The Great Global Warming Blunder: How Mother Nature Fooled the World's Top Climate Scientists* (Encounter Books, 2010). For the political side of the global warming issue, see Raymond S. Bradley, *Global Warming and Political Intimidation: How Politicians Cracked Down on Scientists as the Earth Heated Up* (University of Massachusetts Press, 2011). Two works that focus on what to do about global warming are Robert K. Musil, *Hope for a Heated Planet: How Americans Are Fighting Global Warming and Building a Better Future* (Rutgers University Press, 2009) and William D. Nordhaus, *A Question of Balance: Weighing the Options on Global Warming Policies* (Yale University Press, 2008).

On food production issues and agriculture technologies, see Lester R. Brown, *On the Edge: How to Prevent Environmental and Economic Collapse* (Earth Policy Institute, 2011) and *Plan B 4.0: Mobilizing to Save Civilization* (W. W. Norton, 2009). A work that fears that population growth and human interventions in the environment have dangerous consequences for the future of mankind is Richard A. Matthew, ed., *Global Environmental Change and Human Society* (MIT Press, 2010). Since environmental changes could have devastating effects, many have proposed solutions to these problems. The major term for these changes is "sustainability."

The following works suggest paths to sustainability, most of which require dramatic changes: James Gustave Speth, *The Bridge at the Edge of the World: Capitalism, the Environment, and Crossing from Crisis to Sustainability* (Yale University Press, 2008); Charles J. Kibert et al., *Working Toward Sustainability: Ethical Decision Making in a Technological World* (Wiley, 2012); Russ Beaton and Chris Maser, *Economics and Ecology: United for a Sustainable World* (CRC Press, 2012); Robin Hahnel, *Green Economics: Confronting the Ecological Crisis* (M. E. Sharpe, 2011); Ian Chambers and John Humble, *Developing a Plan for the Planet: A Business Plan for Sustainable Living* (Gower Publishing, 2011); Jennifer Clapp and Peter Dauvergne, *Paths to a Green World: The Political Economy of the Global Environment* (MIT Press, 2011); Costas Panayotakis, *Remaking Scarcity: From Capitalist Inefficiency to Economic Democracy* (Fernwood, 2011); and Milissa Leach et al., *Dynamic Sustainabilities: Technology, Environment, Social Justice* (Earthscan, 2010).

Worldwatch Institute publishes an important series on environmental problems, which includes two annuals: *State of the World* and *Vital Signs*.

Internet References . . .

Sociology—Study Sociology Online

http://edu.learnsoc.org/

Sociology Web Resources

www.mhhe.com/socscience/sociology/resources/index.htm

Sociosite

www.topsite.com/goto/sociosite.net

Socioweb

www.topsite.com/goto/socioweb.com

Selected, Edited, and with Issue Framing Material by:
Kurt Finsterbusch, *University of Maryland, College Park*

ISSUE

Should America Seek the Role of World Hegemon or World Leader?

YES: **Salvatore Babones**, from "The Once and Future Hegemon," *The National Interest* (2015)

NO: **Will Ruger**, from "The Case for Realism and Restraint," *Reason* (2015)

Learning Outcomes

After reading this issue, you will be able to:

- Understand the major views on the proper role for the United States in the world.
- Estimate the military and financial power of the United States relative to the other nations of the world.
- Understand the costs and benefits of taking the role of world hegemon power.
- Understand the costs and benefits of sharing the role of world leader.
- Explain how international terrorism affects America's role as world leader.

ISSUE SUMMARY

YES: Salvatore Babones, an associate professor of sociology and social policy, argues that America has been the hegemonic power since the collapse of the Soviet Union and is still the hegemonic power even though Obama is not currently asserting this power. We work with other countries but none of them are near us in military or economic power.

NO: Will Ruger, an associate professor of political science, agrees that America stands alone in terms of power but advocates restraint in the use of that power. Our goals are better achieved when we share power.

What is the proper role for America in the world today? Some vehemently advocate that the United States should be the world leader and project its power throughout the world. This would require building up its military and being more aggressive in promoting our interests around the world. The other view is represented by the Obama administration, which is not interested in being the world's policeman but tries to work with other countries to contain radicals, terrorists, and warring states or groups. Obama wants to assist the transition to greater democracy, international harmony, and use force as a last resort.

The Project for the New American Century (PNAC) was created in 1997 to promote the forceful world leader view. It declares:

As the 20th century draws to a close, the United States stands as the world's most preeminent power. Having led the West to victory in the Cold War, America faces an opportunity and a challenge: Does the United States have the vision to build upon the achievement of past decades? Does the United States have the resolve to shape a new century favorable to American principles and interests?

[What we require is] a military that is strong and ready to meet both present and future challenges; a foreign policy that boldly and purposefully promotes American principles abroad; and national leadership that accepts the United States' global responsibilities. Of course, the United States must be prudent in how it exercises its power. But we cannot safely avoid the responsibilities of global leadership or the costs that are associated with its exercise.

America has a vital role in maintaining peace and security in Europe, Asia, and the Middle East. If we shirk our responsibilities, we invite challenges to our fundamental interests. The history of the 20th century should have taught us that it is important to shape circumstances before crises emerge, and to meet threats before they become dire. The history of the past century should have taught us to embrace the cause of American leadership.

—From the Project's founding
Statement of Principles

When Bush became president the men who participated in PNAC became leaders in the Pentagon and the White House and with the 9/11 terrorist attack they had the occasion to put their plan into action. Dick Cheney was a founding member along with Defense Secretary Donald Rumsfeld and many other Bush leaders. On September 20, 2001, Bush released the "National Security Strategy of the United States of America," which drew heavily from PNAC documents. It seems clear to many commentators that the Bush administration started carrying out the PNAC doctrine in response to 9/11. The attacks on Afghanistan and Iraq carried out the PNAC plan for American world leadership.

The Obama administration sought to reduce force in both countries with considerable public support. The wars had cost many American lives and economic resources with little or no gains. Hatred toward America increased around the world and our leadership was declining. With the Arab Spring, America avoided boots on the ground and built and worked with a coalition of Arab states. Obama has tried hard not to send troops to fight ISIS. It is likely that America will be drawn into a bigger role fighting ISIS but America's reluctance is the opposite of the PNAC doctrine. Public opinion strongly supports the restraint view of American power. In 2013 the Pew Research Center found that 72 percent favored the "shared leadership role" for America leadership while only 12 percent favored the "single world Leader" role and 12 percent favored "no leadership role."

The above discussion focuses on the military role of America. Another major role is in the economic sphere where massive changes are happening quickly. Globalization is rapidly occurring. Globalization stands for worldwide processes, activities, and institutions. It involves world markets, world finance, world communications, world media, world religions, world popular culture, world rights movements, world drug trade, etc. America's role in these areas has declined significantly in the past 25 years because the economies of other countries have grown so much. The focus of most commentators is on the world economy, which today spreads financial crisis from the United States to the rest of the world. Many believe, however, that globalization promises strong growth in world wealth in the long run. Critics focus on the world economy's negative impacts on workers' wages, environmental protections and regulations, national and local cultures, and vulnerability to economic crises. One thing everyone agrees on is that the impacts of globalization are gigantic. The statistics are mind-boggling. Global trade has grown over 2,000 percent since 1950 and now is over $15 trillion annually. Total international investment exceeds $25 trillion. Multinational corporations dominate global commerce and the 500 largest account for annual sales of over $15 trillion. Another fact that all agree on is that America and its businesses, media, and culture are still at the center of the globalized world. This normally ensures that America gains more than its proportional share of the benefits. But America's centrality is declining and it could be debated whether that is good or bad.

It may be hard to determine the net effects of globalization and American's declining role in this process but we can easily identify many of the benefits or costs that people around the world have experienced. People are communicating by cell phones and Internet around the world. TV and the web bring events from all corners of the world into our living rooms or on our iPods. As a result we feel much more interconnected. Furthermore, we have an abundance of goods at low prices. So each of us personally enjoys many benefits. On the other hand workers lose jobs to cheap foreign workers as companies relocate or invest abroad. World interconnectedness makes us feel more vulnerable to foreign enemies. I have several times had foreigners try to scam money from me. My telephone number has been used for fraudulent international calls. Businesses and government agencies are terrified about the potential damage that hackers can cause. Terrorist experts now believe that cyberattacks could be far more dangerous to us than attacks with weapons of mass destruction, and cyberattacks can be launched from anywhere in the world. Many other problems seem to have their roots in globalization. Therefore, we are both thankful for and fearful of globalization.

We have considered both benefits and costs of America's military leadership and financial centrality in the world today. Salvatore Babones says that America is still the hegemonic power and those who think otherwise are looking at epiphenomena and not the reality. There is no challenging power because both China and Russia lack true partners. Will Ruger agrees that America could assert itself into the role of world hegemon but that would be too costly. America is better off sharing power.

YES ⤶   Salvatore Babones

The Once and Future Hegemon

Is retreat from global hegemony in America's national interest? No idea has percolated more widely over the past decade—and none is more bogus. The United States is not headed for the skids and there is no reason it should be. The truth is that America can and should seek to remain the world's top dog.

The idea of American hegemony is as old as Benjamin Franklin, but has its practical roots in World War II. The United States emerged from that war as the dominant economic, political and technological power. The only major combatant to avoid serious damage to its infrastructure, its housing stock or its demographic profile, the United States ended the war with the greatest naval order of battle ever seen in the history of the world. It became the postwar home of the United Nations, the International Monetary Fund and the World Bank. And, of course, the United States had the bomb. America was, in every sense of the word, a hegemon.

"Hegemony" is a word used by social scientists to describe leadership within a system of competing states. The Greek historian Thucydides used the term to characterize the position of Athens in the Greek world in the middle of the fifth century BC. Athens had the greatest fleet in the Mediterranean; it was the home of Socrates and Plato, Sophocles and Aeschylus; it crowned its central Acropolis with the solid-marble temple to Athena known to history as the Parthenon. Athens had a powerful rival in Sparta, but no one doubted that Athens was the hegemon of the time until Sparta defeated it in a bitter twenty-seven-year war.

America's only global rival in the twentieth century was the Soviet Union. The Soviet Union never produced more than about half of America's total national output. Its nominal allies in Eastern Europe were in fact restive occupied countries, as were many of its constituent republics. Its client states overseas were at best partners of convenience, and at worst expensive drains on its limited resources. The Soviet Union had the power to resist American hegemony, but not to displace it. It had the bomb and an impressive space program, but little else.

When the Soviet Union finally disintegrated in 1991, American hegemony was complete. The United States sat at the top of the international system, facing no serious rivals for global leadership. This "unipolar moment" lasted a mere decade. September 11, 2001, signaled the emergence of a new kind of threat to global stability, and the ensuing rise of China and reemergence of Russia put paid to the era of unchallenged American leadership. Now, America's internal politics have deadlocked and the U.S. government shrinks from playing the role of global policeman. In the second decade of the twenty-first century, American hegemony is widely perceived to be in terminal decline.

Or so the story goes. In fact, reports of the passing of U.S. hegemony are greatly exaggerated. America's costly wars in Iraq and Afghanistan were relatively minor affairs considered in long-term perspective. The strategic challenge posed by China has also been exaggerated. Together with its inner circle of unshakable English-speaking allies, the United States possesses near-total control of the world's seas, skies, airwaves and cyberspace, while American universities, think tanks and journals dominate the world of ideas. Put aside all the alarmist punditry. American hegemony is now as firm as or firmer than it has ever been, and will remain so for a long time to come.

The massive federal deficit, negative credit-agency reports, repeated debt-ceiling crises and the 2013 government shutdown all created the impression that the U.S. government is bankrupt, or close to it. The U.S. economy imports half a trillion dollars a year more than it exports. Among the American population, poverty rates are high and ordinary workers' wages have been stagnant (in real terms) for decades. Washington seems to be paralyzed by perpetual gridlock. On top of all this, strategic exhaustion after two costly wars in Afghanistan and Iraq has substantially degraded U.S. military capabilities. Then, at the very moment the military needed to regroup, rebuild and rearm, its budget was hit by sequestration.

If economic power forms the long-term foundation for political and military power, it would seem that America is in terminal decline. But policy analysts tend to have short memories. Cycles of hegemony run in centuries, not decades (or seasons). When the United

Kingdom finally defeated Napoleon at Waterloo in 1815, its national resources were completely exhausted. Britain's public-debt-to-GDP ratio was over 250 percent, and early nineteenth-century governments lacked access to the full range of fiscal and financial tools that are available today. Yet the British Century was only just beginning. The *Pax Britannica* and the elevation of Queen Victoria to become empress of India were just around the corner.

By comparison, America's current public-debt-to-GDP ratio of less than 80 percent is relatively benign. Those with even a limited historical memory may remember the day in January 2001 when the then chairman of the Federal Reserve, Alan Greenspan, testified to the Senate Budget Committee that "if current policies remain in place, the total unified surplus will reach $800 billion in fiscal year 2011. . . . The emerging key fiscal policy need is to address the implications of maintaining surpluses." As the poet said, bliss was it in that dawn to be alive! Two tax cuts, two wars and one financial crisis later, America's budget deficit was roughly the size of the projected surplus that so worried Greenspan.

This is not to argue that the U.S. government should ramp up taxes and spending, but it does illustrate the fact that it has enormous potential fiscal resources available to it, should it choose to use them. Deficits come and go. America's fiscal capacity in 2015 is stupendously greater than Great Britain's was in 1815. Financially, there is every reason to think that America's century lies in the future, not in the past.

The same is true of the supposed exhaustion of the U.S. military. On the one hand, thirteen years of continuous warfare have reduced the readiness of many U.S. combat units, particularly in the army. On the other hand, U.S. troops are now far more experienced in actual combat than the forces of any other major military in the world. In any future conflict, the advantage given by this experience would likely outweigh any decline in effectiveness due to deferred maintenance and training. Constant deployment may place an unpleasant and unfair burden on U.S. service personnel and their families, but it does not necessarily diminish the capability of the U.S. military. On the contrary, it may enhance it.

America's limited wars in Afghanistan and Iraq were hardly the final throes of a passing hegemon. They are more akin to Britain's bloody but relatively inconsequential conflicts in Afghanistan and Crimea in the middle of the nineteenth century. Brutal wars like these repeatedly punctured, but never burst, British hegemony. In fact, Britain engaged in costly and sometimes disastrous conflicts throughout the century-long *Pax Britannica*. British hegemony did not come to an end until the country faced Germany head-on in World War I. Even then, Britain ultimately prevailed (with American help). Its empire reached its maximum extent not before World War I but immediately after, in 1922.

Ultimately, it is inevitable that in the long run American power will weaken and American hegemony over the rest of the world will fade. But how long is the long run? There are few factual indications that American decline has begun—or that it will begin anytime soon. Short-term fluctuations should not be extrapolated into long-term trends. Without a doubt, 1991 was a moment of supreme U.S. superiority. But so was 1946, after which came the Soviet bomb, Korea and Vietnam. American hegemony has waxed and waned over the last seventy years, but it has never been eclipsed. And it is unlikely that the eclipse is nigh.

When pundits scope out the imminent threats to U.S. hegemony, the one country on their radar screens is China. While the former Soviet Union never reached above 45 percent of U.S. total national income, the Chinese economy may already have overtaken the American economy, and if not it certainly will soon. If sheer economic size is the foundation of political and military power, China is positioned for future global hegemony. Will it build on this foundation? Can it?

Much depends on the future of China's relationships with its neighbors. China lives in a tough neighborhood. It faces major middle-tier powers on three sides: Russia to the north, South Korea and Japan to the east, and Vietnam and India to the south. To the west it faces a series of weak and failing states, but that may be more of a burden than a blessing: China's own western regions are also sites of persistent instability.

It is perhaps realistic to imagine China seeking to expand to the north at the expense of Russia and Mongolia. Ethnic Russians are abandoning Siberia and the Pacific coast in droves, and strategic areas along Russia's border with China have been demographically and economically overwhelmed by Chinese immigration. Twenty-second-century Russia may find it difficult to hold the Far East against China. But that is not a serious threat to U.S. hegemony. If anything, increasing Sino-Russian tensions may reinforce U.S. global hegemony, much as Sino-Soviet tensions did in the 1970s.

To the southeast, China clearly seeks to dominate the South China Sea and beyond. The main barrier to its doing so is the autonomy of Taiwan. Were Taiwan ever to be reintegrated with China, it would be difficult for other regional powers to successfully challenge a united China for control of the basin. In the future, it is entirely possible that China will come to dominate these, its own coastal waters. This would be a minor setback to an America accustomed to dominating all of the world's seas, but it would not constitute a serious strategic threat to the United States.

Across the East China Sea, China faces Japan and South Korea—two of the most prosperous, technologically advanced and militarily best-equipped countries in the world. Historical enmities ensure that China will never expand in that direction. Worse for China, it is quite likely that any increase in China's ability to project power beyond its borders will be matched with similar steps by a wary, remilitarizing Japan.

The countries on China's southern border are so large, populous and poor that it is difficult to imagine China taking much interest in the region beyond simple resource exploitation. Chinese companies may seek profit opportunities in Cambodia, Myanmar and Pakistan, but there is little for China to gain from strategic domination of the region. There will be no Chinese-sponsored Asian equivalent of NATO or the Warsaw Pact.

Farther abroad, much has been made of China's strategic engagement in Africa and Latin America. Investment-starved countries in these regions have been eager to access Chinese capital and in many cases have welcomed Chinese investment, expertise and even immigration. But it is hard to imagine them welcoming Chinese military bases, and equally hard to imagine China asking them for bases. The American presence in Africa is in large part the legacy of centuries of European colonialism. China has no such legacy to build on.

Above all, however, the prospects for future Chinese hegemony depend on the prospects for future Chinese economic growth. Measured in per capita terms, China is still poorer than Mexico. That China will catch up to Mexico seems certain. That China will continue its extraordinary growth trajectory once it has caught up to Mexico is less obvious. In 2011, when the Chinese economy was growing by more than 10 percent a year, I predicted that China was headed for much slower growth. At the time, the IMF was projecting a long-term growth rate of 9.5 percent. Today, the same IMF projections assume 7 percent growth.

Even at 7 percent annual growth, the Chinese economy would account for more than half of total global output by 2050. The United States in its post–World War II heyday never achieved that level of dominance. But exponential extrapolations are inherently tricky. If China continues to grow at 7 percent while the world economy as a whole grows by 3 percent per year, China will account for 90 percent of global economic output by 2100 and

100 percent by 2110. After that, China's economy will be even larger than the world's economy, which of course is impossible unless China moves a large portion of its production off-planet.

A more reasonable assumption is that China's economic growth will eventually settle down to global average rates. The only question is when. Existing demographic trends make it almost certain that the answer is: soon. The U.S. Census Bureau has projected that China's working-age population would reach its peak in 2014 and then go into long-term decline. In the twenty years from 2014 to 2034, China's working-age population will fall by eighty-seven million, while its elderly population will rise by 149 million. In the language of economic punditry, China will "grow old before it grows rich."

The U.S. population, by contrast, is young and growing. In 2034, the U.S. population is projected to be growing at a rate of 0.6 percent per year (compared to −0.2 percent in China), with substantial immigration of talented, productive people (compared to net emigration from China). The U.S. median age of 39.2 will be significantly younger than the Chinese median age of 44.8. Over the long term these trends may change, but the twenty-year scenario is almost certain, because for the most part it has already happened. Economic trends can turn on a dime, but demographic trends are mostly immutable: tomorrow's child-bearers have already been born.

In the ancient Mediterranean world, Rome rose to regional hegemony a century or two after the passing of the Athenian empire. The hegemonic Roman Republic was a hybrid political entity. It consisted of Rome itself, Roman colonies, Roman protectorates, cities conquered by Rome and cities allied to Rome. For four hundred years before 91 BC, the Italian cities allied to Rome were effectively part of the Roman state despite their formal political independence. They participated in Rome's wars under Roman command. They did not pay taxes or tribute to Rome, but they were fully incorporated into a political system centered on Rome. When Hannibal crossed the Alps in 218 BC, most of the Italian cities did not rise up against Rome as he expected. They stood with Rome because they were effectively part of Rome.

In a similar way, the effective borders of the American polity extend well beyond the Atlantic and Pacific coasts. If the Edward Snowden leaks have revealed nothing else, they have shown the depth of intelligence cooperation between the United States and its English-speaking allies Australia, Canada, New Zealand and the United Kingdom. These are the so-called Five Eyes countries. These English-speaking allies work so closely with the United States on security issues that they resemble ancient Rome's Italian allies. Despite their formal political independence, they do not make major strategic decisions without considering America's interests as well as their own.

Curiously, America's English-speaking allies resemble the United States in their demographic structures as well. While East Asia's birthrates have fallen well below replacement levels and parts of continental Europe face outright depopulation, the English-speaking countries have stable birthrates and substantial immigration. The most talented people in the world don't always move to the United States, but more often than not they move to English-speaking countries. It doesn't hurt that English is the global lingua franca as well as the language of the Internet.

One surprising result of these trends is that the once-unfathomable demographic gap between China and the English-speaking world is narrowing. According to U.S. Census Bureau projections, in 2050 the U.S. population will be 399 million and rising by 0.5 percent per year while the Chinese population will be 1.304 billion and falling by 0.5 percent per year. Throw in America's four English-speaking allies, and the combined five-country population will be 546 million—nearly 42 percent of China's population—with a growth rate of 0.4 percent per year. No longer will China have the overwhelming demographic advantage that has historically let it punch above its economic weight.

Is it reasonable to treat America's English-speaking allies as integrated components of the U.S. power structure? Of course, they are not formally integrated into the U.S. state. But the real, effective borders of countries are much fuzzier than the legal lines drawn on maps. The United States exercises different levels of influence over its sovereign territory, extraterritorial possessions, the English-speaking allies, NATO allies, other treaty allies, nontreaty allies, client states, spheres of influence, exclusionary zones and even enemy territories. All of these categories are fluid in their memberships and meanings, but taken together they constitute more than just a network of relationships. They constitute a cooperative system of shared sovereignty, something akin to the power structure of the Roman Republic.

No other country in the world possesses, has ever possessed, or is likely to possess in this century such a world-straddling vehicle for the enforcement of its will. More to the point, the U.S.-dominated system shows no signs of falling apart. Even the revelation that America and its English-speaking allies have been spying on the leaders of their NATO peers has not led to calls for the dissolution of NATO. The American system may not last forever, but its remaining life may be measured in centuries rather than decades. Cycles of hegemony turn very slowly because systems of hegemony are very robust. The American power network is much bigger, much stronger and much more resilient than the formal American state as such.

A recurring meme is the idea that the whole world should be able to vote in U.S. presidential elections because the whole world has a stake in the outcome. This argument is not meant to be taken seriously. It is made to prove a point: that the United States is uniquely and pervasively important in the world. At least since the Suez crisis of 1956, it has been clear to everyone that the other countries of the world, whether alone or in concert, are unable to project power beyond their shores without American support. Mere American acquiescence is not enough. In global statecraft, the United States is the indispensable state.

One widely held definition of a state is that a state is a body that successfully claims a monopoly on the legitimate use of force within a territory. The German sociologist Max Weber first proposed this definition in 1919, in the chaotic aftermath of World War I. Interestingly, he included the qualifier "successfully" in his definition. To constitute a real state, a government cannot merely claim the sole right to use force; it must make this claim stick. It must be successful in convincing its people, civil-society groups and, most importantly, other states to accept its claim.

In the twenty-first century, the United States effectively claims a monopoly on the legitimate use of force worldwide. Whether or not it makes this claim in so many words, it makes it through its policies and actions, and America's monopoly on the legitimate use of force is generally accepted by most of the governments (if not the peoples) of the world. That is not to say that all American uses of force are accepted as legitimate, but that all uses of force that are accepted as legitimate are either American or actively supported by the United States. The world condemns Russian intervention in Ukraine but accepts Saudi intervention in Yemen, and of course it looks to the United States to solve conflicts in places like Libya, Syria and Iraq. The United States has not conquered the world, but most of the world's governments (with the exceptions of countries such as Russia, Iran and China) and major intergovernmental organizations accept America's lead. Very often they ask for it.

This American domination of global affairs extends well beyond hegemony. In the nineteenth century, the

United Kingdom was a global hegemon. Britannia ruled the waves, and from its domination of the oceans it derived extraordinary influence over global affairs. But China, France, Germany, Russia and later Japan continually challenged the legitimacy of British domination and tested it at every turn. Major powers certainly believed that they could engage independently in global statecraft and acted on that belief. France did not seek British permission to conquer its colonies; Germany did not seek British permission to conquer France.

Twenty-first-century America dominates the world to an extent completely unmatched by nineteenth-century Britain. There is no conflict anywhere in the world in which the United States is not in some way involved. More to the point, participants in conflicts everywhere in the world, no matter how remote, expect the United States to be involved. Revisionists ranging from pro-Russian separatists in eastern Ukraine to Bolivian peasant farmers who want to chew coca leaves see the United States as the power against which they are rebelling. The United States is much more than the world's policeman. It is the world's lawgiver.

The world state of so many fictional utopias and dystopias is here, and it is not a nameless postmodern entity called global governance. It is America. Another word for a world state that dominates all others is an "empire," a word that Americans of all political persuasions abhor. For FDR liberals it challenges cherished principles of internationalism and fair play. For Jeffersonian conservatives it reeks of foreign adventurism. For today's neoliberals it undermines faith in the primacy of market competition over political manipulation. And for neoconservatives it implies an unwelcome responsibility for the welfare of the world beyond America's shores.

In fact, it is difficult to avoid the conclusion that the United States has become an imperial world state—a world-empire—that sets the ground rules for smooth running of the global economy, imposes its will largely without constraint and without consideration of the reasonable desires of other countries, and severely punishes those few states and nonstate actors that resist its dictates.

No one ever likes an empire, but despite Ronald Reagan's memorable phrase, the word "empire" is not inseparably linked to the word "evil." When it comes to understanding empire, history is probably a better guide than science fiction. Consider the Roman Empire. For several centuries after the ascension of Augustus, life under Rome was generally freer, safer and more prosperous than it had been under the previously independent states.

Perhaps it was not better for the enslaved or for the Druids, and certainly not for the Jews, but for most people of the ancient Mediterranean, imperial Rome brought vast improvements most of the time.

Ancient analogies notwithstanding, no one would seriously suggest that the United States should attempt to directly rule the rest of the world, and there is no indication that the rest of the world would let it. But the United States could manage its empire more effectively, which is something that the rest of the world would welcome. A winning strategy for low-cost, effective management of empire would be for America to work with and through the system of global governance that America itself has set up, rather than systematically seeking to blunt its own instruments of power.

For example, the United States was instrumental in setting up the International Criminal Court, yet Washington will not place itself under the jurisdiction of the ICC and will not allow its citizens to be subject to the jurisdiction of the ICC. Similarly, though the United States is willing to use UN Security Council resolutions to censure its enemies, it is not willing to accept negotiated limits on its own freedom of action. From a purely military-political standpoint, the United States is sufficiently powerful to go it alone. But from a broader realist standpoint that takes account of the full costs and unintended consequences of military action, that is a suboptimal strategy. Had the United States listened to dissenting opinions on the Security Council before the invasion of Iraq, it would have saved hundreds of billions of dollars and hundreds of thousands of lives. The United States might similarly have done well to have heeded Russian reservations over Libya, as it ultimately did in responding to the use of chemical weapons in Syria.

A more responsible (and consequently more effective) United States would subject itself to the international laws and agreements that it expects others to follow. It would genuinely seek to reduce its nuclear arsenal in line with its commitments under the Nuclear Non-Proliferation Treaty. It would use slow but sure police procedures to catch terrorists, instead of quick but messy drone strikes. It would disavow all forms of torture. All of these policies would save American treasure while increasing American power. They would also increase America's ability to say "no" to its allies when they demand expensive U.S. commitments to protect their interests abroad.

Such measures would not ensure global peace, nor would they necessarily endear the United States to everyone across the world. But they would reduce global tensions and make it easier for America to act in its national interests where those interests are truly at stake. Both the United States and the world as a whole would be better off if Washington did not waste time, money and diplomatic capital on asserting every petty sovereign right it is capable of enforcing. A more strategic United States would preside over a more peaceful and prosperous world.

In pondering its future course, Washington might consider this tale from the ancient world: When Cyrus the Great conquered the neighboring kingdom of Lydia, he allowed his army to loot and pillage Lydia's capital city, Sardis. The deposed Lydian king Croesus became his captive and slave. After Cyrus taunted Croesus by asking him how it felt to see his capital city being plundered, Croesus responded: "It's not my city that your troops are plundering; it's your city." Cyrus ordered an immediate end to the destruction.

SALVATORE BABONES is associate fellow at the Institute for Policy Studies in Washington, DC. and a frequent contributor to Truthout.com. His latest book is *Sixteen for '16: A Progressive Agenda for a Better America*, (Policy Press, 2015)

Will Ruger

NO

The Case for Realism and Restraint

WHAT ROLE SHOULD the United States play in the world? When we ask that question, we are talking about foreign policy: the sum of our defense policy, trade policy, and diplomatic relations with other countries.

The answer: The U.S. should adopt a foreign policy that is both consistent with a free society and aimed at securing America's interests in the world—in other words, libertarian realism. The goal must be to provide security efficiently without sacrificing other important goals that Americans hold in common.

An important caveat up front: There is no universal, one-size-fits-all foreign policy for the ages. A single, comprehensive policy cannot be applied uniformly to any state at any period in history. Geography, institutional constraints, technology, history, and strategic context will always shape how we conduct foreign policy. So the U.S. today might require a very different approach than it needed during, say, the early Cold War or the first years of the republic.

But today, American defense policy should be characterized by strategic restraint; its economic policy must be one of free trade, and its diplomacy ought to be focused on articulating—but not aggressively imposing—liberal values and the benefits of free markets.

Ends and means in politics and war are intimately connected. The primary goal of the state should be to protect the territorial integrity of the United States and the property rights—broadly understood, including throughout the global commons—of the people residing within it. The state is also tasked with securing the conditions that allow for a free people to flourish in America. These elements combine to form the national interest.

The state's role is properly limited to serving these interests rather than meeting the needs of outsiders or of the state itself. However, a libertarian realist foreign policy will have positive benefits for Americans and people of other countries beyond achieving these fairly limited ends.

Realism is important to this schema because, in order to secure our interests properly, we need to understand the world as it is, not as we would like it to be. Realists recognize there are important limiting and complicating factors in politics, just as there are in economics. We can no more wish away the constraints that an anarchic world, the balance of power, and geography impose on statesmen than we can disappear the laws of supply and demand or comparative advantage. We need to understand and adapt to what realism tells us about the laws of international relations.

For example, we might wish we could rely on the rule of law internationally as much as we do domestically, and to maintain a very limited military, if any at all. However, this does not accord with what we've known about international life since Thucydides: The strong often do what they will, while the weak suffer what they must. If you doubt this, look at what is happening in Ukraine.

Realism teaches that power matters significantly in the world, and states can use force to meet a variety of goals, some of them malignant. But even great powers face constraints. As we saw in the Iraq War and aftermath, the world—including the comparatively powerless—also gets a vote, placing limits on what the U.S. can impose. Indeed, the application of power often brings negative unintended consequences and even outright failure.

Ultimately, the long-term security of America rests upon the foundation of a strong economy. Free trade is a key ingredient in the recipe for economic growth, and the U.S. should pursue it maximally. As individuals and firms leverage their comparative advantages in the global economy, the ensuing robust growth will allow Washington to better provide for the common defense at a relatively low cost as a percentage of GDP. There are some rare cases, such as specific strategic goods (missile and weapon technology, nuclear materials, etc.) where trade might be limited on security grounds, but we should be leery of rent seekers who use this rationale as a means to nakedly self-interested protectionism.

In the military realm, the watchword of U.S. policy should be restraint. The restraint approach harkens back to the traditional American thinking about defense that dominated from George Washington's Farewell Address to the beginning of the Spanish-American War in 1898. It finds its most important modern expression in the work of MIT-affiliated scholars such as Eugene Gholz, Daryl Press, Harvey Sapolsky, and Barry Posen, and in the political realm by Sen. Rand Paul (R-Ky.).

Restraint traditionally has two pillars. First, the U.S. should avoid permanent military alliances and be quite wary of making even temporary commitments in times of peace or war. That will maximize U.S. independence and ensure a free hand to avoid or choose engagements on its own terms. It also means that the U.S. ought to carefully wind down its many security commitments around the globe, including NATO. This pillar of restraint does not rule out wartime coalitions like the one that formed in World War II or that would have emerged after 9/11 to counter our enemies in Afghanistan in the absence of NATO.

Second, the U.S. ought to employ the minimal use of force abroad, consistent with the national interest narrowly defined above. Defense and deterrence will be the primary methods of meeting U.S. security needs. However, this is not the absolute noninterventionism or the functional pacifism often advocated by left-liberals and libertarians. Aggressive military action should be on the table where and when warranted, such as what might have been necessary had the French, in the early 1800s, been unwilling to sell New Orleans and threatened to forcibly close off our trade down the Mississippi. Moreover, defense includes pure pre-emption when necessary, as it was for Israel in the Six-Day War or might be in the future for the U.S. should we have absolutely solid intelligence of an imminent forthcoming attack against American soil or U.S. ships.

Restraint, rooted in realism, requires the maintenance of a very strong—but smaller and more focused—military, with the Navy and the Air Force having the most important roles and the Army sustaining the deepest cuts. Naval and air power will be critical to protect America far from shore should deterrence fail. They also provide power projection capability as needed. But restraint will entail less need for the type of large standing army the U.S. currently maintains around the globe. Of course, a highly professionalized, well-equipped Army (and Marine Corps) will still be needed and ought to be designed for expandability in the event of a significant threat. Restraint also requires a capable intelligence community, though one focused abroad and respectful of American civil liberties at home.

Restraint is particularly well-suited to the realities of the modern world. The U.S. is exceptionally safe today, despite what you see on Fox News or in *The Wall Street Journal*. The country has an extremely favorable geographic position, with two huge "moats" separating us from strong or threatening powers. It's continent-sized, with plentiful resources, the world's largest economy, and a large, growing population. The neighbors are friendly and comparatively weak, representing zero military threat.

Importantly, the U.S. also has a major military advantage that will remain unrivaled in the decades ahead, even if right-sized in accordance with a restrained realist strategy. Its superior Navy and Air Force together offer an exceptional deterrent capability and the ability to defeat attackers far from our shores. The U.S.'s secure second-strike nuclear capability in particular gives us virtual invulnerability from traditional threats. It is extremely unlikely that any other country would dare attack the U.S. with nuclear weapons or conventional forces.

Of course, the U.S. should be vigilant about the threat posed by explicitly anti-American terrorist groups, especially those that seek to use weapons of mass destruction. However, we also have to be realistic about the danger terrorism poses. It is rarely an existential threat and often best handled by careful intelligence collection, police work, and special operations forces. Nuclear terrorism is also a very unlikely scenario for a variety of reasons, though still something we should guard carefully against.

Appropriately, then, restraint does not a priori rule out the use of military force against terrorist groups and their state supporters when necessary. Afghanistan in 2001 was one such case where war was justified even within a restraint framework, since the regime in Kabul provided a safe-haven for the notorious terrorist group which carried out the deadly attacks of 9/11.

Another virtue of restraint is that the world today, and especially the balance of power, has changed in a way favorable to American security. Our traditional fear, an emergent Eurasian hegemon, is nowhere on the horizon, not least because any attempt at regional primacy will likely be resisted by neighbors and undermined by nationalism. Russia and China, to name two potential rivals, have internal challenges ahead that dwarf our own domestic problems. Lastly, economic and political developments over the last half-century mean that states such as Japan, South Korea, and our current European allies are plenty rich enough to defend themselves individually or as parts of regional alliances. The U.S. is simply not needed to play the central, stabilizing role it did during the Cold War. Indeed, its continuing deep engagement around the globe only makes it less likely that these countries will take responsibility for their own security, thereby releasing American taxpayers from the cost of their defense.

When your ends are "making the world safe for democracy" or other ambitious do-gooderism, your means are going to involve a permanent and expensive military/foreign policy establishment, always primed for aggressive interventionism. More restrained ends require much more limited means.

Restraint's incompatibility with do-gooderism does not mean that realism is immoral or amoral. There is morality to a realistic foreign policy, especially one connected to liberal values. The state acts justly when it serves its citizens' interests and limits itself to things that people would generally favor contracting out to government (foremost among these is protecting the homeland). But a state with an expansive foreign policy can do a great deal of harm in the world, even if its motives are pure.

A limited, realistic foreign policy is much less likely to require means that threaten the purpose of having government in the first place. State action taken in the name of an activist national security policy can have terrible domestic consequences: civil liberty violations, increased militarization of police, an unaccountable and bloated national security apparatus, more debt and larger deficits, and so on.

The United States, thankfully, can afford to pursue a significantly more restrained foreign policy, spending modestly to maintain forces more than adequate for defense and deterrence. We no longer need to support an extensive web of alliances like those of the early Cold War.

Instead, the country can rely on its own economic and military strength, along with temporary alliances during wartime, just as George Washington counseled.

To quote John Quincy Adams, the U.S. needs to stop going "abroad in search of monsters to destroy." Humanitarian crises in non-democratic/illiberal regimes do not automatically threaten U.S. interests. Americans should not have to spend their own blood and treasure policing the globe, even assuming that we could do so successfully (which recent history has demonstrated otherwise).

Given that war is the health of the state, and a reliable destroyer of domestic liberty, there are great costs to a free society in maintaining a massive military and using it for anything other than true defense of the homeland. A free society is better off opting for realist-inspired restraint, coupled with economic, diplomatic, and personal engagement with the world.

WILL RUGER is an associate professor of political science at the University of Texas-Austin where he also teaches at the LBJ School of Public Affairs. He also serves as Vice President of Research and Policy at the Charles Koch Institute. In addition to his book, *Milton Friedman* (Continuum, 2011), he has published numerous scholarly articles and contributed to a wide variety of media outlets.

EXPLORING THE ISSUE

Should America Seek the Role of World Hegemon or World Leader?

Critical Thinking and Reflection

1. Why would America want to make itself the world hegemon?
2. Why would America want to share world leadership power?
3. How have the Iraq and Afghanistan wars and recent terrorism affected public attitudes toward America's role in the world?
4. What is the position of America in the world economy and how has it changed over the decades?
5. What role will America have in the global economic and military leadership in the future?

Is There Common Ground?

This issue explores the arrangement of world power, both militarily and economically. During the Cold War it was a bipolar world. When the Soviet Union disintegrated it became a unipolar world. Is it still a unipolar world or is America sharing power? Both authors agree that America has the economic and military power to be the unipolar world leader. They disagree on whether America is and should be the world hegemonic power. Both agree that there are both costs and benefits of sharing or retaining world leadership, but Babones asserts that the benefits of leading are greater than the benefits of sharing leadership. In fact, not leading may be dangerous for America. Ruger believes that the costs or exerting world leadership are too large and sharing power is less costly and more beneficial.

One thing that has been demonstrated by the above debate is that military and economic globalization has so many sides to it and so many impacts that any assessment of it can be easily challenged. If we focus on economic globalization we must realize that it cannot be isolated from the military and other aspects. In fact, many believe that economic integration will spawn greater military, political, and cultural integration and this will be to the benefit of mankind. Others believe that it will make the world more dangerous and displace workers.

Additional Resources

Sources that carefully report on hegemon issues are: Bruce B. Bagley and Magdalena Defort, eds., *Decline of the United States Hegemony* (Lexington Books, 2015); Thomas H. Oatley,

A Political Economy of American Hegemony (Cambridge University Press, 2015); Michele Riox and Kim Fontaine-Skronski, eds., *Global Governance Facing Structural Changes* (Palgrave Macmillan, 2015); Peter Balazs, ed., *Europe's Position in the New World Order* (Central European University Press, 2014); Wesley K. Clark, *Don't Wait for the Next War: A Strategy for American Growth and Global Leadership, PublicAffairs* (2014); Bret Stephens, *America in Retreat: The New Isolationism and the Coming Global Disorder* (Sentinel, 2014); Thomas Diez, ed., *A Different Kind of Power: The EU's Role in International Politics* (International Debate Education Association, 2014); Bruce D. Jones, *Still Ours to Lead* (Brookings Institution Press, 2014); Christopher J. Fettwels, *The Pathologies of Power* (Cambridge University Press, 2013); Steven W. Hook, ed., *U.S. Foreign Policy Today: American Renewal?* (CQ Press, 2012); Laurence Pope, *The Demilitarization of American Diplomacy* (Palgrave Macmillan, 2014); James Scott, *Mission Creep: The Militarization of US Foreign Policy?* (Georgetown University Press, 2014); Peter Zeihan, *The Accidental Superpower: The Next Generation of American Preeminence and the Coming Disorder* (Twelve, 2014); and Bryan Mabee, *Understanding American Power* (Palgrave Macmillan, 2014).

For 15 years globalization has been a big issue. Any analysis of globalization should begin with Thomas Friedman's best-selling *The Lexus and the Olive Tree* (Farrar, Straus and Giroux, 1999), which strongly advocated for globalization for the prosperity it brings. He continues his advocacy in *The World Is Flat: A Brief History of the Twenty-First Century* (Picador, 2007) and *Hot, Flat and Crowded* (Farrar, Straus and Giroux, 2008). Friedman sees the United States as the nation that is best able to capitalize on that global economy, so it has the brightest future. Other works on globalization include Jagdish N. Bhagwati, *In Defense of Globalization* (Oxford University Press, 2007); Pankaj Ghemawat, *World 3.0: Global Prosperity and How to Achieve It* (Harvard University Press, 2011); Robert A. Isaak, *The Globalization Gap: How the Rich Get Richer and the Poor Get Left Further Behind* (Prentice-Hall, 2005); Joseph E. Stiglitz, *Making Globalization Work* (W. W. Norton, 2006); Gabor Steingart, *The War for Wealth: The True Story of Globalization or Why the Flat World Is Broken* (McGraw-Hill, 2008); and Rhoda E. Howard-Hassmann, *Can Globalization Promote Human Rights?* (Pennsylvania State University Press, 2010). For relatively balanced discussions of globalization see Dilip K. Das, *Two Faces of Globalization*: *Munificent and Malevolent* (Edward Elgar, 2009); and Alfred E. Eckes, *The Contemporary Global Economy: A History Since 1980* (Wiley-Blackwell, 2011).

Internet References . . .

Sociology—Study Sociology Online

http://edu.learnsoc.org/

Sociology Web Resources

www.mhhe.com/socscience/sociology/resources/index.htm

Sociosite

www.topsite.com/goto/sociosite.net

Socioweb

www.topsite.com/goto/socioweb.com